Globalization against Democracy

Globalization has reconfigured both the external institutional framework and the intrinsic operating mechanisms of capitalism. The global triumph of capitalism implies that the market is embraced by the state in all its variants and that global capitalism is not confined to the shell of nation-state democracy. Guoguang Wu provides a theoretical framework of global capitalism for specialists in political economy, political science, economics and international relations; for graduate and undergraduate courses on globalization, capitalism, development and democracy; and for members of the public who are interested in globalization.

Wu examines the new institutional features of global capitalism and how they reframe movements of capital, labor, and consumption. He explores how globalization has created a chain of connections in which capital depends on effective authoritarianism, while democracy depends on capital. Ultimately, he argues that the emerging state-market nexus has fundamentally shaken the existing institutional systems, harming democracy in the process.

GUOGUANG WU is Professor of Political Science, Professor of History, and Chair in China and Asia-Pacific Relations at the University of Victoria, Canada. He previously served as an editor for the *People's Daily* in Beijing and participated in political reform of China in the 1980s in his capacity as a policy advisor and speechwriter for the national leadership. He is the author and editor of eight books, including *China's Party Congress: Power, Legitimacy, and Institutional Manipulation* (Cambridge University Press, 2015).

Globalization against Democracy

A Political Economy of Capitalism after its Global Triumph

GUOGUANG WU
University of Victoria

CAMBRIDGE
UNIVERSITY PRESS

CAMBRIDGE
UNIVERSITY PRESS

University Printing House, Cambridge CB2 8BS, United Kingdom

One Liberty Plaza, 20th Floor, New York, NY 10006, USA

477 Williamstown Road, Port Melbourne, VIC 3207, Australia

4843/24, 2nd Floor, Ansari Road, Daryaganj, Delhi – 110002, India

79 Anson Road, #06–04/06, Singapore 079906

Cambridge University Press is part of the University of Cambridge.

It furthers the University's mission by disseminating knowledge in the pursuit of education, learning, and research at the highest international levels of excellence.

www.cambridge.org
Information on this title: www.cambridge.org/9781107190658
DOI: 10.1017/9781108116077

© Guoguang Wu 2017

First published 2017

Printed in the United States of America by Sheridan Books, Inc.

A catalogue record for this publication is available from the British Library.

ISBN 978-1-107-19065-8 Hardback
ISBN 978-1-316-64075-3 Paperback

To Alexander and Felix, with love and hope

Contents

Figures and Tables

Figures

Tables

Acknowledgments

To me, writing is always the best way to learn. The writing of a book with a scope of content as great as this one is inevitably a constant and intensive process of learning from numerous and diverse sources, including past thinkers, existing publications, various peers, and never-ending developments in real time. During the years since the major ideas of this book were incepted in September 2007, my great indebtedness to various people has amounted to a degree that has stretched beyond the possibility of listing all of them in any form. To all of those whose publications were consulted in this process (as incompletely recorded in bibliographic footnotes) and who are also concerned with a better future for humankind, I would first like to acknowledge their power in inspiring my thinking and purveying my understanding of the general and concrete themes covered in this book.

I should mention, for the record, the research grant awarded by the Social Sciences and Humanities Research Council (SSHRC) of Canada in its Insight Grant scheme (No. 435–2013-0083). The grant was for a research proposal focusing on China's development in the globalization era, but in the process of research and writing the issue, this book has been completed first. As a general treaty of global capitalism, this book of course carries a scope and set of implications far beyond a regional/ country specialization; its theoretical relevance to understanding the political economy of China's experience in recent decades, however, is obvious and fundamental. It was in the course of conducting the above SSHRC-supported project that I was increasingly convinced of the very limiting or even flawed nature of understanding China's development without a grander view of globalization, thus I came to the decision of resetting my research agenda. Now, following this book, I feel myself to be on more solid ground than before in stepping forward to analyze China's development in some depth, which is expected to make up the second book in a trilogy on global capitalism (of which this book is the first). I don't believe that a better comprehension of either a country case such as that of China or a basic political economy of globalization can be separated from each other; instead, a back-and-forth intellectual path between the two levels of generality and particularity should benefit both.

Although the trend of corporatization of research universities has been accelerating everywhere in the world, I could still find a comparatively favorable circumstance for my academic research and intellectual pondering at the University of Victoria, especially through its Department of Political Science, Department of History, and Centre for Asia-Pacific Initiatives (CAPI), three units on the campus for which I hold a faculty appointment. The ecological, cultural, and social physiognomy of the city of Victoria in British Columbia, I should also mention, does provide an inspiring atmosphere and supportive environment for lifting one's concerns beyond money, commodity, and *guanxi*, or networking for patronage benefits, reaching something which is lofty while fundamental, valuable but invisible for improving human life, something similar, I believe, to those issues on which I have made efforts to dwell in this book. I am glad to have this opportunity to express my appreciation to my colleagues, students, friends, neighbors, and other members of local communities.

Especially, the University of Victoria Library has been very helpful to my research; the CAPI China Chair fund has also been mobilized for covering some research activities that eventually resulted in this book. I thank my colleagues there for their support.

My graduate students, Can Zhao in Political Science and Jack John Hoskins in History, provided excellent research assistance, particularly in data searching and table composition. I very much thank them.

Emma Lansdowne has edited through the manuscript for several rounds with her marvelous writing skills. To her I am greatly indebted and would send my best wishes for the start of her academic career.

At Cambridge University Press, my editor Phil Good has competently steered the entire process of publication. I am deeply grateful to him. Thanks also go to Lucy Rhymer for her enthusiastic help at the initial stage.

The suggestions and criticisms from four reviewers who assessed the book proposal and, at a later stage, the book manuscript were invaluable contributions to the improvement of the book. Errors and mistakes, however, may still remain, all of which are mine.

As an ambitious while sometimes hopeless attempt to catch up with the great transformation of the global political economy we are experiencing in contemporary time, this book has been an ideational exploration, an intellectual adventure, and, accordingly, a personal as well as scholarly devotion to an intellectual course and a human ideal. My wife, Xiaoying, and our sons, Alexander and Felix, with their never-failing love, understanding, and tolerance, have accompanied and consoled me through the adventure; their passionate sympathy to my exploration and their constant and all-around support have helped to pave the way along which I stagger forward to first improve myself while also making some humble attempts to improve the world. This book is dedicated to Alexander and Felix, with daddy's unconditional love and with hope for their generation's better navigating of our globe.

1 | Introduction

What does the global triumph of capitalism mean? How has it changed capitalism and the world? What implications do the changes bring to our life? The world was shocked when on June 23, 2016, more than 30 million voters decided in a referendum that the UK should leave the European Union.[1] Was such a choice a response to globalization, and, if yes, why such a response and why in the UK? No less shocking was the controversial rise of Donald Trump from the right as well as the unanticipated popularity of Bernie Sanders as a self-proclaimed socialist in the 2016 US presidential election;[2] in France, Marine Le Pen's National Front, an ultra-Right-wing party, gained a remarkable number of votes in the 2015 regional elections.[3] Why does a political trend

---

[1] For a quick glance at the referendum, see Brian Wheeler and Alex Hunt, "The UK's EU Referendum: All You Need to Know," *BBC News*, www.bbc.com /news/uk-politics-32810887, posted and accessed June 24, 2016.

[2] When this chapter was nearly finalized, news that Trump won the Republican nomination broke. See, for instance, Emily Stephenson and Amy Tennery, "Beating Rivals and the Odds, Trump Captures Republican Nomination," *Reuters*, www.reuters.com/article/us-usa-election-idUSKCN0ZZ0ZP, posted and accessed July 20, 2016. For Sanders' popularity in the election, see, for example, Jessica Lussenhop, "Who Is Democratic Presidential Candidate Bernie Sanders?" *BBC News Magazine*, www.bbc.com/news/world-us-canada-34532136, posted and accessed January 21, 2016; and Anthony Zurcher, "US Election 2016: Bernie Sanders' and Hillary Clinton's Policies Compared," *BBC News*, www.bbc.com/news/election-us-2016–35666347, posted and accessed February 28, 2016.

[3] See some insightful news reports and analyses in: Reuters, "The Rise of Far-Right Wing Parties in Europe," *The Jerusalem Post*, www.jpost.com/International/ The-rise-of-far-right-wing-parties-in-Europe-354345, posted May 26, 2014, accessed December 15, 2015; Sputnik News, "World Goes 'Right': US, European Right-Wing Parties on Rise," sputniknews.com/politics/20151210/1031546075/ american-european-right-wing-parties-on-rise.html, posted and accessed December 15, 2015; Nick Gutteridge, "Shocking March of the Far-Right across Europe as Migration Fears Reach Fever Pitch," www.express.co.uk/news/world/629022/EU-migration-crisis-far-right-parties-Europe-Germany-Sweden-France, published December 26, 2015, accessed January 3, 2016.

of de-globalization such as that advocated by these Rightist politicians surface in leading industrial democracies from whence global capitalism started its global conquering years before? What is troubling the political world in which democracy has well established itself for centuries?

It is not difficult to see close linkages between the above developments and what has happened in another end of the world, where, as the Global South becomes increasingly and profoundly involved in the global economy, ethnic nationalism, cultural localism, religious fundamentalism, violent terrorism, and political authoritarianism have gained leverage to challenge fundamental principles, political practices, and even the bottom-line preservation of democracy. Economic prosperity, technological progress, and global connections in various aspects of human life, ironically enough, are marching hand in hand with a mounting of strife, hatred, and conflicts across civilizations, nations, groups, and within society. What exactly are the linkages between the resistance in the Global South to globalization and the de-globalization impulse in the Global North? How are these various conflicts relevant to the global triumph of capitalism? Why is such a triumph impotent to deal with those vital challenges?

Moreover, the globe that human beings take as their home is in also crisis, as its basic ecological system has been plagued and shaken with the acceleration of deterioration. The global triumph of capitalism has stimulated the rapid increase of human capacities to acquire wealth from nature, but, paradoxically, it has caused huge ecological predicaments such as climate change and environmental degradation that are seemingly beyond the management and abilities of our governance systems at either the state or the global level and in the form of either democracy or non-democracy. Why does globalization worsen such disasters at such a pressing pace? How can we diagnose and improve the governance systems in this global era to meet such challenges? Would a concentration of public power be more effective than democracy in rescuing the world from these crises?

All of these are big questions that require a systematic exploration of the big picture of globalization. This book is exactly such an attempt and aims to provide a coherent, macro theory of global capitalism with possible explanatory power to help systematically comprehend the institutional nature of the global triumph of capitalism and the various aftermaths brought by this triumph to human economic, social, and political life. In doing so, it joins the ongoing discussion of globalization by suggesting a new political economy of global capitalism, a political economy with three key features.[4]

First, as a systematic treaty of globalization from an institutionalist perspective, this monograph defines globalization as the worldwide institutional triumph of capitalism whose origins lie in the ideological conciliation and institutional collaboration between the state and the market, and seeks to sketch a grand picture of globalization by depicting the major institutional features that frame global capitalism in a wider setting. It highlights an observation that globalization is unfolded with two contradictory but overlapping trajectories of grand institutional change: On one hand, the shaping of the state-market nexus as the institutional backbone of globalization leads to the rise of the economic state, which commits the world to intensive economic competition for materialistic development; on the other hand, two great splits have emerged, one between capitalism that has gone global and democracy that remains confined within boundaries of the sovereign state, and another between all national economies that have now combined the market with state command and the global market that operates with the absence of effective authorities of global governance, both leading to a breakdown of the historical and institutional match between pre-global capitalism and political democracy. Global capitalism, therefore, lives in an institutional circumstance that is fundamentally different from those in which it arose in its early stages and under which it competed with communism during the Cold War; it is exposed to two political matches, either democracy or authoritarianism, but a variety of factors incline to empower political authoritarianism to the degree that capitalism depends on "effective authoritarianism" while nation-state democracy is impotent to govern global capitalism. This is a grand transformation of human institutions, which leaves the fate of human societies greatly vulnerable and uncertain.

---

[4] There is a huge body of literature on globalization; thus here it is impossible to list even only the major publications in this regard. For some useful overviews of the debates around globalization, see, for instance, David Held and Anthony McGrew, *Globalization/Anti-Globalization: Beyond the Great Divide*, Cambridge: Polity, 2007, 2nd ed.; Andrew Jones, *Globalization: Key Thinkers*, Cambridge: Polity, 2010; Barrie Axford, *Theories of Globalization*, Cambridge: Polity, 2013.

Second, it further provides a comprehensive investigation of how globalization has transformed the intrinsic dynamics of capitalism as embodied and operated in its three fundamental elements, namely, capital, labor, and consumption, and their complicated mutual interactions.[5] The global triumph of capitalism also signifies capitalism's encounter with its global limit; joined by the information revolution and institutional factors, this has altered the movements of capital, labor, and consumption, often resulting, on one hand, in the concentration of capital and the disproportional accumulation of wealth, the high organization of production, commerce, and finance in terms of their networking and coordination, and the powerful commercial promotion of products and its shaping of social mentality, and, on the other hand, the increasing but still limited fluidity of labor and the deformation of labor's strength, a plummeting and even a pauperization of the middle classes, and the dispersion of consumers' power to the degree that a new anarchy of consumption is created. In summation, this book explores how its global reach has refashioned capitalism further in the direction of capital's concentration along with labor's dispersion and consumer's atomization that structurally and institutionally strengthens the domination of capital over others.

Third, by experimenting with a methodology termed "inter-institutionalism" that emphasizes the interplays of different sets of institutions to motivate and constrain human behavior, it highlights interconnections and interactions between the two layers of exterior and interior institutions listed above with which global capitalism operates, and analyzes how all of these rudimentary changes wrought with the global triumph of capitalism point to making democracy socioeconomically undermined, institutionally dysfunctional, and politically impotent, thus, reciprocally lending global capitalism a "nude" status, in other words, existing without a political "shell" to overcome various crises of public affairs.

The major, perhaps the most important, consequences of these transformations, it argues, are rising inequalities in particular and,

[5] Though many general treatments of globalization do not include labor or consumption, let alone parallel them with capital, there should be no dispute over the fundamental significance of these three elements to capitalism. For a brief discussion, see James Fulcher, *Capitalism: A Very Short Introduction*, Oxford University Press, 2004, pp. 14–16.

accordingly, the victimization of democracy in general, as globalization has been unfolded at the cost of rights, power, and the influence of average citizens in political economy.[6] This is not a rationalization of a theme of globalization against democracy; by contrast, the central argument of the book traces the major contemporary troubles that perplex and challenge human societies to an institutional root that is deeply embedded in the negative effect of capitalist globalization over democracy. It is not, however, simply a moral denouncement of capitalism; rather, it emphasizes the necessity for and urgency of institutional innovations in the political realm to revitalize democracy, re-connect democracy with capitalism, and rewire the political-economic logic between democracy and the market in order to remedy the inability and often the absence of participatory public power in steering global capitalism.

The Age of Global Capitalism, the Age of Great Transformation: The Global Triumph of Capitalism as Both Expansion and Limit

Capitalism has gained its global triumph since the late twentieth century in many senses, but observers and analysts have often either neglected or misread its most significant dimension, namely, the institutional triumph of capitalism. This triumph, in this book's interpretation, means that as nearly all states have embraced the market as their fundamental economic institution, the market, as the rudimentary institution around which capitalism is originated, organized, and operated, has overcome its institutional obstacles and competitors to become virtually the only choice worldwide for not only organizing human material life but also influencing every aspect of human activity.[7] As the world is, in reality,

---

[6] There are existing publications that have pointed out globalization's effects of undermining democracy and public goods, as two of the best in the type have exemplified: Dani Rodrik, *The Globalization Paradox: Democracy and the Future of the World Economy*, New York: W. W. Norton, 2011; William I. Robinson, *Global Capitalism and the Crisis of Humanity*, Cambridge University Press, 2014. This book aims to develop the line of reasoning with an institutionalist political economy of globalization.

[7] David Harvey, a major contemporary critic of capitalism, sees such a development as "almost all states" embracing neoliberalism. David Harvey, *A Brief History of Neoliberalism*, Oxford University Press, 2005, p. 3. The current book, however, defines it as the embracement of the market in

divided into territories belonging to different state sovereignties, this global triumph of capitalism is firstly, therefore, a geographic and territorial expansion crossing state borders to reach every corner of this globe, leading to unprecedented developments in commerce, technology, transportation, and communication and their profound aftermaths in shaping a so-called global village.[8] The more important global triumph of capitalism, however, is institutional in a double sense: the market triumphs over any contending institutions, especially the state-planning economy, to become the globally adopted fundamental institution through which human beings now organize their economic activities; it also substantially expands into other spheres of human activity, where other human institutions once dominated but where these institutions have now become collaborators in various ways with the market, driving and defining human life in tandem.

With these two fundamental expansions, namely, the capitalist coverage of the globe both geographically and institutionally, the latest wave of globalization in the post–Cold War era has differentiated itself from earlier waves of globalization and, accordingly, made global capitalism distinctive from pre-global capitalism.[9] Global capitalism,

general, while viewing neoliberalism as just one form of the various expressions of the state-market nexus – a point that will become clear in later discussions.

[8] Numerous publications have examined these aspects of globalization and their aftermaths. For a concise introduction, see Manfred B. Steger, *Globalization: A Very Short Introduction*, Oxford University Press, 2009, 2nd ed.

[9] There is, of course, a historical process of globalization, but the institutional definition of globalization contributed here distinguishes the current incarnation of globalization from earlier waves of globalization. This institutional perspective of globalization, accordingly, is different from historical perspectives on globalization. For globalization in history and globalization in various historical perspectives, see, for instance, A. G. Hopkins ed., *Globalization in World History*, New York: W. W. Norton, 2002; Geoffrey C. Gunn, *First Globalization: The Eurasian Exchange, 1500–1800*, Lanham, MD: Rowman & Littlefield, 2003; Robbie Robertson, *The Three Waves of Globalization: A History of a Developing Global Consciousness*, London: Zed Books, 2003; Jürgen Osterhammel and Niels P. Petersson, *Globalization: A Short History*, translated by Dona Geyer, Princeton University Press, 2005; Peter N. Stearns, *Globalization in World History*, London: Routledge, 2010; Stephen Broadberry and Kevin O'Rourke eds., *The Cambridge Economic History of Modern Europe*, Vol. II: *1870 to the Present*, Cambridge University Press, 2010; John M. Hobson, "Orientalization in Globalization: A Sociology of the Promiscuous Architecture of Globalization, c. 500–2010," in Jan Nederveen Pieterse and Jongtae Kim eds., *Globalization and Development in East Asia*, New York: Routledge, 2012, pp. 12–35.

therefore, is not simply a convenient term in use; it has specific but profound meanings for redefining capitalism.[10] Among these meanings, this book emphasizes three, all being institutional but referring to different domains in which capitalism runs as a set of institutions, as will be briefly presented immediately below.

First of all, this book would like to emphasize the limit that capitalism has encountered with its global triumph. This is in contrast to the prevailing celebration of the institutional unbinding of the market with globalization. The limit is primarily geographic and spatial,[11] which is easy to understand as capitalism is now global in the sense of extending its coverage everywhere, so much so that few regions are untouched by the complex networks of the capitalist market and flows of capital, goods, services, information, and people along with global market channels,[12] implying a fundamental limit to the continuous discovery of possible new frontiers for expansion. This limit is simultaneously institutional, because, having nearly reached the end of its extensive expansion, capitalism that is by nature expansive encounters a basic dilemma of being expansive but having nowhere to expand to.[13]

Logically, introversive restructuring follows, and, accordingly, institutional reconfiguration takes place. This is a great transformation of capitalism; from pre-global to global, capitalism has been under fundamental changes in both its external and internal logics. The second and third institutional meanings of globalization that help to redefine capitalism in its global incarnation, therefore, refer to, on the one hand, the

---

[10] The emphasis on "global capitalism" as a conceptual entity does not mean any justification of the ignorance of the internal diversity and richness of capitalism in its global age. Instead, this author pays close attention to varieties of capitalism (VofC), a well-developed theme in comparative political research. In a similar vein, there are many different types of the state, of which this book is fully aware, but that never prevents social scientists from employing the state (at least since Max Weber) as a useful concept of analysis. To this author, this is a question of a level of analysis.

[11] Outer space? At this stage it is not practical, and in the foreseeable future it will not become significant enough to change the nature of the market in terms of its current global boundaries.

[12] David Held, Anthony McGrew, David Goldblatt, and Jonathan Perraton, *Global Transformations: Politics, Economics and Culture*, Stanford University Press, 1999; James H. Mittleman, *The Globalization Syndrome: Transformation and Resistance*, Princeton University Press, 2000.

[13] For the expansive nature of capitalism, see, for instance, Joyce Appleby, *The Restless Revolution: A History of Capitalism*, New York: W. W. Norton, 2010.

restructuring of the connections between capitalism and other human institutions, primarily the state, and, on the other hand, the reshaping of the movements of and interactions among the immanent elements of capitalism, namely, capital, labor, and consumption. To investigate how capitalism is reconfigured along these two fundamental external and internal logics will be the central content of this book; the later sections of this introduction will accordingly summarize why the global triumph of capitalism inevitably brings about such reconfigurations and will outline the updated institutional portrait of global capitalism.

It is necessary to take the "global limit" thesis further, however, before we turn to the impact of the global limit on the external and internal logics of capitalism, from two angles in particular: political and historical. From the political-institutional angle, the global limit thesis emphasizes that the global triumph of capitalism has reshaped the relationship between the two intrinsic organizations of capitalism, namely, the market that supposedly carries free competition and the firm that institutes resource concentration and management efficiency to win competition. The global limit of capitalism obviously implies that the outward expansion of the market is virtually over; the firm has, accordingly, been restructuring in the direction of gaining a bigger share within the last frontiers of the global market. This book maintains, therefore, that global capitalism is greatly effective in promoting material wealth through the concentrative movements of various resources on a global scale, but, as such movements lead to monopoly and oligopoly, the spirit of free competition is institutionally undermined and restricted.

For a long time, there has been an intellectual tradition in studies of capitalism to depict its self-contradiction. For Max Weber, capitalism is torn between two competing ethical ideals: one is Puritan asceticism and self-denial, the other is a eudaimonism that seeks worldly happiness through wealth accumulation and property.[14] In a similar way, American sociologist Daniel Bell has found "the cultural contradictions of capitalism" between the Puritan ethic of accumulation, which emphasizes work, discipline, and deferred gratification, and a hedonistic ethic of consumption for enjoyment, pleasure, and the limitless pursuit of

---

[14] Max Weber, *The Protestant Ethic and the Spirit of Capitalism*, translated by Talcott Parsons, New York: Charles Scribner's Sons, 1958. See a thoughtful elaboration in Steven B. Smith, *Political Philosophy*, New Haven: Yale University Press, 2012, pp. 174–176.

happiness.[15] A contemporary political philosopher, Steven B. Smith, affirms that "this tension still remains at the core of our capitalist system as we try to find a way to manage our contradictory impulses toward our urge to save and our urge to spend, our Calvinism and our hedonism."[16] Here I would take this argument further to the institutional domain, where the market and the firm, as the two organizational bodies of the capitalist system, stand to explain why and how capitalism is torn in its fundamental institutions.[17] I would maintain emphatically that there is an institutional resonance between the market mechanism and democracy as a political institution, on one hand, and between the organizational principle of the firm and authoritarian political institutions, on the other hand.[18] The global limit of capitalism has inevitably reshaped the dynamism of this intrinsic contradiction of capitalism and its institutional connections with democracy and authoritarianism; the trend of new movements in capitalism, this book would argue, increasingly possesses more political proximity with authoritarianism than with democracy.

From a historical-institutional perspective, the relationship between capitalism and democracy has been curiously complicated, but capitalism during the Cold War era was nevertheless mutually associated with and supported by political democracy. The end of the Cold War, which is viewed in this book as the watershed between the pre-global

[15] Daniel Bell, *The Cultural Contradictions of Capitalism*, New York: Basic Books, 1978.

[16] Smith, *Political Philosophy*, p. 176.

[17] For the significance of the firm and the market in capitalist institutions, see R. H. Coase, *The Firm, the Market and the Law*, University of Chicago Press, 1988; Oliver E. Williamson, *The Economic Institutions of Capitalism: Firms, Markets, Relational Contracting*, New York: The Free Press, 1985.

[18] The similarity between market and democracy has been a well-established point. As early as 1929, Harold Hotelling drew a parallel between market competition for consumers and political competition for votes. Harold Hotelling, "Stability in Competition," *Economic Journal* 39 (1929): 41–57. Joseph Schumpeter reinforced the point in 1942 by arguing that political leaders and parties should be treated as firms competing for votes. Joseph A. Schumpeter, *Capitalism, Socialism and Democracy*, New York: Harper & Row, 1975 [1942]. For a brief, contemporary discussion, see Donald P. Green and Ian Shapiro, *Pathologies of Rational Choice Theory: A Critique of Applications in Political Science*, New Haven: Yale University Press, 1994, p. 1. This book, however, does not follow the Schumpeterian argument that economic logic can be unquestionably applied in politics; instead, it emphasizes the separation, interconnections, and interactions between the political and economic logics, which are supposedly different.

and global eras of capitalism, has transformed such an association, thus, as the next section will highlight, capitalism in its global expansion grows out of its "political shell" of democracy while it encounters the limit set by authoritarian states. Simply in this sense, global capitalism is not a geographic extension of pre-global capitalism because it inhabits a different institutional circumstance; a great transformation has been unfolding with globalization due to the fundamental changes in the relationships among capitalism, the state, and democracy, which, each long being a grand design and device for the order of human societies, have jointly framed the fundamental institutional structure of human life over the course of modern history since the Industrial Revolution and the French and American Revolutions.[19]

Global capitalism, therefore, is an institutional concept, as capitalism in the wake of its global triumph is a distinctly new institutional version of pre-global capitalism, rather than simply being the globally enlarged geographic version. It is different from the Marxist notions of the "highest stage" of capitalism or "late capitalism";[20] it denies the linear approach that is inclined to extend the logics of pre-global capitalism into an understanding of global capitalism. The world has been fundamentally changed by the rise of global capitalism, and human thinking needs time, intelligence, and input to acknowledge and understand not only the details but also the big picture of its brave new world. This book is a humble attempt to do so through its efforts to synthesize, systemize, and theorize the political economy of globalization.

Global Capitalism without a Political Shell: Why Is Globalization against Democracy?

In depicting the institutional framework of global capitalism, this book identifies four features: the prevailing of the state-market nexus, the rise of the economic state, the emergence of the great disjuncture between global capitalism and state democracy, and the split between national mixed-economies and the ill-governed global market. As they will be

---

[19] For this order and its features, see Eric J. Hobsbawm, *The Age of Capital, 1848–1875*, New York: Vintage Books, 1996 [1975], p. 1.

[20] For example, V. I. Lenin (1939), *Imperialism: The Highest Stage of Capitalism*, New York: International Publishers, 1990; Ernest Mandel, *Late Capitalism*, London: Verso, 1999, 2nd ed.

systematically discussed in Chapter 2, the following is a brief introduction to outline this grand structure and its position in the book.

The state is, in traditional practice and conventional perception, the most powerful among competitors to the market, as it regulates the market to define the market's boundaries, organizes the state-planning economy to antagonize the market, and, in situations where state-planning is not adopted, most powerfully influences all non-economic spheres against which the market has to operate. It is considered a fundamental conception to acknowledge the distinction, competition, and even confrontation between the state and the market, a lasting, fundamental paradigm that shapes contemporary human thinking of social phenomena. The global triumph of capitalism in the late twentieth century, however, meant the market's conquest of virtually all states, which has transformed the relationship between the state and the market from ideological confrontation and institutional competition to ideological conciliation and institutional collaboration. Hence globalization. It is through this institutional triumph gained by the market, marked by the worldwide collapse of communism, that the latest wave of globalization has, since the 1990s and up to this century, swept the world. This, I argue, is the institutional origin of twenty-first-century globalization.

This global triumph of capitalism, however, does not mean, as a euphonic perception of it describes, that the world has become "flat";[21] rather, this book would argue, the world is now deeply split by the dynamics of globalization, better understood with two overlapping, interplaying, but sometimes opposite institutional developments which together have fundamentally transformed the exterior structure in which capitalism operates. Yes, one of them works to connect, couple, and integrate, primarily, the state and the market, though this development of connection and integration also causes the intensification of market competition and the deformation of the state, specifically, this book would suggest, the rise of the state-market nexus and "the economic state"; on another trajectory, globalization is propelled with great might to disconnect, decouple, and disintegrate the global political economy and the nation-state, chiefly manifested in the decoupling between global capitalism and nation-state democracy,

---

[21] Thomas L. Friedman, *The World Is Flat: The Globalized World in the Twenty-First Century*, New York: Penguin Books, 2005.

and meanwhile, the mixed economy prevails in virtually all nations, but so does the absence, or at least impotence, of governance in the global economy. For this book, only an awareness of these fundamental institutional developments can help to grasp the secret of globalization, and thorough scrutiny of them can lead to an understanding of both the triumph and the crisis of global capitalism.

The state-market nexus emerges in globalization alongside ideological conciliation and operational collaboration between the state and the market. In the contemporary world, there is no state disallowing market operation within its jurisdiction,[22] and there is no market that operates without cooperation with the state; these two sets of institutions have joined each other as collaborators – this is the basic meaning of the state-market nexus. Of all human institutions, now both the state and the market are omnipresent via their collaboration, though separately they are already hugely powerful; in combination their power has more than doubled their joint influence in dominating human life. Together, there are no other human institutions as powerful as these two, nor is it possible for other institutions to escape from the decisive influences of or control by these two. The state-market nexus, therefore, has shaped the institutional backbone for globalization.[23]

As institutional allies, both the market and the state are institutionally reconfigured by their conciliation and collaboration. Intrinsic tensions yet remain between the state and the market, but the state-market nexus provides huge motivations and multiple channels for inter-fertilization between state institutions and market institutions. On the side of the state, this book would highlight primarily the rise of the economic state as history in the post–Cold War era has witnessed. Globalization means the intensification of international economic competition involving all states in the world via their institutional

---

[22] Even North Korea and Cuba, the very few cases in which the state in principle insists on the state-planning economy, have also relaxed their opposition to the market by experimenting with the introduction of some market elements within their economies. More on this will be presented in Chapter 2.

[23] Many scholars have criticized the dichotomy that confronts the state and the market, and have emphasized state-market synergy in economic development (relevant literatures will be cited in Chapter 2 where the discussion of the point is unfolded). But the normative concern of the current book is different from many of those pioneers. While they see it to be a preferable mechanism in promoting economic development, this book traces it as the institutional root of globalization and its various pitfalls.

collaboration with the market; the global spread of materialism and consumerism has both enticed and compelled the state everywhere to respond as effectively as possible to these trends. In general, the state greatly increases its concern over the economy, which often means the built-in attention and interest, self-perceived responsibility and commitment, and wide-ranging, market-concerned, and market-appropriate efforts of the state in regards to various economic affairs. From an institutionalist point of view, these are inevitably crystalized in a transformation of state legitimacy from various possible sources, be it utopian ideology, traditional lineage, or democratic process, to become primarily based on economic performance via the state's gains in international competition. An authoritarian state can justify its repression over political freedom by its performance in "feeding" residents; political accountability in a democracy has shifted to bank-notes rather than ballots.

As capitalism goes global, it leaves behind democracy that is inherently associated with the nation-state.[24] The historically established affinity between capitalism and democracy has been broken; the previous institutional connection between capitalism and democracy has been uncoupled, as there is yet to be such a thing as global democracy to match global capitalism. This is a great disjuncture, the emergence of which has transformed capitalism in many ways, most primarily in the sense of depriving the market of its so-called integrated political shell on the global scale it now inhabits. Global capitalism grows into a giant, necessarily traveling out of the political framework of national democracies, which, by contrast, are dwarfed in being "local" and parochial. Public affairs, therefore, become a domain where participatory power is not able to govern in both domestic and global arenas.

The observation of this great disjuncture obviously contradicts many prevailing theses, including the once-influential argument of the "end of history." To this book, intellectual reflections upon our time have not been sufficiently updated to address the long-discussed connections and contradictions between democracy and capitalism against the new context of post–Cold War globalization, thus misleading ideas can be

---

[24] For an insightful emphasis of "stateness" as a precondition to democracy, see Juan J. Linz and Alfred Stepan, *Problems of Democratic Transition and Consolidation: Southern Europe, South America, and Post-Communist Europe*, Baltimore: Johns Hopkins University Press, 1996, ch. 2. Also, Robert A. Dahl, *Democracy and Its Critiques*, New Haven: Yale University Press, 1989, ch. 15.

surprisingly popular.[25] The "end of history" theory, for example, mistakenly assumes that the end of resistance to the market naturally means the end of resistance to democracy;[26] its conceptual assumption that the market and democracy is one set of inseparable institutions is simply wrong. Yes, the "mutual recognition" between market and democracy once emerged in the late 1980s and early 1990s,[27] but it has quickly been changed by the new logic of global capitalism. Mutual recognition actually occurs between the market and the state, as this book emphasizes, especially and remarkably between the market and those states that in the pre-global era, in one way or another, resisted the market while simultaneously being non-democratic. As a matter of fact, the triumph of the market does not necessarily democratize the state; rather, it first wins the cooperation of all states, regardless of regime type. Then, as this book will demonstrate, it goes on to under-mine democracy in democratic nations and hinder democratization in non-democratic states.

With this disjuncture, global capitalism now operates in relationship with two different political matches: post–Cold War democracy and contemporary authoritarianism. These two political matches, further-more, are not in balance with one another in terms of their relationships with global capitalism. Authoritarian states, specifically those "who govern," in Samuel Huntington's old term,[28] are empowered by the above-discussed reconfigured institutions of the global political econ-omy, while democracy, on the other hand, is impaired. Without the democratic delegation of power from popular voters, authoritarian political legitimacy badly needs materialist support that can, with the rise of the economic state, be obtained from economic prosperity. As these effective authoritarian states work well with global capital

---

[25] For how capitalism and democracy are not necessarily connected to each other, see, for example, Bob Jessop, "Capitalism and Democracy: The Best Possible Political Shell?" in Gary Littlejohn, Barry Smart, John Wakeford, and Nira Yuval-Davis eds., *Power and the State*, New York: St. Martin's Press, 1978, pp. 10–51. More relevant publications will be cited in Chapter 2.

[26] Francis Fukuyama, "The End of History?" *The National Interest*, 16 (Summer 1989): 3–18.

[27] See, for instance, Laurence Whitehead, "Stirrings of Mutual Recognition," in Laurence Whitehead ed., *Emerging Market Democracies: East Asia and Latin America*, Baltimore: Johns Hopkins University Press, 2002, pp. 1–15. Detailed discussions will be developed in Chapter 2.

[28] Samuel P. Huntington, *Political Order in Changing Societies*, New Haven: Yale University Press, 1968, p. 1.

due to their capacity of governance in creating better conditions for profit-making, they provide a new, favorite "political shell" for capitalism, while democracy comes up against the constraints from sovereign boundaries which global capital is able to cross but which so far democracy is not. This institutional gap between the global stretch of capitalism and the local absence of democracy in effective authoritarian countries can greatly help to nurture economic prosperity, such as that which has been achieved in China, and it is also the conceptual key to understanding both the advantages and pitfalls of economic development in the era of globalization.

In tandem with the great disjuncture between capitalism and democracy, another disjuncture also arises to define a feature of the institutions of globalization. With state-market conciliation and collaboration, virtually "all societies are mixed economies, with elements of market and command."[29] The global economy, however, is not one with an element of command from a central authority, thus in this sense being a purely market economy at the global level; the mixed economies of different societies at the sub-global level, by contrast, are fragmented because of separated state-authority jurisdictions. This book will argue that such a split between national mixed economies and global laissez-faire capitalism motivates the state to further transform itself into the economic state and to pursue a seemingly contradictory but essentially complementary strategy of adopting neoliberal policies of deregulation of the market and, at the same time, increasing state roles in economic affairs, as both sides of this strategy help to strengthen national competitiveness on the global market. Deregulation unleashes nation-based market power, and statist economic functions support such power in non-market methods. Together, the states are to different extents corporatized; their domestic behavior and, accordingly, institutions are intended to play up authority, hierarchy, discipline, and even repression, while their outward, global engagement is more competition-driven but less concerned with citizen's diverse domestic preferences and global public goods. The political impact is the same as that which the capitalism-democracy disjuncture entails, which is the rise of a new authoritarian trend everywhere, not only in a form of the state but also as an institutional norm of power, authority, and management, including within existing democracies.

---

[29] Paul A. Samuelson and William D. Nordhaus, *Economics*, Boston: McGraw-Hill/Irwin, 2010, 19th ed., p. 8.

The world of globalization, therefore, is far from being "flat," for it contains a variety of disconnections, gaps, and bumps that dominate at least the political, if not economic, landscape. The most significant political gap, this book maintains, lies in the absence of a coherent political framework for global capitalism. Operating in relationship with the two political contenders of democracy and authoritarianism, global capitalism becomes intimate with the latter in the institutional sense while estranging itself from the former, thereby creating a chain of "dependency reversed": As what can be called "authoritarian advantage" emerges in globalization, capital aspires to seek political auspices from effective authoritarianism at the cost of democracy; when political authoritarianism is able to harness capitalism, democracy, by contrast, becomes dependent on capitalism as it is politically and institutionally economized, corporatized, and provincialized; the so-called dependency of developing nations on leading capitalist countries has been reversed. The general aftermath is a phenomenon in which authoritarian advantages are pitted against democracy's dysfunctions not only in the sense of authoritarianism and democracy being different organizational forms of the state, but also in the sense that they are different norms, principles, and, in general, institutions to organize various human activities. It is this political economic aftermath of globalization that leads human societies to deep-rooted pitfalls and crises.

Capital Concentration versus Labor Segmentation and Consumer Atomization: How Is Globalization against Democracy?

With capitalism's globalization transformation, all of its fundamental elements, namely, capital, labor, and consumption, and their relationships with one another are inevitably restructured. This is a comprehensive, complicated, and encompassing transformation; it is impossible to present an exhaustive research of all aspects of the transformation, but this monograph will devote its major content to outlining some major trends, with a focus on how the movement of capital, labor, and consumption, respectively, is reshaped, and on how their interactions are reconfigured under the new institutions of global capitalism. In other words, the institutional framework of the political economy of global capitalism sketched in the last section shall be embedded primarily in examinations of the operation of the market and the reconstruction of various relationships around the milieu of the market, including those between capital and labor, between production/sale and consumption, and even between capital and capital, labor and labor, and consumer and consumer. Furthermore, the social and political implications of these reconfigurations will be taken into account for the purpose of demonstrating how the socioeconomic bases of democracy are undermined.

The global triumph of capitalism has first meant the global triumph of capital. The great transformation of capitalism caused by globalization, accordingly, is primarily embedded in the new movement, structure, and power of capital, the most fundamental and dynamic element of capitalism. It has long been argued that capitalism has already entered its monopoly stage, and that finance capital has overwhelmed production and other capital forms to dominate capitalism.[30] Such arguments, however, are historically and theoretically associated with the rise of the ideational and social forces that aim to denounce and destroy capitalism, namely, with the Marxist tradition that was carried to Leninism in the early twentieth century, mainly around the historical events of the First World War and the communist world revolution. Capitalism, with its incredible capacity for learning and adjustment, has since improved itself by incorporating some of those criticisms into its operation, as exemplified in the promotion of competition, the increase of state intervention, and the delivery of social welfare. Democracy, as the political framework within which capitalism had to work during this short twentieth century, in my point of view, tremendously contributed to capitalism's capacities in learning, adaptation, and reform. The trend of monopoly, therefore, was to some extent interrupted and reduced. The global triumph of capitalism has fundamentally changed this landscape, however; capital has gained the world, of which not only many parts, but also the whole, are beyond democratic governance. Flowing on a global scale is not new for capital, but two factors are different from the past: the globally favorable institutional conditions for capital's fluid mobility across various borders and the globe in its entirety as the boundary that will eventually confine the size of the capital market within which capital flows. Joined by the information revolution that provides convenient facilities for the

---

[30] See a systematic survey of this line of reasoning in Anthony Brewer, *Marxist Theories of Imperialism: A Critical Survey*, London: Routledge, 1990, 2nd ed.

movement and management of capital, these factors have shaped the new political economic institutions that nurture the actualization of the intrinsic and inevitable demand of capital monopoly into reality at its new global level. Capital moves more freely around the globe, leading it to accumulate and concentrate quickly and remarkably for the purpose of gaining and maintaining global competitiveness. Monopoly, this book shall argue based on its relevant empirical investigation, has since become the normality for global capitalism, whether it be in the form of monopoly, duopoly, or oligopoly. That is to say, monopoly is not only more possible for global capitalism than before in a practical sense, but it is also intrinsically demanded by global capital as a result of various factors, ranging from fewer state regulations congenital in the state-market nexus to the technical standardization embedded in the information revolution.

Labor is also increasingly involved in global mobility in various forms, primarily in cross-state immigration and domestic migration. With evidence drawn from various sources, however, this book will argue that the seemingly parallel movements of capital and labor are in fact fundamentally asymmetrical. While capital's movements strategically strengthen the power of investment, international immigration and domestic dislocation of migrants make mobile laborers into "economic men" in the sense of exchanging various facets of their life, including identities, cultural belongings, social fabrics, and their political ability to participate in public life, for possible opportunities to make a better material life. It is indisputable that those in mobility make up a small percentage of labor; therefore they must, this book suggests, be examined in their connections to those in immobility, which are the overwhelming majority on the global labor market. In this analytical connection, the global labor market is dialectically becoming more segmented in its global integration; internal competitions are inevitably intensified within labor when all segments are more or less involved in and affected by globalization. Moreover, as labor's global mobility is largely directed one way from developing countries to industrialized democracies, the economic inequalities and the erosion of social capital and political capacity at both ends of such mobility are worsened. Altogether, the rise of labor mobility within the institutional framework of global capitalism has to some degree undone what the political transformation since the French Revolution has achieved, a feat summarized by Reinhard Bendix as "the laboring poor have become citizens, recognized participants in the political process."[31]

Consumption is often an enchanting and esoteric weapon of capitalism to conquer the world; via globalization it further makes human beings into "economic men" through the global expansion of the consumption market and the global rise of consumerism. The "economic man" in this context, however, embodies a version (termed "economic man 2.0" in this book) different from the "economic man" as laborer in the capitalist system; while the labor version of "economic man" has to struggle to find an employment opportunity in a firm where discipline, hierarchy, and authority dominate, "economic man 2.0" is seemingly liberated to enjoy the freedom of market consumption based upon his/her individual power of making his/her own decisions. This is an illusion, this book will argue, because, with its various institutional, cultural, operational, and/or technological elements, global capitalism standardizes consumption on a global scale, implying that all consumers become similar to each other through their consumption behaviors, thus losing their individuality. This further means the atomization of consumers, as they are isolated from each other in this process of consumption without effective horizontal communication, let alone possible coordination or effective collective action. Anarchy is, therefore, created in global consumption, but it is, ironically, a caged anarchy, due to the power of the state-market nexus in general and capital in particular in shaping, confining, and making decisions in the universe of consumption.

A decreasing curve has emerged in global capitalism connecting capital, which is well networked and increasingly prone to concentration, with labor, which is globally segmented, and the consumer, who is standardized and atomized. This curve from power concentration to dispersion indicates a great imbalance of power in terms of the degree of organization, internal coordination, and collective influence in the decision-making of contemporary political economy. The world of global capitalism, accordingly, is witness to an enlarging gap between those who are in various ways closely and substantially connected with capital and the state everywhere regardless of democracy, on one hand, and those who have no such connections, on the other. Their disparity is primarily economic in terms of income, ownership, and, in general,

---

[31] Reinhard Bendix, *Force, Fate, and Freedom: Historical Sociology*, Berkeley: University of California Press, 1984, p. 69.

wealth; but the inequality also concerns way of life, social status, political power, and every other significant aspect of human life.

The information revolution that accompanies and enables the rise of globalization has powerfully facilitated the above trends in many effective ways. As will be investigated in the relevant chapters of this book, it requires natural monopoly and promotes oligopoly; it enforces the power of commercial advertisement to conquer the consumption markets; it makes individuals more isolated from each other and more atomized in terms of real-life social interactions, thus making it more difficult for ordinary people to take group action or other possible steps to strengthen their collective power against well-coordinated capital, state, and their coalitions.[32]

The consequences and ramifications of the rise of global capitalism are underlying and tremendously far-reaching, while, this book maintains, those that are directed toward various undermining effects against democracy are especially harmful and intractable, as they challenge and impair the very mechanism of popular participation and public deliberation for governing and improving public affairs. It is a triple crisis, in fact: It is the crisis of capitalism; it is the crisis of global governance; and, most fundamentally, it is the crisis of democracy. In short, though it has always been fraught with internal tension, the originally coherent institutional framework consisting of capitalism, democracy, and the nation-state system that governs human societies comes to a crossroad; the future of capitalism, in fact the future of human societies, is subject to the will and whim of human societies, including capitalists.

Inter-Institutional Perspective of Political Economy: Methodological Experimentation and Ideological Transcendence

The book is designed to sketch a grand picture of global capitalism with both its internal movements of capital, labor, and consumption, and its external interactions with the state system. As it is impossible in such a relatively short space to present an exhaustive treatise of every major aspect of the political-economic transformation caused by the rise of

---

[32] Robert D. Putnam, *Bowling Alone: The Collapse and Revival of American Community*, New York: Simon & Schuster, 2000.

globalization, the book's devotion to original empirical research of various topics is often limited. Instead, the book in general and the chapters on the operation of global capitalism and its social aftermaths in particular make attempts at possible syntheses of existing studies in relevant aspects, which are extremely rich and diverse to a degree that is often beyond this author's command. Many facts might seem familiar to readers, but they are reanalyzed, reassessed, and re-conceptualized in a comprehensive, systematic, and interactive way under the theoretical lens the book employs to focus on the new institutional framework of global capitalism.

It is through the highlighting of the various institutional dimensions of globalization, including the institutional origins, institutional nucleus, and institutional consequences of the rise of global capitalism, that this book differentiates itself from those perspectives of globalization that pay a majority of their attention to the material, technological, and economic contents of the latest wave of globalization since the end of the twentieth century. Basically it adopts the now classic concept of institutions as the "rules of the game" suggested by Douglass North,[33] but some further considerations and revisions of the concept will be developed throughout the analyses presented in this monograph. The major revision in this regard will be coined "inter-institutionalism" of comparative political economy, an approach suggested here to highlight interplays of multiple sets of institutions, rather than any single set of institutions. Specific to political economy, this approach focuses on interconnections and interactions of the state as the primary political institution and the market as the prevailing economic institution, not the state or the market alone as a relatively independent or isolated institution.

According to the fundamental methodology this book employs, a theoretical re-comprehension of institutions, first of all, points to the

---

[33] Douglass C. North, *Institutions, Institutional Change, and Economic Performance*, Cambridge University Press, 1990, p. 3: "Institutions are the rules of the game in a society or, more formally, are the humanly devised constraints that shape human interaction." The current book also incorporates to its understanding Stephen Krasner's conception of "regimes" that includes principles, norms, rules, and decision-making procedures. Stephen D. Krasner, "Structural Causes and Regime Consequences: Regimes as Intervening Variables," in Stephen D. Krasner ed., *International Regimes*, Ithaca: Cornell University Press, 1983, pp. 1–21 (p. 1).

"rules of the game" as not only constraints but also incentives.[34] Therefore, institutions can be defined as ways to organize various relationships via which human activities are simultaneously incentivized and constrained toward the realization of certain purposes. Furthermore, at the center of the "inter-institutional" perspective lies an assumption that institutions in human life exist in a complicated network. A human actor, therefore, rarely takes action following a single, clear-cut set of institutions as though it were isolated from other institutions, but, more often than not, in a manner involving different sets of institutions interacting with each other.

Imagine a basketball player in a high school match. It is possibly one of the most isolated circumstances in which the game is guided by a clear set of rules familiar to the player and without the risk of other rules having influence upon the process and the result, but the player's performance can still be affected by, say, the presence of his/her beloved person in the audience watching the play and by the specific condition of this player's relationship with that person in attendance. The player, therefore, may be diverted to some extent from what the rules of the basketball game require and constrain in order to attain the goal of showing the beloved his/her individual superiority in the game, even though the coach may not like such a show-off because its overall effect can have a negative impact on the player's team attaining their collective goals in the sport. In other words, sets of rules other than those of the basketball match may also work to shape the game, or at least to affect a player's behavior in the game; those rules may not be as clear, direct, observable, and enforceable as the rules of a basketball play, but they can also be forceful and influential in shaping the dynamic, process, and result of the game.

This is not a metaphor, but a simple, real-life example of a situation in which multiple sets of rules work simultaneously and interactively to shape a player's behavior. In those more complicated social circumstances, such inter-influencing of one's behavior by different sets of

---

[34] North also mentions the role of institutions for incentives (North, *Institutions, Institutional Change and Economic Performance*, p. 3), but it seems that he does not think it is necessary to differentiate between "constraints" and "incentives." This author, however, has attempted to emphasize that institutions are enabling and motivating as well as constraining. For the discussion, see Guoguang Wu, *China's Party Congress: Power, Legitimacy, and Institutional Manipulation*, Cambridge University Press, 2015, ch. 2.

rules can be widely observed. In any case, the assumption that in a given context there is only one set of institutions at work is not a valid tack in understanding human activity; the "inter-institutional" perspective, therefore, gets closer to understanding a social dynamic in which multiple sets of institutions often present themselves to mutually interact.

Political economy is especially suitable as a subject to the lens of "inter-institutionalism," because it must, by default, be a mutual field in which two-way interactions between politics and economy take place.[35] The market is a series of institutions, and so is the state. Political economy in this book is viewed as a way of thinking that focuses on the interrelationships between various economic and political elements, especially between the state and the market.[36] This book's examination of global

[35] There are theoretical foundations well established in political economy in this regard with a diversity of perspectives, as exemplified or elaborated in, to name a few, Charles E. Lindblom, *Politics and Markets: The World' Political-Economic Systems*, New York: Basic Books, 1977; Robert H. Bates, *Markets and States in Tropical Africa: The Political Basis of Agricultural Policies*, Berkeley: University of California Press, 1981; Robert H. Bates, *Essays on the Political Economy of Rural Africa*, Berkeley: University of California Press, 1983; Robert Gilpin, *The Political Economy of International Relations*, Princeton University Press, 1987; Charles S. Maier ed., *In Search of Stability: Explorations in Historical Political Economy*, Cambridge University Press, 1987; Robert H. Bates ed., *Toward a Political Economy of Development: A Rational Choice Perspective*, Berkeley: University of California Press, 1988; James E. Alt and Kenneth A. Shepsle eds., *Perspectives on Positive Political Economy*, Cambridge University Press, 1990; James A. Caporaso and David P. Levine, *Theories of Political Economy*, Cambridge University Press, 1992; Jeffrey S. Banks and Eric A. Hanushek eds., *Modern Political Economy: Old Topics, New Directions*, Cambridge University Press, 1995; Jeffery A. Frieden and David A. Lake, *International Political Economy: Perspectives on Global Power and Wealth*, Boston: Bedford, 2000; 4th ed.; Robert Gilpin, *The Challenge of Global Capitalism: The World Economy in the 21st Century*, Princeton University Press, 2000; Robert Gilpin, *Global Political Economy: Understanding the International Economic Order*, Princeton University Press, 2001; Joseph M. Grieco and G. John Ikenberry, *State Power and World Markets: The International Political Economy*, New York: W.W. Norton, 2003; Robert O'Brien and Marc Williams, *Global Political Economy: Evolution and Dynamics*, New York: Palgrave Macmillan, 2004; Benjamin J. Cohen, *International Political Economy: An Intellectual History*, Princeton University Press, 2008.

[36] This book does not follow the approach that defines political economy as the "methodology of economics applied to the analysis of political behavior and institutions." Barry R. Weingast and Donald A. Wittman, "The Reach of Political Economy," in Barry R. Weingast and Donald A. Wittman eds., *The Oxford Handbook of Political Economy*, Oxford University Press, 2006, pp. 3–25 (p. 3).

capitalism, therefore, follows two interplaying and interwoven paths: The first, from economics to politics, analyzes the political economy of the global market; the other, from politics to economics, investigates the political economy of the state that embraces the global market. Or, to be more precise, they are one path defined by two fundamental sets of institutions: All actors under global capitalism are motivated and constrained simultaneously by the interactions of the state and the market.

In this way, the present research emphasizes "mutual contextualization" of politics and economy, power and wealth, global integration and local varieties, and, most importantly, the state and the market by viewing the market in the context of how the state runs and simultaneously the state in the context of how the market operates.[37] The capitalist institutions, in this methodology, must be investigated and understood in their mutual contextualization with other institutions, primarily institutions of the state in political democracy or authoritarianism; within the economic sphere of capitalism, the movements of capital, in a similar vein, should be examined and analyzed in regards to their interconnections with movements of labor and the consumer. In stressing both how political phenomena take place in the economic context and how economic phenomena take place in the political context, it is expected that we may gain some conceptual and methodological strengths in drawing a wider picture of political economy.

This "inter-institutionalism" certainly follows the theoretical track of new institutionalism of social science analyses, especially historical institutionalism in comparative politics.[38] But it develops the paradigm

---

[37] This author in an earlier research suggests a methodology of "mutual contextualization" in comparative political studies, but that is between informal politics and formal institutions. Wu, *China's Party Congress*, ch.1.

[38] For the line of reasoning of new institutionalism that the discussion here follows, see, for example, James G. March and Johan P. Olsen, *Rediscovering Institutions: The Organizational Basis of Politics*, New York: The Free Press, 1989; Sven Steinmo, Kathleen Thelen, and Frank Longstreth eds., *Structuring Politics: Historical Institutionalism in Comparative Analysis*, Cambridge University Press, 1992; John L. Campbell and Ove K. Pedersen eds., *The Rise of Neoliberalism and Institutional Analysis*, Princeton University Press, 2001; James Mahoney and Dietrich Rueschemeyer eds., *Comparative Historical Analysis in the Social Sciences*, Cambridge University Press, 2003; Ian Shapiro, Stephen Skowronek, and Daniel Galvin eds., *Rethinking Political Institutions: The Art of the State*, New York University Press, 2006; Elizabeth Sanders, "Historical Institutionalism," in R. A. W. Rhodes, Sarah A. Binder, and Bert

of new institutionalism by paying special attention to three methodological elements that might otherwise be neglected in the application of new institutionalism, namely, the possible presence of institutions of different sets at multiple layers, their interconnections and interactions, and the implications of such a grand institutional map for various social-science topics. It is, perhaps, bold in its attempt to blend comparative political analysis into studies of international political economy; its perception that globalization makes domestic and global institutions interact more intensively than before and even, in fact, to integrate with each other helps to justify such an experiment.[39] Though it is far beyond this book's scope to systematically explore the methodology, it is clear to this author that the unfolding of globalization does occur along multiple levels, including the global and domestic. Inter-institutionalism or mutual contextualization, therefore, here also means interactions of domestic and global institutions beyond the separate focus of comparative politics on the former and international relations on the latter, thus implying that domestic political economy should be understood in the context of global political economy while global political economy cannot be analyzed without in-depth studies of domestic political economy.

A. Rockman eds., *The Oxford Handbook of Political Institutions*, Oxford: Oxford University Press, 2008, pp. 39–55; James Mahoney and Celso M. Villegas, "Historical Enquiry and Comparative Politics," in Carles Boix and Susan C. Strokes eds., *The Oxford Handbook of Comparative Politics*, Oxford University Press, 2009, pp. 73–89.

[39] This author views the post–Cold War flourishing of the approach in international relations emphasizing foreign-domestic linkage as an intellectual response to the effect of globalization in blending domestic and international institutions, though a discussion shall not be unfolded here due to limited space. For pioneer research with the foreign-domestic linkage in IR studies, see Peter Gourevitch, "The Second Image Reversed: The International Sources of Domestic Politics," *International Organization* 32, 4 (Autumn 1978): 881–912; Robert D. Putnam, "Diplomacy and Domestic Politics: The Logic of Two-Level games," *International Organization* 42, 3 (Summer 1988): 427–460; for the post–Cold War flourishing, see, for example, Peter Evans, Harold K. Jacobson, and Robert D. Putnam eds., *Double-Edged Diplomacy: International Bargaining and Domestic Politics*, Berkeley: University of California Press, 1993; Robert O. Keohane and Helen V. Milner eds., *Internationalization and Domestic Politics*, Cambridge University Press, 1996; Helen V. Milner, *Interests, Institutions, and Information: Domestic Politics and International Relations*, Princeton University Press, 1997; Linda Weiss ed., *States in the Global Economy: Bringing Domestic Institutions Back In*, Cambridge University Press, 2003.

In social sciences, a possible methodological rigor can be compromised by a given ideological attachment. The debate around capitalism has always been highly ideological, as viewpoints are often divided by pro- or anti-capitalism in a normative sense with strong ideological inclinations to either neo-liberalism or neo-Marxism. In regards to globalization, it can be simply extended to defend or blame the market mechanism. To the neoliberal perspective, free market is the remedy to almost all problems, and it blames state power in theory while choosing to neglect the fact that the market works under the auspices of the state in the post–Cold War era.[40] In a similar vein that runs in an opposite direction, neo-Marxist approaches condemn capitalism for its rapacious profit-making and uncontrollable capital accumulation, which leads, as in the example of its expansion to one of the last geographic reserves that is China, into the pitfalls of privatization and class confrontation.[41] It often turns to the state for rescue, in this case the state ideally being Maoist, although for many the current Chinese state is better than both the market mechanism and the capitalist state. Both lines of reasoning, however, dichotomize state and market as contending alternatives among human institutions, thus equally sharing the blindness to the fact that state-market collaboration now works as the institutional backbone of global capitalism and presents new challenges to the political economy of human life.

Instead, this book's critical evaluation of global capitalism lies exactly in its findings of the institutional collaboration between global capitalism and the state in general and the updated communist and other effective authoritarian regimes in particular. "Inter-institutionalism," this author believes, can help to avoid ideological biases. In drawing ideational resources from both Marxism and market liberalism as well as from other streams of ideas, this book attempts to go beyond the dichotomy of capitalism versus socialism, neoliberalism versus statism, the Right versus the Left, or the conservatives versus the radicals. In its boldest ambition, this books attempts to sound an alarm that calls for an ideational revolution in the reflection of capitalism beyond those paradigms of pre-global capitalism. As the global triumph of capitalism has reconfigured the social reality in which we live, it is time to systematically

---

[40] See a review of such arguments in Harvey, *A Brief History of Neoliberalism.*
[41] See an example in Minqi Li, *The Rise of China and the Demise of the Capitalist World-Economy*, New York: Monthly Review Press, 2008.

refresh our conceptualization and comprehension of the reality of global capitalism. More than thirty years ago, Albert Hirschman wrote a book to explore "political arguments for capitalism before its triumph," due, in his own words, to "the incapacity of contemporary social science to shed light on the political consequences of economic growth and, perhaps even more, in the so frequently calamitous political correlates of economic growth . . . "[42] To this author, this is a prophecy of our time, and it still applies to our age of capitalism after its global triumph.

Plan of the Book

Immediately following this introductory chapter, Chapter 2 will elaborate the institutional framework within which globalization originates, unfolds, and operates around the political-economy linchpin that is global capitalism's connection with the state system. It will first investigate how the state-market relationship has been transformed with the global triumph of capitalism, a transformation characterized by the shaping of the state-market nexus and the rise of the economic state; both help to couple the most powerful economic mechanism and the most powerful political organization, thus having formed the institutional backbone of global capitalism. Then it will proceed to examine the uncoupling track of institutional change wrought by the global expansion of capitalism, which features two splits: the great disjuncture between global capitalism and nation-state democracy, and the political-economic gap between national mixed economies and the global neoliberal market. Bringing these two tracks of connecting and disjointing into one grand picture, the chapter outlines the institutional reconfiguration of capitalism and, furthermore, contributes an institutionalist interpretation to the long-time intellectual tradition that emphasizes the self-contradiction of capitalism by presenting an argument of "dependency reversed," in which global capitalism struggles between its two political matches but often falls into the role of protégé to political authoritarianism while democracy increasingly depends on capital.

The three chapters that follow will investigate how global capitalism within the institutional framework depicted above operates with its

---

[42] Albert O. Hirschman, *The Passions and the Interests: Political Arguments for Capitalism before Its Triumph*, Princeton University Press, 1977, p. 3.

three fundamental elements, namely, capital, labor, and consumption, in terms of the new trends of their individual movements and their mutual interactions. Chapter 3 focuses on capital, the most dynamic and dominant element of capitalism. It shall first present empirical evidence indicating the concentrative movements of capital in various ways; then it shall clarify the conceptual meaning of "monopoly" against the background of globalization. In analyzing why global capitalism intrinsically requires and institutionally motivates capital's concentration and coordination, the chapter argues that such coordination has already arrived to the degree that getting organized has become the norm of capitalist production, finance, and service-providing on the global scale.

In contrast with capital's concentration, labor and consumption have moved toward further dispersion. Chapter 4 examines how labor is more disadvantaged than before as, on one hand, global mobility increases and, on the other, immobility still dominates. It also argues that, with these two tracks merging into one, the global labor markets are increasingly interconnected but institutionally fragmented, which stirs intensive global competition among different segments of labor. The chapter shall emphatically discuss how those in mobility are trapped in social poverty and political incapability, how those in illegal mobility are disadvantaged in labor relations with capital, and how those in immobility are left behind at the bottom of the globalizing world. All have to struggle to exchange their human existence for possibilities of better material well being, a struggle that makes them "economic men."

Laborers have another role in the capitalist system, which is that of the consumer. In this capacity, they are even more dispersed, as demonstrated in Chapter 5 by supplying the third component that will complete the diminishing curve in the relationships among three fundamental elements of capitalism, namely, capital's coordination, labor's segmentation, and consumer's atomization. The chapter will extend the examination by discussing how the making of "economic men" unfolds in the global expansion of capitalist consumption and, accordingly, the global rise of consumerism, as well as scrutinizing the restructuring of power relations among consumer, capital, and the state. It subsequently argues that these trends and relationships in globalization greatly contribute to the standardization of consumption and the atomization of consumers, thus shaping a new anarchy of human societies.

All the institutional and dynamic features of global capitalism have yielded profound social and political impacts, among which Chapter 6 will highlight inequality in both cross-state and intra-society dimensions and its disastrous sociopolitical consequences in undermining democracy. Around a scheme of global social stratification that will be termed the "three worlds" of globalization, the chapter will discuss a new great divergence in world history, and spell out how global capitalism undermines social bases of democracy, impairs democratic institutions of governance, and obstructs democratization of authoritarian polities. Chapter 7, the conclusion, will extend such discussions further, especially the implications of the absence of a coherent "political shell" of global capitalism to the following themes: the theorization of our time, the paradigm of development, the challenges facing global governance, the epistemological reframing of the ideological spectrum, and, finally, the search for a future of global capitalism.

2 | Capitalism in Institutional Reconfiguration by Globalization
A Theoretical Framework

The global triumph of capitalism is an institutional triumph, reaching far beyond the physical, technological, economic, social, cultural, and political, as all of these dimensions and their global ideological, material, and ecological aftermaths are embedded in post–Cold War globalization as a series of institutional reconfigurations of capitalism.[1] This triumph, this book would suggest, is signaled by the fact that virtually all states in the world now accept the market as the sole effective institution for economic life and, accordingly, collaborate with the market, resulting in state-market ideological conciliation and practical collaboration which has cleared away the ideological and institutional obstacles for capitalism to sweep across the globe – this is the rise of globalization. It is the institutional origin of post–Cold War globalization, the latest wave of globalization, that distinguishes itself from those earlier waves, not only with its unprecedented geographical reach, but also with an institutional universality of capitalism across various borders.[2]

Globalization has reconfigured capitalism, meaning that the global triumph of capitalism has fundamentally changed previously existing institutions of capitalist political economy; global capitalism operates under an institutional framework that differs greatly from pre-global capitalism, particularly Cold War capitalism. For the purpose of understanding such institutional changes and the new institutional

---

[1] In a succinct discussion of globalization and some of its dimensions, Manfred B. Steger does not discuss institutional meanings of globalization. Manfred B. Steger, *Globalization: A Very Short Introduction*, Oxford University Press, 2009, 2nd ed. For lengthier and more comprehensive treatments of globalization, see relevant notes below.

[2] See ft. 9, ch. 1 for some historical studies of different waves of globalization in human history. To this author, however, their attention to the institutional essence of the post–Cold War globalization as distinct from earlier waves is very much insufficient.

configuration of capitalism, this book highlights a great two-layered transformation through which capitalism has shifted both its external and internal logics during post–Cold War globalization. In the "outward" or "external" layer concerning capitalism's relationships with other major institutions in human life – prominently the state as a coercive, sovereign organization and democracy as a public-decision-making mechanism employing popular participation – lives global capitalism with new forms of integration and new instances of disconnection in its global movements, all set against a political background that is still dominated by the nation-state system; the "inward" or "interior" layer points to the remodeling of capitalism via the rise of new features of capital, labor, consumption, and their complicated mutual relationships. As the chapters that follow will take on the task of investigating institutional changes of capitalism within the second layer, the current chapter shall focus on the transformation within the first layer, namely, how the general institutional structure shared by capitalism, democracy, and the nation-state has been reconfigured through the global triumph of capitalism.

In sketching such an extensive picture, four features shall be identified and investigated, which together constitute the institutional framework of twenty-first-century globalization. At the center lies the first institutional feature that is termed the "state-market nexus," which arises in the form of a crystallization of the post–Cold War ideological conciliation and operational collaboration between the state and the market, and which occurs through the state-market institutional coupling that serves to dominate the major aspects of human life. Inevitably, the state is engaged primarily in global market competition as well as other interstate competitions, which promotes a profound shift in the various qualities of the state, ranging from its concern, role, and function to its foundation of legitimacy. The state's reliance on the capability to promote economic prosperity thus makes the state parallel to the market institutions whose primary role is economic. This phenomenon, as the second institutional feature of globalization, is conceptualized in this book as the rise of the "economic state," which can be defined as a coercive, sovereign authority for the purpose of gaining material wealth. It features an internal transformation of the state stimulated by the state-market nexus; these two features together have made a trend of closer connections, institutional coupling, and, to some extent, functional integration between the market and the state.

Disconnections have also taken place within the institutions that frame global capitalism. Of them, this chapter highlights two, both occurring above the state level. One fundamental disjuncture emerges simply because capitalism now moves globally, beyond any national scale, while democracy remains within the boundaries of the sovereign nation-state. For this simple reason, the previous historical institutional match between capitalism and democracy has been dismantled; unsurprisingly, its implications are profound. In the real world, global capitalism has found a "flat" world in its ability to escape from the checks and constraints of "local" democracies; in the ideational domain, however, the traditional conception that generalizes the historically specific Cold War inseparability between market and democracy still prevails, which consequently traps mainstream human epistemology in being too impotent to grasp the institutional essence of global capitalism. Similarly, another fundamental uncoupling occurs between national economies and the global economy, as the former have become mixed economies across the board in terms of converging both state and market functions, while the latter runs without effective governance due to the absence of a central, coercive authority. These two cleavages have formed the third and fourth institutional features that frame global capitalism; they highlight the various bumps, cracks, and gaps found in the world of globalization.

Capitalism, beyond democracy, does not operate in a political vacuum where authoritarianism could not possibly govern; as long as authoritarianism governs effectively, global capitalism may find a new paradise for fortune-making under its auspices. The new institutional political economy of global capitalism, this chapter shall argue, empowers those effective authoritarian states while harming democracy; global capitalism now lives with two different, separate political bodies, that of democracy and authoritarianism. The absence of a coherent political "shell" for capitalism – which for Cold War capitalism was, at least at one time, democracy – yields a dual political consequence: authoritarianism as both a state regime and a political institution is favored by global capital for its institutional advantage that is rooted in a condensed power which helps promote global competitiveness at the expense of civic rights, social equality, and ecological sustainability; democracy, on the other hand, in its renderings as both a state regime and a political institution, becomes increasingly dysfunctional and is inclined to depend on capital in order to maintain political legitimacy. A new chain of dependency, in which democracy depends on global capital, is shaped, which can help improve material performance, thereby lending the government legitimacy; however, global capital depends on effective authoritarianism in order to successfully generate financial success. In contrast to the "dependency theory" once suggested in studies of development, this chapter terms the chain "dependency reversed." Each of the above arguments shall be elaborated upon in detailed discussions below.

The Emergence of the State-Market Nexus: The Global Triumph of Capitalism as the Institutional Origin of Globalization

Commonly the state and the market are regarded and practiced as contending agencies for organizing social activities, two fundamentally different mechanisms not only following divergent principles and operating under distinct norms, but also working in separate spheres of human life.[3] The market is usually seen as a social mechanism that operates through voluntary involvement of people in the mutual exchange of facilities for material benefits based on the private ownership of properties; by contrast, the state features a monopoly of coercive power that is supposed to govern public affairs and, important to the discussion here, for a considerable portion of the twentieth century, was given a significant role as an alternative to the market for owning properties, planning production, and, in general, organizing economic activities.[4] The idea and practice of the state-planning economy gained

---

[3] See, for example, Charles Wolf, Jr., *Markets or Governments: Choosing between Imperfect Alternatives*, Cambridge, MA: MIT Press, 1993, 2nd ed.;
Daniel Yergin and Joseph Stanislaw, *The Commanding Heights: The Battle Between Government and the Marketplace That Is Remaking the Modern World*, New York: Simon & Schuster, 1998.

[4] For the coercive nature of the state, see Max Weber, *Economy and Society*, Guenther Roth and Claus Wittich ed., Berkeley: University of California Press, 1978, pp. 54, 318; for some general but concise discussions of the state, see, for example, Martin Carnoy, *The State and Political Theory*, Princeton University Press, 1984; John A. Hall and G. John Ikenberry, *The State*, Minneapolis: University of Minnesota Press, 1989; Gianfranco Poggi, *The State: Its Nature, Development and Prospects*, Stanford University Press, 1990; for the state-planning economy as an alternative to the market economy, see, for instance, Phyllis Deane, *The State and the Economic System: An Introduction to the History of Political Economy*, Oxford University Press, 1989.

its momentum and prominence during the Cold War era.[5] This created
the overall confrontation between capitalism, which was organized
around the market as the institutional nucleus, and communism, an
advocate of state planning as a substitute for the market, further
strengthening the conceptual as well as institutional antagonism
between the state and the market.[6]

Ideological conciliation and practical collaboration between the
state and the market, however, had also started early as a long,
historical process of institutional change in which several different,
sometimes opposite but always overlapping trends can be recognized
in bringing the state and the market to work together. One trend of
such state-market collaboration can be traced back to Keynesian
economics, occurring in mature capitalism, which began to admit
some necessity for state intervention in the market, leading to the so-
called Keynesian revolution that has had profound implications in the
capitalist state-market relationship.[7] In the words of an historian of
political economy, "the most significant and revolutionary feature
of Keynesian macro-economic analysis lay in the beneficent role it
indicated for direct government intervention in the modern market
economy."[8] To the current author, this indicates a capability of
capitalism, which was at the time historically and institutionally
associated with political democracy, for self-adjustment and institutional adaptation, allowing different, even contending mechanisms to
work together in a kind of balance to remedy the problems and
challenges that capitalism encounters. The so-called convergence

---

[5] Barrington Moore, Jr., *Terror and Progress – USSR: Some Sources of Change and
Stability in the Soviet Dictatorship*, New York: Harper & Row, 1954, ch. 2; Carl
J. Friedrich and Zbigniew K. Brzezinski, *Totalitarian Dictatorship and
Autocracy*, Cambridge, MA: Harvard University Press, 1965; Alec Nove,
The Soviet Economic System, Boston: Allen & Unwin, 1977; Jan Prybyla,
"The Chinese Communist Economic State in Comparative Perspective," in
David Shambaugh ed., *The Modern Chinese State*, Cambridge University Press,
2000, pp. 188–215.

[6] Dwight H. Perkins, *Market Control and Planning in Communist China*,
Cambridge, MA: Harvard University Press, 1966; J. M. Roberts, *The Penguin
History of the Twentieth Century: The History of the World, 1901 to the Present*,
London: Penguin Books, 2000.

[7] Lawrence R. Klein, *The Keynesian Revolution*, London: Macmillan, 1950;
Peter Hall ed., *The Political Power of Keynesian Ideas: Keynesianism Across
Nations*, Princeton University Press, 1989. Also, John Hicks, *The Crisis in
Keynesian Economics*, Oxford: Blackwell, 1974.

[8] Deane, *The State and the Economic System*, p. 166.

theory can be seen as a theoretical epitome of the trend that believes in the convergence between capitalism and socialism as an indication of a future of human societies, primarily a convergence between the market economy and state-planning measures.[9]

For the relatively later arising capitalist states, the state often played a much larger role in economic affairs than in those early capitalist countries; their success in catching up prompted a conception of the "developmental state," conceived in the 1970s and 1980s, based on various experiences such as the post–Second World War "Japanese miracle" of economic development.[10] Meanwhile, the second oil shock joined other factors in attesting to the competitiveness of states that have wider economic functions and more state autonomy than other capitalist states.[11] This trend was further reinforced by the rise of newly industrialized economies on the global periphery, exemplified by "Asian tigers", and by the good performance of small corporatist states in Europe on the world market.[12] Their conceptual confluence led to

[9] For some general elaborations of "convergence theory" of industrial societies, see, for instance, Pitrim A. Sorokin, *The Basic Trends of Our Times*, New Haven: Rowman & Littlefield, 1964; Clark Kerr, *Industrialism and Industrial Man*, New York: Penguin Books, 1973; Clark Kerr, *The Future of Industrial Societies: Convergence or Continuing Diversity?* Cambridge, MA: Harvard University Press, 1984; for "convergence" particularly between capitalism and communism, see, for example, Ramesh Mishra, "Convergence Theory and Social Change: The Development of Welfare in Britain and the Soviet Union," *Comparative Studies in Society and History*, 18, 1 (1976): 28–56; John Kenneth Galbraith and Stanislav Menshikov, *Capitalism, Communism, and Coexistence: From the Bitter Past to a Better Prospect*, Boston: Houghton Mifflin, 1988.

[10] Chalmers Johnson, *MITI and the Japanese Miracle: The Growth of Industrial Policy, 1925-1975*, Stanford University Press, 1982; Chalmers Johnson, *Japan: Who Governs? The Rise of the Developmental State*, New York: W. W. Norton, 1995; Masahiko Aoki, Hyung-Ki Kim, and Masahiro Okuno-Fujiwara eds., *The Role of Government in East Asian Economic Development: Comparative Institutional Analysis*, Oxford: Clarendon Press, 1997; Mark Robinson and Gordon White eds., *The Democratic Developmental State: Politics and Institutional Design*, Oxford University Press, 1998; Meredith Woo-Cumings ed., *The Developmental State*, Ithaca: Cornell University Press, 1999.

[11] Peter Gourevitch, *Politics in Hard Times: Comparative Responses to International Economic Crises*, Ithaca: Cornell University Press, 1986.

[12] For "Asian tigers," see, for example, Frederic C. Deyo ed., *The Political Economy of the New Asian Industrialism*, Ithaca: Cornell University Press, 1987; Stephan Haggard, *Pathways from the Periphery: The Politics of Growth in the Newly Industrialized Countries*, Ithaca: Cornell University Press, 1990; Gary Gereffi and Donald L. Wyman eds., *Manufacturing Miracles: Paths of Industrialization in Latin America and East Asia*, Princeton University Press,

reflections based on the theses of "governing the economy" and "governing the market," with empirical references as wide as the covering of advanced industrial economies in Western Europe and newly industrialized economies in East Asia.[13] Even in the United States, which is commonly and traditionally viewed as an economy with limited state involvement,[14] such a trend has accelerated to make the state cooperate with the market.[15] More generally, the call for "bringing the state back in" has revitalized a state-centered paradigm in studies of political science, calling for increasing state capacity in wider domains including the economy.[16] All of these developments, however, in either the practice of capitalism or the ideation of it in order to reflect and inspire, are still unfolded in various ways within the framework of the state versus the market in the sense of increasing roles and functions of the state within the market-framed economy, thus often suggesting the state as a remedy to overcome market failures and as an agency to address public concerns that the market tends to overlook.

Another trend in the historical process of state-market conciliation and collaboration, one which moves in an entirely different political direction, is the rise of neoliberalism. During approximately the same period discussed above,[17] the so-called neoliberal revolution took place

1990. For small corporatist states in Europe, see Peter J. Katzenstein, *Corporatism and Change: Austria, Switzerland, and the Politics of Industry*, Ithaca: Cornell University Press, 1984; Peter J. Katzenstein, *Small States in World Markets: Industrial Policy in Europe*, Ithaca: Cornell University Press, 1985.

[13] Peter A. Hall, *Governing the Economy: The Politics of State Intervention in Britain and France*, Oxford University Press, 1986; Robert Wade, *Governing the Market: Economic Theory and the Role of Government in East Asian Industrialization*, Princeton University Press, 1990.

[14] This common perception, however, is challenged by some research, which finds that the American economy has actually not been so non-interventionist. See a latest publication along this line in Stephen S. Cohen and J. Bradford DeLong, *Concrete Economics: The Hamilton Approach to Economic Growth and Policy*, Cambridge, MA: Harvard Business Review Press, 2016.

[15] Marc Allen Eisner, *The American Political Economy: Institutional Evolution of Market and State*, New York: Routledge, 2011. Also, Wyatt Wells, *American Capitalism, 1945-2000: Continuity and Change from Mass Production to the Information Society*, Chicago: Ivan R. Dee, 2003.

[16] Peter Evans, Dietrich Rueschemeyer, and Theda Skocpol eds., *Bringing the State Back In*, Cambridge University Press, 1985.

[17] David Harvey regards the years 1978–1980 as a "revolutionary turning-point" seeing the rise of neoliberalism. David Harvey, *A Brief History of Neoliberalism*, Oxford University Press, 2005, p. 1. Also see Christian Caryl, *Strange Rebels: 1979 and the Birth of the 21st Century*, New York: Basic Books, 2013.

in both major industrial democracies and communist economies, then sweeping across other parts of the world, and has since maintained an overwhelming influence on the economy, society, and politics along with the rise and progress of globalization.[18] With this trend, as some already observed in the early 1990s, "there is indeed a clear-cut shift in the opinions of commentators and policymakers. In fact, public discourse shows an overwhelming tendency toward simplistic trust in 'the market' and skeptical rejection of the state's role in the economy."[19] In the United States, scholars observed the "grand truce with capital."[20] Citing Karl Polanyi's conclusion that the spread of universal suffrage and democratic associationalism worked as a reaction against the tyranny of the market forces that the gold standard had helped to unleash, a scholar commented in the first decade of the twenty-first century that "what would have surprised him, presumably, was the resurgence of market forces ... "[21] In a summary by one of its major

[18] Harvey, *A Brief History of Neoliberalism*; John L. Campbell and Ove K. Pedersen, "Introduction: The Rise of Neoliberalism and Institutional Analysis," in John L. Campbell and Ove K. Pedersen eds., *The Rise of Neoliberalism and Institutional Analysis*, Princeton University Press, 2001, pp. 1–23; Manfred B. Steger and Ravi K. Roy, *Neoliberalism: A Very Short Introduction*, Oxford University Press, 2010; Colin Crouch, *The Strange Non-Death of Neoliberalism*, Cambridge: Polity, 2011; Jonathan Swarts, *Constructing Neoliberalism: Economic Transformation in Anglo-American Democracies*, University of Toronto Press, 2013.

[19] Louis Putterman and Dietrich Rueschemeyer, "State and Market in Development: An Introduction," in Louis Putterman and Dietrich Rueschemeyer eds., *State and Market in Development: Synergy or Rivalry?* Boulder: Lynne Rienner, 1992, pp. 1–6 (p. 1). Other contributors to the same volume have similar statements. For example, paralleling it to the Keynesian revolution, Haggard and Kaufman state: "In the 1980s, a similar sea change took place in economic thinking in the developing world. ... There was a growing perception of the limits of state intervention in markets and of inward-looking developmental strategies, although substantial debate remained about how far to go in a more liberal direction." Stephen Haggard and Robert Kaufman, "The State in the Initiation and Consolidation of Market-Oriented Reform," in Putterman and Rueschemeyer, *State and Market in Development*: p. 237.

[20] Leo Panitch and Sam Gindin, *The Making of Global Capitalism: The Political Economy of American Empire*, London: Verso, 2012, p. 59.

[21] Barry Eichengreen, *Globalizing Capital: A History of the International Monetary System*, Princeton University Press, 2008, 2nd ed., pp. 230–231. For Polanyi's point of view, see Karl Polanyi, *The Great Transformation: The Political and Economic Origins of Our Time*, Boston: Beacon Press, 1957 [1944], pp. 133–134, 227–229. For a general investigation of this trend, see Steger and Roy, *Neoliberalism*; for such a resurgence particularly in the United

critics, David Harvey, neoliberalism is described as believing that "human well-being can best be advanced by liberating individual entrepreneurial freedoms and skills within the institutional framework characterized by strong private property rights, free markets, and free trade," and is often embedded in government policies of promoting privatization and deregulation.[22]

The last sentence of Harvey's quotation is particularly interesting, as it indicates that neoliberalism paradoxically requires state actions, though often in the form of "actions to reduce actions," so to speak. The significant role of the state in initiating, promoting, and implementing neoliberal economic policies, though it may sound self-contradictory for those who are stuck in the state-market dichotomy, should be highlighted here.[23] In a mature market economy such as the United Kingdom's, as thoughtfully pointed out by an early analyst of Thatcherism, neoliberalism signifies a broad-ranging and distinctive program aimed at promoting economic recovery through the privatization of public enterprise and the *restoration of the authority of the state*.[24] The free economy and the strong state, as this analyst explicitly indicated in the book title, were reinforced at the same time. The victory of the market, therefore, cannot be interpreted simply as a retreat of the state; rather, it is a conversion of the state to work in line with the market principle. Neoliberalism, therefore, is an ideational reflection of the emerging state-market collaboration rather than a pure market doctrine; it has transformed the state into a servant of the market, making the realm of the state one that is being "privatized" for materialist interest, rather than being a convergence of public interests as it otherwise would be, at least in theory.[25] This transformation has profound implications, which shall be discussed later concerning the rise of the economic state.

The above two trends, namely, increasing state intervention in the market economy and neoliberal deregulation of the market by the state,

States, see a historical review in John L. Kelley, *Bringing the Market Back In: The Political Revitalization of Market Liberalism*, London: Macmillan, 1997.

[22] Harvey, *A Brief History of Neoliberalism*, p. 2.

[23] Jonah D. Levy ed., *The State after Statism*, Cambridge, MA: Harvard University Press, 2006.

[24] Andrew Gamble, *The Free Economy and the Strong State: The Politics of Thatcherism*, Durham: Duke University Press, 1988.

[25] I use the term "privatize" here in the sense of being contrary to socialization, as defined in E. E. Schattschneider, *The Semisovereign People: A Realist's View of Democracy in America*, Fort Worth: Holt, Rinehart & Winston, 1983.

to this author, ironically but dialectically display the same institutional change: the trend of state-market conciliation. Conceptually, both assume that the state and the market can work together, albeit with different emphases on either the state or the market. Diachronically, they may be regarded as pendulum movements between the state and the market to adjust their relationships and seek a proper mechanism of how the capitalist state coexists and collaborates with the market. To learn from Isaiah Berlin's distinction between "positive" and "negative freedoms,"[26] this chapter suggests an understanding of the difference between the trend of increasing state roles in the economy and the rise of neoliberalism as "positive" and "negative" roles of the state in the market: conventional state interventionism emphasizes the active role of the state and its positive impact; neoliberalism believes in the passive role of the state in benefiting the market, allowing the latter a negative freedom. They both, however, contribute to the shaping of the state-market nexus.

The decisive turn in the emergence of the state-market nexus, however, took place in communist states, where – in circumstances fundamentally different from those discussed above – the state, since its establishment, had held an anti-market ideology while practicing a state-planning economy. However, about the same time that the above-discussed changes were transforming capitalist economies, market-oriented reform was being carried out in order to incorporate market elements into the statist framework. State-market antagonism began to relax across the Eurasian continent from Berlin to Beijing, initially with the introduction of limited market elements into these communist systems, but then turning into comprehensive marketization programs, first in Eastern European countries and subsequently spreading to the Soviet Union and China, the two largest and most powerful communist economies. Up to the 1980s, market-oriented economic reform became a major program in most communist states.[27] Eventually, history witnessed in the late 1980s

---

[26] Isaiah Berlin, *Four Essays on Liberty*, Oxford University Press, 1969, pp. 121–144.
[27] For marketization reform in the Soviet Union and Eastern European countries, see, for example, Stephen White, *Gorbachev in Power*, Cambridge University Press, 1990; Anders Aslund, *Gorbachev's Struggle for Economic Reform*, Ithaca: Cornell University Press, 1991; János Mátyás Kovács and Márton Tardos eds., *Reform and Transformation in Eastern Europe: Soviet-Type Economics on the Threshold of Change*, London: Routledge, 1992;

and early 1990s two outcomes for these communist states. Some, such as in the Soviet Union and Eastern Europe, collapsed;[28] an observer of contemporary capitalism pointed out that this resulted from "the eagerness of the new democratic governments in Europe to embrace the project of a fast transition toward market mechanisms," making "the triumph of free marketers overwhelming in the early nineties."[29] Other

Walter Adams and James W. Brock, *Adam Smith Goes to Moscow*, Princeton University Press, 1993; James Leitzel, *Russian Economic Reform*, London: Routledge, 1995; Jerry F. Hough, *The Logic of Economic Reform in Russia*, Washington, DC: Brookings Institution Press, 2001; Oleh Havrylyshyn and Saleh M. Nsouli eds., *A Decade of Transition: Achievements and Challenges*, Washington, DC: IMF Institute, 2001; Vladimir Gel'man, Otar Marganiya, and Dmitry Travin, *Reexamining Economic and Political Reforms in Russia, 1985-2000: Generations, Ideas, and Changes*, Lanham: Lexington Books, 2014. For that in China, see, for instance, Harry Harding, *China's Second Revolution: Reform After Mao*, Washington, DC: Brookings Institution, 1987; Sheng Hua, Xuejun Zhang, and Xiaopeng Luo, *China: From Revolution to Reform*, London: Macmillan, 1993; Barry Naughton, *Growing Out of the Plan: Chinese Economic Reform, 1978–1993*, Cambridge University Press, 1995; Jonathan Story, *China: The Race to Market*, London: Prentice Hall, 2003; Scott Kennedy, *China's Capitalist Transformation*, Stanford University Press, 2011; Nicholas R. Lardy, *Markets over Mao: The Rise of Private Business in China*, Washington, DC: PIIE Press, 2014. For Asian communist countries' acceptance of market, see, for instance, Sujian Guo, *The Political Economy of Asian Transition from Communism*, Aldershot: Ashgate, 2006; Janos Kornai and Yingyi Qian eds., *Market and Socialism: In the Light of the Experiences of China and Vietnam*, New York: Palgrave Macmillan, 2009. For some comparative studies, see, for example, Minxin Pei, *From Reform to Revolution: The Demise of Communism in China and the Soviet Union*, Cambridge, MA: Harvard University Press, 1994; Bernard Chavance, Charles Hauss, and Mark Selden, *The Transformation of Communist Systems: Economic Reform Since the 1950s*, Boulder: Westview, 1994.

[28] For the collapse of communism in Eastern Europe and the Soviet Union and its implication for these countries' marketization, see, for instance, Adam Przeworski, *Democracy and the Market: Political and Economic Reforms in Eastern Europe and Latin America*, Cambridge University Press, 1991; Larry Diamond and Marc F. Plattner eds., *Economic Reform and Democracy*, Baltimore: Johns Hopkins University Press, 1995; Grzegorz Ekiert and Stephen E. Hanson eds., *Capitalism and Democracy in Central and Eastern Europe: Assessing the Legacy of Communist Rule*, Cambridge University Press, 2003; John E. Jackson, Jacek Klich, and Krystyna Poznanska, *The Political Economy of Poland's Transition: New Firms and Reform Governments*, Cambridge University Press, 2005.

[29] Robert Boyer, "The Variety and Unequal Performance of Really Existing Markets: Farewell to Doctor Pangloss?" in J. Rogers Hollingsworth and Robert Boyer eds., *Contemporary Capitalism: The Embeddedness of Institutions*, Cambridge University Press, 1997, pp. 55–93 (p. 57).

communist states explicitly abandoned their anti-market ideology and their state-planning economic practices, instead embracing the market for a fundamental restructuring of their economies, as China and Vietnam may best demonstrate.[30]

To a much lesser extent, but symbolically important nonetheless, even nations like Cuba and North Korea also began at a later time to limitedly explore the introduction of market measures in order to revitalize their economies, including the initiation and inception of Special Economic Zones, a widely adopted policy for a communist state in testing water of marketization.[31] The historical track is clear in showing that the state-planning economy has been seriously questioned and even blamed for its inefficiency, and it has been reformed and restructured in all communist countries using various measures, paces, and determinations, eventually resulting in its abandonment as a political-economic system for an ideal society, sealed into history as an ever-most-powerful contending political-economic institution opposing market institutions. The market, the rudimentary institution of capitalism which was once condemned in these countries as the "devil" in human life,[32] has now been adopted as the fundamental mechanism of the economy.

At this juncture, capitalism was able to claim its global triumph, as the collapse of world communism erased all traces of the state system that

---

[30] China's successful marketization is a well-known story around which a huge body of scholastic literature emerged in the past decades. For some overviews of China's early marketization in the late twentieth century, see ft. 27. For Vietnam's experience of marketization, see, for instance, Geoffrey Murray, *Vietnam: Dawn of a New Market*, New York: St. Martin's Press, 1997; Jennie Litvack and Dennis A. Rondinelli eds., *Market Reform in Vietnam: Building Institutions for Development*, Westport, CT: Praeger, 1999; Stéphanie Balme and Mark Sidel eds., *Vietnam's New Order: International Perspectives on the State and Reform in Vietnam*, New York: Palgrave Macmillan, 2006.

[31] For the experiments of economic liberalization in Cuba, see, for example, Richard Feinberg, *Open for Business: Building the New Cuban Economy*, Washington, DC: Brookings Institution Press, 2016; for those in North Korea, see, for instance, Hazel Smith, *North Korea: Markets and Military Rule*, Cambridge University Press, 2015.

[32] For an extreme case against the market such as the Maoist economic doctrine and practice during China's Cultural Revolution, see, for example, Carl Riskin, *China's Political Economy: The Quest for Development since 1949*, Oxford University Press, 1987; Richard Curt Kraus, *The Cultural Revolution: A Very Short Introduction*, Oxford University Press, 2012, ch. 4. Also see Perkins, *Market Control and Planning in Communist China*; Prybyla, "The Chinese Communist Economic State in Comparative Perspective."

explicitly opposed the doctrine, practice, and institutions of the market. Instead, as an expert claims, since the 1990s "there has emerged a common ideology that markets are basically the most efficient methods for coordinating the economies of modern societies ... "[33] The market has become the "hegemonic liberal bourgeois ideology," which, some say, is "omni-present today and begins to pervade a person even before he or she learns how to walk."[34] This prevaling of the market, I would add, has not been simply ideological; more importantly, it has been institutional. It stands to reason, in fact, that a person in the post–Cold War era has to live with the market even before he or she is born.

To this book, this is the institutional origin of the twenty-first-century globalization that defines our age. This chapter, therefore, argues emphatically that the collapse of world communism has cleared the way for a global triumph of the market; this makes the actualization of the world market possible with much greater integration than before. As virtually all states embrace the market mechanism, the market is able to connect and integrate every part of the globe into something we have called global capitalism. Globalization, in this book's definition, simply refers to this phenomenon. In other words, starting from state-market collaboration, globalization has gained an institutional momentum that galvanizes all elements or conditions involved in trade, investment, technology, communication, transportation, and the like, unleashing the market "unbound," as some authors have described, to cause the unprecedentedly global reach of capitalism.[35]

The state-market nexus, therefore, has emerged along with the global triumph of capitalism as the first new institutional feature of the political economy of global capitalism. This nexus, generally speaking, is the institutional convergence of all the above-discussed trends in the exploration of a variety of state-market compatibilities along differing lines; it is the organizational crystallization of the globalizing momentum of capitalism in reconfiguring its connections and relationships with the state. Analytically, the nexus means, first of all, that all states

---

[33]   Boyer, "The Variety and Unequal Performance of Really Existing Markets," p. 56.

[34]   Jose Brendan Macdonald, "The Challenge of a Democratic Economy," in Jeff Shantz and Jose Brendan Macdonald eds., *Beyond Capitalism: Building Democratic Alternatives for Today and the Future*, New York: Bloomsbury, 2013, pp. 1–23 (p. 7).

[35]   Lowell Bryan and Diana Farrell, *Market Unbound: Unleashing Global Capitalism*, New York: John Wiley, 1996.

accept the market as the fundamental mechanism to organize the economy, without any inspiration or attempt to build up an alternative series of economic institutions, especially such institutions solely dominated by the state, to replace the market. Secondly, all states in the post–Cold War world make efforts to work with the market, rhetorically for the purpose of remedying market failures but in practice often for stimulating market power; the state is not seen as something irrelevant to market operations, while the market is not a domain separated from coverage by the state. This operational collaboration between the state and the market ties the two most powerful institutions in human life together more closely than they have ever been. Thirdly, as this chapter shall investigate, the state and the market in their collaborations have influenced each other in institutional ways, and have developed their common goals, shared interests, codependent operations, and mutually fertilized institutions.

In short, the state-market nexus means ideological conciliation, operational collaboration, and institutional compatibility between the state and the market in together laying down the institutional foundation of globalization. In the nexus, the state and the market institutionally couple, are compatible, and collaborate with each other, albeit with some intrinsic tensions, in order to work together, rather than confronting, competing, or isolating themselves from one another. With the nexus, the state and the market coincide in their coverage of human life, reinforcing each other and operating within virtually the same jurisdiction while increasingly dispelling any other human institutions from being powerful enough to compete or parallel them. In other words, in signaling the global triumph of capitalism in the institutional sense, the state and the market as two different sets of institutions have now joined each other as collaborators in making possible their domination of human life, primarily within but not limited to the economic realm.

Many earlier studies have emphasized that "the role of states and markets in fostering economic efficiency are intricately intertwined. If this is true about economic growth in mature industrial societies, it is even truer when it comes to creating and maintaining the institutional conditions required for sustained economic growth."[36] My theorization of the post–Cold War state-market nexus, however, is different in the analytical, conceptual, and normative sense. Analytically, such earlier

---

[36] Putterman and Rueschemeyer, "State and Market in Development," p. 2.

arguments, as quoted above, still hold a zero-sum-game assumption between the state and the market, though they emphasize a kind of balance or combination of the two institutions within such a game. My argument, however, tries to show that with the neoliberal turn, the involvement of the state in economic activity has not been reduced but has dramatically increased simultaneously with the expansion of the market mechanism both geographically and institutionally. In other words, the state and the market within the state-market nexus co-work in the direction of both increasing their roles in shaping the political economy of global capitalism. Conceptually, a notional and institutional relationship between the state and the market must not be understood as that in which the state works to correct market failures, a prevailing assumption underlining earlier observations of state-market cooperation; instead, this chapter, in reflecting the development of global capitalism, highlights the possibility of a new conceptualization of state-market codependence and inter-fertilization. The involvement of the state in the economy, as analyzed above in this section, reinforces the market in various ways rather than balancing, constraining, or correcting it. Finally, while earlier propositions of state-market synergy usually recommend it as an avenue for better development, this book views the state-market nexus as the institutional root of globalization and its numerous pitfalls and normatively negative consequences.

It is clear that the shaping of the state-market nexus is a fundamental institutional change to modern human history, but its profound implications have been insufficiently investigated and understood. The traditional, specifically Cold War–era, ideological coordinate that defines the Rightist-Leftist spectrum along with the state-confronting-market axis has become outdated, but our way of thinking is still, more often than not, trapped in the stereotype of highlighting state-market antagonism in values, principles, and mechanisms. Accordingly, the institutional essence of globalization embedded in the state-market nexus is often neglected or, as is sometimes noticed, inadequately elaborated. This chapter, however, takes the state-market nexus as the conceptual ground for exploring further its institutional ramifications in the sense of how the state per se is institutionally affected by this nexus, as in the rise of the economic state, and how the relationship between global capitalism and the political economy of the nation-state changes through major decoupling. They together set up the institutional framework within which globalization unfolds.

The Rise of the Economic State: State-Led Development and Economization of Political Power

In its ideological conciliation, operational collaboration, and institutional cross-fertilization with the market, the state is inevitably reconfigured; the rise of the economic state is the most prominent change regarding fundamental state institutions and inherent features of the state. As the state is primarily occupied by concern over its economic performance, attempting to function in either positive (statist) or negative (neoliberal) ways to promote economic development, and increasingly lays its legitimacy and institutional foundations on the delivery of material or other economy-related benefits to its population rather than on the protection and provision of public goods, it has become, this author suggests, the economic state. The economic state often shares a common goal with the market as a whole, which is to increase the movement of private goods of participants into market exchanges; it may "govern" or "deregulate" the market for the actualization of this goal, but, either way, its efforts lie solely in the creation of political utility for the purpose of serving market operations. Or, in a rather gentler sentence by two leading scholars of international political economy, "nation-states have keen interests in the workings of markets."[37] Economic performance, often in the form of growth or development, rises as "governmentality," to use a Foucaultian term, [38] or as ideology to dominate politics, and material-based legitimacy grows to such a degree that it may overwhelm other types of legitimacy, accordingly undermining procedural, participatory, and democratic legitimacy.

This "economization" of the state is, of course, contradictory to classic conceptions of the state. Traditionally and conceptually, the state and the market work in different spheres of human activity; when they interact with each other, they check over one another, acting as a constraint to the other's operation, function, and impact. Now, however, they are mutually reinforcing each other. Such a change, in the state-market-nexus perspective, is quite natural, as the state-market nexus makes the two sets of institutions mutually influence and alter

---

[37] Joseph M. Grieco and G. John Ikenberry, *State Power and World Markets: The International Political Economy*, New York: W.W. Norton, 2003, p. 9.

[38] Michel Foucault, "Governmentality," in Graham Burchell, Colin Gordon, and Peter Miller eds., *The Foucault Effect: Studies in Governmentality*, University of Chicago Press, 1991, pp. 87–104. Also see, Mitchell Dean, *Governmentality: Power and Rules in Modern Society*, London: Sage, 1999.

each other's organizational principles and institutional functions. This institutional codependence reinforces both the state and the market, but also distorts or reconfigures both via various methods of cross-fertilization.

Globalization, moreover, intensifies the international economic competition that engages virtually all states, which further increases economic concerns and strengthens relevant economic functions of the state.[39] Against the background of state-market conciliation and collaboration across regime types of various states, international economic competition intensifies not only because the scope of the market has been expanded through globalization and the concomitant stretch of multinational corporations to occupy the market, but also due to domestic pressures everywhere that the state must tackle in order to gain or maintain the legitimacy that was once ideologically or procedurally supported. The state has unprecedentedly taken an increased interest in its own economic performance in both interstate and domestic political economies, though such economic engagement of the state can take different paths, including, as discussed earlier, expanding the role of the state in economic affairs or, in a functionally opposite direction, allowing the market to operate in a "freer" manner through decreasing state regulations over the market for the purpose of promoting the market's successes in delivering wealth.

The rise of the economic state is, perhaps, most observable in the Global South, where, as many scholars – most prominently Atul Kohli – point out, state-led development prevails.[40] "The creation of effective states within the developing world," Kohli argues, "has generally preceded the emergence of industrializing economies," and this is "because state intervention in support of investor profits has proved to be a precondition for industry to emerge and flourish among late-late-developers."[41] In post–Cold War studies of development, the

[39]   John Micklethwait and Adrian Wooldridge, *The Fourth Revolution: The Global Race to Reinvent the State*, New York: Penguin Press, 2014.

[40]   Atul Kohli, *State-Directed Development: Political Power and Industrialization in the Global Periphery*, Cambridge University Press, 2004. Also, Peter Evans, *Embedded Autonomy: States and Industrial Transformation*, Princeton University Press, 1995; Linda Weiss and John M. Hobson, *States and Economic Development: A Comparative Historical Analysis*, Cambridge: Polity, 1995; David Waldner, *State Building and Late Development*, Ithaca: Cornell University Press, 1999.

[41]   Kohli, *State-Directed Development*, p. 2.

"developmental state" or "governing the market" perspective has gained further rigorous intellectual power, as exemplified in notions such as "combining states and markets," "strategic capitalism," and "state-led" or "state-directed development."[42] The state, therefore, is increasingly viewed, analyzed, and appreciated as an economic agency.

In industrialized democracies, the disappearance of political, military, and ideological confrontations between democracy and communism with the collapse of the Soviet bloc greatly promoted an economy-centered mentality among voters, as epitomized in Bill Clinton's first campaign slogan, "It's the economy, stupid!"[43] The Clinton years are, accordingly, remembered and celebrated for their economic achievements, a time of unprecedented wealth, of breathtaking progress in technology, and, therefore, a "golden age" in which American society was "so favored as it entered a new millennium that its people could be excused for believing they were experiencing their very best of times."[44]

It is true that the economization of the state has been an underlying trend for a great length of time over the course of modern history. As touched upon earlier in this chapter, the trend can be traced back at least to the Cold War era, when, despite the ideological and political confrontation between the state-planning system and market capitalism, the imperative, policy, and practice that emphasized and increased state functions in market operations had never failed in its attempts to restructure state-market relations toward the direction of "economizing" the state. The capitalist state in industrial democracies, not to mention the communist state that carried the tremendous weight of both the ownership of properties and its indispensable role of state-planning, has experienced a constant enlargement in order to take increasing care of the economy. This can be sketched in three versions of the state emerging in sequence over history: the regulatory state, which functions to maintain the order of the market and whose economic role is often termed "gate-keeper"; the welfare state, in which the capitalist state expands its concern, role, and functions into the realm of distribution; and the developmental state, which further

---

[42] Weiss and Hobson, *States and Economic Development*; Kohli, *State-Directed Development*.

[43] For the slogan and its background, see, for example, Wikipedia, https://en .wikipedia.org/wiki/It's_the_economy,_stupid, accessed June 15, 2015.

[44] Haynes Johnson, *The Best of Times: America in the Clinton Years*, New York: Harcourt, 2001, p. 1.

expands into the realm of production.[45] Even the regulatory state, though some argue it has little intervention in market operation, for our point obviously contradicts the belief in a self-regulating market, thus implying the existence of economic roles and functions of the state, albeit greatly limited ones. It is commonly acknowledged that autonomous market operation is inclined to increase inequality, thus arises the welfare state in capitalism in order to remedy this fateful market problem by emphasizing the state's role in distribution.[46] In late and late-late capitalist nations, the role of the state is further extended into the sphere of production, thus placing upon the developmental state growing economic responsibilities to create various "miracles" represented by "manufacturing miracles."[47] The state has been, in general, increasingly interventionist, though to various degrees in given national environments, while the market everywhere has been acting increasingly under state governance despite the seemingly un-statist phenomenon of neoliberalism.[48] This trajectory, though taking diverse paths, clearly indicates the growing economization of the capitalist state, and eventually results in the rise of the economic state through the merging of various earlier developments of the economization of the state as a new, institutional crystallization.

---

[45] This is the current author's interpretation of the types of the so-called capitalist state in terms of their different relations with the market. For the regulatory state, especially in the US, see, for example, Kelley, *Bringing the Market Back In*. For the welfare state, see, for instance, Francis G. Castles, Stephan Leibfried, Jane Lewis, Herbert Obinger, and Christopher Pierson eds., *The Oxford Handbook of the Welfare State*, Oxford University Press, 2010; Nicholas Barr, *Economics of the Welfare State*, Oxford University Press, 2012, 5th ed.; Kees van Kersbergen and Barbara Vis, *Comparative Welfare State Politics: Development, Opportunities, and Reform*, Cambridge University Press, 2013; David Garland, *The Welfare State: A Very Short Introduction*, Oxford University Press, 2016. For the developmental state, see ft. 10.

[46] Gøsta Esping-Andersen, *The Three Worlds of Welfare Capitalism*, Princeton University Press, 1990; Albert O. Hirschman, *The Rhetoric of Reaction: Perversity, Futility, Jeopardy*, Cambridge, MA: Belknap Press of Harvard University Press, 1991.

[47] Gereffi and Wyman, *Manufacturing Miracles*. See also, Johnson, *MITI and the Japanese Miracle*; Johnson, *Japan: Who Governs*; Deyo, *The Political Economy of the New Asian Industrialism*; Haggard, *Pathways from Periphery*; Wade, *Governing the Market*; Aoki et al., *The Role of Government in East Asian Economic Development*; Woo-Cumings, *The Developmental State*; Alice H. Amsden, *Asia's Next Giant: South Korea and Late Industrialization*, Oxford University Press, 1992.

[48] Peter A. Hall and David Soskice eds., *Varieties of Capitalism: The Institutional Foundations of Comparative Advantage*, Oxford University Press, 2001.

Post–Cold War globalization, however, does establish new features within this long-existing trend. It creates a political and ideological boundary that restricts an increase of the state's economic role, which is exemplified in the collapse of the state-planning economy. The market is now the foundation for all state functions in economic affairs while, by the same token, state governance of the market is no longer trying to replace the latter. The state now respects the market, but it also governs the market by various methods. Now they jointly, rather than separately or antagonistically, set the framework for economic activities. When state-market collaboration replaces state-market confrontation, both the state and the market have to compromise, which means that each gains and each loses. The type of state that aims for the elimination of the market disappears, yet the state in general has won new ground in economic affairs; the "free" market that denies all state intervention, on the other hand, ebbs, but with the insertion of new roles of the state, the market in its post–Cold War incarnation prevails. The rise of the economic state, therefore, should be understood in this context of institutional interweaving between the state and the market, standing at the mutually reinforced point that connects the two.

The prevailing of the neoliberal state, therefore, is not a contradiction to the above-observed trend. Rather, I would argue that the rise of the neoliberal state is simply a specific form of the rise of the economic state, as it employs a specific strategy based on its specific belief in the reduction of the state's "positive" intervention in the market, paradoxically for the purpose of strengthening the state's attention to the economy and promoting an economic efficiency that the state has expected and that is in the state's interest.[49] It is a rather too-narrow perspective to view neoliberalism simply as a project of disengaging the state from the economy; neoliberalism, in a deeper sense, can mean a kind of "service" that the state provides to the market, as "services" to the market by the state can be through either "negative" or "positive" means, according to Berlin's line of reasoning.

In a similar vein, here it can be proposed that state intervention may be carried out on two levels that correspond to a fundamental division of spheres in economics, namely "micro-interventions" and "macro-interventions" or, in two-way and political terms, "tactic interventions" and "strategic interventions." There is no clear-cut distinction

---

[49] Harvey, *A Brief History of Neoliberalism.*

between the two, but I would suggest that macro- or strategic interventions are often manifested in the overall increasing governmental attention to and concern over market operation and its economic performance within a given state's jurisdiction. They can include the increased importance and, accordingly, functions and influence of the central bank in the state's overall governance of a nation, for example; they especially include the state's greatly strengthened role in international economic competition.

The economic state can do either or both; the neoliberal state nevertheless is inclined to reduce micro-interventions while increasing macro-interventions. In fact, the rise of state-led development and neoliberal dominance can be regarded as two sides of the same coin, both reflecting the underlining trajectory of the rise of the economic state and accordingly demonstrating how the state and the market are reconfigured by each other as they become locked in the state-market nexus during the transformation of the state brought about by the global triumph of capitalism.

With the state-market nexus, the triumph of the market does not necessarily mean the substantial retreat of the state, although many scholars had predicted and described such a decline of the state with the rise of globalization.[50] As Robert Gilpin points out, "for better or for worse, this is still a state-dominated world." He maintains that "the importance of the state has even actually increased in some areas, certainly with respect to promoting international competitiveness through support for R & D, for technology policy, and for other assistance to domestic firms."[51] Concerning some wider and deeper changes in the economic role of the state, here I would push Gilpin's judgment further by arguing that, despite various erosions to state sovereignty – as exemplified by the rise of multilateralism in international relations,[52] the many adjustments of state functions in economic

---

[50] Susan Strange, *The Retreat of the State: The Diffusion of Power in the World Economy*, Cambridge University Press, 1996; Vincent Cable, 'The Diminished Nation-State: A Study in the Loss of Economic Power," *Daedalus* 124, 2 (Spring 1995): 23–53, see the point in 44–46.

[51] Robert Gilpin, *Global Political Economy: Understanding the International Economic Order*, Princeton University Press, 2001, p. 363.

[52] For the rise of multilateralism in international relations and its constraint over states, see, for instance, John Gerard Ruggie ed., *Multilateralism Matters: The Theory and Praxis of an Institutional Form*, New York: Columbia University Press, 1993.

affairs, and the rise of competitors to sovereign states[53] – the involvement of the state in economic affairs has been increasing continually and has expanded to the degree that there is no state in today's world that does not exercise any economic role and function. Overall, the economy plays a much more significant role in the life of the state than before, which is what this section refers to as the rise of the economic state.

The state does decline, on the other hand, if it is viewed under the lens of public goods. Such declines, however, in this book's point of view, simply support the argument of the rise of the economic state by highlighting how the economization of the state implies the transformation of the state from a public venue to one that is privatized, thus reducing the responsibilities of the state in providing social benefits and public goods for all citizens, while its capacity for unleashing market power and promoting material prosperity is increasingly and often single-mindedly sought. The consequences of the rise of the economic state, in fact, are profound, often including growing socioeconomic inequality, deterioration in the quality of public governance, and impotence in dealing with human security challenges. Two prominent impacts over state institutions, however, deserve special attention: the shift of the basis of state legitimacy, which will be briefly discussed immediately below, and the corporatization of the state, a point that will be analyzed in the section concerning the disjuncture between the global free market and the mixed national economy.

A significant aftermath of the rise of the economic state is the shift of state legitimacy toward being materialistic, often depending upon the leadership's economic performance. This shift is prominent in the developing world, as both Gilpin and Kohli suggest from different angles.[54] In Kohli's words, since "the way state power is organized and used has decisively influenced rates and patterns of industrialization in the global periphery," "legitimate states that govern effectively and dynamic industrial economies are widely regarded today as the defining characteristics of a modern nation-state,"[55] which powerfully motivates those left behind, namely, the developing states, which have no choice except to try to catch up.[56] This economic catching-up

---

[53] Hendrik Spruyt, *The Sovereign State and Its Competitors: An Analysis of System Change*, Princeton University Press, 1994.
[54] Gilpin, *Global Political Economy*, p. 376; Kohli, *State-Directed Development*.
[55] Kohli, *State-Directed Development*, p. 9.   [56] Ibid., p. 1.

becomes more urgent in the globalization age than before, for the following reasons:

1) The demise of communism shut down a major, if not the only, alternative to capitalism for promoting development, and the developing nations now have no option but to bring themselves into a comparative global context with the industrialized capitalist states;

2) Because many of the developing countries have newly inaugurated democracies through the "third wave" of democratization,[57] domestic political contestation intensifies politicians' competition to offer "beef," namely economic performance and material benefits to gain voters' support, as seen in stable democracies but often with greater vigor;

3) If political authoritarianism maintains power in a developing nation, the urgency of delivering material improvement becomes even more pressing to the regime's interest, because the ideological victory of democracy, though limited in comparison with that of the market, has further reduced the political legitimacy of such an authoritarian regime. This forces it to turn to economic performance to remedy its politically and ideologically handicapped authority;

4) Involvement in globalization intensifies international economic competition, in which the developing countries have to strengthen their state functions for economic purposes, as they now directly encounter those developed nations which have supposedly greater advantages, at least in economic and technological aspects.

The economic state operationally bends politics to economics, and conceptually it desires citizens' convenient acceptance of the proposition of "economics as politics." The rise of the conception of a political legitimacy that is rooted in economic performance is, to this author, simply an ideational reflection as well as, intentionally or not, a justification of the change.[58] As economics is propelled toward becoming the central focus of politics, political power, whether in the form of

---

[57] Samuel P. Huntington, *The Third Wave: Democratization in the Late Twentieth Century*, Norman: University of Oklahoma Press, 1991.

[58] For a discussion and criticism of economic performance-based political legitimacy, see Guoguang Wu, *China's Party Congress: Power, Legitimacy, and Institutional Manipulation*, Cambridge University Press, 2015, ch. 2.

democracy or not, needs effective delivery of economic benefits to bolster its legitimacy over the ruled; politicians now often rely on their propagandized promises and positive performance in promoting economic prosperity either to gain power, as in a democracy, or to maintain power, as with authoritarianism. Political accountability, therefore, is for banknotes rather than for ballots; prosperity can support power without sufficient consideration of the people. Moreover, state power is now more than ever before tainted by exchange, thus governmental corruption prevails everywhere. The rise of the economic state, in sum, is a huge institutional change alongside globalization; its profound ramifications explain many of the significant post–Cold War developments in the political economy of capitalism, including their seemingly self-contradictory manifestations. As these shall be investigated later in their appropriate places, this chapter shall now turn to institutional changes in the global structure beyond the internal nature of the state.

Global Capitalism Out of the Political Shell of Nation-State Democracy: The Great Disjuncture of Globalization

As capitalism expands onto a global scale, democracy is, by contrast, still confined within the boundaries of the nation-state; a great disjuncture, therefore, emerges between global capitalism and nation-state democracy. This great disjuncture is obviously essential for understanding the new political economy of global capitalism; it speaks volumes in explaining twenty-first-century globalization and its aftermaths.

This proposition challenges a prevailing idea that interprets the global triumph of capitalism in the late twentieth century as a triumph of both market and democracy, an idea being exemplified in arguments such as the "mutual recognition" between markets and democracy, the "end of history," and the so-called liberal logic of marketization leading to democratization.[59] In a metaphor used by

---

[59] For the argument of "mutual recognition" between market and democracy, see, for example, Laurence Whitehead, "Stirrings of Mutual Recognition," in Laurence Whitehead ed., *Emerging Market Democracies: East Asia and Latin America*, Baltimore: Johns Hopkins University Press, 2002, pp. 1–15; for the "end of the history" thesis, see Francis Fukuyama, "The End of History?" *The National Interest*, 16 (Summer 1989): 3–18; Francis Fukuyama, "At the 'End of History' Still Stands Democracy," *Wall Street Journal*, June 6, 2014, http://www.wsj.com/arti cles/at-the-end-of-history-still-stands-democracy-1402080661; Francis Fukuyama,

South Korean democratic-dissident-turned-President Kim Dae-jung, democracy and the market are, as it is widely held, as complementary as "two wheels of a cart."[60] This is a vital mistake, which has misled human thinking towards various inaccurate perceptions of the post–Cold War international political economy and, therefore, to the fundamental misperception of our age that causes significant conceptual and practical pitfalls. Contrary to these prevailing arguments that have greatly shaped the post–Cold War human mentality, this book asserts that the global triumph of capitalism has caused a major disjuncture between global capitalism and nation-state democracy, which manifests itself in both space and institutions. As the market expands globally, democracy remains local within separated jurisdictions of state sovereignty; this is the space implication of the great disjuncture. More importantly, the historically established previous coupling between capitalism and democracy has been broken; this is the institutional manifestation of the great disjuncture. Therefore, if democracy and the market are "two wheels of a cart," the global triumph of capitalism causes them to run at different speeds, on different paths, and even in opposite directions. In one sentence, as capitalism has conquered the globe, democracy has been undermined; global capitalism often makes democracy the major institutional prey of its geographic expansion and institutional triumph.

The relationship between capitalism and democracy has been a classic question in studies of comparative politics, especially for radical and

Political Order and Political Decay: From the Industrial Revolution to the Globalization of Democracy, New York: Farrar, Straus & Giroux, 2014. The "liberal logic" of marketization leading to democratization is held often as common sense, as exemplified in Bill Clinton's "engagement" policy toward China. See discussions and criticism of Clinton's such policy in Stefan Halper, *The Beijing Consensus: Legitimizing Authoritarianism in Our Time*, New York: Basic Books, 2010, p. 194, and Michael Mandelbaum, *Mission Failure: America and the World in the Post-Cold War Era*, Oxford University Press, 2016, ch. 1. Its scholastic foundation, however, lies in modernization theory. For a representative work in this line of reasoning, see Seymour Martin Lipset, "Some Social Requisites of Democracy: Economic Development and Political Legitimacy," *American Political Science Review* 53, 1 (March 1959): 69–105; for this line of reasoning in post–Cold War publications, see, for example, Larry Diamond, *Developing Democracy: Toward Consolidation*, Baltimore: Johns Hopkins University Press, 1999.

[60] South Korean President Kim Dae-jung's speech, included in Farrukh Iqbal and Jong-Il You eds., *Democracy, Market Economies, and Development: An Asian Perspective*, Washington, DC: World Bank, 2001, p. 1.

critical scholars of capitalism.[61] From the literature inspired by the debate, we have learnt that capitalism and democracy are not conceptually identical to one another, and that their practical connections are historical rather than general. To highlight the great disjuncture between global capitalism and nation-state democracy, this book refashions the long-standing theoretical debate around the so-called political shell issue of capitalism against the background of the global triumph of capitalism; the disjuncture, therefore, should be understood with three institutional features that emerge as new. First, rather than simply being conceptual, it is now a real institutional gap that emerges between the global stretch of capitalism and the local nature of nation-state democracy. Second, this gap empowers capitalism through its global leverage to escape from, resist, and oppose democracies when it is convenient or of interest and benefit to do so, while democracy, which by nature is "local" in comparison with global capitalism, becomes impotent, unable to create a "shell" for capitalism, in this sense for the purpose of containment or providing checks. Thirdly, the gap also manifests in authoritarian nations as that between the countries' involvement in global capitalism and the local absence of democracy, forcing global capitalism that has now stretched into these "new territories" of business to face, adapt, and often cooperate with the new "political shell" of political authoritarianism. Later sections of this chapter will analyze the second and third points to investigate how globalization transforms the relationships between capitalism and practical democracies and, respectively, global capitalism

---

[61] See, for example, Bob Jessop, "Capitalism and Democracy: The Best Possible Political Shell?" in Gary Littlejohn, Barry Smart, John Wakeford, and Nira Yuval-Davis eds., *Power and the State*, New York: St. Martin's Press, 1978, pp. 10–51; Samuel Bowles and Herbert Gintis, *Democracy and Capitalism: Property, Community, and the Contradictions of Modern Social Thought*, New York: Basic Books, 1987; Dietrich Rueschemeyer, Evelyne Huber Stephens, and John D. Stephens, *Capitalist Development and Democracy*, University of Chicago Press, 1992. Also, Polanyi, *The Great Transformation*; Anthony Giddens, *Capitalism and Modern Social Theory: An Analysis of the Writings of Marx, Durkheim, and Max Weber*, Cambridge University Press, 1971; Robert R. Alford and Roger Friedland, *Powers of Theory: Capitalism, the State, and Democracy*, Cambridge University Press, 1985; Adam Przeworski, *Capitalism and Social Democracy*, Cambridge University Press, 1985; Ellen Meiksins Wood, *Democracy Against Capitalism: Reinventing Historical Materialism*, Cambridge University Press, 1995; Bob Jessop, *The Future of the Capitalist State*, Cambridge: Polity Press, 2002; Timothy K. Kuhner, *Capitalism v. Democracy: Money in Politics and the Free Market Constitution*, Stanford Law Books, 2014.

and political authoritarianism. However, the discussion immediately below shall focus on the general picture of the gap, its historical emergence, and its conceptual implications.

Yes, capitalism and democracy are two different concepts and institutions, however their match with each other over a long period of human history is not simply accidental. To this author, capitalism has an inherent feature that leads it to couple with democracy, while simultaneously having other inherent features that cause its tension, contradiction, and conflict with democracy. Capitalism, as a set of economic institutions, is constituted on two fundamental organizational forms: private ownership, often in the form of the incorporated firm, and market competition via the existence of countless firms as well as consumers' spontaneous decisions in transactions. Individual autonomy rooted in private ownership and competition understood as the market spirit, therefore, can be viewed as a feature that is naturally compatible with and mutually reinforced by political democracy, while the organizational form of the firm that requires the internal hierarchy of authority for achieving efficiency can be roughly viewed with an inclination toward authoritarianism. To this author, these two organizational bodies of capitalism are significant for understanding the political economy of capitalism. More specifically, the compatibility of both individual autonomy and market competition with democracy is the institutional reason why capitalism and democracy can be coupled with each other in the historical circumstances of the classic Western democratic revolution,[62] and, more importantly to our discussion, why the capitalist world during the Cold War era was, essentially, the democratic world in confrontation with the communist bloc.[63] In other words, the Cold War's capitalism-democracy coupling

---

[62] For a historical account of this democratic revolution, see R. R. Palmer, *The Age of the Democratic Revolution: A Political History of Europe and America, 1760-1800*, Vol. I: *The Challenge*, Princeton University Press, 1959/1989; R. R. Palmer, *The Age of the Democratic Revolution: A Political History of Europe and America, 1760-1800*, Vol. II: *The Struggle*, Princeton University Press, 1964/1989; for an analytical history, see Reinhard Bendix, *Kings or People: Power and the Mandate to Rule*, Berkeley: University of California Press, 1978. For the connection between the bourgeois and the rise of democracy, see, for example, Barrington Moore, Jr., *Social Origins of Dictatorship and Democracy: Lord and Peasant in the Making of the Modern World*, Boston: Beacon Press, 1966.

[63] Roberts, *The Penguin History of the Twentieth Century*; Martin Walker, *The Cold War: A History*, Toronto: Stoddart, 1994.

was not entirely fortuitous; it was also due to both historical and institutional inevitabilities.

These inevitabilities reached their historical zenith in the late 1980s and the early 1990s, namely, during the period when the Cold War came to its end. The peak, however, caused some fatal misunderstandings of the relationship between capitalism (or the market) and democracy, as epitomized in the argument that the end of the Cold War meant the victory of *both* the market and democracy. This once influential argument, in its historical context, does have reason; its contribution to our understandings of the fundamental change of the late twentieth century can be threefold: First, it correctly highlights the triumph of Western capitalism over its most powerful rival, that is, the communist-state-planning political economic system;[64] second, it also takes into account the so-called third wave of democratization in the late twentieth century in its interpretation of historical changes;[65] third, it implicitly emphasizes the historical fact of the institutional coupling between the market and democracy during the Cold War. However, the mistake of the "both-victories" thesis is vital. In historical development, it chooses only "convenient facts" to make an argument, while ignoring the "inconvenient" reality that challenges its generalization.[66] In some cases, as in former communist countries of Eastern Europe, democracy and the market did in fact become interconnected institutions that took effect;[67] in other cases, as in some East Asian newly industrialized countries, the existing market mechanism also helped in this way or that to inaugurate democratic politics.[68] There are still other cases, however, in which the market has been accepted but democracy has been denied. China is obviously a prominent case in the latter regard;[69] most of those remaining

[64] Francis Fukuyama, *The End of History and the Last Man*, New York: Free Press, 1992.

[65] For the third wave of democratization, see, Huntington, *The Third Wave*.

[66] Max Weber, "Science as a Vocation," in H. H. Gerth and C. Wright Mills eds., *From Max Weber: Essays in Sociology*, Oxford University Press, 1958, pp. 129–156. Here I extend Weber's definition of the concept of "inconvenient facts" from being "inconvenient for their party opinions" to a wider sense for an author's conceptual generalization.

[67] For a thoughtful analysis of the development, see Przeworski, *Democracy and the Market*.

[68] Laurence Whitehead ed., *Emerging Market Democracies: East Asia and Latin America*, Baltimore: Johns Hopkins University Press, 2002.

[69] For China's embracing of the market mechanism but its resistance to democracy, see, for example, Andrew J. Nathan, *China's Crisis: Dilemmas of*

undemocratic countries fall into the same category.[70] And while it is already incomprehensible why the advocates of the "end of the history" thesis erase these nations from their map of the world, it is even more curious that, after a quarter of a century, they still insist that "at the end of history stands democracy,"[71] as though the emerging literature on hybrid regimes has contributed nothing to the field, let alone the continuous resistance of authoritarianism to democracy, and even the decline of democracy itself.[72]

The most fundamental mistake of the "both-victories" or the "end-of-history" theses lies in the conceptual assumption about the inseparability of capitalism and democracy. The market during the Cold War era had been described as "free," and apparently being "free" had deeper political significance; it was, at that time, institutionally

Reform and Prospects for Democracy, New York: Columbia University Press, 1990; Merle Goldman and Roderick MacFarquhar eds., *The Paradox of China's Post-Mao Reforms*, Cambridge, MA: Harvard University Press, 1999; Minxin Pei, *China's Trapped Transition: The Limits of Developmental Autocracy*, Cambridge, MA: Harvard University Press, 2006; Guoguang Wu and Helen Lansdowne eds., *Socialist China, Capitalist China: Social Tension and Political Adaptation under Economic Globalization*, London: Routledge, 2009; Teresa Wright, *Accepting Authoritarianism: State-Society Relations in China's Reform Era*, Stanford University Press, 2010.

[70] For instance, see Martin K. Dimitrov ed., *Why Communism Did Not Collapse: Understanding Authoritarian Regime Resilience in Asia and Europe*, Cambridge University Press, 2013.

[71] Fukuyama, "At the 'End of History' Still Stands Democracy."

[72] For hybrid regimes, especially those emerging after the third wave of democratization, see, for example, Fareed Zakaria, *The Future of Freedom: Illiberal Democracy at Home and Abroad*, New York: W. W. Norton, 2003; Andreas Schedler ed., *Electoral Authoritarianism: The Dynamics of Unfree Competition*, Boulder: Lynne Rienner, 2006; Steven Levitsky and Lucan A. Way, *Competitive Authoritarianism: Hybrid Regimes After the Cold War*, Cambridge University Press, 2010. For the continuous resistance of authoritarianism to democracy, see, for instance, Dimitrov, *Why Communism Did Not Collapse*; Jie Chen and Bruce J. Dickson, *Allies of the State: Democratic Support and Regime Support among China's Capitalists*, Cambridge, MA: Harvard University Press, 2010. For the decline of democracy itself, see, for instance, Eva Bellin, *Stalled Democracy: Capital, Labor, and the Paradox of State-Sponsored Development*, Ithaca: Cornell University Press, 2002; Joshua Kurlantzick, *Democracy in Retreat: The Revolt of the Middle Class and the Worldwide Decline of Representative Government*, New Haven: Yale University Press, 2013; Larry Diamond, Marc F. Plattner, and Christopher Walker eds., *Authoritarianism Goes Global: The Challenge to Democracy*, Baltimore: Johns Hopkins University Press, 2016.

connected and interwoven with political democracy.[73] But this historical compatibility does not equate to their notional and institutional inseparability, let alone their identification as such. Globalization has highlighted the institutional difference between democracy and the market, and it has even gone so far as having broken their institutional connections, as the market becomes global but democracy does not. Still, "stateness" is an indispensable precondition of democratization and democracy,[74] and struggles for democracy now often push different states in diverse and dispersive directions rather than simply enabling them to become "free" or "liberal."[75] Once capitalism gains its global triumph, as this book attempts to demonstrate, it is these contradictions and this incompatibility that arise to dominate the relationship between capitalism and democracy. This chapter argues, therefore, that with the end of the Cold War, the history of pre-global capitalism has also ended, but another history has since begun: the history of global capitalism, a capitalism that is no longer parochial, provincial, or national; a capitalism now carrying a logic different from its previous incarnations, primarily concerning its relationship with democracy. Cold War institutional logic can be anachronistic when it is applied to analyses of global capitalism, most importantly because it still views capitalism and democracy as being inseparable.

The nation-state system is obviously key to understanding the great disjuncture between global capitalism and local democracy, as it stands between the global expansion of the market and the confinement of democracy within state sovereignty. An institutional fault line can, therefore, be observed between the domestic political institutions within industrialized nations and these nations' economic outreach. As its economic expansion reaches virtually every corner of the world through the market, the globalization that originated from leading industrialized countries leaves its domestic political bases behind, which means that domestic democracy in industrialized nations is not able to travel with the nations' global economic outreach, at the

---

[73] Charles E. Lindblom, *Politics and Markets: The World' Political-Economic Systems*, New York: Basic Books, 1977; Amartya Sen, *Development as Freedom*, New York: Anchor Books, 1999.

[74] Juan J. Linz and Alfred Stepan, *Problems of Democratic Transition and Consolidation: Southern Europe, South America, and Post-Communist Europe*, Baltimore: Johns Hopkins University Press, 1996.

[75] Zakaria, *The Future of Freedom*; Schedler, *Electoral Authoritarianism*.

very least being far behind in its pace and scope to match market globalization.[76] Market globalization thus becomes politically naked, with no political protection to support such globalization across national borders. This means that global capital can, for the most part, avoid the political checks and constraints created by local voters' preferences in a nation-state democracy. It also lays bare the propensity of capitalism, when no political and legal checks are in effect, to incline toward avarice and unscrupulousness.

This institutional nudity, more importantly, makes capitalism vulnerable to non-democratic political power. The market is, perhaps, virtually the same mechanism everywhere, but the practical varieties of capitalism have still attracted enormous academic attention that has borne remarkable research findings.[77] Politics often matter much in creating such variety; in this book's terminology, at the other end of the state-market nexus, various forms of the state are a vital element in determining how the state works with market operations and in yielding profound institutional implications. Political differences between democracy and authoritarianism, therefore, do matter in economic

---

[76] The imperative for "exporting democracy" once appeared and even became powerful at times, but it ebbed quickly after the world came into globalization. For the imperative, see, for example, Tony Smith, *America's Mission: The United States and the Worldwide Struggle for Democracy in the Twentieth Century*, Princeton University Press, 1994; Laurence Whitehead ed., *The International Dimensions of Democratization: Europe and the Americas*, Oxford University Press, 2001, expanded ed. For an analysis of the waning of international efforts at democratizing post–Cold War authoritarianism, see Chapter 6.

[77] This is a huge body of literature jargoned as VofC (varieties of capitalism), with which many leading scholars of comparative politics do their research. See, for example, Suzanne Berger and Ronald Dore eds., *National Diversity and Global Capitalism*, Ithaca: Cornell University Press, 1996; Herbert Kitschelt, Peter Lange, Gary Marks, and John D. Stephens eds., *Continuity and Change in Contemporary Capitalism*, Cambridge University Press, 1999; Hall and Soskice, *Varieties of Capitalism*; Ben Ross Schneider, *Hierarchical Capitalism in Latin America: Business, Labor, and the Challenges of Equitable Development*, Cambridge University Press, 2013; Kathleen Thelen, *Varieties of Liberalization and the New Politics of Social Solidarity*, Cambridge University Press, 2014. Also, Bruno Amable, *The Diversity of Modern Capitalism*, Oxford University Press, 2003; William J. Baumol, Robert E. Litan, and Carl J. Schramm, *Good Capitalism, Bad Capitalism: And the Economics of Growth and Prosperity*, New Haven: Yale University Press, 2007; Andrew Walter and Xiaoke Zhang eds., *East Asian Capitalism: Diversity, Continuity, and Change*, Oxford University Press, 2012.

development in many significant ways, especially in their individual relationships with global capitalism. In fact, the global expansion of capitalism by nature means that the market is cooperating with almost all states, regardless of whether they are democratic or not.[78] Political authoritarianism, with its highly concentrated political and economic power, is able, therefore, to take the opportunity to "hijack" the economic development that is propelled by market globalization and turn such development against freedom, primarily at home but also, to a lesser but increasing degree, abroad.

Globalization, per se, is a political economic dilemma, as it carries itself as a market expansion without a universal political arrangement to match it. Historically speaking, the modern market economy took shape when both the nation-state and political democracy arose to form the framework of human life. But globalization changes this with uneven effect; as the market goes beyond national borders, political democracy is left behind, while the nation-state remains powerful and carries ever-increasing functions. The political conditions of market operation, therefore, become unbalanced: bottom-up constraints, which are institutionalized via democracy, are globally absent and locally weak; but top-down constraints, which are often imposed by the state, especially from effective authoritarian states, can be stronger than before. This imbalance, as this chapter shall argue, defines the basic dilemma that globalization encounters. Globalization goes wild, on one hand, as it interacts with citizens who, without an arrangement like democracy, have little power to influence the direction, pace, and contents of global capitalism; it is tamed, on the other hand, by political power that concentrates in the niche of authoritarianism, often in the form of the state but also in many other organizational forms such as the firm.

National Mixed Economies Compete on the Global Free Market: State Capitalism in Tandem with Neoliberalism

Parallel to the great disjuncture between global capitalism and nation-state democracy, another huge, fundamental cleavage has also emerged with the global expansion of capitalism, which, to this book, forms the

[78] Mancur Olson, *Power and Prosperity: Outgrowing Communist and Capitalist Dictatorships*, New York: Basic Books, 2000.

fourth institutional feature joining the above three to frame the current globalization phenomenon. This is a split between the different sets of political-economy institutions of national and global economies. On the national level, with state-market conciliation and collaboration, according to a standard and authoritative textbook of economics, "all societies are mixed economies, with elements of market and command."[79] In a similar vein, Amartya Sen has suggested that now "capitalism has lost its meaningfulness because nearly all the countries of the world allow more or less private ownership of productive means, but also practice considerable government intervention in the market."[80] In other words, as the state-planning economy is buried in history, a pure market economy no longer functions in any nation in the world. This is a reconfirmation of our analysis on the shaping of the state-market nexus. On the global level, however, it is hard to conclude that the global economy at this point is under any effective command from coercive authorities, let alone a central authority.[81] Though the institutionalization of international politics has grown to an unprecedented and unimagined degree since the end of the Cold War, leading to some scholars' argument that state strategies among the major Western powers were guided by existing international rules and expectations that were legalized,[82] virtually nothing exists that can function as

[79] Paul A. Samuelson and William D. Nordhaus, *Economics*, Boston: McGraw-Hill/Irwin, 2010, 19th ed., p. 8.

[80] Amartya Sen, "Capitalism Beyond the Crisis," *New York Review of Books*, March 26, 2009, http://www.nybooks.com/articles/2009/03/26/capitalism-beyond-the-crisis/.

[81] For the anarchy in international relations, see Hans J. Morgenthau, *Politics Among Nations: The Struggle for Power and Peace*, New York: Knopf, 1949; Kenneth N. Waltz, *Man, State, and War*, New York: Columbia University Press, 1954; Robert J. Art and Robert Jervis eds., *International Politics: Anarchy, Force, Imperialism*, Boston: Little, Brown, 1973, Part I; Hedley Bull, *The Anarchical Society: A Study of Order in World Politics*, New York: Columbia University Press, 1977; Brian C. Schmidt, *The Political Discourse of Anarchy: A Disciplinary History of International Relations*, Albany: State University of New York Press, 1998. But the point that the global economy can be anarchic in the sense of the absence of a central authority has not been highlighted in existing literature.

[82] Robert O. Keohane, Joseph S. Nye, and Stanley Hoffmann eds., *After the Cold War: International Institutions and State Strategies in Europe, 1989-1991*, Cambridge, MA: Center for International Affairs, Harvard University, 1993; Judith Goldstein, Miles Kahler, Robert O. Keohane, and Anne-Marie Slaughter eds., *Legalization and World Politics*, Cambridge, MA: MIT Press, 2001. For more discussions of the trend in world political economy, see, for example,

sovereign institutions to make and enforce laws in global political economy.[83] In this sense, global capitalism is a purely market economy, or at least more pure than national ones. Therefore, a grand picture of the global political economy occurs in which the global economy as a whole very much borders on being laissez-faire, but its sub-global levels are composed of the mixed economies of different societies that are fragmented because of separated state-authority jurisdictions. This split between the global free market and national mixed economies is no less significant than the disjuncture between global capitalism and nation-state democracy; its implications are profound to the state, capitalism, and globalization.

The absence of effective governance of the global economy, first of all, means the intensification of global competition with few enforceable rules, thus making the global free market closer to the "Hobbesian jungle" in which there are no rules governing who owns which resources, rather than to the civil state of society to which we are accustomed in normal life.[84] The global limitedness that we earlier discussed in the Introduction should now be further understood in the context of this "jungle" proposition. The introversive pressure of global competition continuously mounts due to a global reach of the eventually finite boundaries of this globe as a geographic entity and the global market in expansion; the global Hobbesian jungle allows "freedom" in the primitive sense of the stronger preying upon the weaker without effective regulations.

The prevalence of neoliberalism, to this author, is simply an ideational crystallization, ideological justification, and policy adaptation of/to the jungle that is the political economy of global capitalism. It becomes natural for states to follow neoliberal economic philosophy and its policies, as doing so can unleash the economic elements in their sovereign jurisdictions that will allow them to become involved in the global market with fewer restraints than otherwise. Like many

Robert O. Keohane, *After Hegemony: Cooperation and Discord in the World Political Economy*, Princeton University Press, 1984; Robert O. Keohane and Joseph S. Nye, *Power and Interdependence*, New York: Harper Collins, 1989, 2nd ed.

[83] This is Hobbes' theory, which suggests that the sovereign is the source of the law. For a discussion of the theory, see Alan Ryan, "Hobbes's Political Philosophy," in Tom Sorell ed., *The Cambridge Companion to Hobbes*, Cambridge University Press, 1996, pp. 208–245.

[84] Thomas Hobbes, *Leviathan*, Cambridge University Press, 1991 [1651], ch. 13.

scholars, Robert Boyer has noticed this linkage, asserting that the intensification of global competition is why "most governments have deregulated their national financial and labor markets, precisely in order to respond more efficiently to the changing patterns and recurrent disturbances associated with the globalization of most economic activities."[85]

Meanwhile, this split between the global "jungle" political economy and the domestic state-market mixed economy inevitably drives the trend toward concentration of power in many ways, as all the players involved in globalization are propelled to make efforts to concentrate, or to further concentrate if they have already done so, possible resources, be it material, organizational, or any other kind, in order to gain a competitive edge. For the state, this implies its momentum moving closer toward economization and, moreover, toward corporatization. As national economies engage more intensively than before in competing in the global economy, they become similar to individual corporations competing on the market. The state, a sovereign entity that now is locked in the state-market nexus and runs a mixed economy within its society, behaves more and more like a corporate board in many ways. Economically, the state is now inclined to coordinate, organize, and even issue certain commands to direct its national economy for the purpose of pursuing "comprehensive national power," similar to the way a corporate board seeks profits; this motivates the further economization of the state. Politically, the hierarchical line of authorities, the discipline of its members, and even the repression of any behavior that is viewed by the state as disturbing to national interests are, in principle, justified and exercised at the price of freedom, rights, and individual autonomy, regardless of whether a state is organized within a democracy or not.

Moreover, the state is inclined to increase state support of corporations in global competition through various methods of "positive" intervention.[86] Actually, the state in global market competition often likes to mobilize various political and other means to empower corporations of their own nations, through means that roughly fall into

[85] Boyer, "The Variety and Unequal Performance of Really Existing Markets," p. 56.

[86] "Positive" here holds no normative meaning, as, to repeat, this chapter follows Isaiah Berlin's way of distinguishing between "positive" and "negative." See ft. 26.

two basic categories in terms of state-economy relations: namely, governmental deregulation and state intervention. While intellectual reflections and criticism legitimately focus on neoliberal deregulations, the latter side of the state-market collaboration in globalization has been comparatively less noticed, often being thought of as a regional phenomenon prevailing in East Asia as a specific variety of capitalism, or at least not scrutinized with sufficient attention to its dialectic connection with the rise of neoliberalism.[87] As we will not repeat our earlier point on the distinction between "positive/tactic" and "negative/strategic" interventions, here what can be added in demonstrating closer state-business cooperation in the institutional sense is the rise of state-owned or state-supported corporations, a phenomenon that will be empirically investigated in Chapter 3. For individual corporations, the global economy provides a free field in which to expand their size, power, coverage, and influence in various ways, and the tendency towards monopoly and oligopoly has been substantially and momentously encouraged and escalated; in turn, their global power helps enable them to influence the local state, to penetrate into the national political economy, and to escape domestic constraints, especially those constraints rooted in popular participation in a democracy.

State capitalism, therefore, arises in at least the above two senses, namely, in the sense of increasing and even dominating the role of the state in the capitalist domestic economy and in the sense of closer state-enterprise collaborations. Conceptually, state capitalism can be viewed as a special type of the economic state, perhaps the stronger version. State capitalism, as elaborated earlier concerning the dialectic relationship between the economic state and the neoliberal state, is not a phenomenon in contradiction with the rise of the neoliberal state; rather, they are the same movement in which the state has been transformed into a coercive, administrative, and public machine with

---

[87] In the case of China, for example, the relevant studies often emphasize either economic liberalization as the retreat of the state or the desirable role of the state in promoting economic development. For some recent representative works in the analysis of China's state-market relations, see Shahid Yusuf, Dwight H. Perkins, and Kaoru Nabeshima, *Under New Ownership: Privatizing China's Enterprises*, Stanford University Press, 2006; Edward S. Steinfeld, *Playing Our Game: Why China's Economic Rise Doesn't Threaten the West*, Cambridge University Press, 2010; Roselyn Hsueh, *China's Regulatory State: A New Strategy for Globalization*, Ithaca: Cornell University Press, 2011; Lardy, *Markets Over Mao*.

economic (read, first of all, as materialist) concerns taking precedence over other roles assumed by the state. Neoliberal policies are not as paradoxical to the rise of the economic state as they are at first glance. With such policies the state reduces its regulation of the market, to this book's interpretation, in order to enforce its governmentality of promoting national competitiveness on the global market. To repeat what this chapter has earlier highlighted, the neoliberal state is a type of state that also makes efforts to "govern" the economy, "govern" in this sense meaning that the state is involved in economic activities in various ways, which in this context primarily includes its deregulation of market activities. In fact, the global-national structural cleavage of organizing the economies further helps to explain why neoliberalism and state capitalism arise at the same time and merge with each other in the globalization age. This split between national mixed economies and global laissez-faire capitalism, it can be additionally argued, motivates the state to pursue the two seemingly contradictory but essentially complementary strategies of adopting neoliberal policies of deregulation of the market and, at the same time, increasing state roles in economic affairs. Both sides of this strategy help to strengthen national competitiveness on the global market; deregulation unleashes nation-based market power, and statist capitalism supports a given national economy by organizing and managing it as a business firm.

At this point in our discussion we come back to the political-economic impact of the two fundamental institutional organizations of capitalism, namely, the firm and the market; it can be further argued that the cleavage between the global free market and national mixed economies has, to a huge extent, transformed the institutional match in which market freedom resonates with freedom in other domains such as civic and political and democratic, while the organizational principle of the firm corresponds to authoritarian institutions. With the emergence of the structural split highlighted in this section, now such linear matches have been distorted or transmuted: the authoritarian, or pro-efficiency, propensity of the firm becomes stronger, but the consonance between market freedom and civic freedom as well as democratic principles is garbled and mangled, mainly because globalization forms no political sphere in which non-economic freedoms apply; one-dimensional economic freedom, therefore, becomes the freedom of the strongest in preying upon the weak. This is the institutional and philosophical ground upon which this book stands to argue that market freedom of globalization is combined with authoritarianism. Both institutional features of capitalism, in other words, the firm and the market, in this context, are inclined to function against civic freedoms and popular democracy.

Together, the state is corporatized to various extents; its domestic behavior and, accordingly, institutions tend to play up authority, hierarchy, discipline, and even repression, while its outward, global engagement is more competition-driven but less concerned with the domestic context and citizen's diverse preferences. The absence of effective governance of the global economy, furthermore, lends huge possibilities to economic competitors for ignoring public goods, especially global public goods such as "human security."[88] Market failures at the global level cannot be effectively corrected or remedied; instead, a race to the bottom prevails in achieving competitive advantages and, eventually, profits at the cost of labor rights, human dignity, moral principles, ecological environments, and anything else that could hinder maximization of profit-making. The state is not only unable to expand its governance to the global realm, but also, due to its economization, "privatization," and corporatization, is inclined to ignore public goods when the causes and implications of such global issues appear within its domestic jurisdiction. This, as a macro-structural cause, further brings the state-market nexus toward mutual reinforcement, rather than the state being a remedy for market failures. Neoliberalism and state capitalism, accordingly though ironically, are entangled in a complicated reinforcing relationship.

In tandem with the great disjuncture between capitalism and democracy, this structural split in global-state economies very much contributes to a new, seemingly contradictory political economy of global capitalism, in which the global economy combines strong economic roles of the state engaging in global competition with the overall laissez-faire status of the global economy in terms of weak regulations, if not the absence of regulations altogether. This differs from previous political economies of capitalism, especially that of Cold War capitalism, in which the state's engagement in economic affairs was by nature contending and confrontational towards the possibility of a laissez-faire economy. Why is such a strange combination possible, or even

---

[88] See, for example, Guoguang Wu ed., *China's Challenges to Human Security: Foreign Relations and Global Implications*, London: Routledge, 2013.

practical and inevitable for global capitalism? The answer lies in the emergence of the globality with which capitalism now runs: As long as there is no global polity emerging as of yet, the existence of the global economy across and beyond national economies is more similar to jungle politics in the Hobbesian sense of the stronger preying upon the weak at the cost of civic freedoms and associational democracy. The political impact is the same as that of the capitalism-democracy disjuncture, which sees the rise of a new authoritarian trend every-where while democracy and democratization are undermined.

Authoritarian Advantages, Dysfunctional Democracy, and Dependency Reversed: The Political-Economic Consequences of Globalization

In this globalizing world of such institutional features discussed above, a dual political aftermath becomes inevitable: Authoritarianism as an institution in general, and authoritarian states in particular gain var-ious advantages in globalization, while, by the same token, democracy is undermined, handicapped, and made increasingly dysfunctional. Altogether, a chain of "dependency reversed" emerges, in which, at one end, global capitalism depends on effective authoritarianism, but on the other end, democracy depends on global capitalism.

Our discussion of authoritarian advantages versus dysfunctional democracy may be given a prelude with sixteenth-century rural England, the time when industrial capitalism rose with England as a flowerbed of this historical development. Contrary to the conven-tional perception about the close connection between modern cities and capitalist industrialization, capitalists at that time, according to two leading historians of the rise of capitalism, found freedom of enterprise in rural regions rather than in central cities. It is recorded that, by moving operations from the city to rural areas, a newborn capitalist was able to seek the favorable institutional environment provided by the countryside:

In a rural village where he had his headquarters he was free of municipal taxes and the burdens of public office, unhampered by the old guild and municipal regulations which formerly limited the number of employees he could hire and minutely regulated the quality of his materials and the nature of his manufacturing methods. Here he could hire or contract with whom he pleased, offer whatever wages or piece rates would secure him workers, order their work in any way he liked. He determined the quality, quantity, and price of what he produced in response to the varying demands of the international market. He was free to experiment with machines in order to reduce labor costs and increase production.[89]

Gaining economic prosperity by expanding capitalist productions, this migration of factories and business from cities to rural regions "marked the beginning of a new stage in the development of capitalist industry."[90]

More than four hundred years later, in the world of the twenty-first century, such industrial migration can again be observed, but this time on a global scale. It, too, follows a path of industrial and business mobility from urban centers to rural peripheries, but now they are from the "global center" of capitalism in the leading industrial world to the "global countryside" of industrially less-developed countries where capitalists again find a paradise for their industrial production and fortune-making.[91] The "global countryside" is more or less a metaphor, as scholars may now show a preference for the terms "global peripheries" or "Global South"; in any case, today's developing nations do provide elements similar to those that sixteenth-century rural England was able to offer, elements that are attractive in terms of what the now globally flowing capital seeks for business prosperity. Again, behind these elements that nourished the spread of industrialization and supported economic development lies an institutional core which empowers capital with economic freedom while suppressing citizens' rights and social justice, social and political conditions that were difficult for capital to accommodate in sixteenth-century London and for international business in today's industrialized democracies.

This historical analogy between rural England and the Global South cannot go further, however, as, through the theoretical lens provided by our earlier discussions, several differences between sixteenth-century

---

[89] Eugene F. Rice, Jr. and Anthony Grafton, *The Foundations of Early Modern Europe, 1460-1559*, New York: W. W. Norton, 1994, 2nd ed., p. 59.

[90] Ibid.

[91] Immanuel Wallerstein creatively elaborates the argument with his influential "world-systems" theory of capitalism. See, for example, Immanuel Wallerstein, *World-Systems Analysis: An Introduction*, Durham, NC: Duke University Press, 2004.

capitalism and twenty-first-century global capitalism are obvious and significant. The state-market nexus and the rise of the economic state, first of all, have altered the spontaneity of industrialization in early capitalism, as now the state is deeply involved in the later industrialization of Global South; second, state sovereignty embedded in territorial control can stand to hinder the spread of political institutions that govern industrialized nations to authoritarian countries. Third, the global limit that capitalism now encounters can dramatically increase the gravity of the emerging markets in their relationship with global capital; many such markets, however, are under the political jurisdiction of authoritarian or new, hybrid regimes. The absence of, or at least fundamental limits to, a new frontier of capitalist expansion, can make international capital, which now has limited options in finding new markets, require the local cooperation of the authoritarian state more than ever before when it is in search of global financial opportunities. This makes international capital vulnerable, in addition to creating intensified competition among firms on the global scale that are often dependent upon those authoritarian states which effectively control foreign admission into their domestic economies, as will be discussed below. Altogether, unlike in earlier centuries during which democracy arose to govern capitalism against political authoritarianism, these historical and institutional differences empower "effective authoritarianism," the contemporary authoritarian state that governs and functions well in general and embraces the market under the state-market nexus for effectively delivering economic performance.

With the rise of global capitalism, it is, therefore, "effective authoritarianism" that has gained a series of institutional advantages in the competition among economic states on both fronts, versus democracies and versus global capitalism. These advantages can be analyzed in many aspects; this section shall highlight three institutional factors below regarding, respectively and with overlap, the politicization of the market, political accountability, and the density of state power.

Politicization of the market is simply another side to the story of the rise of the economic state and the economization of political power through the state-market nexus. Robert Bates once argued, though in another context, that "government regulation may transform markets into political organizations, ones in which too few transactions take place at too high a cost but ones that can be used to build organizations supportive of those in power."[92] As the market expands across nations in the process of globalization, state sovereignty may arise to either hinder or help expansion into its jurisdiction depending on its own interests, interests often defined by "those in power" for their own benefit. The authoritarian state naturally defines such interests in building up an "organization supportive of" itself; the democratic leadership, on the other hand, despite such "organizational support," must, due to its institutional design, eventually be tested by popular elections. While all states in general cooperate with the market mechanism, this does not mean that a specific state allows all specific firms to enter into the domestic market under its jurisdiction. Rather, the state retains its coercive power to fend off those firms for various reasons, often political, as, again to cite Bates, "political elites are behaving in ways economically irrational, they are behaving in ways that are politically rational."[93] The effective authoritarian state has both strong incentives and capabilities of political control of the market, and even monopolization of its domestic market, especially in terms of market admission for global business. All of these strengthen rather than reduce the state's bargaining position in dealing with international capital.

This politicization of the market, in general, indicates that the more effectively authoritarian the state is, the more powerfully it is able to play the politics that structure the market. In this sense, the well-functioning authoritarian state becomes a "gatekeeper" of market operation, though not in the traditional sense of little intervention. It is a gatekeeper of its national market in the sense that it has the power and function to grant access to capital and business, or not, as the case may be. In other words, state sovereignty guarantees such an authoritarian state the power to give, or not give, international capital an "entry permit" to its domestic market. The permission can be politically selective, as it often is, in accordance with both the political and economic interests of the state. In fact, the authoritarian state is much more politically inclined and institutionally empowered to do so than a democratic state.[94] This is

---

[92] Robert H. Bates, "Toward a Political Economy of Development," in Robert H. Bates eds., *Toward a Political Economy of Development: A Rational Choice Perspective*, Berkeley: University of California Press, 1988, pp. 239–244 (p. 244).

[93] Ibid.

[94] There can be a variety of authoritarian politics that affect the working of markets. See a systematic consideration in Ronald Wintrobe, *The Political Economy of Dictatorship*, Cambridge University Press, 1998.

a new kind of "gatekeeper" state that is able to rise for the purposes of either smoothing or handicapping the global expansion of capitalism; this simultaneously implies the political dependence of global capital on the authoritarian state.

The institutional difference of political accountability between authoritarianism and democracy also empowers the former in global competition while undermining the essence of the latter. The rise of the economic state, as mentioned earlier, stimulates a shift of the base of political legitimacy to economic performance, which, obviously, reduces the weight of democratic procedures in creating political legitimacy. The Schumpeterian understanding of democracy has often been criticized as proceduralist, and various efforts in both conceptual and practical realms to remedy this shortcoming have been made in order to add greater substance to democratic institutions.[95] Democratic procedures, however, are still an unavoidable starting point for the establishment and improvement of democracy; or, in Przeworski's emphasis, they work as a form of "minimal democracy" that is often crucial for both mature democracy and democratization.[96] When procedures are undermined but money becomes prominent in politics, democracy as a whole is, at the very least, undermined, if not hijacked.

The global stretch of capitalism, moreover, enables international capital and big business to go beyond popular checks at home in the

---

[95] For the Schumpeterian concept of democracy, see Joseph A. Schumpeter, *Capitalism, Socialism, and Democracy*, New York: Harper & Row, 1975 [1942], p. 269. For this definition's contemporary application, see Huntington, *The Third Wave*, pp. 5–13. For the variety, development, and degrees of democracy, see, for example, Suzanne Berger ed., *Organizing Interests in Western Europe: Pluralism, Corporatism, and the Transformation of Politics*, Cambridge University Press, 1981; Benjamin Barber, *Strong Democracy: Participatory Politics for a New Age*, Berkeley: University of California Press, 1984; Robert A. Dahl, *A Preface to Economic Democracy*, Berkeley: University of California Press, 1985; Robert A. Dahl, *Democracy and Its Critics*, New Haven: Yale University Press, 1989; John Dunn ed., *Democracy: The Unfinished Journey, 508BC to AD1993*, Oxford University Press, 1992; David Held, *Models of Democracy*, Stanford University Press, 1996, 2nd ed.; Jon Elster ed., *Deliberative Democracy*, Cambridge University Press, 1998; Arend Lijphart, *Patterns of Democracy: Government Forms and Performance in Thirty-Six Countries*, New Haven: Yale University Press, 1999; Stuart N. Soroka and Christopher Wlezien, *Degrees of Democracy: Politics, Public Opinions, and Policy*, Cambridge University Press, 2010.

[96] Adam Przeworski, "Minimalist Conception of Democracy: A Defense," in Ian Shapiro and Casiano Hacker-Cordon eds., *Democracy's Value*, Cambridge University Press, 199, pp. 23–55.

democratic countries from where global capital often originates. This means, as the far reach of market globalization travels across national borders, that participatory democracy on the national scale is not able to extend its political influence over global business to the degree that it might do so in the domestic context. In turn, the dominating influence of global capital and big business over democracy can be strengthened. The line of accountability in a democracy, which by design either ideally or at least institutionally equates to the account-ability of everybody, including capital and business, to the law and, furthermore, accountability of government as lawmaker and law enforcer to citizens, can be turned, in the reality of global capitalism, vice versa. Thus a dilemma of political accountability arises in a democracy in at least two senses: It is a dilemma of substance versus procedures, which helps transform state legitimacy to become increasingly based on the leadership's performance in promoting material wealth; it is also, accordingly, a dilemma with which the state becomes increasingly responsible to the economy while decreas-ingly responsible to citizens.

The replacement of democratic accountability by economic account-ability has some further profound normative implications, including political, social, and ecological. Generally speaking, the authoritarian advantage often lies in its ignorance of, and even repression over, civic freedoms and human rights, thereby justifying political repression with the successful delivery of material wealth; the so-called strong-strong combination (the strong state with powerful multinational corpora-tions) tends to victimize the weak,[97] which increases socioeconomic disparity and creates enormous social problems; with the sponsorship of, rather than political checks from, the state, especially due to the absence of the political checks under authoritarianism that are nor-mally provided by democratic facilities, market failures in promoting public goods become consequential, escalating, and disastrous, most

---

[97] For the latter's power, see, for instance, Richard J. Barnet and Ronald E. Müller, *Global Reach: The Power of the Multinational Corporations*, London: Jonathan Cape, 1974; Robert Gilpin, *U.S. Power and the Multinational Corporation*, New York: Basic Books, 1975; Thomas J. Biersteker, *Multinationals, the State, and Control of the Nigerian Economy*, Princeton University Press, 1987; Geoffrey Jones, *Multinationals and Global Capitalism: From the Nineteenth to the Twenty-First Century*, Oxford University Press, 2005; Baumol, Litan, and Schramm, *Good Capitalism, Bad Capitalism*.

prominently in ecological and environmental protection.[98] These failures explain why an authoritarian state's effective improvement of the materialist quality of people's lives often prompts further social disparity and ecological catastrophes,[99] as will be discussed later in this book.

The third institutional cause of authoritarian advantages (AA), lies in the density of state power and, accordingly, state capacity in actualizing the economic state. Two comparisons can be drawn in this regard: the first concerns that between the authoritarian state and the market, and the second between effective authoritarianism and democracy. In comparison with market forces, which are, in principle, decentralized, the state is much more centralized and its power is in much higher density.[100] State power is particularly concentrated under political authoritarianism, which further strengthens the state's bargaining power in dealing with various decentralized (albeit more concentrative under globalization than before) market players, primarily individual corporations. As the game of "market admission" is played, for example, the authoritarian state acting as gatekeeper decides, among various individual corporations of global business, whom to allow into the domestic market under its jurisdiction and whom to exclude. Such decisions can be based on the calculation of national economic interests, but, as Bates clearly indicates, they are more likely to be political decisions that reflect the state's political considerations.

With a democratic system, societal factors have more opportunities to reduce the state's autonomy in making such decisions; effective authoritarianism, on the other hand, is stronger, more efficient, and more capable of imposing its political willpower on both its domestic population and, perhaps to a lesser degree but more relevant to our discussion here, foreign business. As an expert argues, the impact of the multinational corporation depends on the host government's ability to manage its relations with the firm, especially on the advantages of

---

[98]   Robert Kuttner, *Everything for Sale: The Virtues and Limits of Markets*, University of Chicago Press, 1996.

[99]   James C. Scott, *Seeing Like a State: How Certain Schemes to Improve the Human Condition Have Failed*, New Haven: Yale University Press, 1998.

[100] Bertrand Badie and Pierre Birnbaum, *The Sociology of the State*, translated by Arthur Goldhammer, University of Chicago Press, 1983; Michael Mann, *The Sources of Social Power, Vol. II: The Rise of Classes and Nation-States, 1760-1914*, Cambridge University Press, 1993.

a host state in the bargaining relationship.[101] Moreover, as Chapter 3 shall demonstrate, an effective authoritarian state can promote and support those business corporations it owns or favors to their various advantages in global economic competition; the point Lenin highlighted about state-backed capitalist competition now, ironically, emerges prominently with effective authoritarian states, especially former communist states which now embrace globalization, rather than, as in Lenin's analysis, with Western democratic capitalist countries.[102]

The effective authoritarian state, generally speaking, is often stronger in terms of state capacity than an average democracy;[103] this is particularly the case in global economic competition because, as globalization features the flow of global capital across state borders to seek a maximization of profit, the effective authoritarian state provides better opportunities for capital to make its fortunes than would be obtainable under an industrial democracy. In the latter circumstance, not only have socioeconomic conditions increased the price of labor, but government accountability in the formal (or even only formalistic) democratic sense requires the state to consider many issues with which the public is concerned, such as environmental protection, in a way that further raises the cost for investment and production. Political authoritarianism, by

[101] David Fieldhouse, "'A New Imperial System'? The Role of the Multinational Corporations Reconsidered," in Jeffry A. Frieden and David A. Lake eds., *International Political Economy: Perspectives on Global Power and Wealth*, Boston: Bedford/St. Martin's, 2000, pp. 167–179 (p. 167).

[102] For Lenin's point of view, see V. I. Lenin, *Imperialism: The Highest Stage of Capitalism*, New York: International Publishers, 1990 [1939]. Also, Anthony Brewer, *Marxist Theories of Imperialism: A Critical Survey*, London: Routledge, 1990, 2nd ed., ch. 6.

[103] Atul Kohli, "Democracy and Development," in John P. Lewis and Valeriana Kallab eds., *Development Strategies Reconsidered*, Washington, DC: Overseas Development Council, 1986, pp. 152–182; Jose Maria Maravall, "The Myth of the Authoritarian Advantage," in Larry Diamond and Marc F. Plattner eds., *Economic Reform and Democracy*, Baltimore: Johns Hopkins University Press, 1995, pp. 13–27; for discussions of state capacity in contemporary political economy, see Evans et al., *Bringing the State Back In*; for state capacity under democracy, see Ralph Miliband, *The State in Capitalist Society*, New York: Basic Books, 1969; for it in developing nations, see Alfred Stepan, *The State and Society: Peru in Comparative Perspective*, Princeton University Press, 1978; Joel S. Migdal, *Strong Societies and Weak States: State-Society Relations and State Capabilities in the Third World*, Princeton University Press, 1988. But it can be argued that it is impotent in many regards, as in dealing with human security challenges – an issue that shall be analyzed in Chapter 7.

contrast, is more likely to be "capable" of "overcoming" public preferences in social justice, civic freedom, and ecological protection to provide a business environment in which global capital may care less about labor, social, and ecological considerations than with a democracy, in spite of the general cost human societies have to pay for such carelessness. For example, the authoritarian state can relatively easily make its laws and regulations with little citizen participation, and the laws and regulations can often become political tools of authoritarianism as well as being legitimate means of governance to give convenience to international capital, which is not as easy for a democracy to accomplish. With globalization, therefore, effective authoritarian states can more easily than advanced democracies offer those economic and institutional factors sought by international capital, such as cheaper labor and lighter regulation, thus more possibly creating new paradises for global capital.

In general, globalization provides international capital with a wider spectrum of institutional options in choosing its cooperation with a home country but a narrower geographic space in choosing the target market in the territorial sense, both of which assist effective authoritarianism to demonstrate its greater capability over democracy for inducing global capital. Democracy can have an advantage in economic development, as many have observed, particularly during the Cold War era;[104] this institutional convenience, however, has been weakened by the globalization from which authoritarian advantages emerge.

Authoritarian advantages and democratic disadvantages are not only running in simple parallel; rather, they are locked in a chain of uneven power distributions that can be termed "dependency reversed." The chain consists of two major relationships: the market, especially global capital, depends on the effectively governed authoritarian state to strengthen its global competitiveness and maximize profit-making, while the democratic state, as the economic state arises, often depends on capital and market for delivering materialist performance in order to strengthen its domestic legitimacy.[105] It is different from what the dependency theory of comparative political economy in the 1960s and the 1970s once suggested, based on the Latin American experience,

[104] Adam Przeworski, Michael E. Alvarez, Jose Antonio Cheibub, and
       Fernando Limongi, *Democracy and Development: Political Institutions and
       Well-Being in the World, 1950-1990*, Cambridge University Press, 2000.
[105] Adam Przeworski and Michael Wallerstein, "Structural Dependence of the
       State on Capital," *American Political Science Review*, 82 (1988): 12–29.

that, in promoting economic development, the global periphery increases its dependence on the advanced capitalist countries, as the developing countries, especially those under political authoritarianism, have to rely on transnational corporations and, more generally, international capital in making a political alliance for economic benefits.[106] In "dependency reversed," however, global capitalism, which is nurtured under industrial democracies, increasingly depends on political authoritarianism, which effectively governs at the global periphery; an imbalance of power is created by post–Cold War globalization tilting toward the direction that lends greater leverage to developing authoritarianism.

Moreover, the logic of "dependency reversed" can be extended beyond relationships among states to the general domain of political institutions. As globalization involves all nations in global competition, authoritarian advantages can both force and lure democratic states to be engaged in a race in which democracy is also inclined to ignore citizens' preferences in competing against less democratic states, thus in general reducing the commitment to democratic institutions. The intrinsic trend of corporatization of the state alongside globalization, of course, also applies to a democratic state, thus one may argue that the decline of democracy can mean an impulse toward the authoritarianization of a democratic state. In fact, virtually all social organizations are involved in such a process of corporatization as an institutional "colonization" by the organizational form of the capitalist firm; authoritarianism as a set of institutions, namely as rules of the game, arises to reduce and replace democracy as such. The proposed argument of globalization enhancing authoritarian advantages against democracy, therefore, is not only a state-centered argument, as is often adopted in international politics to read the rise of authoritarian states like China against developed democracies such as the United States, but, more fundamentally, it is an institutionalist proposition that emphasizes democracy (here defined according to Douglass North as "the rules of the game" in governing public affairs[107]) as being victimized due to its seeking of resource

[106] Fernando Henrique Cardoso and Enzo Faletto, *Dependence and Development in Latin America*, Berkeley: University of California Press, 1979; Peter Evans, *Dependent Development: The Alliance of Multinational, State, and Local Capital in Brazil*, Princeton University Press, 1979.

[107] Douglass C. North, *Institutions, Institutional Change, and Economic Performance*, Cambridge University Press, 1990, p. 3.

concentration and market competitiveness for the purpose of promoting material wealth. In this wider sense, the theory of "dependency reversed" highlights how the global triumph of capitalism has reconfigured its institutional connections with authoritarianism and democracy by increasing the dependency of global capitalism as a mechanism of material production on authoritarian norms and principles, such as resource concentration, power centralization, political hierarchy, and repressive governance, while dissolving the weight, power, and magnetism of democratic norms and principles, such as citizens' participation in legislation and decision-making, inherent autonomy and freedom of members, and equality of everyone in terms of dignity, rights, and joining competitions.

Concluding Remarks

The global triumph of capitalism has transformed the institutional linkages between capitalism and other institutions, most prominently the state and regime types of the state as organized into either democracy or authoritarianism; the institutional framework under which capitalism, as a set of economic institutions, lives with various political institutions has therefore been fundamentally reconfigured. This chapter has attempted to sketch out the new institutional framework that defines capitalism's relationships with the state vis-à-vis democracy and authoritarianism, and has, accordingly, spelled out the general political-economic consequences found within the institutional essence of globalization.

The chapter has depicted four fundamental features of the new institutional framework of global capitalism, namely, the shaping of the state-market nexus; the rise of the economic state; the disjuncture between global capitalism and nation-state democracy, and the cleavage between the global free market and national mixed economies. To elaborate upon them, the chapter has started from a historical transformation of state-market relations from their Cold War confrontation to post–Cold War ideological conciliation and institutional collaboration, which has signaled the global, institutional triumph of capitalism and, accordingly, shaped the state-market nexus as the institutional backbone of post–Cold War globalization. The long-standing ideological, institutional, and functional boundaries between the market and the state, therefore, are melted, blurred, and cross-fertilized, though internal tensions still exist; the state-market nexus has since become the major locomotive that propels the development of global capitalism. It has brought about a series of institutional changes in global political economy, especially in state-market relations, to the degree that institutional changes have altered the fundamental principles of both the state and the market. The rise of the economic state is a most significant outcome of such institutional changes in the mutual context of state-market interactions.

Capitalism's global reach obviously has to interact with the existing nation-state system that still dominates in either domestic or international political realms, thus a great disjuncture emerges between global capitalism and nation-state democracy, simply because capitalism now expands over the globe but democracies are confined within national borders. This historical transformation, however, has been virtually neglected in intellectual reflections of the end of the Cold War and the rise of globalization, as the former is widely regarded as the victory of both market and democracy, and the latter as making the globe "flat." This chapter has disputed such prevailing interpretations of our age by suggesting that the collapse of communism as the victory of the market is overwhelming, but the victory of democracy in the "third wave" is much more limited, and that the rise of globalization advances the victory of the market further while at the same time restricting democracy even more substantially than before.

The global expansion of market capitalism within the state system also creates another institutional cleavage that has been given even less attention in the existing literature: As the global market runs virtually "free" across states in the sense of lacking effective command, the state-market nexus has transformed all national economies into being more or less "mixed" by involving state governance in market operations. This cleavage splits the world economic picture into two different levels, in resonance with the two organizational bodies of capitalism: The global economy as a whole is the under-regulated market where neoliberalism prevails, while a national economy can be compared in the way it is run to a capitalist firm in its efforts to enhance its competitiveness.

Together, these institutions make global capitalism operate in a new way that is rudimentarily different from pre-global capitalism, especially from Cold War capitalism. As pushing and pulling factors, the four institutions of globalization deprive capitalism of its earlier

political "shell" of democracy and, instead, provide it with two separate, inconsistent political bodies: nation-state democracy that is institutionally uncoupled with global capitalism and post–Cold War
authoritarianism that has survived the "end of history" by embracing
the global market. As the national economy is increasingly similar to
a firm competing on the global market, these two political bodies fall
into an uneven relationship of power vis-à-vis the two organizational
bodies of capitalism: On one hand, national democracies are not only
weak in their ability to govern global capitalism with their "local"
democratic procedures or citizens' preferences, but are in return undermined by a variety of local impacts of global capitalism; effective
authoritarianism, on the other hand, has gained leverage vis-à-vis
both democracy and global capitalism. They are locked in a two-link
chain termed "dependency reversed."

   The first link is embedded in global capital's dependence on authoritarian institutions in general and the effective authoritarian state in
particular, which provide organizational facilities and favorable circumstances for global capital to gain fortune and, joined by other
factors like the global limit of capitalist expansion, the bargaining
position of the authoritarian state is strengthened in dealing with global
capital. This makes possible the new political economy of development
in the globalization age: Economic prosperity is often achieved with,
institutionally, a strong state working together with the world market
and, in consequence, growing economic inequality, social injustice, and
a tremendous ecological cost. It also casts a political shadow on civil
rights and political freedoms at home and abroad. Authoritarian
advantages fit as a fundamental feature of capitalism in pursuing
efficiency via well-managed corporations, but they sacrifice the ordinary population's rights and interests and human public goods.

   This "dependency reversed" chain further extends to the relationship
between capitalism and democracy, in which the latter as another political body of global capitalism is not able to contain the former and has
simultaneously been undermined by various social, economic, political,
and even cultural and ideational impacts of globalization to the degree
that democracy has become increasingly dysfunctional. International
capital gains more leverage than before due to its "freedom" in stretching globally to undemocratic territories; in return, it becomes more
dominating in its home political bases of democracy for the purpose of
reducing democracy's accountability to ordinary citizens. Taking the

two links together, globalization enforces authoritarianism while under-mining democracy, which is, this book maintains, the institutional root of various crises in democracy, democratization, and the global govern-ance of our age.

Within this grand, institutional framework, how does global capit-alism coordinate all its major elements in the economy, namely, capital/production, labor, and consumption? As various relationships among these elements are also inevitably reconfigured with globalization, what will be their political-economic consequences, especially, in turn, on the state and institutions of authoritarianism versus democracy? Now our investigation shall address the "internal" realms of the institutions of global capitalism, starting from that of capital and production.

3 | Institutional Oligopoly and Embedded Coordination
Concentrative Movements of Capital

Globalization, at least in its early twenty-first century form, is primarily manifested in global movements of capital. In concert with the trend of state deregulation, capital, as the most dynamic element of the market economy, goes global with increased freedom and fewer restrictions, thus extending itself to an unprecedented scale, intensity, and frequency of movement, crossing various boundaries of political, economic, social, and cultural divisions, thereby making itself truly global not only in the physical and geographical sense but in the organizational and institutional sense. A prevailing interpretation of such movement often emphasizes the intensification of business competition as a major consequence; by contrast, this chapter shall demonstrate how capital now moves toward concentration on a global scale, and, furthermore, argue that the variety of concentrative movements intrinsically leads to monopoly and oligopoly of the global economy by capital.

The underlying observation, to echo the previous chapter's analysis of global capitalism, is institutionalist in the sense that it is greatly concerned with the structural and organizational dimensions of capital operation in general, and on capital's connections with the state in particular. The emergence of global capitalism, to this book, clearly makes the geographic space within which global capital operates in a limited rather than unlimited capacity; further dispersion, differentiation, and diversification of capital in the process of globalization, therefore, are at most partial in the spatial and geographic sense, let alone in its institutional operation. Neoliberal deregulation by the state at first gives capital a larger unrestricted space than what was previously accessible within state sovereignty, but the essence of globalization goes much further than such "unleashing"; rather, the capital that has now gained freedom and leverage of global movement soon butts up against global geographic and physical limits, thus it must turn to introversive concentration after its extensive spread. Capital concentration, therefore, emerges as a dynamic process of globalization; the concentrative movements of capital have, accordingly, established a fundamental feature of the operation of global capitalism.

The consequences of such concentrative movements are the embedded network and coordination of capital and, accordingly, institutional oligopoly, both of which can be identified as new forms of market monopoly. New form reveals new essence, this chapter will further argue and, thus, will attempt to redefine the concept of monopoly in relation to the age of global capitalism. Monopoly is, of course, a politically and ideologically sensitive topic. The intellectual tradition concerning monopoly capitalism originated from earlier critical thinkers of capitalism, who worked primarily following the last round of globalization that took place prior to the First World War in the early twentieth century. They argued that monopoly is a major indicator of capitalism coming into its late period, since competition as a general rule is thought to be the essence of the market economy while monopoly aims to diminish market competition into extinction.[1] Mainstream economists at one point began to incorporate this conception into their analyses of capitalism, as exemplified by Samuelson's *Economics*,[2] but today it is still novel to employ the concept of monopoly in mainstream discussions of capitalist finance and production. The rise of global capitalism, in particular, has often been regarded as the intensification of competition on a global scale rather than anything indicating monopoly; in the aftermath of the 2008 financial crisis, it is still rare to encounter the term "monopoly" in the flourishing publications that diagnose and remedy the problems of capitalist globalization. This chapter, however, shall go beyond the ideological and sensational use of the notion by borrowing ideas from both mainstream and radical observers of capitalism; its exploration of how capital's power institutionally dominates the global economy shall shed new light on the conceptual understanding of monopoly and oligopoly.

In highlighting the global reach of capitalism, this book recognizes the new historical and institutional circumstances in which global

---

[1] See a fine survey of early critical theories of monopoly in Anthony Brewer, *Marxist Theories of Imperialism: A Critical Survey*, London: Routledge, 1990, 2nd ed.

[2] Paul A. Samuelson, *Economics: An Introductory Analysis*, New York: McGraw-Hill, 1958, 4th ed., p. 42.

capitalism operates, and, accordingly, it highlights new momentum, new forms, and new paths that the movements of global capital take. All of these make the global movements of capital fundamentally characterized by concentration rather than dispersion. More exactly, there is a dialectic process in which capital now moves toward dispersion across nations while on the global scale it moves toward concentration. The intensification of global competition does not reduce concentration of capital; by contrast, it requires further concentration of capital in order to gain further competitiveness in the global market. Moreover, with the state-market nexus and the rise of the economic state, global competition involves not only market forces but also the state to an increasing degree, which likewise contributes to the mutually reinforcing interactions between concentration and competition that must be read against such new institutional backgrounds.

The information age in which contemporaries live is, of course, an important difference between global and pre-global capitalism. The information and technology revolution is often thought to be a democratic force in the sense that it "democratizes" the power of the spreading of information into the hands of mass users which number in the millions. But this chapter shall demonstrate that the connection between the information revolution and movements of capital points to an opposition of this "dispersion" assumption, as the former not only reinforces the latter's inclination to concentrate, but, more vitally, it also makes networking and coordination of capital technically convenient and institutionally ingrained, thus generating monopoly and oligopoly of capital as the normality of global capitalism.

Below this chapter shall undertake two tasks in developing and demonstrating the above arguments. The first task is empirical, through which some major global movements of capital shall be investigated to display how they make the structures and organizations of global capitalism concentrative in terms of capital's operation, and how such concentration institutionally underlines monopoly and oligopoly. In its attempts to cover three significant layers of contemporary monopolies and oligopolies, specifically regarding production, services, and finance, the major avenues of concentrative movement under investigation will include the global expansion of multinational corporations and their global dominance; the developments of chain stores in consumer services, especially in retailing, and of clusters in the amalgamation of production, research, innovation, and industrial services; and institutional changes in the financial sector due to globalization, a sector often emphasized as the headquarters of monopoly capitalism. The second task shall be conceptual and analytical, regarding which two questions will be asked: what forms do monopolies and oligopolies take today under global capitalism; and why does globalization promote monopoly and oligopoly? In unfolding these discussions, the chapter will make an effort to clarify the new characteristics of monopoly and oligopoly in the globalization age, spell out the conceptual implications of such new features, and answer how and why the global triumph of capitalism in the information age is necessarily connected with such monopoly and oligopoly as a norm of economic activities. Together with these two tasks, below this chapter will depict a general picture of capital movements in globalization and outline the institutional change that such movements have brought to capitalism.

Big Businesses Dominate the Global Economy: Multinational Corporations in Capitalist Globalization

The age of globalization is the age of big business, primarily in the form of multinational or transnational corporations (MNCs or TNCs), "capitalist firms which operate in more than one country."[3] True, MNCs are not a new organizational form of capitalist firms, but they have gained tremendous momentum in concert with the global triumph of capitalism. They have therefore concentrated an unprecedentedly huge amount of wealth, especially in the form of capital, into the hands of a small number of organizations, and these organizations are managed non-democratically. In any possible form of measurement, MNCs now represent a new scale, degree, and density of capital concentration that goes far beyond the imagination of earlier studies on capitalist monopoly.

Many researchers have reported that MNCs have been well developed since the 1990s, when globalization began to sweep the world. With data from the UN's *World Investment Report*, a textbook of international political economy states,

By the late 1990s, there were some 53,000 MNCs in the world, with 450,000 foreign affiliates. Most are relatively small, but the top several hundred are so huge and so globe straddling as to dominate major portions of the world

---

[3] Brewer, *Marxist Theories of Imperialism*, p. 261.

economy. MNCs' foreign affiliates are worth about $3.5 trillion, and they produce goods worth $9.5 trillion every year. These foreign affiliates account for one-third of world exports and a very substantial proportion of world output. Indeed, the largest MNCs have annual sales larger than the gross national product (GDP) of all but a few of the world's nations.[4]

In a similar vein, some other experts conclude that "today, the globalization of production is organized in large measure by MNCs. Their preeminence in world output, trade, investment and technology transfer is unprecedented."[5] According to them, these MNCs are "the linchpins of the contemporary world economy. Around 53,000 MNCs account for at least 20 per cent (some estimate 30 per cent) of world output and on some estimates up to 70 per cent of world trade." These MNCs, they continue,

play a much more central role in the operation of the world economy than in the past and they figure prominently in organizing extensive and intensive transnational networks of coordinated production and distribution that are *historically unique*. MNCs and global production networks are critical to the organization, location and distribution of productive power in the contemporary world economy.[6]

The 2008 world financial crisis did not change this fundamental trend of big-business development. In 2010, multinational companies numbered some 80,000, more than double the levels of 2000.[7] In posting "Global 500 2014," Deputy Managing Editor of the *Fortune* magazine Stephanie N. Mehta writes,

Global business is back. After limping through a worldwide financial crisis and economic slowdown, the 500 largest companies ranked by revenues shattered all sorts of performance records in 2013: They racked up combined revenues of $31.1 trillion, up 2.5% from 2012, and profits soared 27% to nearly $2 trillion. China's 95 companies (up from 89 last

---

[4] Jeffry A. Frieden and David A. Lake eds., *International Political Economy: Perspectives on Global Power and Wealth*, Boston: Bedford/St. Martin's, 4th ed., p. 141.

[5] David Held, Anthony McGrew, David Goldblatt, and Jonathan Perraton, *Global Transformations: Politics, Economics and Culture*, Stanford University Press, 1999, p. 282.

[6] Held, McGrew, Goldblatt, and Perraton, *Global Transformations*, p. 282. Emphasis added.

[7] Gary Clyde Hufbauer and Kati Suominen, *Globalization at Risk: Challenges to Finance and Trade*, New Haven: Yale University Press, 2010, p. 6.

year) posted $5.8 trillion in revenues. The U.S. has four fewer companies on the list than last year but remains (for now) the country leader, with 128 corporations on the list – including No. 1 Wal-Mart Stores – reporting $8.6 trillion in revenues.[8]

To make a note, 31.1 trillion equates to 40.23 percent of the GDP of the entire world that same year.[9]

In world trade, MNCs take a higher percentage of the total volume. Some commentators have estimated that multinationals – parents and affiliates combined – are responsible for 75 percent of the world's commodity trade;[10] an authoritative report indicates that MNCs accounted for two-thirds of world trade in 2007.[11] As much as 90 percent of US trade is estimated to flow through multinationals of all nationalities operating in the United States.[12] The Bureau of Economic Analysis calculates that US MNCs alone account for more than 50 percent of US exports and more than a third of American imports – as well as for a quarter of US GDP and 20 percent of private-sector jobs. The worldwide operations of US MNCs account for half of all profits in the United States. In China, MNCs are estimated to account for a third of output and a half of exports of the nation.[13]

The economic power of those top MNCs, therefore, can be larger than most countries in the world. In 2013, the top three global MNCs, in terms of their annual revenues, are ranked above all except twenty-six of the largest economies, which means that Wal-Mart (with a revenue of $476.294 billion), Royal Dutch Shell ($459.599 billion),

[8] http://fortune.com/global500/, accessed November 3, 2014.
[9] The total GDP of the world in 2014 was US$77.3 trillion according to www
     .statista.com/statistics/268750/global-gross-domestic-product-gdp/, accessed
     May 13, 2015.
[10] John H. Dunning, *Multinational Enterprises and the Global Economy*,
     Wokingham: Addison-Wesley, 1993; quoted in Howard J. Shatz and Anthony J.
     Venables, "The Geography of International Investment," in Gordon L. Clark,
     Maryann P. Feldman, and Meric S. Gertler eds., *The Oxford Handbook of
     Economic Geography*, Oxford University Press, 2000, pp. 125–145 (p. 126).
[11] United Nations Conference on Trade and Development (UNCTAD), *World
     Investment Report 2008*, Geneva: UNCTAD, 2008.
[12] A. B. Bernard, J. B. Jensen, and P. K. Schott, "Importers, Exporters and
     Multinationals: A Portrait of the Firms in the U.S. that Trade Goods,"
     Cambridge, MA: National Bureau of Economic Research, NBER Working
     Paper No. 11404, June 2005; quoted in Hufbauer and Suominen, *Globalization
     at Risk*, p. 88.
[13] Hufbauer and Suominen, *Globalization at Risk*, p. 88.

and Sinopec Group ($457.201 billion) could be ranked the 27th, 28th, and 29th largest economic entities only after those countries ranging from the United States (1st, with a GDP of $16,768.1 billion) to Norway (26th, $512.58 billion).[14] A comparison of GDPs and corporate sales for 2015 reveals that 43 of the world's 100 largest economies are multinational corporations, while 57 are countries.[15] It is not difficult to find a multitude of similar statements such as the following: "Enterprises like General Motors, Wal-Mart, Exxon-Mobil, Mitsubishi, and Siemens belong to the 200 largest TNCs, which account for over half of the world's industrial output";[16] "Rivaling nation-states in their economic power, these corporations control much of the world's investment capital, technology, and access to international markets";[17] "Small countries rely heavily on MNCs to supply capital and create jobs. Today, Luxembourg, Belgium, Hong Kong, and Singapore are more than 60 percent 'transnationalized'."[18] As a side note, the countries named here may be seen as small in popular perception, but they are actually ranked as large economies in the world.[19]

To emphasize the enormous power of MNCs in almost every aspect of life is nearly cliché; various terms are created to refer to such power in global capitalism, for example "corporate globalization" as cited by Manfred Steger; Robert Gilpin highlights the "age of the multinational" and Paul Bowles describes "corporatist capitalism"; and David Korten entitles a relatively early work *When Corporations Rule the World*, to name a few among many others.[20] What this chapter chooses to highlight as a follow up to these discussions,

[14] World Bank, World Development Indicators database, December 16, 2014, https://issuu.com/world.bank.publications/docs/9781464801631.
[15] Knoem, "World GDP Ranking 2015," http://knoema.com/nwnfkne/world-gdp-ranking-2015-data-and-charts; Forbes, "Global 2000," www.forbes.com/global2000/list/#tab:overall; both accessed February 20, 2016.
[16] Manfred B. Steger, *Globalization: A Very Short Introduction*, Oxford University Press, 2nd ed., 2009, p. 49.
[17] Steger, *Globalization*, p. 50.
[18] Hufbauer and Suominen, *Globalization at Risk*, p. 6; pp. 87–88.
[19] In 2013, Belgium is ranked the 24th largest economy in the world; Singapore, 36th; Hong Kong, 39th; Luxembourg, 73rd. World Bank, World Development Indicators database, December 16, 2014.
[20] Steger, *Globalization*, p. 50; Robert Gilpin, *The Challenge of Global Capitalism: The World Economy in the 21st Century*, Princeton University Press, 2000, ch. 6; Paul Bowles, *Capitalism*, Harlow: Pearson Longman, 2007, p. 17; David Korten, *When Corporations Rule the World*, London: Earthscan, 1995.

however, shall be, in particular, some new features of the development around MNCs in globalization and their dominance in the global economy.

One such feature is the continuous trend of MNCs growing larger and larger through mergers completed on a global scale. Although the growth in size of MNCs takes various forms, corporation merging and acquisition have become prevalent in global business in the globalization age. According to an expert,

In order to maintain their prominent positions in the global marketplace, TNCs frequently merge with other corporations. Some of these recent mergers include the $160-billion marriage of the world's largest Internet provider, AOL, with entertainment giant Time-Warner; the purchase of Chrysler Motors by Daimler-Benz for $43 billion; and the $115-billion merger between Sprint Corporation and MCI WorldCom.[21]

Two other scholars have recorded that "in 2007, the cross-border mergers and acquisitions rose to total a record $1.8 trillion, 21 percent above the levels attained at the turn of the millennium."[22] As Table 3.1 demonstrates, the historical trend of increasing numbers of business merger and acquisition is remarkable if comparing the late 1980s, when the annual average of five years was 7,005, to the early 2010s, when the same indicator was multiplied to be 42,588. In fact, 1989 had already indicated a jump from immediately previous years, as its number is 3.7 times that in 1985. This trend obviously makes large MNCs continuously larger in order to extend their global influence and, accordingly, causes capital to be further concentrated in the fewer number of firms on the global scale. As will be seen in later discussions, this combination of geographic extension and organizational concentration of capital repeatedly appears in many aspects of globalization, and this book views it as a key to understanding the essence of global capitalism.

Another significant feature regarding MNCs in globalization is the emergence of state-backed or even state-owned multinational enterprises, a phenomenon that seems to conflict with the spread of market forces, but, in the theoretical lens of this book elaborated upon in the previous chapter, it in fact well illustrates how the state-market nexus as the general institutional framework of global capitalism has been

---

[21] Steger, *Globalization*, p. 50.
[22] Hufbauer and Suominen, *Globalization at Risk*, p. 6.

Table 3.1 *Increase of Merger and Acquisition Worldwide: A Historical Comparison between the Late 1980s and the Early 2010s*

Historical Period	Year	Number of Merger and Acquisition	Annual Average during the Period
Late 1980s	1985	3,286	7,005.40
	1986	4,674	
	1987	5,992	
	1988	8,892	
	1989	12,183	
Early 2010s	2010	44,804	42,587.17
	2011	43,912	
	2012	41,409	
	2013	39,437	
	2014	43,473	
	2015	42,488	

Source: The author's composition based on the information available in http://imaa-institute.org/resources/statistics-mergers-acquisitions/, accessed February 20, 2016.

carrying MNCs into a new stage of development. More specifically, state-backed and state-owned MNCs arise mainly from the Global South, in which such MNCs have, to use a metaphor, been turning into "nuclear weapons" for those emerging economies to gain a foothold in global competition. Many developing states, prominently in East Asia, very much prefer a policy of promoting the growth of their multinationals.[23] The institutional nature of it, needless to say, is that the state throws its weight to support specific firms; with this, state-market symbiotic collaboration is most successfully institutionalized in economic operations.

The East Asian model of development has in particular been characterized for a long time by the state's endorsement of large firms, as is

---

[23] Shatz and Venables, "The Geography of International Investment," p. 142. Also, see some empirical studies in Ilan Alon and John R. McIntyre eds., *Globalization of Chinese Enterprises*, New York: Palgrave Macmillan, 2008, esp. James P. Johnson, "Paths to Globalization: The Korea *Chaebol* and Chinese State-owned Enterprises," pp. 133–145; A. Goldstein and F. Pusterla, "Emerging Economies' Multinationals: General Features and Specificities of the Brazilian and Chinese Cases," *International Journal of Emerging Markets*, 5 (2010, 3–4): 289–306.

well exemplified in the experience of South Korea and China.[24] In the Chinese case, for example, scholars have found "unique features" in the international expansion of these Chinese firms:

These unique features include that the dominant type of Chinese multinationals are SOEs, and their international expansion is promoted and supported by the Chinese government. These Chinese SOEs have operated in different ownership structures and in different institutional environments than multinationals in developed countries and other emerging economies. They have been characterized by a high level of control by the central government, strong bargaining power with the government, easy access to political and economic privileges, and soft budgets.[25]

Another study confirms the above observation:

Even though these firms are legally incorporated into joint stock companies, direct government ownership and indirect ownership through SASAC [State-owned Assets Supervision and Administration Commission, a ministerial-level department of the national government] remain common ... Despite modern firm ownership structure, these incorporated firms are de facto SOEs.[26]

These Chinese SOEs are small in number, but they "possess large assets" and "often monopolies with significant legal and technical entry barriers ... "[27]

These Chinese state-owned MNCs have in recent years started to become more globalized through increasing outward FDI, not only stretching to other developing economies but also to industrialized nations in Europe and North America.[28] In this process,

---

[24] Alice H. Amsden, *Asia's Next Giant: South Korea and Late Industrialization*, Oxford University Press, 1992; Peter Nolan, *China and the Global Economy: National Champions, Industrial Policy, and the Big Business Revolution*, New York: Palgrave, 2001.

[25] Xiaohua Yang and Clyde Stoltenberg, "Growth of Made-in-China Multinationals: An Institutional and Historical Perspective," in Ilan Alon and John R. McIntyre eds., *Globalization of Chinese Enterprises*, New York: Palgrave Macmillan, 2008, pp. 61–76 (p. 69).

[26] Sea-Jin Chang, *Multinational Firms in China: Entry Strategies, Competition, and Firm Performance*, Oxford University Press, 2013, p. 74.

[27] Ibid.

[28] B. Ramasamy, M. Yeung, and S. Laforet, "China's Outward Foreign Direct Investment: Location Choice and Firm Ownership," *Journal of World Business*, 47 (2012, 1): 17–25; S. Meunier, "'Beggars Can't Be Choosers': The European Crisis and Chinese Direct Investment in the European Union," *Journal of European Integration*, 36 (2014, 3): 283–302.

It is widely recognized that the Chinese government has played a crucial role in shaping the country's O-FDI. . . . The Chinese government has adopted a strategic posture in framing both their I-FDI and O-FDI policies to meet the demands of new global challenges and their own domestic economic interests. The government's attitudes and actions in relation to multinational activity and growth have been integral parts of allocation and upgrading of national resources. The Chinese government has placed the creation of an internationally competitive industrial base on the national agenda of economic liberalization.[29]

Thus some leading Chines SOEs have quickly grown to be among the top global MNCs, often larger in size than a large national economy in the world. Table 3.2 is a simple attempt to draw a comparison for the purpose of listing their ranks in the world's 100 largest economic entities. It is quite astonishing, at least to this author, to see that China's largest SOEs possess larger economic power than countries such as Norway, Thailand, and Israel.

China is not alone in supporting state-backed corporations, as outward investment from the Global South, "nontraditional sources," has already become phenomenal in the twenty-first-century world economy, with "nontraditional sources" including the Middle East and Russia, as well as China. In promoting this development, the government in these countries plays a vital role:

Direct investment in the United States from Russia has increased about five times between 2003 and 2008; from China, six times; and from the Middle East, perhaps thirty times. It is not clear that the new investors are reading the same commercial playbook as Western firms, since much of their investment is tied up with governing circles in the home country. In fact, a quarter of the top one hundred multinational companies in developing countries are government-owned, as opposed to only five of the world's one hundred largest MNCs.[30]

It is obvious that "MNCs do constitute concentrations of immense economic power";[31] with the direct or indirect involvement of the state in this regard, often for the purpose of favoring MNCs' global competitiveness, the collaboration and even combination of a strong state and strong companies further makes the state-market nexus the institutional

---

[29] Yang and Stoltenberg, "Growth of Made-in-China Multinationals," p. 69.
[30] Hufbauer and Suominen, *Globalization at Risk*, p. 234.
[31] Gilpin, *The Challenge of Global Capitalism*, p. 192.

Table 3.2 *Chinese SOEs against Large National Economies: A Rough Comparison*
(Number indicates the rank in 2015 in the world's 100 largest economic entities that include both corporations and countries. Those top 24 largest national economies are omitted here; other omitted ranks are occupied by non-Chinese MNCs)

Chinese SOE-MNCs	Selected National Economies
	25: Sweden
	26: Poland
	27: Belgium
28: Sinopec	
	30: Norway
	31: Islamic Republic of Iran
	33: Thailand
	34: Austria
	36: United Arab Emirates
37: PetroChina	
	38: South Africa
	39: Malaysia
	40: Hong Kong SAR
	41: Philippines
	42: Israel
	43: Singapore
	44: Denmark
	45: Colombia
	46: Pakistan
	49: Chile
	50: Finland
	54: Bangladesh
	56: Vietnam
	57: Portugal
	59: Kazakhstan
	61: Greece
	62: Qatar
	64: Czech Republic
	65: Peru
	66: Algeria
	67: Romania

Table 3.2 (*cont.*)

Chinese SOE-MNCs	Selected National Economies
	70: New Zealand
	72: Iraq
	86: Venezuela
89: China Construction Bank	
90: Agricultural Bank of China	
100: China State construction Engineering	97: Kuwait

Sources: The author's composition based on the information available in http://knoe
ma.com/nwnfkne/world-gdp-ranking-2015-data-and-charts, and www.forbes.com/
global2000/list/#tab:overall, both accessed February 20, 2016.

linchpin around which the concentration not only of "immense economic power" but also immense political power is realized and established. Where power exists, however, it can be abused; where power is
enormously concentrated, it can be willful, perverse, and intractable in
such abuse. The MNCs, as a leading scholar of international political
economy points out, "like all large and powerful social institutions
(including government bureaucracies and even nonprofit organizations)," can "behave in corrupt, arrogant, and socially irresponsible
ways."[32] The most severe aftermath of the growing power of MNCs in
generating such an unprecedented concentration of wealth and capital
among a handful of oligarchically organized business firms can be identified as what is usually termed monopoly, duopoly, or oligopoly. As a
later section shall focus on the conceptual aspects of the topic covering
the notion of monopoly, its variation, ideological debates around it, and
how to define it in the globalization age, here we will skip over it and turn
instead to some additional concentrative movements of global capital.

Concentration of Capital in Both Stretch and Proximity: The Rise of Chain Stores and Regional Clusters

The outgrowing of MNCs is only one institutional way, though a most
significant one, of capital becoming globally concentrative; many other

[32] Ibid.

structural and organizational facilities are innovated and created in the global expansion of capitalism to actualize the expansion while promoting concentration of wealth, capital, and business decision-making power, especially through increasing networks, interdependence, and coordination among various corporations as well as between business firms and governments. "The key feature of oligopoly is the interdependence among firms."[33] This interdependence has greatly developed in the post–Cold War era with the rise of globalization, and it now manifests itself in diverse forms. This section chooses two prominent forms of such manifestation for closer scrutiny, two forms that seem to run in opposite directions, but both reveal the same quintessence of global capital's trend toward concentration. We will see, on one hand, how chain stores prevail with an organizational stretching-out onto the expanding global market, particularly stretching to those traditionally dispersive sectors such as retail and services, while, on the other hand, the rise of clusters suggests the rapid increase of production networks in geographic proximity with the amalgamation of industrial production, scientific and technological innovation, relevant logistical support, and local government's economic engagement. Each of the two has received insufficient attention in the field of macro political economy of globalization, however. A leading expert regarding retail, for example, complains in a 2000 publication that "a myopic neglect" has taken hold in globalization studies of retail-industry MNCs such as Gap Inc., Royal Ahold, and Carrefour.[34] In regards to clusters, it is often a subject of research that is limited to economic geography and regional studies, with greater emphases being placed on its function to promote economic development rather than on its comprehensive implications for global capitalism in general. More importantly, the rise of clusters is predominantly seen as indicating a trend of regionalization that attempts to balance globalization, while chain stores are regarded as being more extensive and dispersive rather than concentrative. This section below shall argue, however, that despite their different trajectories of geographic movement and organizational structuring, chain

[33] James A. Caporaso and David P. Levine, *Theories of Political Economy*, Cambridge University Press, 1992, p. 168.

[34] Neil Wrigley, "The Globalization of Retail Capital: Themes for Economic Geography," in Gordon L. Clark, Maryann P. Feldman, and Meric S. Gertler eds., *The Oxford Handbook of Economic Geography*, Oxford University Press, 2000, pp. 292–313. The later two are Dutch and French food retailers.

stores and regional clusters by their very essence share fundamental institutional features that are more significant than their business appearances in disclosing how capital works with globalization: namely that via these entities, capital is gaining intrinsic concentration, internal interdependence, and overall oligopoly.

Actualizing Institutional Concentration in Global Stretching: Chain Stores in Retail and Services

The chain-store system is not a creation of globalization, as in fact it began to emerge in the late nineteenth century, primarily in Britain and the United States.[35] In the early half of the twentieth century, it was, particularly in the US, already "recognized as an established feature" of the distribution setup.[36] The global triumph of capitalism in the post–Cold War era, however, has powerfully energized the system to the extent of transforming retail capital in three prominent ways. First, chain stores have experienced an unprecedented global expansion, which has yielded profound consequences in commerce, consumption, and, more generally, economy and society. Second, capital giants of retail have emerged in this wave of globalization not only with an astonishingly rapid speed but also in startlingly colossal sizes, to the extent that such giants are now able to be top global MNCs, as well exemplified by Wal-Mart.[37] Thirdly, the information and technology revolution has provided new momentum and creative paths to

[35] Hermann Levy, *The Shops of Britain: A Study of Retail Distribution*, London: Routledge & Kegan Paul, 1948. It noticed that "This tendency toward large-scale retail business came almost 100 years later than the Industrial Revolution; the Bon Marche came in 1852, the first departmental stores in the United States in the later 'fifties, Whiteley's in 1860" (p. 3).

[36] Godfrey M. Lebhar, *Chain Stores in America, 1859–1950*, New York: Chain Store Publishing, 1952, p. ix.

[37] For research and debates around Wal-Mart, see, for example, Bill Quinn, *How Wal-Mart Is Destroying America (and the World)*, Berkeley: Ten Speed Press, 2005; Stanley D. Brunn ed., *Wal-Mart World: The World's Biggest Corporation in the Global Economy*, New York: Routledge, 2006; Charles Fishman, *The Wal-Mart Effect: How the World's Most Powerfully Company Really Works – and How It's Transforming the American Economy*, New York: Penguin Books, 2006; Anthony Bianco, *Wal-Mart: The Bully of Bentonville: How the High Cost of Everyday Low Prices Is Hurting America*, New York: Doubleday, 2007; Rebekah Peeples Massengill, *Wal-Mart Wars: Moral Populism in the Twenty-First Century*, New York University Press, 2013. Also, Anita Chan ed., *Wal-Mart in China*, Ithaca: Cornell University Press, 2011.

actualize such speedy development and the gigantic sizes of MNCs, including many chain stores, in retail and services.

The growth of chain stores can be better understood through a brief historical review of its development. In the US, retailing was still dominated in the mid-twentieth century by small independent firms operating just a single store; in 1948, 70 percent of total US retail sales were accounted for by such firms and only 18 percent by the larger chains operating more than ten stores (this is obviously too small a number in comparison with a chain store of today). By the early 1980s, however, the share of total US retail sales accounted for by the single-store independent firms had fallen to just 48 percent whilst that of the larger chains had risen to over 40 percent. Similar trends had also occurred in Britain so that, by 1984, 58 percent of total retail sales had been captured by equivalent chains.[38] In 2015, the top 121 retail chains in the US had 60.4 percent of the US retail market, dwarfing the rest at 39.6 percent; the same year in the UK, the top 133 retail chains had 73.6 percent of the UK retail market, while the rest had only 26.4 percent.[39]

The rise of the retail corporation – the mega chains – is the more important development. In the USA and Britain, retail census figures show that the relatively small number of very large chains (defined conservatively as those operating more than 100 stores), which had previously comprised just a tiny proportion – less than 1 percent – of all retail firms, had dramatically increased their share of total retail sales.[40] In the US, their share almost tripled from 12 percent in 1948 to 30 percent by 1982, while in Britain it more than doubled in the same period to 42 percent by 1984. By the early years of the twenty-first century, as Table 3.3 helps to indicate, the largest retailers' sales had skyrocketed, sending these corporations into the top ranks of MNCs.

Moreover, these overall figures concealed much greater levels of dominance that the mega-chains had begun to achieve in particular sectors of the industry.[41] Established retail-industry MNCs, according to an authoritative publication, "were by the late 1990s very significant global firms," such as, for example, Royal Ahold operating in 17 countries,

---

[38] Neil Wrigley and Michelle Lowe, *Reading Retail: A Geographical Perspective on Retailing and Consumption Spaces*, Oxford University Press, 2002, p. 22.

[39] www.portal.euromonitor.com.ezproxy.library.uvic.ca/portal/statistics/change measure, accessed May 1, 2016.

[40] Wrigley and Lowe, *Reading Retail*, p. 22.   [41] Ibid, p. 23.

Table 3.3 *The Largest US Retailers, 2013*

Corporation	Worldwide Sales (US$ million)
Wal-Mart	473,979,000
Costco	105,100,000
Kroger	93,598,000
McDonald's	89,126,000
7-Eleven	84,008,000
The Home Depot	78,812,000
Amazon.com	77,551,000
Target	72,596,000
Walgreen	70,096,000
CVS Caremark	66,682,000

Source: The author's composition based on the information available in https://nrf.com/2014/top100-table, accessed February 24, 2016.

Carrefour in 21 (26 countries with annual sales exceeding $55 billion following the completion of Carrefour's merger with Promodes), and these were "obtaining a large proportion of their sales and profits from their international activities" – 75 percent in the case of Ahold and 40 percent for Carrefour/Promodes.[42]

The emergence of e-commerce has accelerated such a process of capital concentration in some retail firms, as "the late 1990s has seen both rapidly developing new economic geographies of globalizing retail capital, and the rise of e-commerce as a potentially destabilizing force within those geographies."[43] Online retailers, some of which are listed in Table 3.4, and their world of e-commerce arose quickly with the information and, technology revolution; more importantly, they indisputably indicate "the increasingly global nature of retail distribution."[44] As will be emphatically discussed later in this chapter, the promotional rather than negative effect of the information and communication technology revolution for the continuous trend of capital concentration is distinct, here best exemplified in the development of new e-commerce MNCs into mega chains.

---

[42] Wrigley, "The Globalization of Retail Capital," p. 293.   [43] Ibid, p. 311.
[44] Ibid, p. 294.

Table 3.4 *Top Online Companies, Ranked by Assets*

Corporation	Assets (US$ billion)	Annual Revenues (US$ billion)	Year the Firm Formed
Google	147.461	75	1998
Amazon.com	65.444	107.1	1994
Facebook	49.41	17.928	2004
Alibaba	45.494	12.29	1999
Yahoo!	45	4.62	1995
Tencent	40.204	12.099	1998
Rakuten	37.812	6.321	1997
Baidu	19.077	7.905	2000
eBay	17.785	8.592	1995
Priceline.com	16.614	8.442	1997
JD.com	13.070	18.535	1998
Yahoo! Japan	11.494	3.794	1996
Salesforce.com	10.692	5.37	1999
Netflix	10.202	6.779	1997
LinkedIn	7.011	2.991	2002
NetEase	5.226	2.0	1997
Twitter	4.38	1.403	2006
Naver	2.534	2.254	1999
Vipshop	2.364	3.773	2008

Sources: The author's composition based on the information available in the following webpages: For Google: https://abc.xyz/investor/news/earnings/2015/Q4_google_earning s/index.html; www.marketwatch.com/investing/stock/goog/financials; for Facebook: http://investor.fb.com/releasedetail.cfm?ReleaseID=952040; for Amazon: https://finance .yahoo.com/q/bs?s=AMZN+Balance+Sheet&annual; for eBay: https://finance.yahoo.co m/q/bs?s=EBAY+Balance+Sheet&annual; for Baidu: http://ir.baidu.com/mobile.view?c= 188488&v=203&d=1&id=2104539; for Priceline.com: https://www.google.ca/finance %3Fq=NASDAQ:PCLN%26fstype=ii; https://www.google.ca/finance?q=NASDAQ:PC LN&fstype=ii; for Yahoo!: www.wikinvest.com/stock/Yahoo!_%28YHOO%29/Data/ Total_Assets; www.wikinvest.com/stock/Yahoo!_%28YHOO%29/Data/Key_Metrics; for Netflix: https://finance.yahoo.com/q/bs?s=NFLX+Balance+Sheet&annual; www.sta tista.com/statistics/272545/annual-revenue-of-netflix/; for LinkedIn: https://finance.yaho o.com/q/bs?s=LNKD+Balance+Sheet&annual; www.marketwatch.com/investing/stock/ lnkd/financials; for Twitter: https://investor.twitterinc.com/releasedetail.cfm?relea seid=894844; www.marketwatch.com/investing/stock/twtr/financials/balance-sheet; for Yahoo! Japan: http://ir.yahoo.co.jp/en/bizres/q_index.html; for Rakuten: www.gurufo cus.com/term/Total%20Assets/RKUNF/Total%252BAssets/Rakuten%252 C%2BInc; for NetEase: www.gurufocus.com/term/Total%20Assets/NTES/Total%252BAssets/Net Ease%2BInc; for Vipshop: www.gurufocus.com/term/Total%20Assets/VIPS/Total%2B Assets/Vipshop%2BHoldings%2BLtd. All accessed February 24–25, 2016.

Neil Wrigley, a world-leading expert in studies of chain stores, identifies four general trends in the globalization of retail industry by the late 1990s, all of which indicate concentration of capital:

1) the massive growth in scale of many of these retail firms during the 1990s, particularly since the midpoint of the decade, powered by a wave of acquisition- and merger-driven consolidation of retail markets throughout the world;
2) the increasingly international nature of much of that merger and acquisition activity;
3) the rapid emergence within this listing of the world's largest retailers of an elite group of firms with proven international capability and ambition – Ahold, Carrefour/Promodes, Kingfisher, Casino, Delhaize, Metro, Auchan, and so on – with international sales in the 25 to 75 percent range, active across a range of developed (mature) and emerging (growth) markets, and potentially including within their number firms such as Wal-Mart and Tesco who prior to the mid-1990s had very little international exposure;
4) the importance of food retailing, both within the real-terms growth in scale of the world's largest retailers during the 1990s, and as a core component of the activities of that elite group of retail-industry TNCs.[45]

Daily-life experience as a consumer can help give a sense of the growing significance and dominance of chain stores in retailing; everywhere one looks, be it in a shopping mall or a business district, from New York City to Paris, from Shanghai to São Paulo, one can easily find outlets of the same brands across the globe. Department stores (as "cathedrals of consumption"[46]), spacious retail outlets, supermarket chains, menswear and women's fashion chains, and restaurants (we need not mention McDonald's, but think about even a Vietnamese rice noodle chain such as Pho Ha, a much less flamboyant "brand")[47] and

---

[45] Ibid, p. 296.   [46] Wrigley and Lowe, *Reading Retail*, p. 21.
[47] For McDonald's expansion to, for example, East Asia, a region whose food tastes are traditionally quite distinguished from the West's, see James L. Watson ed., *Golden Arches East: McDonald's in East Asia*, Stanford University Press, 2006, 2nd ed. Also, Warren K. Liu, *KFC in China: Secret Recipe for Success*, Singapore: John Wiley, 2008. Similar stories are found in other places of the world, as exemplified in McDonald's opening of its first franchise in Moscow in 1990 "to a tremendous welcome from the Russian people and press." Ilan Alon, Dianne H. B. Welsh, and Cecilia M. Falbe, "Franchising in Emerging Markets,"

coffee shops (yes, Starbucks now runs 24,395 shops worldwide as of the first quarter of 2016,[48] including a big one on the Champs-Élysées – could this have been imaginable before the 1990s?) all operate with numerous branches dotted across the globe, announcing the triumph of corporate retail and dispelling individual shops, small businesses, cultural diversities, and the social values affiliated with these things.[49]

In order to better comprehend this phenomenon, especially its nature of expansion under the institutional framework provided by global capitalism, below we shall briefly analyze two topics relevant to chain stores: franchising as a specific method of capital expansion and the role of government in franchising. Mergers and Acquisition (M&A), as employed among MNCs, also plays a significant role in these retail MNCs' securing of their place in global competition.[50] Franchising, in particular, is a convenient way for retail giants to expand their global map, especially to emerging markets, as, according to experts, "Retail franchising allows firms to achieve the expanded reach and efficiencies associated with internationalization more rapidly and effectively than the firms could accomplish on their own."[51] It is seen as a "means of obtaining scare capital as the franchisee is generally required to make a substantial investment in the business," through which firms can "maximize revenues through administrative efficiency and protection of the franchise brand while minimizing operational costs."[52] In practice, retail franchises were established in emerging markets primarily at the turn of the twenty-first century through master franchises and corporate franchise agreements, and, to a lesser extent, joint venture franchising and conversion franchising. By 1997, the top 50 US food chains had $33.1 billion in international sales as a result of significant efforts by large US-based food retail franchisors.[53]

In their rapid expansion to emerging markets and other parts of the global periphery, where conditions for reproducing MNCs' business

in Ilan Alon ed., *Franchising Globally: Innovation, Learning and Imitation*, New York: Palgrave Macmillan, 2010, pp. 11–35 (p. 12).

48 Knoema, "Number of Starbucks Stores Globally, 1992–2016," https://knoema .com/kchdsge/number-of-starbucks-stores-globally-1992-2016, accessed May 25, 2016.

49 Chapters 5 and 6 will explore this topic from perspectives of consumption and social consequences, respectively.

50 Wrigley, "The Globalization of Retail Capital."

51 Alon, Welsh, and Falbe, "Franchising in Emerging Markets," p. 19.

52 Ibid, p. 13.   53 Ibid, p. 12.

format against heterogeneous locations around the globe can vary and be uncertain, MNCs often choose to promote their cooperation with local governments in host countries to increase their chances of success in investment. In reciprocity, as they increasingly become aware of the benefits to their country that franchising can offer, "many governments are in the process of improving their country's business environment in order to attract high quality franchises" through legislative, organizational, financial, and other possible means.[54] This helps to highlight the significant role of government in capital's global search for profits, a theme implied in the state-market nexus as the institutional backbone of global capitalism. It also adds flesh to this book's argument of "dependency reversed."

All of the above developments, often termed the retail revolution, the shopping revolution, or "Wal-Martization,"[55] signal a reconfiguration of corporate structures in retailing and, accordingly, the concentration of capital in the industry into a smaller number of hands. As two experts point out, "the increasing level of retail concentration" has been "such a market feature of many western economies" particularly over the past twenty-five years, and such concentration "has been accompanied by the growth of large retail corporations whose concern has been both to create and maintain what might be termed their 'competitive space'."[56] Thus, retailing has been "transformed via a strong trend towards the concentration of capital into an industry increasingly dominated by 'big capital' in the form of large corporations," with the years since the 1990s having been "characterized by the development of global empires" of those giant firms.[57] The geographic extension of capital working in tandem with the rise of chain stores, therefore, reveals institutional concentration rather than dispersion of capital, in resonance with the general trend of big businesses dominating global capitalism.

Geographical Proximity as a Nucleus of Institutional Congregation of Industrial Production: The Case of Clusters

Different from the chain stores that represent the concentration of capital and business power often in the form of sector oligopoly, the

---

[54] Ibid, p. 20.
[55] For example, Carl Gardner and Julie Sheppard, *Consuming Passion: The Rise of Retail Culture*, London: Unwin Hyman, 1989, p. 24; Greville Havenhand, *Nation of Shopkeepers*, London: Eyre & Spottiswoode, 1970, ch. 1.
[56] Wrigley and Lowe, *Reading Retail*, p. 21.   [57] Ibid, p. 22.

rise of clusters indicates a geographic concentration of capital, usually having production as its core while agglomerating other increasingly significant elements for global capitalist production, primarily technology innovation. Especially important to our discussion, the rise of clusters also helps to exemplify the critical role of government, often through its local agencies, in promoting capital concentration, which supports a central argument made by this book about the significance of state-capital collaboration for global capitalism.

Like chain stores, regional concentration is not a new idea, as Alfred Marshall in the late nineteenth century was already aware of "the advantages" of "a large business over small ones" that were conspicuous in manufacturing because a large business had "special facilities for concentrating a good deal of work in a small area."[58] However, as pointed out by a group of experts specializing in European clusters, "it is only quite recently that policy makers joined the wave and began to include clusters in the set of instruments they can use for their industrial or regional policy agenda."[59] That is to say, the involvement of government in clustering is a new but decisive development in "this type of concentration."[60] Moreover, government engagement in clustering can be unprecedentedly wide, because "cluster policies can be implemented by all levels of governments."[61] For example, in the United States, where the federal government has traditionally been reluctant to conduct either industrial or regional policy, many sub-national jurisdictions have turned to cluster policy instead.[62] In Europe, where "this movement in favour of cluster policies has impacted many European countries and regions in the last thirty years," the European Commission, national governments, and sub-national administrations all play important roles in this regard.[63] At the Pan-Europe level, the European Commission, which in 2006 and 2008 published two policy papers in which "it encouraged member states to integrate cluster strategies in their national innovation programmes," made various efforts to promote clusters, efforts ranging from financial policy to

---

[58] Alfred Marshall (1890), *Principles of Economics: Unabridged Eighth Edition*, New York: Cosimo Classics, 2009, p. 239.
[59] Gilles Duranton, Philippe Martin, Thierry Mayer, and Florian Mayneris, *The Economics of Clusters: Lessons from the French Experience*, Oxford University Press, 2010, p. 1.
[60] Ibid.   [61] Ibid, p. 3.   [62] Ibid.
[63] Ibid, p. 4. The European Cluster Observatory provides detailed reports in this regard: www.clusterobservatory.eu.

assistance in cross-country experience-sharing.[64] At the nation-state level, government intervention can be important in clustering, as in the French case, where "there is a long tradition of strong government intervention regarding the location of economic activity."[65] Sub-national government's enthusiasm in clustering has been particularly strong in Europe, with pioneers like the Spanish Basque region, as well as other examples in Germany and France.[66] In all cases, the role of the state in the economy in promoting competitiveness is obvious and pivotal.

The Global South, in an attempt to catch up with industrialization, is equally, if not more, keen on the promotion of clustering. The World Development Bank in 2009 published a report entitled *Reshaping Economic Geography*, which clearly recorded a strong policy interest in developing countries in the various issues concerning clusters.[67] Successes have been achieved in some emerging economies, such as in Dongguan, China, which is "certainly best described as one of a successful cluster story that exemplifies the economic gains of agglomeration."[68] Special economic zones can also be regarded as a special type of regional clustering, which has become a widely adopted measure in developing economies for promoting industrialization, science and technology innovation, and its integration with globalization.[69]

Obviously the state-market nexus now extends to all levels of government, including intergovernmental organizations; the rise of clusters is a

[64] Duranton, Martin, Mayer, and Mayneris, *The Economics of Clusters*, pp. 5–6. For the European Commission's reports, see *Putting Knowledge into Practice: A Broad-Based Strategy for the EU*, COM (2006) 502; *Towards World-Class Clusters in the European Union: Implementing the Broad-Based Innovation Strategy*, COM (2008) 652.

[65] Duranton, Martin, Mayer, and Mayneris, *The Economics of Clusters*, p. 10.

[66] Ibid, pp. 4–5.

[67] World Bank, 2009; quoted in Duranton, Martin, Mayer, and Mayneris, *The Economics of Clusters*, p. 13.

[68] Duranton, Martin, Mayer, and Mayneris, *The Economics of Clusters*, p. 13.

[69] Douglas Zhihua Zeng ed., *Building Engines for Growth and Competitiveness in China: Experience with Special Economic Zones and Industrial Clusters*, Washington, DC: World Bank, 2010; Thomas Farole and Gokhan Akinci eds., *Special Economic Zones: Progress, Emerging Challenges, and Future Directions*, Washington, DC: World Bank, 2011; Thomas Farole, *Special Economic Zones in Africa: Comparing Performance and Learning from Global Experiences*, Washington, DC: World Bank, 2011; Connie Carter and Andrew Harding eds., *Special Economic Zones in Asian Market Economies*, Abingdon: Routledge, 2011.

good case in which both the state and capital not only benefit from their collaboration, but also, as this book has earlier pointed out, from their institutional coupling and functional overlapping. The "benefits from concentration" in terms of the competitive edge that clusters can provide is a major reason that governments are engaged in promoting relevant policies.[70] In those exemplary cases of successful clusters such as Silicon Valley and Route 128, development strategies of the state, which are often local states, play a vital role in attracting investments.[71] It has been observed that since the end of the 1990s, another round of policy innovation has emerged with the encouragement of industry clusters.[72]

The information revolution and the wider technology revolution both powerfully stimulate the rise of clusters, as reflected in Silicon Valley's "iconic example" that serves as a model for the popularity of cluster policies. It is reported that, "following its success, clusters have come to be seen by many as the magical formula for regional development, innovation, and growth."[73] Thus observers have witnessed, for example, in Europe the establishment of the cluster of Cambridge (sometimes called SiliconFen) and the French cluster Minalogic in Grenoble in the fields of microelectronics and software, and the Biovalley (Strasbourg, Basle, and Freiburg); Stockholm, Munich, and Cambridge have become leading clusters in biotechnologies.[74] In

---

[70] Duranton, Martin, Mayer, and Mayneris, *The Economics of Clusters*, pp. 2, 8–9.

[71] Amy K. Glasmeier, "Factors Governing the Development of High Technology Clusters: A Tale of Three Cities," *Regional Studies*, 22 (1987): 287–301; Amy K. Glasmeier, "Economic Geography in Practice: Local Economic Development Policy," in Gordon L. Clark, Maryann P. Feldman, and Meric S. Gertler eds., *The Oxford Handbook of Economic Geography*, Oxford University Press, 2000, pp. 559–579 (p. 561).

[72] Glasmeier, "Economic Geography in Practice," p. 563.

[73] Duranton, Martin, Mayer, and Mayneris, *The Economics of Clusters*, pp. 1–2. For Silicon Valley, see a classic work in AnnaLee Saxenian, *Regional Advantage: Culture and Competition in Silicon Valley and Route 128*, Cambridge, MA: Harvard University Press, 1994.

[74] For competitive advantage of clusters, see, for example, Michael Porter, *The Competitive Advantage of Nations*, New York: Free Press, 1990; Michael Porter, "Clusters and Competition: New Agendas for Companies, Governments, and Institutions," in *On Competition*, Cambridge, MA: Harvard Business School Press, 1998, pp. 213–304; Michael Porter, "Clusters and New economics of Competition," *Harvard Business Review*, 76, 6 (1998): 77–91; Michael Porter, "Locations Clusters and Company Strategy," in Gordon L. Clark, Maryann P. Feldman, and Meric S. Gertler eds., *The Oxford Handbook of Economic Geography*, Oxford University Press, 2000, pp. 253–274; Michael Porter,

addition, relatively traditional industries now carry new momentum from the technology revolution in cases such as the British Motor Valley.[75] The common thread is that all are featured with technology innovation as the core of a cluster, and all successfully demonstrate the intimate connection between the technology and information revolutions and the rise of clusters.[76] To gain such benefits of proximity, local cooperation necessarily includes not only firms and local governments but also universities and other kinds of research organizations concerning production and circulation of new knowledge,[77] indicating that the concentration of various elements of the capitalist economy has reached a higher level of amalgamation.

Some analysts regard clustering as a balance against the dominance of MNCs in globalization, or a trend of "localization in globalization."[78] For them, clusters have the potential to "connect these localities within and across nations; to create an enterprise economy that appropriately includes all actors in all communities," thus challenging the assertion that "the world is in a position where the enterprise economy has been to some extent globalized through the activities of large corporations, but where community economies have remained fixed within localities."[79] Here I would argue, however, that clustering

"Location, Competition, and Economic Development: Local Clusters in a Global Economy," *Economic Development Quarterly*, 14, 1 (2000): 15–34; Michael Porter, "The Economic Performance of Regions," *Regional Studies*, 37, 6–7 (2003): 549–578. For how Michael Porter's argument on clusters' competitive advantage influenced governmental policy in European countries, see, for example, Duranton, Martin, Mayer, and Mayneris, *The Economics of Clusters*, p. 2.

[75] N. Henry and S. Pinch, "Spatialising Knowledge: Placing the Knowledge Community of Motor Sport Valley," *Geoforum*, 31, 2 (2000): 191–208.

[76] P. Maskell, "Towards a Knowledge-based Theory of the Geographical Cluster," *Industrial and Corporate Change*, 10, 4 (2001): 921–943.

[77] Duranton, Martin, Mayer, and Mayneris, *The Economics of Clusters*, pp. 8 and 12; P. Cooke, "Regional Innovation Systems, Cluster, and the Knowledge Economy," *Industrial and Corporate Change*, 10, 4 (2001): 945–974; H. Bathelt, A. Malmberg, and P. Maskell, "Clusters and Knowledge: Local Buzz, Global Pipelines and Process of Knowledge Creation," *Progress in Human Geography*, 28, 1 (2004): 31–56.

[78] Christos Pitelis, Roger Sugden, and James R. Wilson, "Introduction," in Christos Pitelis, Roger Sugden, and James R. Wilson eds., *Clusters and Globalisation: The Development of Urban and Regional Economics*, Cheltenham: Edward Elgar, 2006, pp. 1–16. Also, Michael Storper, *The Regional World: Territorial Development in a Global Economy*, New York: Guilford, 1997.

[79] J. Robert Branston, Lauretta Rubini, Silvia Sacchetti, Roger Sugden, Ping Wei and James R. Wilson, "The Development of Local Economies and the Possible

as a form of concentration is more complementary than contradictory to the dominance of MNCs. As clustering develops a method intrinsically leading to a concentration of economic power, it accordingly creates socioeconomic consequences similar to those caused by other forms of monopoly and oligopoly such as the MNCs, of which, in the case of clusters, regional inequality stands prominent. From a historical perspective, the state promotes clusters as a reversion to earlier state policies of which "the main objective was to avoid growing economic disparities between regions and help regions in decline";[80] but now such an objective has been greatly compromised, as the earlier policies emphasizing decentralization and regional equity "started to be viewed as failures," and "traditional industrial and regional policies were both abandoned or reduced to a minimum by the turn of the century."[81] As some experts point out, "Unlike old-style regional policy, equity considerations are not officially the main concern of cluster policies. Quite the opposite, by actively pushing firms to cluster, this type of strategy could deprive poor regions of any chance to attract economic activities."[82] Therefore, as the rise of clusters in globalization has "exacerbated the divide between cores and peripheral regions, and between competitive and backward regions,"[83] the "geographical hierarchy of regional centers," as Cantwell and Iammarino have termed them, prevails.[84] In this sense, it can be argued that, with the rise of clusters, regional inequality between cores and peripheries has penetrated deeper, from the world system into domestic domains and local economies.

It is clear that chain stores and industrial clusters have shared a fundamental feature, the concentration of business, though they

---

Impact of Public Policy: A Framework for Case Studies," in Christos Pitelis, Roger Sugden, and James R. Wilson eds., *Clusters and Globalisation: The Development of Urban and Regional Economics*, Cheltenham: Edward Elgar, 2006, pp. 82–95 (p. 85).

[80] Duranton, Martin, Mayer, and Mayneris, *The Economics of Clusters*, p. 11.

[81] Ibid, p. 3.   [82] Ibid.

[83] Lisa De Propris and Nigel Driffield, "FDI, Clusters and Knowledge Sourcing," in Christos Pitelis, Roger Sugden, and James R. Wilson eds., *Clusters and Globalisation: The Development of Urban and Regional Economics*, Cheltenham: Edward Elgar, 2006, pp. 133–158 (p. 133).

[84] John Cantwell and Simona Iammarino, "The Technological Relationships between Indigenous Firms and Foreign-owned MNCs in the European Regions," in Philip McCann ed., *Industrial Location Economics*, Cheltenham: Edward Elgar, 2002, pp. 286–318 (p. 293).

adopt divergent paths in the concentrative movement. Surely this is an institutional concentration, meaning that the concentration of capital, wealth, and production is realized in the concentration of decision-making power within few organizations; such institutional concentration can appear in geographic extension or organizational stretch, while it can also be actualized through amalgamation and coalescence. In fact, economic convergence often goes beyond business factors, reaching out to the arenas of policy, government, and research. It is a trend in which distributional concerns have been replaced by a focus on the promotion of competitiveness, and in which, for business firms, getting bigger is helpful and, for governments, working closer with business to their own advantage is at the same time lending favor to themselves as agencies of the economic state. Theoretically, the geographical explanation of the early concentration of capital in urban centers is enlightening in its emphasis on the interplay of capitalism and state-making,[85] and in the current context of global capitalism, various programs of rescaling, of which clustering is one example and chain stores may be viewed as another, do have rich significance for understanding the interactive dynamics of globalization vis-à-vis the state and market.[86] Though here we have no space to go further in discussing such theoretical implications, it is not difficult to see a direction toward which state-building as a process of the concentration of public power and the concentration of capital and business power along with globalization often go on hand in hand, thus mutually empowering each other.

Money Speaks Aloud: The Financial Sector as the Gravity Center of Global Capitalism

The rise of global financial markets has since the late 1970s become an eye-catching phenomenon, indicating the intensive flow of money across state borders and into global movements. "All sorts of transactions flourished," according to an expert:

[85] Charles Tilly, "The Geography of European Statemaking and Capitalism Since 1500," in Eugene D. Genovese and Leonard Hochberg eds., *Geographic Perspectives in History*, Oxford: Basil Blackwell, 1989, pp. 158–181.
[86] See, for example, Markus Perkmann and Ngai-Ling Sum eds., *Globalization, Regionalization and Cross-Border Regions*, New York: Palgrave Macmillan, 2002, esp. Bob Jessop, "The Political Economy of Scale," pp. 25–49.

Perhaps most emblematic was foreign exchange trading, necessary for many cross-border capital flows and essentially nonexistent in 1945. By 1973 the average daily turnover in foreign currency markets was $15 billion, then a nearly inconceivable sum. By 1998 $1.5 trillion changed hands each day in the markets. In 2004 the daily turnover was $1.9 trillion.[87]

The deeper change has taken place in global financial institutions, meanwhile, ranging from the development of new financial instruments and the deregulation of national financial markets to the growth of international banks and other financial institutions, all of which "have created a functioning global financial system."[88]

Financial liberalization is the major program that has shaped such transformations of the global financial system through both the increasing size of transactions and the institutional infrastructures with which these huge transactions take place. In the financial world of the late twentieth century, "the rules were liberalized, managers and investors enjoyed an era of extraordinary freedom."[89] A publication in 2000 states,

[i]nternational finance has rapidly changed shape during the last two decades. The large-scale dismantling of regulatory structures such as exchange and capital controls and cross-border investment rules and increased foreign ownership has widened the geographical scope of international finance. The revolution of information technology has allowed the implementation of financial operations at lightning speed.[90]

It is a cliché to say that financial globalization features the current system of capitalism; the core position of the global financial system in global capitalism, however, still needs to be emphasized against new historical circumstances. The conclusion that capitalism has come into its global stage, it can be argued, does not change the dominant position of the financial system in capitalism; rather, it reinforces such dominance in comprehensive ways. Yes, "the financial system is a core component of any capitalist market economy,"[91] and global capitalism

---

[87] Rawi Abdelal, *Capital Rules: The Construction of Global Finance*, Cambridge, MA: Harvard University Press, 2007, p. 2.

[88] Held, McGrew, Goldblatt, and Perraton, *Global Transformations*, p. 189.

[89] Abdelal, *Capital Rules*, p. 2.

[90] Risto I. Laulajainen, "The Regulation of International Finance," in Gordon L. Clark, Maryann P. Feldman, and Meric S. Gertler eds., *The Oxford Handbook of Economic Geography*, Oxford University Press, 2000, pp. 215–229 (p. 215).

[91] Adam D. Dixon, *The New Geography of Capitalism: Firms, Finance, and Society*, Oxford University Press, 2014, p. 18.

is no exception; for global capitalism, however, the global financial system becomes even more indispensable, vital, and active than ever before, because the global reach of capitalism is primarily carried out in economic domains by the global flow of money and its necessarily accompanying global extension of the financial system. Therefore, not only do "finance and global financial integration provide in many respects the foundation" for the realization of "one world of production,"[92] but also "finance pervades almost all aspects of contemporary economic activity and social life, from the way firms are managed, to the built environment of urban centers, and the prospects for one's quality of life in retirement."[93] In one sentence, the financial system plays a linchpin role in shaping the foundational institutions of global capitalism.

The financial system of global capitalism, as the central facilitator of the movements of capital and the core of its institutional integration, is also undertaking concentrative movements. For the purpose of analyzing such concentrative movements of the global financial operation and their effects, this chapter suggests four aspects, namely, geographic concentration, institutional standardization, operational coordination, and the state-market nexus embodied in financial decision-making, each briefly discussed below.

Geographic concentration of the global financial system deserves a discussion because, generally speaking, "location really matters in the modern [capital] trading industry" as it is "an integral part of business strategy, affecting competition and its outcomes."[94] There is a prevailing misunderstanding, however, that globalization has made the world financial system more and more decentralized and dispersive; our analysis here will dispute this point of view. Despite the global stretch of capitalism, according to an authoritative book on globalization, the world financial system is "heavily concentrated in the three main centres of London, Tokyo and New York."[95] Take the global stock market, one of the most significant institutions of capitalist financing, as an example. It is found that "London headquartered exchanges in 2010 controlled 44 per cent of European stock trading activity"; in the same year, "no less than 66 per cent of European stock trading value

---

[92] Ibid, p. 24.   [93] Ibid, p. vii.

[94] Dariusz Wójcik, *The Global Stock Market: Issuers, Investors, and Intermediaries in an Uneven World*, Oxford University Press, 2011, p. 144.

[95] Held, McGrew, Goldblatt, and Perraton, *Global Transformations*, p. 189.

executed on matching engines within 30 miles from the centre of London." And, "this is a level of dominance comparable to that in foreign exchange trading, where London also accounts for approximately two-thirds of the European total."[96] The same author believes that "it is safe to say that geographical concentration of the exchange industry has also taken place across the Atlantic" in New York City.[97]

Different from a common perception that the information revolution makes geographic dispersion possible, geographic concentration in capital markets prevails and, similar to the emergence of industrial-technology clusters examined in the last section, is reinforced for the purpose of gaining proximity. "Distance," in global competition of stock trading, "is critical, as the race for speed approaches its natural limit – the speed of light," an expert explains. "Proximity between computers," therefore, "is important because of latency – the speed with which an order can reach the matching engine of the exchange, be executed, and the confirmation of its execution return to the computer from which it was sent."[98] A spiral effect thus appears, as "The value of proximity between people and computers combined creates a virtuous circle of network externalities; where customers attract matching engines, matching engines attract more customers and more matching engines. This virtuous circle has clearly taken root in London."[99] In conclusion, "The geography of the exchange industry implies that this network has nodes in large financial centres"; while there has been a revolution in their business model, "internationally, the revolution seems to reinforce the New York City-London axis of global financial centres."[100]

Again using the global stock market as an example, observers can find "the *network externalities* that characterize international monetary arrangements,"[101] or, in plainer language, institutional contagion and standardization, the second element of the global financial system that helps promote dominance, coordination, and monopoly/oligopoly in the financial decision-making of global capitalism. An expert explains it in this way:

When most of your friends and colleagues use computers with Windows as their operating system, you may choose to do likewise to obtain technical

[96] Wójcik, *The Global Stock Market*, p. 144.   [97] Ibid, p. 146.
[98] Ibid, p. 145.   [99] Ibid, p. 146.   [100] Ibid, pp. 148–149.
[101] Eichengreen, *Globalizing Capital*, p. 4. Emphasis in original.

advice and ease the exchange of data files, even if a technologically incompatible alternative exists (think Linux or Leopard) that is more reliable and easier to learn when used in isolation. These synergistic effects influence the cost and benefits of the individual's choice of technology ... Similarly, the international monetary arrangement that a country prefers will be influenced by arrangements in other countries.[102]

This standardization inevitably strengthens the network effect in coordinative operation of the global financial system. Many experts have indeed pointed out such coordination, as exemplified in an analyst's emphasis on the "coordination" by the Bank for International Settlements (BIS), the European Union (EU), the International Organization of Securities Commissions (IOSCO), and similar organizations – all with "comparatively recent origin," meaning, in other words, a new phenomenon arising with globalization.[103]

The financial sector, moreover, plays the vital role of coordinating the entire capitalist economy; it has been so since its historical development from merchant capitalism through industrial capitalism to financial capitalism.[104] In the early twentieth century, Hilferding, a major critic of imperialism, contributed the concept of "finance capital" to highlight the existence of such a role, identifying "the fusion of industrial and financial capital into huge interlocking groups." According to Brewer's summary of Hilferding's point, "These groups do not compete with each other by price cutting: they enlist state support to gain control of whole industries by financial and political means."[105] This observation is not entirely outdated; it seems that global capitalism unfolds in the same way, simply on a larger, global scale. For example, today almost nobody would deny that "multinational activity now dominates international economic exchange,"[106] while, important to the discussion here, the rise of the multinational corporation is inseparably connected to foreign direct investments (FDI),[107] a means of global financial flow that is operated via the global financial system.

The state-market nexus that has emerged in globalization helps to enforce such coordination embedded in the financial system in particular

[102] Ibid.   [103] Laulajainen, "The Regulation of International Finance," p. 215.
[104] Bowles, *Capitalism*, p. 15.
[105] Brewer, *Marxist Theories of Imperialism*, p. 20.
[106] Shatz and Venables, "The Geography of International Investment," p. 126.
[107] Held, McGrew, Goldblatt, and Perraton, *Global Transformations*, p. 242.

and in the entire economic system in general. Yes, commentators have talked about how the global financial system converges across countries[108] or, in other words, "how individual country financial and economic systems are competitively merging into one global system,"[109] but what must be emphasized here is that this globalization of the system does not necessarily mean the dispersion of financial power. Instead, a seemingly self-contradictory trend emerges on parallel but overlapping and interactive tracks, namely, the increasing weight of the private sector in global financial power, on one hand, and the increasing involvement of the state in financial operation on the other, often designing its policies to fit and promote the interests of the private sector. As an observer has noticed:

Economic and financial power has shifted from the public sector to the private sector as individuals throughout the world invest in pension funds, mutual funds, and other private pools of capital. *This weight of capital will have the final word over government policy.* Central government policymakers must attract, entice, and encourage investment in their countries. To ensure success they must continuously compete with other countries in making their economic and financial environment attractive at all times. This process is dynamic, and as competitive as any private sector industry. The freedoms of movement of capital throughout the world, tax levels, both corporate and personal, regulation, and the rule of law are all part of this equation . . .[110]

In this sense, one may argue that the state has, as a partner, also joined the coordination mechanism around the operation of the global financial system. Yes, the state may have its autonomy and may sometimes make regulations against the wishes of the bankers, but, even as such a scenario occurs, the imbalance of power tilting toward the financial sector can easily invalidate this effort from the state. When "the financial scene is evolving rapidly and the $1-million people are those behind the change," as an above-cited scholar asks: "Can any regulator really keep a tight rein on people making $1 million a year in bonuses?"[111]

---

[108] See, for example, Dixon, *The New Geography of Capitalism*.
[109] Michael H. Hyman, *The Power of Global Capital: New International Rules – New Global Risks*, Mason, OH: Thomson/South-Western, 2004, p. 223.
[110] Ibid, p. 223. Emphasis added.
[111] Laulajainen, "The Regulation of International Finance," p. 228.

Doubtlessly, government regulation "has also played a part in the concentration of trading industry" in finance,[112] which can be understood as both "positive" and "negative" interventions as defined in Chapter 2. With neoliberalism, the state can promote the concentration of financial industry with the absence of regulations against such concentration. On the other hand, the state-market nexus in global finance can also be positive and even aggressive, and it is in this nexus that state capitalism works. For example, an investigation of the People's Bank of China (PBC, the central bank of the country) has found that "the rise of the PBC reflects the growth of strong mutual dependencies between the PBC and the leadership of the Communist Party, which has helped underpin the growing authority of the PBC within the steep hierarchy of the party-state."[113] In a wider picture of the global economy, the role of the state is often explicit and significant in promoting FDI, as "FDI is spatially more clustered than other forms of production."[114] To explain why "although all locations will have some production, only some locations will have FDI," experts refer to the possibility that firms "herd" in the sense of following signals of government policy in a host country for the purpose of assuring that firms find "a good location for FDI."[115] There are simply too many practical cases in which, when the competition for FDI inflows has grown fiercer, various countries, especially transitional economies and other developing countries, make state efforts to attract multinationals.[116] Bringing together these different tactics employed by the state in its financial movements, this book argues that against the new backdrop of globalization, neoliberalism and state capitalism work intertwined in the same direction toward a shared goal and with the same aftermath, which is the concentration of power in global financial operation and, accordingly, the concentration of capital via its global flow through the channels provide by this global financial system.

It should be clear that various concentrations, convergences, and coordination have emerged to cement and integrate both the global financial system in itself as well as this system with other systems of global capitalism, including the MNCs and the state, the two most powerful

[112] Wójcik, *The Global Stock Market*, p. 146.
[113] Stephen Bell and Hui Feng, *The Rise of the People's Bank of China: The Politics of Institutional Change*, Cambridge, MA: Harvard University Press, 2013, p. 299.
[114] Shatz and Venables, "The Geography of International Investment," p. 132.
[115] Ibid, p. 133.   [116] Ibid, p. 142.

organizations in the political economy of globalization. As such coordination functions beyond the financial sector per se, it is reminiscent of the conclusion made by many in earlier years that the financial system is a core of the capitalist economy. Altogether, in the global financial system rests the decision-making power of global capitalism, a point beyond ideological dispute; Hilferding from the Left held such a point of view, and in mainstream economics, a widely accepted conclusion since Schumpeter has been that the locus of power in capitalism lies in the monetary and credit markets, which "determine when and where production takes place and how far credit-financed consumption can absorb it."[117] I would assume that no one would deny the heavy weight of the following names and their firms: Bill Gates of Microsoft, Steve Jobs of Apple, and Mitch Kapor of Lotus; however, standing behind them and their successes is capitalist finance. "In each case," according to a relevant study, "these men were helped by a formal process known as venture capital, a system created to build new business." And, "The venture capital process not only invests risk capital in a new business but also nurtures that fledgling company until it grows and becomes profitable."[118] It means that, behind these firms that soon grow to monopolize within their sectors, financial capital played the role of deciding their fates when they were still in a stage of infancy; these decision-makers of capital financing, it can be said, monopolize the power, money, and resources to nurture those who monopolize industries.

To further demonstrate the relationship between the financial market and capitalist monopoly, just one more example shall be cited, which is, again, the global stock market, seemingly the most "democratic" among various capital markets. According to an expert, "It is an irony that while trading corporate ownership rights in a way epitomizes capitalism, the institutional architecture of the stock exchange industry in Europe until recently –made of national monopolies operating like public utilities – could hardly be further from a model of free competitive markets."[119] So, who are the major winners and losers of the stock exchange revolution? "The winners are investment banks and firms that can capture a share of the booming trading activity stimulated by the revolution"; on the other hand, "The benefits of the stock

[117] Geoffrey Ingham, *Capitalism*, Cambridge: Polity, 2011, p. 51.
[118] Robert J. Kunze, *Nothing Ventured: The Perils and Payoffs of the Great American Venture Capital Game*, New York: Harper Business, 1990, p. 1.
[119] Wójcik, *The Global Stock Market*, p. 148.

exchange revolution may however be uncertain for small- and medium-sized companies."[120] This helps to reveal the spirit of the financial sector of global capitalism: it draws more and more participants into the capitalist economy by expanding across virtually the entire world, which gives the appearance of global capitalism being more "democratic" or at least more dispersive than pre-global capitalism, but the system and, in general, the global economy are concentrative even in the geographic and operational sense, let alone in an institutional and political-economy sense. As the above section has showed, the financial industry in globalization is highly concentrative in geographic allocation and operational mechanism; the power of decision-making rests with bankers and their collaborators, who include government leaders, and accordingly the benefits go largely into their pockets.

Global Oligopolistic Coordination of Capital Operation: Re-comprehending Monopoly in the Global Age

The above investigations on multinational corporations, service-based chain stores, regional clusters, and the global financial system have all pointed to the conclusion that monopoly and oligopoly have since the end of the Cold War reached a new stage in which the concentration of capital, production, and the supply of various products and services has reached an unprecedented degree of operation running on a global scale and has dominated the global economy in a variety of forms at multiple levels. Such a prominent and fundamental development of global capitalism, however, fails to foment much relevant discussion on monopoly. John Kenneth Galbraith in 2004 critically observed that "the phrase 'monopoly capitalism,' once in common use, has been dropped from the academic and political lexicon."[121] My observation draws the same conclusion, though one observer, at least, thinks that this lack of recognition has since been changed.[122] Even a book focusing on the debates around Wal-Mart, for example, does not index the term "monopoly";[123] it seems that both critics and defenders of Wal-Mart often engage themselves in

---

[120] Ibid, p. 150.
[121] John Kenneth Galbraith, *The Economics of Innocent Fraud: Truth for Our Time*, Boston: Houghton Mifflin, 2004, p. 12.
[122] John Bellamy Foster, *The Theory of Monopoly Capitalism: An Elaboration of Marxian Political Economy*, New York: Monthly Review Press, 2014, p. vii.
[123] Massengill, *Wal-Mart Wars*.

moral debates with little concern over the institutions that make such a global behemoth. Moreover, when discussing the global financial system and its crisis, authors often place emphasis on the monetary issues instead of the monopoly question.[124] Why has this strange death of attention to monopoly occurred when in fact monopoly presents itself in real life almost everywhere? Is monopoly still a useful concept for our understanding of global capitalism? If yes, how and why?

Some ideological biases, perhaps, work against discussions of monopoly, as monopoly is often negatively labeled a Marxist concept that denounces capitalism.[125] This alone, however, cannot fully explain this fundamental intellectual ignorance; even in the high years of the Cold War confrontation between Western capitalism and Soviet communism, Paul Samuelson still admitted the prevalence of monopoly in capitalism by concluding that "[T]his is a realistic fact, not a moral condemnation."[126] For the current book, discussions beyond ideological biases and hostilities ought to be presented, as the following paragraphs shall attempt to do. Below, the concept of monopoly will be clarified against the new historical background of globalization, especially in terms of the conceptual confusions over monopoly that are brought about by the intensification of global competition, by state competition in international political economy, and by institutional changes of the global market. As the concept of monopoly must be refashioned in order to understand its practical prevalence in the globalization age, it will be argued that the new characteristics of global capitalism make monopoly a normality – that is to say, global capitalism lives inherently and inevitably alongside updated forms of monopoly.

Monopoly and Competition: A Zero-Sum Dichotomy or a Spiral Effect?

Monopoly is usually viewed as an antonym of competition,[127] therefore the intensification of competition inspired by globalization may

---

[124] See, for example, Martin Wolf, *The Shifts and the Shocks: What We've Learned – and Have Still to Learn – from the Financial Crisis*, New York: Penguin Books, 2014.

[125] In the introduction to the new edition of *The Theory of Monopoly Capitalism*, John Bellamy Foster highlights monopoly as a Marxist or Marxian concept.

[126] Samuelson, *Economics*, p. 42.

[127] The Kalecki tradition of economics in particular views monopoly as the opposite of competition (Ben Fine and Andy Murfin, *Macroeconomics and*

explain why many economists have, for all intents and purposes, remained blind toward the new development of monopoly. This conceptualization, however, is problematic. Capitalism, according to Samuelson's classic statement, is always operating with the mixed presence of both competition and monopoly, which implies that monopoly can coexist with competition. In Samuelson's own words, "All economic life is a blend of competitive and monopoly elements. Imperfect, or monopolistic, competition is the prevailing mode, not perfect competition."[128] On the other end of the ideological spectrum of economics, "Marxist theory rests upon the central role assigned to the accumulation of capital. Consequently, it also recognizes monopolization as coterminous with, and not exclusive of, competition."[129] To this author, therefore, the coexistence of monopoly and competition is a point beyond ideological dispute, and, more importantly, neither the existence of competition nor its intensification equates to the absence of monopoly.

There can be such a circumstance, in other words, in which both monopoly and competition become intensified; the global reach of capitalism is such a case. As globalization destabilizes the existing market structures that have been in place for decades, if not centuries, it requires that, to quote a leading expert, "each firm, region, or nation must now compete in the international arena and can no longer be protected by stabilized oligopolistic national markets, which tended to be the case during the fifties and sixties."[130] The logic that once shaped the "stabilized oligopolistic national market," however, may now also be applied on a global scale, thus global markets can also become "stabilized oligopolistic" global markets.

In stretching beyond their national markets, businesses come to new, foreign surroundings that can vary from nation to nation; this puts greater pressure and greater uncertainties in market

    Monopoly Capitalism, Brighton, UK: Wheatsheaf Books, 1984), while the post-Keynesians share a similar view (M. C. Sawyer, *Macroeconomics in Question: The Keynesian Monetarist Orthodoxies and the Kaleckian Alternatives*, Brighton: Wheatsheaf Books, 1982).

[128] Samuelson, *Economics*, p. 42.
[129] Fine and Murfin, *Macroeconomics and Monopoly Capitalism*, p. 78.
[130] Robert Boyer, "The Variety and Unequal Performance of Really Existing Markets: Farewell to Doctor Pangloss?" in J. Rogers Hollingsworth and Robert Boyer eds., *Contemporary Capitalism: The Embeddedness of Institutions*, Cambridge University Press, 1997, pp. 55–93 (p. 56).

competition upon those firms that are involved in globalization. Moreover, these firms now compete on a global scale over a larger economic space and in a game much bigger than ever before. Both these factors intensify competition as well as increase the feeling of such intensification along with globalization. To quote the same author above,

Competition within the world market is now perceived as a strong constraint on national compromises and distinctive forms of organized national institutions. In some extreme cases, the troubles, or even the quasi-bankruptcy, of some national champions have clearly exhibited the important role attributed to market mechanisms, which are currently identifying the world's more efficient firms and productive organizations.[131]

Bankruptcy of Firm A, however, can simply mean an extension of the market share of Firm B, or, often more realistically, of firms B, C, D, and the like; concentration of economic power in the form of a bigger share of a firm, or oligopoly, always emerges through such ruthless competition. This is exactly how capitalism operates. If, as some say, "The capitalist entrepreneur is a prisoner of competition,"[132] then he/she can also be a winner or loser of competition; and, as competition is intensified by globalization, there could be a greater number of losers, but the winners are also more greatly rewarded with the losers as their prey. The most highly rewarded winners, it deserves repeating, are, nevertheless, growing beyond their previous monopoly/oligopoly of their national markets to join global monopoly/oligopoly.

That is why, in the economic reality of globalization, intensification of competition in many senses promotes the concentration of capital, and, in general, competition and its intensification can coexist with monopoly and oligopoly. Earlier investigations in this chapter of MNCs, chain stores, regional clusters, and the financial system have all implied this point. For example, in the case of the global stock market, "stock trading has become a much more competitive, technology driven and efficient industry," but this has simply promoted

---

[131] Ibid.

[132] Jose Brendan Macdonald, "The Challenge of a Democratic Economy," in Jeff Shantz and Jose Brendan Macdonald eds., *Beyond Capitalism: Building Democratic Alternatives for Today and the Future*, New York: Bloomsbury, 2013, pp. 1–23 (p. 7).

various concentrations including a geographic concentration of the industry.[133] In terms of MNCs, as David Harvey has observed,

While the virtues of competition are placed up front, the reality is the increasing consolidation of oligopolistic, monopoly, and transnational power within a few centralized multinational corporations: the world of soft-drinks competition is reduced to Coca Cola versus Pepsi, the energy industry is reduced to five huge transnational corporations, and a few media magnates control most of the flow of news, much of which then becomes pure propaganda.[134]

In principle, "Cooperative may face capitalist competition more efficiently";[135] bigger cooperatives, namely, firms with an oligopolistic capability, are thus encouraged by fiercer competition to strive to be even bigger and more oligopolistic, if not monopolistic.

Furthermore, competition among giants can be even more intense than competition among small firms, as, obviously, the stakes in competition are accordingly higher. While the concept of "monopolistic competition" cannot concisely capture the essence of such competition among giants,[136] this chapter would suggest a concept of "oligopolistic competition" to describe the situation in which the number of competitors are much fewer than in perfect competition but the market share of each is considerably large to the degree that it has the potential to monopolize the market. Conceptually, competition can be understood in two dimensions: its scope, or the number of competitors involved; and its intensity, or the degree concerning the vitality of survival of competitors. Oligopolistic competition, therefore, refers to a competition with fewer competitors but greater intensity. With globalization, "MNCs are central to globalizing competition"; "the growth of transnational production has made it [competition] more intense and enhanced its geographical reach."[137] Competition among MNCs is the best example of oligopolistic competition, which combines, rather than confronts, intensification of competition with the trend of oligopolization.

[133] Wójcik, *The Global Stock Market*, p. 147.
[134] David Harvey, *A Brief History of Neoliberalism*, Oxford University Press, 2005, p. 80.
[135] Macdonald, "The Challenge of a Democratic Economy," p. 7.
[136] "Monopolistic competition" is defined as a situation in which "a large number of sellers produce differentiated products." Paul A. Samuelson and William D. Nordhaus, *Economics*, Boston: McGraw-Hill/Irwin, 2010, 19th ed., p. 171.
[137] Held, McGrew, Goldblatt, and Perraton, *Global Transformations*, p. 278.

Competition and monopoly/oligopoly, therefore, are conceptually not only inseparably coexistent, but in fact codependent in market practice. Put simply, monopoly and oligopoly often emerge from competition in the normal market economy, thus intensification of competition can increase intensification of monopoly and oligopoly. Yet competition and monopoly/oligopoly are also antagonistic to each other, although the antagonism does not occur reciprocally; the existence and intensification of market competition does not prevent the emergence of monopoly and oligopoly, but monopoly and oligopoly, as long as they emerge, in turn can reduce and prevent competition, at least in scope. Competition, in other words, can provide an institutional mechanism to foster monopoly and oligopoly, but not vice versa. The prevailing observations and emphases on the intensification of competition within globalization, logically, cannot deny the emergence of global monopoly and oligopoly.

As monopoly reduces and even prevents competition, however, why does competition continue to become intensified once monopoly has emerged? There is a spiral effect, which should be explained by non-market factors, as the markets never operate within a vacuum; furthermore, market operation, as this book emphasizes methodologically, must be understood with regards to inter-institutionalism. In his seminal book *Kings or People*, Reinhard Bendix highlights that capitalism cannot explain every change of the last four to five hundred years; for example, he highlights the significance of ideas in social change, and addresses "intellectual mobilization" referring to "the growth of a reading public and of an educated secular elite dependent on learned occupations "as an "independent cause of social change."[138] Moreover, Bendix criticizes the classic theories of capitalism for the fact that they do not taken into account a sufficient number of international factors.[139] For the discussion here, globalization is obviously one of the most powerful factors that build competition into the new, upgraded circle of competition leading to a global monopoly and oligopoly that occur on a scale previously unknown.

Monopoly, in one sentence, is not a stationary but dynamic and historical phenomenon. It means that there is always a dynamic

---

[138] Reinhard Bendix, *Kings or People: Power and the Mandate to Rule*, Berkeley: University of California Press, 1978, pp. 265, 266.
[139] Ibid, p. 268.

development that can be roughly sketched in cycles of competition versus monopoly/oligopoly. This interpretation is fundamentally different from the classic notions of monopoly which, in either the Marxist tradition or the Kalecki school, conclude that monopoly in the twentieth century has displaced the free competition of the nineteenth century, and that as a result, for Leninists, capitalism comes to its "highest stage," thereby approaching its own death.[140] This is a dialectic historical approach rather than a linear historical approach, as the latter simply divides capitalism into "its early competitive phase and the subsequent, twentieth-century, monopoly phase driven and dominated by large corporations."[141] For this book, in addition to their synchronous coexistence, competition and monopoly/oligopoly can repeatedly occur to diachronically dominate various stages of capitalism. And, even in the global stage of capitalism, as a later chapter shall argue, capitalism may not come to its end. Global capitalism does, however, come to a new, higher stage of monopoly/oligopoly, which has been promoted, dialectically, by intensified global competition.

State Competition and Market Competition: Conceptual Confusion or Institutional Reinforcement?

Another conceptual confusion concerning the complicated relationship between competition and monopoly comes, perhaps, from a misreading of the reality that with globalization, interstate competition also becomes intensified to a great degree. Such a misreading, in being insufficiently aware of the new institutional phenomena of globalization that this book has highlighted in Chapter 2, which include the state-market nexus and the rise of the economic state, often takes competition among the firms with different state-affiliations in general, and among state-backed corporations in particular to be competition between states and corporations. This is a multilayered confusion in which both conceptual muddles and practical misinterpretations are entangled, resulting in a series of intentional or unintentional misperceptions of monopoly and

---

[140] Michael Kalecki, *Dynamics of the Capitalist Economy*, Cambridge University Press, 1971. Also, Josef Steindl, *Maturity and Stagnation in American Capitalism*, Oxford University Press, 1952; Paul Baran and Paul M. Sweezy, *Monopoly Capital: An Essay on the American Economic and Social Order*, New York: Monthly Review Press, 1966.

[141] Bowles, *Capitalism*, p. 16.

oligopoly in global capitalism. Conceptually it is often assumed that multinational corporations, in their global rise, are encountering intensive competition with nation-states, as exemplified in the assumption of a leading expert on globalization David Held and his collaborators that there is a "structural impact" of globalization which is "corporate power versus state power."[142] This chapter argues that such a thesis of state-versus-corporate competition is misleading, albeit misleading with reason. Yes, competition among states is intensified with globalization; competition among corporations, as discussed above, is also intensified, and, furthermore, state-corporate collaboration emerges as a major institutional phenomenon. These three dimensions of global competition are, of course, overlapping and interactive with each other, but they are nevertheless different dimensions, and they should not be conceptually muddled together.

One significant source of confusion comes from the classic Marxist judgment that the state is simply an agent, tool, and spokesman of the ruling class, in other words, the capitalist class for the capitalist state.[143] In this line of reasoning, Bukharin, for example, asserted that in entering the monopoly stage capitalist "competition thus becomes competition between 'state capitalist trusts'."[144] The world system theory and various branches of dependency theory have continued this conceptual tradition against new historical backdrops. For example, world system

[142] Held, McGrew, Goldblatt, and Perraton, *Global Transformations*, p. 281.
[143] Karl Marx (1852), "The Eighteenth Brumaire of Louis Bonaparte," in Robert C. Tucker ed., *The Marx-Engels Reader*, New York: W. W. Norton, 1978, 2nd ed., pp. 594–617. See discussions in Gianfranco Poggi, *The State: Its Nature, Development and Prospects*, Stanford University Press, 1990, pp. 93–97; Richard W. Miller, "Social and Political Theory: Class, State, Revolution," pp. 55–105 and Alan Gilbert, "Political Philosophy: Marx and Radical Democracy," pp. 168–195; both in Terrell Carver ed., *The Cambridge Companion to Marx*, Cambridge University Press, 1991. Yet the theory of state autonomy, originally within the tradition of Marxism but in its theoretical development going beyond it, modifies and revises this judgment. See Ralph Miliband, *The State in Capitalist Society*, New York: Basic Books, 1969; Peter Evans, Dietrich Rueschemeyer, and Theda Skocpol eds., *Bringing the State Back In*, Cambridge University Press, 1985. Also Bob Jessop, "Recent Theories of the Capitalist State," pp. 81–103; Claus Offe, "Structural Problems of the Capitalist State: Class Rule and the Political System, on the Selectiveness of Political Institutions," pp. 104–129; Fred Block, "The Ruling Class Does not Rule: Notes on the Marxist Theory of the State," pp. 130–245; and Margaret Levi, "The Predatory Theory of Rule," pp. 146–175; all in John A. Hall ed., *The State: Critical Concepts*, London: Routledge, 1994, Vol. I.
[144] As discussed and quoted in Brewer, *Marxist Theories of Imperialism*, p. 21.

theory maintains that capitalist exploitation takes place not only in class relations, but also in terms of areas or regions concerning state-state relations, in which the global "metropolis" or "core" exploits "satellites" or "periphery" regions.[145] Dependency theory usually regards MNCs as agents of industrial states to exploit developing countries, as authoritarian states in the latter provide local support to the former.[146] For example, contemporary Marxist scholar John Bellamy Foster in a very recent publication concludes that the notion that the countries at the center of the capitalist system exploit and hinder the development of those in the periphery is fundamental for understanding monopoly capitalism.[147]

Such analyses, I would argue, have four problems which can be summarized as follows: First, the issue of uneven development of global capitalism is mixed with the issue of market competition and monopoly; second, the conceptual power of class analyses is undermined, as domestic class divisions are displaced with an analysis of interstate exploitations; third, and most significant to the discussion here, capital monopoly in the markets is equated to the domination of a given state (or states) in interstate relations, thus market competition is mixed with state competition; and fourth, the political differences between a democratic state and an authoritarian state are entirely neglected, thus any possible check that the functional democratic state may impose over capital is ignored.

The emergence of state-backed and even state-owned multinational corporations is, in itself, a way of the owner-state seeking an advantage in global competition, which inevitably helps to mix state competition with market competition. However, it is a greater reflection of the state-market nexus and the rise of the economic state as institutional features of globalization rather than a competition between state-owned MNCs and other states. It is clear that such state-owned MNCs indicate the state's increasing engagement in economic activities, including global economic competition; furthermore, the globalizing world makes it not only possible but also more effective that one state's policy can easily

[145] Ibid, pp. 17–18.
[146] See, for example, Fernando Henrique Cardoso and Enzo Faletto, *Dependence and Development in Latin America*, Berkeley: University of California Press 1979; Peter Evans, *Dependent Development: The Alliance of Multinational, State, and Local Capital in Brazil*, Princeton University Press, 1979.
[147] Foster, *The Theory of Monopoly Capitalism*, p. xiv.

affect corporate interests in another country.[148] This can be a cause for confusion involving geopolitical or geo-economic interpretations, as stated by a leading expert of international political economy:

> Another threat to global capitalism came from its very essence, competition. As country after country joined the global economy, competitive pressures threatened many powerful interests. The threat was symbolized by the reentry of the world's largest country into the world economy. 'The China price,' reported *Business Week*, had become 'the three scariest words in U.S. industry'.[149]

It is clear that in those situations discussed above, competition among states in the global market via corporations should not be read as a competition of state versus corporation.

The rise of global finance also greatly contributes to the misperception of the global political economy as being competition driven, and further-more, it contributes to a state-competition-centered interpretation of global capitalism. Globalization arose with the "breakdown of the territorial monopolies that national governments have historically claimed,"[150] an assertion which could foster the misperception of com-petition between currencies as competition among states, and, more importantly to our analysis, as the absence, or at least the reduction, of monopoly in comparison with intensification of competition. This book never denies the intensification of interstate economic as well as wider competitions; competition via global finance can be of particular concern to the state. Furthermore, as discussed earlier, the financial system is the niche of the capitalist economy, within which corporate firms operate. Yet although all such players including the state and corporations are involved in the same game of global financial competition, these players don't necessarily all compete with each other at the same level.

All of the above developments do contribute to intensification of competition on a global level, and the state is now engaged in such

---

[148] For example, see a discussion in Richard B. Freeman, "Are Your Wages Set in Beijing?" in Jeffry A. Frieden and David A. Lake eds., *International Political Economy: Perspectives on Global Power and Wealth*, Boston: Bedford/St. Martin's, 4th ed., pp. 343–352.

[149] Jeffry A. Frieden, *Global Capitalism: Its Fall and Rise in the Twentieth Century*, New York: W. W. Norton, 2006, p. 464.

[150] For such spatial reorganization of currency relations in the early stage of post–Cold War globalization, see Benjamin J. Cohen, *The Geography of Money*, Ithaca: Cornell University Press, 1998. Quotation is from p. xi.

competition in various ways. Globalization fuels interstate competition, thus the political concept of such competition is often used to displace the market concept of competition. The engagement of the state in market competition, however, does not simply intensify competition but also, more importantly, promotes monopoly and oligopoly; this is the first point that should be clarified regarding the complicated situation of state involvement in competition. Second, competition among regions, states, and/or, particularly, between so-called center and periphery should not be equated to competition among corporations; its intensification, therefore, does not conceptually mean the intensification of competition among firms. Thirdly, in both a conceptual and empirical sense, MNCs do not compete with nation-states, though interstate competition does in a variety of ways shadow corporate competition. In one sentence, market competition on the global scale is not conceptually equal to interstate competition in the international economy.

These two types of competition, namely, state competition in international relations and corporation competition in the global market, do interconnect and mutually reinforce each other, especially with the emergence of the state-market nexus and the rise of the economic state. Therefore, although this chapter challenges the conceptual confusion between state competition and corporative competition, it does emphasize the practical reinforcement between state competition and corporative competition in the global economy. Furthermore, it maintains that such mutual reinforcing in general, and the reinforcement of corporative competition by state competition in particular inevitably strengthen the trend toward monopoly and oligopoly.

From Price Monopoly to Institutional Monopoly: Structural Power in Perspective

One more conceptual pitfall concerning monopoly seems to lie in the traditional emphasis on the impact of monopoly over market price.[151] According to Samuelson, "The mere presence of a few rivals is not enough for perfect competition. Actually, the economic definition of an 'imperfect competition' is this: *anyone who buys or sells a good in large*

---

[151] See such a discussion in John Kenneth Galbraith, *The New Industrial State*, Boston: Houghton Mifflin, 1967, pp. 179–188.

enough quantities to be able to affect the price of that good."[152] The neoclassical model emphasizes that competition among firms will prevent any single enterprise from achieving an oligopolistic position, thereby influencing a "distorting" of the market price.[153] Highlighting that "economic relations have increasingly been influenced by monopolization," the Kalecki school of economic thought also maintains that, due to monopoly, "The result within each sector of the economy is for output to be restricted and for prices to be higher."[154] Therefore, as summarized by two leading scholars of political economy,

Large firms might be able to affect prices, thus affecting their terms of exchange with others (consumers and other firms). Firms in competitive markets are price takers. Firms in concentrated markets may be price makers. Power in this sense means the capacity to impose a higher price and by implication inferior terms of exchange on other economic agents than would exist under more competitive market conditions.[155]

In all these lines of reasoning, monopoly is primarily understood and analyzed in terms of the dominant influence of price in seeking "monopoly profits"; small businesses can be controlled by large firms via monopsony.

This chapter, however, suggests viewing monopoly in a wider sense, through the lens of institutions. Monopoly, therefore, can first of all be embodied in ownership; it is, accordingly, reflected in shares of the market. In their discussion of "power-centered approaches to political economy," Caporaso and Levine state: "Oligopolies occur when several firms control a large share of the market (or assets) in a particular sector."[156] Thus,

What are the implications of producer concentration for power? Firms that possess a large share of the market are said to possess 'market power' ... Large firms might also be able to affect other economic parameters, including output levels, technology, and even tastes (through allocating resources to advertising) ... Firms have the power to affect other firms in oligopolistic

---

[152]   Samuelson, *Economics*, p. 42. Emphasis in original.
[153]   E. K. Hunt, *History of Economic Thought: A Critical Perspective*, Armonk, NY: M. E. Sharpe, 1979; quoted in Mark Beeson, *Competing Capitalisms: Australia, Japan and Economic Competition in Asia-Pacific*, London: Macmillan, 1999, p. 84.
[154]   Fine and Murfin, *Macroeconomics and Monopoly Capitalism*, p. 77.
[155]   Caporaso and Levine, *Theories of Political Economy*, p. 167.
[156]   Ibid, p. 96.

environments ... [I]n oligopolistic conditions, firms can, by pursuing different strategies, affect what other firms do, how much they produce, their price levels, and even whether they enter or leave an industry.[157]

In this chapter's analysis, it means that monopoly over price is actually a manifestation of a deeper monopoly over property and, accordingly, shares of the market.

Concentration of capital, as discussed earlier, through firm mergers, acquisitions, franchising, and other possible methods of business organizational reconfiguration, inevitably reduces the number of existing firms. Accordingly, the weight of an individual giant firm is increased in many aspects, including its amount of wealth and market share, thereby leading to the shaping of monopoly and oligopoly. As an expert emphasizes, "monopoly capitalism occurs when large corporations are in control." And, "These large corporations are typically seen as manipulating markets, through mergers and acquisitions on the supply side and through advertising on the demand side, to control the economy for their own benefits."[158] This point is well echoed by Caporaso and Levine with a description of a contrasting picture in which monopoly does not apply:

In a perfectly competitive market, there are a large number of buyers and sellers. Each producer is so small in relation to the rest of the market that he or she cannot affect aggregate market properties, especially prices. In fact, under perfectly competitive conditions, individual firms have very little power at all. Their choices are limited to which products to produce and how much. For firms to be restricted in this fashion is simply to say that markets are functioning as they should.[159]

That is to say, "a perfectly competitive market is characterized by diversity and numerous options, in short by choice," while "in oligopoly, there are few producers – that is, a small number control larger shares of the market (in total production, sales, and so on)."[160] In this sense, we may say that "market power" is controlled by a small number of firms, "power" in this case being more comprehensive that simply as it relates to pricing.

A fundamentally important feature of monopoly or oligopoly is the exclusion of newcomers from market entry. The market as an

---

[157] Ibid, p. 167.   [158] Bowles, *Capitalism*, p. 16.
[159] Caporaso and Levine, *Theories of Political Economy*, p. 95.
[160] Ibid, pp. 166, 167.

institution, in fact, is intrinsically connected with free entry and free exit of voluntary participants in limitless numbers, in contemporary economies often in the form of firms (as well as individuals as consumers). Oligopoly, however, is "characterized by higher barriers to entry and sometimes by producing and selling heterogeneous products," because, to once again cite Caporaso and Levine,

Barriers to entry seem to be the most important feature in maintaining the privileged position of the oligopolist. These barriers may have economic origins (such as economies of scale) or they may owe their existence to political practice (such as licenses, subsidies, tariffs). In either case, firms already in the market have an advantage over those outside.[161]

Globalization, especially, is a situation in which the phenomenon described above is well noticed and recorded by many experts. For Robert McChesney, "successful firms get larger and larger over time, so it requires much more capital for newcomers to enter their markets and attempt to seize some of their profits. Larger firms have distinct advantages of scale over small firms, and they come to rule the roost."[162] For Robert Branston and his collaborators, "the strength of these incumbents denies freedom and openness to the others that are unable to act. The incumbents are well placed to form repressive coalitions furthering their aims and thereby denying governance in the public interest."[163] In general, it is concluded that "The evolution of the Washington Consensus and encouragement of a certain sort of private sector economy have been associated with monopoly power and a denial of access to the 'global' economy for the vast majority of potential participants."[164]

To follow the scholars cited above, this chapter thus suggests the concept of "institutional monopoly" in order to seize the essence of monopoly and oligopoly as structural power reflected in the weight of market shares for deciding the norms and rules of the market. Such power, to summarize, may include the following aspects: First, it structures the market per se by setting up the barriers to enter markets

---

[161] Ibid, p. 167.
[162] Robert W. McChesney, *Digital Disconnect: How Capitalism Is Turning the Internet against Democracy*, New York: New Press, 2013, pp. 36–37.
[163] Branston, Rubini, Sacchetti, Sugden, Wei, and Wilson, "The Development of Local Economies and the Possible Impact of Public Policy," p. 85.
[164] Ibid.

in favor of the existing firms' interests; second, it can structure the scope of competition on the market by reducing the number of firms; and third, it shapes decision-making on the market on both macro and micro levels, the former concerning resource distribution in investment, production, etc. of the entire economy, while the latter can refer to an individual company's business decisions. In essence, institutional monopoly transforms the market into a place housing a variety of hierarchies that are now globally structured; monopoly and oligopoly are thus institutionalized through the exercise of such market structuring power. Monopoly/oligopoly over or via price, therefore, is simply one of a number of expressions of such institutional monopoly/oligopoly; or, to put it another way, the power that can structure market price is embedded in a set of deeper and wider institutions. A thorough understanding of monopoly/oligopoly, therefore, must not be restricted to price monopoly, but must look to big capital's structural power in shaping institutions of market operation, which is what we have termed "institutional monopoly."

Networks and Coordination as Oligopolies: How Does Global Capitalism Get Organized?

Two more issues should be analyzed briefly in addition to the above three fundamental clarifications around the concept of monopoly/oligopoly. One of the issues is about the geographical dispersion of capital, production, and, more generally, economic forces alongside the global reach of capitalism, which is often emphasized by thinkers of imperialism and, recently, observers of globalization. For example, Bukharin in the early twentieth century highlighted the tendency of the "acceleration of the geographical spread of capitalism and its integration into a single world capitalist economy."[165] Regarding late-twentieth-century globalization, some scholars also talked about the emerging of a "global manufacturing system" in which "production capacity is dispersed to an unprecedented number of developing as well as industrialized countries."[166] Earlier investigations in this

---

[165] Brewer, *Marxist Theories of Imperialism*, p. 20.

[166] Gary Gereffi, "The Organization of Buyer-Driven Global Commodity Chains: How U.S. Retailers Shape Overseas Production Networks," in Gary Gereffi and Miguel Korzeniewicz eds., *Commodity Chains and Global Capitalism*, Westport, CT: Praeger, 1994, pp. 95–122.

chapter, however, have shown various concentrative movements of economic forces, including capital, production, innovation, and services (even retail services, which are by nature inclined toward geographic dispersion), that have been unfolding with globalization, which should be helpful in clarifying that, in general, the global reach of capitalism cannot be identified solely with the global dispersion of economic power within the capitalist system, and, in particular, when geographic dispersion takes place alongside globalization, it can be combined with an institutional concentration of economic power. In any sense, capitalism's geographic coverage of the globe does not necessarily mean an institutional decentralization of the capitalist mechanism; instead, concentration of capital can be stimulated in various ways by such geographic expansion, especially by the global limitedness that capital now encounters.

The coexistence and mutual promotion between geographic extension/limitedness on a global scale and institutional concentration of economic power in limited numbers of firms/players require and facilitate capital to increase its engagement in networks, not only among corporations but also among business, government, and other relevant elements such as research organizations in scientific and technology innovation. With the growing intensity of such networks, furthermore, coordination within the involved parties with regards to decision-making and economic measures has inevitably become prevalent in running the economy. Many years ago, Charles Lindblom had already observed that

For big companies in national markets, a common pattern is oligopoly, as in the American automobile industry where four companies account for 99 percent of output or the farm machine industry where four firms account for over half the output. Perhaps as much as 60 percent of manufactured goods in the United States are produced by enterprises that *make their production plans and set their prices in light of their interaction with two or three other dominant firms in their industry.*[167]

For post–Cold War globalization, in noticing that "It was characterized by the very rapid expansion of global trade in manufactures, fueled by the systematic reduction in the barriers to trade," a scholar, in a similar vein, points out that "increasingly, this trade was in semi-processed

[167] Charles E. Lindblom, *Politics and Markets: The World' Political-Economic Systems*, New York: Basic Books, 1977, p. 149. Emphasis added.

manufactures, produced *in coordinated global production net-works.*"[168] Following them, this chapter argues that, first, the global triumph of capitalism provides even more momentum and facilities than did pre-global capitalism for increasing and actualizing interdependence, networks, and coordination; second, such networking and coordination can be viewed as an institutionally imbedded form of monopoly and oligopoly; and third, inherent coordination of capital indicates a new, significant feature of global capitalism.

This understanding of monopoly/oligopoly, with the theoretical lens provided by Chapter 2, should be positioned within the institutional context framed by features of the institutions of globalization, especially the state-market nexus. The investigations in earlier sections have helped to show that state-capital synthesis works well as the institutional locus of capital's concentration, oligopoly, and networking. A variety of industrial, strategic trade, regional, and generally increased governmental policies, as we have seen, become not only a possibility but also a necessity for capitalist economies in globalization; and, all such policies help indicate the state's vital role in fabricating the network and coordination of capitalism, making the state-market nexus dynamic in shaping the operation of global capitalism. Monopoly and oligopoly in the global stage of capitalism is, therefore, mainly embodied in such augmentations of the organizational degree of the capitalist economy in general, and in the increasing oligopolistic coordination of capital and production in particular. This is a deeper comprehension of what was termed earlier as "institutional monopoly."

According to this institutional logic, capitalist crisis does not cause a breakup of concentrative movements of capital and therefore reduce the institutional aftermaths of such movements, in other words, monopoly and oligopoly. By contrast, crisis often promotes further concentration of capital and oligopolies. For example, in the 1930s, capitalist crisis ruined small stores, since at that time corporate retail growth coincided with significantly increased small business failure rates during the Depression years.[169] In general, "in the crisis period, firm restructuring takes place in order to create the conditions for renewed profitability.

---

[168] Raphael Kaplinsky, *Globalization, Poverty and Inequality: Between a Rock and a Hard Place*, Cambridge: Polity, 2005, p. 233. Emphasis added.
[169] Neil Wrigley, "Antitrust Regulation and Restructuring of Grocery Retailing in Britain and USA," *Environment & Planning*, A, 24 (1992): 727–749.

This restructuring takes the form of mergers and acquisitions with the result that monopolies ... are another integral and inevitable feature of capitalism."[170]

In a more general view, the increase of networking and coordination of capital and production has gradually but fundamentally transformed capitalism from what Marx depicted as anarchy to a highly organized and often well-coordinated system. The global triumph of capitalism, therefore, also means the unprecedented growth of the organizational degree of capitalist production; its profound implications will be discussed in connection with labor, consumption, and social consequences in the chapters that follow. Both global spread and economic crisis, in this perspective, can be seen as among the most powerful factors that are pushing and pulling capitalism toward change in the direction of increased networks and coordination; geographic extension requires better coordination, and getting organized in various ways, including networks, is taken up by capitalism as a remedy to overcome its crisis, said to be caused by anarchy. Therefore, a fundamental transition has been unfolding before us in which capitalism becomes increasingly organized in its global age, and through which monopolies and oligopolies are naturally dominating the economy.

The Flat World for Capital: Why Does Globalization Call for Monopoly and Oligopoly?

Why does the global triumph of capitalism make capitalism inevitably inclined to increase coordination of capital and its oligopolistic monopoly of the global market? This section will be devoted to an analysis of those prominent underlining causes through which globalization intrinsically demands, momentarily promotes, and institutionally supports monopolies and oligopolies. They include, not exhaustively, the global size of the markets, the information revolution, the increasing significance of knowledge and the rise of intellectual property rights due to globalization, the rise of late late-developmental economies, the prevalence of public services, and mass mentality to worship big brands. Below some of them will be discussed.

---

[170] Bowles, *Capitalism*, p. 71.

Why Does the Gigantic Size of the Global Markets Favor Oligopoly?

Globalization in general intensifies both competition and monopoly, but competition-driven concentration of capital eventually leads to the inclination towards monopoly and oligopoly. The unprecedentedly huge size of the market and its cross-national nature, in particular, foster big businesses, because only big businesses, rather than smaller firms, are able to operate beyond national borders and can remain competitive in a market of such global size. This helps to explain why the seemingly self-contradictory tandem emerges between geographic extension and institutional concentration.

Globalization, first of all, opens new space for the continuous enlargement of already-large corporations, and what has become a restless pursuit of becoming gigantic dominates the trend of business operations. A few firms, never a large number in comparison with the growing size of the markets and the countless number of consumers, are getting larger and larger in several senses, ranging from the size of their organization to the sum of their revenues or the amount of the business deals in which they are involved, and from their geographically global coverage across nations to the cross-sector penetration of their business empires in terms of diversity. Inevitably, these companies' market share becomes increasingly huge. Meanwhile, via various methods such as merger, acquisition, and franchising, as demonstrated earlier, they keep growing to a size that easily dwarfs other companies and even the national economies of most countries in the world.

Second, the global size of the markets has greatly raised the threshold for market entry, the cost of business operation, and the requirements for the capacity to maintain and expand a market share, raising them to be nearly insurmountably high for relatively smaller business firms, let alone the truly small ones. Now, for example, "the management is professional and distinct, overseeing a vast bureaucracy and competing in several different product categories,"[171] which is not affordable to smaller businesses. This is only one reason among many others, such as the formidably and insurmountably high requirement of initial capital, why an economic philosopher maintains that "economies of scale" are among the major "barriers to entry that enable companies already in

---

[171] McChesney, *Digital Disconnect*, pp. 36–37.

the market to exert market power."[172] To use a metaphor, globalization makes the market a vast ocean beyond the reach of small boats.
Only those corporations large enough, therefore, are qualified to join
the game of global competition, which by nature leads to oligopolistic
structures of the global market.

Moreover, even local business circumstances for small firms are made
hostile with globalization, because big businesses can easily invade with
better competitiveness in terms of economic efficiency. For example, retail
is a business traditionally comprised of numerous small shops (single-
outlet independents) or small-scale firms, and such composition simply
reflects "the fundamental ease of entry, in terms of low initial capital
requirements, into the industry."[173] As this chapter earlier examined,
however, this has been transformed by globalization, as "international
retail franchising often has the effect of displacing local industry, particularly 'mom-and-pop' stores. These stores cannot compete effectively with
the distribution and marketing expertise of multinational franchisors."[174]

A fourth factor that favors big business in globalization is institutional, which has roots in the reality of the global economy as a sphere
lacking effective regulations and public governance. As discussed in
Chapter 2, this reality inspires the states to cast their economic and
non-economic weight behind those corporations they choose in order
to promote their global competitiveness. It also, furthermore, makes
global competition more similar in nature to "jungle politics" than
domestic economies where citizens' preferences can more or less exercise their influence, thus implying more geniality in the principle and
practice of the strongest and wildest preying upon the weak. With the
four causes presented above, therefore, it is clear that the global expansion of the capitalist economy intrinsically favors and inspires big
business and, accordingly, its oligopolies over others.

How Does the Information Revolution Demand and Facilitate Monopoly?

When David Harvey discusses "monopoly power," he simply refers to
that "of the sort that Google, Microsoft and Amazon wield these

---

[172] Julian Reiss, *Philosophy of Economics: A Contemporary Introduction*,
       London: Routledge, 2013, p. 232.
[173] Wrigley and Lowe, *Reading Retail*, p. 22.
[174] Alon, Welsh, and Falbe, "Franchising in Emerging Markets," p. 20.

days"; in a similar vein, he exemplifies "oligopoly" with what "the 'Seven Sisters' major global oil companies possess" and "monopsony" with "the power that Wal-Mart and Apple exert over their suppliers." According to him, "now in both Europe and North America questions are being asked concerning the excessive market power of Google, Microsoft and Amazon."[175] Here he does not distinguish between Internet-based corporations and otherwise, but he does emphatically mention many of those new firms born with the information and communication technology (ICT) revolution which enjoy power of monopoly or oligopoly on a global scale. It is not accidental that these new, Internet-based firms have quickly become typical examples of monopoly; behind them stands the power of the information revolution that has transformed the business world.

The information revolution is usually regarded as a force for further decentralization and democratization in various ways.[176] I don't deny such impacts, but, as the information revolution is a complicated and multifaceted development, I would argue that such impacts coexist with other consequences that point to the promotion of concentration, coordination, and monopolistic oligopoly of the capitalist economy. It is obvious that the information revolution makes coordination and monopoly of capital more convenient and more possible on a global scale than otherwise; furthermore, it makes it necessary, inevitable, and desirable because compatibility, standardization, and networks are intrinsic demands when the revolution applies. That is why, for example, Microsoft gained a monopoly in a much shorter time than a firm in a traditional industry could have. In the eyes of a leading economist, Bill Gates simply "profited from a virtual monopoly on operating

---

[175] David Harvey, *Seventeen Contradictions and the End of Capitalism*, Oxford University Press, 2014, pp. 131–132.

[176] Lawrence K. Grossman, *The Electronic Republic: Reshaping Democracy in the Information Age*, New York: Viking, 1995; Barry N. Hague and Brian D. Loader eds., *Digital Democracy: Discourse and Decision-Making in the Information Age*, London: Routledge, 1999; Bruce Bimber, *Information and American Democracy: Technology in the Evolution of Political Power*, Cambridge University Press, 2003; Norbert Kersting and Harald Baldersheim eds., *Electronic Voting and Democracy: A Comparative Analysis*, New York: Palgrave Macmillan, 2005; Philip N. Howard and Muzammil M. Hussain, *Democracy's Fourth Wave? Digital Media and the Arab Spring*, Oxford University Press, 2013; Jessica Baldwin-Philippi, *Using Technology, Building Democracy: Digital Campaigning and the Construction of Citizenship*, Oxford University Press, 2015.

systems (as have many other high-tech entrepreneurs in industries ranging from telecommunications to Facebook, whose fortunes were also built on monopoly rents)."[177]

Furthermore, the development of communication technologies has generally facilitated the networks of the capitalist economy, because networks, as discussed earlier in this chapter, help capitalism organize and coordinate into oligopoly. To quote an expert who points out the opportunities that the information revolution provides to global connectivity of the capitalist economy,

New information and communication technologies, based on microelectronics, telecommunications and network-oriented computer software, have provided the infrastructure for this new [global, capitalist] economy. While internationalization of economic activities is certainly not new, this technological infrastructure is. Network-oriented information and communication technologies allow for unprecedented speed and complexity in the management of the economy. Thus, economic transactions and production are able to increase their size dramatically without hampering their connectivity.[178]

This chapter would further emphasize, in addition to the above "facility" argument, the necessity of standardization in such globalization, which is even more fundamental in driving the global economy to be monopolized. Back to the example of Microsoft, imagine that there were a hundred suppliers of software of the computer operation system, which is not a big number in a traditional industry considering the huge size of the global market; what would happen? Incompatibility among these different hundred programs would certainly very much annoy consumers, not to mention the huge inconveniences they would cause in allowing people to get connected with each other in the Internet age through the World Wide Web.[179] From a more general point of view, globalization requires much more intensive and

---

[177] Thomas Piketty, *Capital in the Twenty-First Century*, Cambridge, MA: Belknap Press of Harvard University Press, 2014, p. 444.

[178] Manuel Castells, "Information Technology and Global Capitalism," in Will Hutton and Anthony Giddens eds., *Global Capitalism*, New York: New Press, 2000, pp. 52–74 (pp. 52–53).

[179] Martin Campbell-Kelly and William Aspray, *Computer: A History of the Information Machine*, New York: Basic Books, 1996; John Naughton, *A Brief History of the Future: The Origins of the Internet*, London: Weidenfeld & Nicolson, 1999.

extensive global communication, thus a standard computer language/
program is what people prefer to choose.[180] Therefore, standardization
is inherent to the development of the information revolution, as standardization technically benefits consumers. In the reality of business,
however, the successful unfolding of standardized products demands
merger, acquisition, and/or bankruptcy of the many by the few gigantic
firms. Eventually one either uses Microsoft or Apple, as the third option
is least popular, and only at a point of time approaching this do the
oligopolists begin to develop compatibility between their software
programs in technology and, I would emphasize, the coordination of
their businesses in the world of market institutions.[181] In this sense,
monopoly/oligopoly is desirable for consumers as well as business
tycoons and more irresistible than it would have been in a pre-ICT-
revolution world (ICT refers to information and communication technologies). Therefore, on these three levels, namely, for an individual
MNC in the information industry to become a monopoly power, for
global capitalism to be enabled to operate in well-connected coordination, and for the standardization of such operations to be required, the
ICT revolution contributes tremendously to global monopoly and
oligopoly.

One more issue relevant to the ICT revolution is the increasing
significance of knowledge and the rise of intellectual property rights,
both of which also enhance monopoly. Innovation, for example, is
surely an intrinsic feature of the ICT revolution; however, "one important way to create temporary monopolies is by innovation," according
to an expert on economic philosophy. "An innovating firm creates a
new product and is able to charge higher prices until imitators have
come up with substitutes that are good enough. The monopoly profit
an innovator makes in the period he can charge a higher price is an
important incentive to innovate in the first place."[182] Moreover,

A situation analogous to that of the natural monopoly can arise when the
value of a good to a user increases with the number of other users; that is,

---

[180]   A similar trend even emerges with globalization in the world of "real" (as
        against "digital") language, where English has more and more become
        "globish." See Robert McCrum, *Globish: How the English Language Became
        the World's Language*, Toronto: Doubleday Canada, 2010.
[181]   See an interesting story in James Wallace, *Overdrive: Bill Gates and the Race to
        Control Cyberspace*, Hoboken, NJ: Wiley, 1997.
[182]   Reiss, *Philosophy of Economics*, p. 232.

when there are network effects. Think of the position Microsoft occupies in the market for PC operating systems. When there are network effects, the first company in the market (or the company whose product is adopted as standard) can have an enormous advantage quite independently of the quality of the good. Other barriers to entry include the control of natural resources (for instance, OPEC's control over oil in the 1970s) and the technological superiority of a large firm that is better able to acquire, integrate and use the best possible technology in producing its goods.[183]

In either of the two main forms, namely patents and copyright, intellectual property rights give the creator of an idea monopoly rights over the use of the idea for a period of time, and therefore they tend to prevent competition. Scientific and technological innovations have "the property of non-rivalry";[184] they are, by nature, monopolistic.

No one would deny the increasing importance of knowledge in general and of intellectual property rights in particular in the information age, but this intrinsic connection between them and monopoly is not appreciated as widely as it should be for an understanding of global capitalism. In fact, big business in global expansion is inclined to strengthen rather than spread its core technology. It is observed that the preeminence of multinationals is

concentrated heavily in industries characterized by high levels of research and development, a large share of professional and technical workers, and production of technically complex or differentiated goods. Firms that invest often have some type of intangible asset they want to keep within the firm, rather than exploit through licensing. Furthermore, investing firms are often the larger firms in their industries.[185]

Therefore, because of both the general trait of technological innovation in terms of property rights and the strategy specific firms take in technology transfer, the rise of increasing significance of knowledge and the rise of intellectual property rights both incline toward monopoly.

How Does the Increasing Economic Role of the State Promote Monopoly?

In fact, all the grand institutions of globalization discussed in Chapter 2, namely, the state-market nexus, the rise of the economic state, the great

---

[183] Ibid.   [184] Ibid, p. 241.
[185] Shatz and Venables, "The Geography of International Investment," p. 126.

gap between global capitalism and national democracy, and the disjuncture between various national mixed-economies and the unregulated global market, promote monopoly and oligopoly. In general, that the state has joined global capitalism has strengthened monopoly overall while reducing checks from public power over capital's monopoly. This statist impact, however, is most prominently reflected in the rise of late late-developmental economies to global capitalism, as exemplified in the fact that emerging economies compete against industrial nations often with their concentration of economic power directed into a small number of state-backed corporations, and that the state plays a dominant role in supporting and even organizing such corporate monopolies and oligopolies.

What deserves special attention is the value change to the popular perception of markets as institutions brought by the rise of late and late late-developmental economies, a change from valuing freedom to emphasizing competitiveness and efficiency. According to a comparative study of Japanese and Australian capitalisms,

> In the orthodox view that informs economic policy-making in the Anglo-American economies, market power, oligopolization and the absence of competition are seen as necessarily bad, both theoretically and normatively. In Japan, by contrast, 'excessive competition' is seen as dangerous and potentially destructive, and therefore something to be avoided where possible by the careful interventions of government officials. Consequently, as we have seen, the state has been at the centre of attempts to encourage the development of major corporations in which their oligopolistic positions are seen as a source of national competitive advantage, not a distortion to be overcome.[186]

Yet the Japanese economic problems were due to "some of the structural weaknesses in the Japanese economy, the most prominent being the cozy relationship between its leading banks and corporations and the government ... The Japanese had had antimonopoly legislation since 1945, but these laws were weakly enforced."[187]

People have not learned from the Japanese lesson, however; instead, many countries, especially East Asian nations such as South Korea, Singapore, and now China have followed suit, as exemplified by

---

[186] Beeson, *Competing Capitalisms*, p. 84.
[187] Joyce Appleby, *The Restless Revolution: A History of Capitalism*, New York: W. W. Norton, 2010, p. 356.

China's "large enterprise strategy,"[188] a phenomenon upon which this chapter has earlier touched. In any case, when government enforcement of big business becomes a preferred norm of state behavior for gaining a competitive edge in the global market, monopolies and oligopolies gain huge momentum. In a wider sense, some leading scholars argue that "the *best* form of 'good capitalism' is a blend of 'entrepreneurial' and 'big-firm' capitalism";[189] considering "competitiveness," it is often a truth even for "business" in news reporting that "scale is everything" as "audiences and advertisers shift to big outlets and big platforms."[190] This is indeed a "new gilded age" in both reality and mentality.[191]

In a similar vein theoretically, though often different in practice, the prevalence of public services also adds to the momentum of monopolization, because public service demands monopoly. According to Albert Hirschman,

Public services are typically sold or delivered by a single public or publicly regulated supplier, for various reasons: (1) some services (railroads, postal services, electric power, etc.) are supplied by a technical or legal monopoly; and (2) some services (education, health) are not paid for directly, because all citizens regardless of income are considered to be entitled to them – hence they cannot be supplied through the market; (3) in some cases society holds that a service should be supplied in conditions of uniform, publicly controlled quality regardless of the variation of consumer preferences.[192]

Hirschman discusses problems stemming from this that include "maintaining productive efficiency and quality,"[193] but the most serious problem is monopoly itself.

---

[188] Sarah Eaton, "The Gradual Encroachment of an Idea: Large Enterprise Groups in China," an unpublished manuscript.

[189] William J. Baumol, Robert E. Litan, and Carl J. Schramm, *Good Capitalism, Bad Capitalism: And the Economics of Growth and Prosperity*, New Haven: Yale University Press, 2007, p. ix. Emphasis in original.

[190] Joshua Benton, "Scale Is Everything: Can Local News Survive as Audiences and Advertisers Shift to Big Outlets and Big Platforms?" *Nieman Reports* (Summer 2015): 50–51.

[191] For the term, and a thoughtful investigation of its consequences, especially on inequality and democracy, see Larry M. Bartels, *Unequal Democracy: The Political Economy of the New Gilded Age*, Princeton University Press, 2008.

[192] Albert O. Hirschman, *Rival Views of Market Society: And Other Recent Essays*, Cambridge, MA: Harvard University Press, 1986/1992, p. 87.

[193] Ibid.

Globalization promotes in various ways the prevalence of public services. For example, regional clusters demand ample supplies of local public services. As a relevant study points out, "The concept of 'local public services' is associated with the idea of an infrastructure that is a natural monopoly in the supply of services within a local system (a city, an industrial district, a rural system, etc.) ... "[194] In general, all the situations described by Hirschman have obviously been further promoted by globalization, joining the state-market nexus and the increasing role of the state overall in most aspects of citizen life to powerfully strengthen a trend of public services and monopoly.

There are many other factors in globalization joining the trends described above to underline the concentration of capital and mono-poly/oligopoly in a variety of ways, but limited space here does not allow more thorough discussion. Before wrapping up this section, however, just one more development should be pointed out for its enforcement of oligopoly, which is consumers' prevailing mentality to worship big brands. Obviously it provides the mass social foundations for the psychological roots of monopoly/oligopoly, as consumers flood in to purchase goods from a limited number of well-known brands. The phenomenon itself is not only psychological, however; it has an institutional background in the global triumph of capitalism. Globalization, in this regard, means the rapid expansion of the world consumer market to those who were previously not involved in the consumption of goods and services provided by leading global corporations; they are now exposed to such opportunities, but are also having to face the problem of making choices among different brands. Not only does the shortage of product knowledge of new consumers help to promote big brands; other issues such as these consumers' social mentality, the style of consumption of the nouveau riche, mass distrust over the qualities of goods and services offered by those lesser-known names, powerful advertising of famous brands, and the like (see more discussions in Chapter 5), all help to shape a spiral effect between monopoly by big business and mass consumption.

Various developments of global capitalism, in sum, incline to promote monopoly and oligopoly; moreover, they are now shaping a

---

[194] Marco Bellandi, "A Perspective on Clusters, Localities, and Specific Public Goods," in Christos Pitelis, Roger Sugden, and James R. Wilson, eds., *Clusters and Globalisation: The Development of Urban and Regional Economics*, Cheltenham: Edward Elgar, 2006, pp. 96–113 (p. 100).

powerful trend in which monopoly and oligopoly become a dominating norm of the capitalist economy. In other words, monopoly and oligopoly are now not simply considered a business strategy and an inevitable evil, but often a preferred value of economics, a desired convention arising alongside the information revolution, an ingrained rule of the game in global competition, and a state-backed formula to promote economic development and residents' benefits. In one sentence, globalization makes monopoly and oligopoly a normality, which in turn has fundamentally transformed the market institutions.

Concluding Remarks

Capital is the most dynamic, powerful, and dominating element in capitalism, on which this chapter has focused its investigation in order to look at how the global triumph of capitalism has greatly transformed the nature, institutions, and characteristics of capitalism in this fundamental domain. The chapter's major empirical finding is that the global triumph of capitalism has promoted various concentrative movements of capital on the global scale, a development embodied in, first of all, those traditional economic phenomena of capitalism occurring since the early twentieth century that are now reenergized by globalization, which include the unprecedented growth of multinational corporations and the unrivaled power of the capitalist financial system; it is also characterized by many other new or renewed movements and organizations of capital that have since the late twentieth century gained momentum through the global reach of capitalism and its institutional reframing, these forms being exemplified in the rise of state-owned corporate behemoths from the Global South, the increasing importance of clusters in economic geography, and the worldwide coverage of markets by chain stores. The chapter is, of course, in no way a comprehensive survey of all issues raised by globalization-driven movements of capital, as it has been impossible for such a book to systematically present empirical studies regarding all of the movements. The selected forms of movement under examination, however, do cover wide and diverse realms and trajectories that demonstrate the macro trends in global capitalism of the operation of capital and its expressions in production, selling, services, and finance.

Based on such investigations, the chapter has argued that all of those concentrative movements of capital have further strengthened monopoly and oligopoly of capital on a global scale. In doing so, it has made efforts to re-comprehend the manifestations of monopoly and oligopoly in the global age of capitalism, and has contributed new understandings of monopoly/oligopoly in particular, and the operation of capital in global capitalism in general.

Monopoly, with its rich expressions in practice, is a concept with complicated and diverse aspects; it has, moreover, experienced a long historical development in both reality and conception. Various notions, such as "natural monopoly," "oligarchic monopoly" or oligopoly, "state monopoly," and relevantly, "monopolistic competition," have been coined to highlight its variety, aspects, and developments.[195] More often than not, existing understandings of monopoly, in terms of viewing the internal structure of capitalism, emphasize "finance monopoly"; for example, a leading scholar of monopoly states that "Monopoly capital has evolved, in its more advanced phase, into global monopoly-finance capital."[196] When it comes to external domains, monopoly and oligopoly, as understood with a focus on big businesses' domination of production, selling, and services, can be put in different and contending perspectives that point to various different relationships in which such domination may operate alongside many other factors in distinguished contexts – for example, the domination of big businesses is more often than not interpreted as something that is acting against the state, a crucial point for ideological demarcation between the Right (which is inclined to support business) and the Left (which prefers bigger roles of government). Accordingly, connections and interactions between monopoly and competition are also explained in different but often linearly accentuated ways.

For the purpose of drawing together different lines to understand and clarify the concept of monopoly in the globalization age, this chapter has proposed the notions of "oligopolistic competition" and "institutional monopoly," with the former attempting to highlight the dialectic interactions between global intensification of competition and its impact of promoting monopoly and oligopoly, and the latter emphasizing the power of monopoly and oligopoly to structure and determine principles, norms, rules, and decision-making procedures alongside

---

[195] Brewer, *Marxist Theories of Imperialism*, p. 78.
[196] Foster, *The Theory of Monopoly Capitalism*, p. vii.

which the market operates, or, in short, rules of the market game.[197] Together, the oligarchic dynamics and institutionalization of monopoly have made the operation of capital in particular, and global capitalism in general, much more well-networked, coordinated and, therefore, organized, rather than anarchic, as Marx maintained, through developments of capital's concentration, its internal communication, and its various interdependence.

With globalization in general and the ICT revolution in particular, monopoly and oligopoly have become a normality of global capitalism, a normality in the sense that monopoly and oligopoly are now inherent to capital's movements, natural in business operation, and desirable for consumption. This chapter has tried to analyze why the intensification of monopoly emerges with globalization, and how various developments running alongside globalization stimulate and necessitate this new high degree of monopoly. Among such developments, the size of the global markets, the ICT revolution, state-market collaboration, the expansion of state functions, and the global involvement of late late-developing nations are the most significant in pushing the momentum forward and shaping the characteristics of global monopolistic oligopoly.

The global triumph of capitalism, therefore, means the historical and institutional triumph of capital in its predominance over other elements of the market as well as society. And, needless to say, global monopoly has entailed tremendous and profound economic, social, cultural, political, and ecological consequences to human life. Employing inter-institutional methodology, the book must now turn to two other fundamental elements of capitalism, namely labor and consumption, for further examination of global capitalism to see how capital's concentration and institutional monopoly interact with, respectively in the next two chapters, the globalization of labor markets and the rise of global consumption markets, while leaving an investigation of the consequences of the global institutional monopoly of capital to Chapter 6. That is to say, labor, consumption, and, more generally, politics and society in the age of global capitalism, all have to be examined in the chapters that follow against their relationships with capital.

---

[197] Ft. 33, ch. 1.

4 | Human (Im)mobility, Social Poverty, and Political Inability

"Economic Man" on the Segmented Labor Market

One of the major reconfigurations of capitalism effected by globalization concerns labor, especially labor's increasing geographic mobility and its impact over global labor markets. Pre-global capitalism, as emphasized in the last century by Arghiri Emmanuel in elaborating his theory of the determination of prices of production in a world economy, features a contrast between capital's capability of high international flow and labor's impotency to move across locations and nations.[1] This is often considered a vital principle in understanding capitalism. The global triumph of capitalism, however, as it is frequently argued, has fundamentally changed the reality in which various forms of migration have now arisen and, in general, so-called human capital has gained increasing freedom in relocation;[2] accordingly, those interpretations based on the above contrast have been challenged. How

[1] See Anthony Brewer, *Marxist Theories of Imperialism: A Critical Survey*, London: Routledge, 1990, p. 22 and ch. 9.

[2] For brief summaries of the history of human migration since the rise of capitalism, see, for example, Doreen Elliott, Nazneen S. Mayadas, and Uma A. Segal, "Immigration Worldwide: Trends and Analysis," in Uma A. Segal, Doreen Elliott, and Nazneen S. Mayadas eds., *Immigration Worldwide: Policies, Practices, and Trends*, Oxford University Press, 2010, pp. 17–26; Anthony J. Marsella and Erin Ring, "Human Migration and Immigration: An Overview," in Leonore Loeb Adler and Uwe P. Gielen eds., *Migration: Immigration and Emigration in International Perspective*, Westport, CT: Praeger, 2003, pp. 3–22. For the high tide of human migration during the turn from the nineteenth to the twentieth century in particular, see detailed studies in, for instance, Jürgen Osterhammel, *The Transformation of the World: A Global History of the Nineteenth Century*, Princeton University Press, 2014, ch. 4; Roger Daniels, *Coming to America: A History of Immigration and Ethnicity in American Life*, New York: Harper Collins, 1990; Leslie Page Moch, *Moving Europeans: Migration in Western Europe since 1650*, Bloomington: Indiana University Press, 1992; Walter Nugent, *Crossings: The Great Transatlantic Migrations, 1870–1914*, Bloomington: Indiana University Press, 1992.

does the increasing mobility of labor affect the global labor market? Has such freedom of relocation strengthened labor's bargaining position and overall power in its relationship with capital? How do institutions of global capitalism promote and/or constrain laborers in achieving their interests? These will be the questions to which this chapter attempts to provide macro answers.

While fully recognizing labor's increasing mobility due to globalization, this chapter attempts to draw a larger picture of the global labor markets, in which those who are not engaged in geographic mobility and their interconnections with labor mobility will be considered, and in which the interactions among labor, capital, and the state will be highlighted. In considering labor as a whole in terms of it being a fundamental element of the capitalist political economy, labor's fluidity in either the relative or the absolute sense is greatly limited – relative in comparison with capital's degree of movement and absolute in labor per se in terms of the tiny portion of laborers in mobility emerging out of the gigantic bases of laborers in a state of immobility. Although migration studies have flourished as a field of academic research and policy analysis since the end of the Cold War and have resulted in numerous publications and profound contributions, this chapter is not designed to investigate migration as a relatively independent topic; instead, it will bring the issue of labor mobility into contrast with labor's immobility. It is easy to understand why people who are on the move have attracted greater attention in globalization studies, especially when these moves involve such a vast number of people, a number which is consistently increasing over time. It is even easier, however, to be aware of the fact that these people still make up a tiny portion of the world population. It is, therefore, somehow surprising that it is not a prevailing fashion in globalization studies to consider the weight of those who are not on the move within the studies of those who are; this surprise becomes greater still if one can claim that those who are not on the move are also inevitably and equally involved in global capitalism. Therefore, what should be placed in the spotlight, this chapter maintains, is the connection and interaction between those people in mobility and those who are not in order to examine the fate of either category or both. The global labor market as a whole would not be comprehensively understood without each.

Under such a lens, it can be argued that the global labor market is highly segmented; in fact, it is further fractured and fragmented by the global reach of capitalism that connects and involves different parts of global labor. Increasing mobility of labor across various borders, accordingly, helps to strengthen the hierarchical structure of labor in terms of different layers of people gaining and actualizing the freedom to be mobile in varying degrees. Internal competition among different segments of labor, therefore, is intensified, which much explains the new economy and new politics of labor under global capitalism, including a growing socioeconomic inequality and the decline of union movements.

Standing as the operational linchpin of capitalist markets, including the labor market, is capital. One of the most significant consequences of increasing labor mobility and segmentation of the global labor market, this chapter argues, is the enhancement of the advantages and domination that capital holds against labor and the institutionalization of such advantages and domination on the global labor markets. It will examine labor moves and non-moves in their close relationship with capital's movements that have been investigated in the previous chapter, attempting to draw connections, comparisons, and interactions between the movements of capital and so-called human capital in order to understand the nature, characters, and impacts of the latter as an indispensable element of global capitalism. The seemingly parallel movements of capital and labor are, in fact, fundamentally and significantly divergent, often running in opposite directions that can be summarized as the concentration of capital versus the dispersion, fragmentation, and dislocation of labor.

Especially significant is the state's different functions of facilitating capital flow while hindering labor's movement, an expression of the institutional framework centered on the state-market nexus as elaborated in Chapter 2. Thus, in addition to the two connections that exist between labor mobility and labor immobility, and between labor and capital, the third connection, which exists between economic elements as manifested in labor versus capital and political elements such as the state, sovereignty, and governance, should also be highlighted. Only through the inter-institutional lens this book has suggested does it become clear that all movements of capital and labor and their interactions are stimulated and constrained, respectively, by institutions of the political economy of global capitalism.

This inter-institutional logic naturally extends studies of labor beyond simply considering it as a market element, but also viewing it in its social, cultural, and political contexts and how these contexts interact with the market to characterize the ongoing movements of migration in particular and labor in general. Whereas capital globalizes to network and to maximize the return, the global market further uproots labor from its deep, comprehensive social fabrics and increasingly makes the laborer an "economic man" in the sense of being a one-dimensional person in sole pursuit of the improvement of material life at the expense of other human identities and qualities. Everywhere, through either labor's mobility or immobility, the institutional framework of global capitalism has to some degree undone what the political transformation since the French Revolution has achieved, as summarized by Reinhard Bendix as "the laboring poor have become citizens, recognized participants in the political process,"[3] the dismantling of which generates social poverty and political inability of labor.

Global Moves of Labor and the Making of "Economic Man": One-Dimensional Globalization, One-Dimensional Human Beings

Migration, or the geographic movement of people, now attracts huge attention, argued to be a phenomenon that is increasing in tandem with globalization.[4] The global triumph of capitalism inevitably means the expansion of the capitalist labor market to cover this globe and, therefore, the involvement of an increasing number of people in the global networks of exchange of labor and money. People in mobility, of course, have formed the most active part of the global labor market; prominent among them are those who cross national borders via international immigration to seek new settlement in foreign countries. Our examination of globalizing labor, therefore, shall begin with this group of people.

Yes, immigration, migration, and various dislocations have since the end of the Cold War quickly risen to dominate human movement and labor market fluidity. In terms of international immigration, it is reported that "nearly 215 million persons now live in a country

---

[3] Reinhard Bendix, *Force, Fate, and Freedom: Historical Sociology*, Berkeley: University of California Press, 1984, p. 69.

[4] For a updated overview of migration, see Stephen Castles, Hein de Haas, and Mark J. Miller, *The Age of Migration: International Population Movements in the Modern World*, New York: Guilford Press, 2013, 5th ed.

where they were not born, so immigrants account for about 3 percent of the world's population."[5] This figure, as pointed out by some scholars, is equivalent to the population of Brazil, the fifth largest country in the world.[6] In addition, there are massive numbers of illegal immigrants who have crossed national borders without the permission of relevant sovereign authorities. "More than 11 million illegals," for example, "live in the United States"; illegal immigrants now constitute 5 percent of the workforce in the US, the largest economy in the world.[7]

The increasing significance of global immigration cannot be sufficiently estimated looking only at its percentage of the world population, however; other indicators should be emphasized in this regard. First of all, global immigration now involves all nations in the world, thus making the phenomenon truly "global." As the 2005 report of the World Migration Organization noted, "no country remained untouched by international migration."[8] Second, the number of people involved in international migration has been growing quickly, indicating a speeding-up of this trend. Table 4.1 shows this acceleration across different historical periods, in which those years from 1965 to 1970 saw the world population of immigrants increased at a rate of 0.8 million per year, then 2.8 million between 1985 and 1990, more than 4 million between 1990 and 1997, and then, between 2000 and 2005, the average annual number of immigrants jumped to 6 million, making 190 million the total number of migrants around the world 2005, more than twice the 1970 level of 82.5 million.[9] It is reported that "the world's population of immigrants has increased at a rate exceeding world population growth and the potential for future growth in international migration is

[5] George J. Borjas, *Immigration Economics*, Cambridge, MA: Harvard University Press, 2014, p. 1.
[6] Uma A. Segal, Doreen Elliott, and Nazneen S. Mayadas eds., *Immigration Worldwide: Policies, Practices, and Trends*, Oxford University Press, 2010, p. vii.
[7] Carol M. Swain, "Introduction," in Carol M. Swain ed., *Debating Immigration*, Cambridge University Press, 2007, pp. 1–24 (p. 3).
[8] International Organization for Migration, "World Migration Report 2005," www.iom.int/world-migration-report-2005, accessed May 20, 2015. For change in Japan's case of traditionally excluding immigrants, see for example, Seisoh Sukemune, "Migration from and to Japan," in Leonore Loeb Adler and Uwe P. Gielen eds., *Migration: Immigration and Emigration in International Perspective*, Westport, CT: Praeger, 2003, pp. 243–249.
[9] David Held and Anthony McGrew, *Globalization/Anti-Globalization: Beyond the Great Divide*, Cambridge: Polity, 2nd ed., 2007, p. 95.

Table 4.1 *The Acceleration of Global Immigration, Selected Periods Between 1965 and 2005*

Historical Period	Increasing Rate of World Population of Immigrants per Year (in millions)
1965–1975	0.8
1985–1990	2.8
1990–1997	4.0+
2000–2005	6.0

Source: The author's composition based on the information available in Douglas S. Massey and J. Edward Taylor, "Introduction," in Douglas S. Massey and J. Edward Taylor eds., *International Migration: Prospects and Policies in a Global Market*, Oxford University Press, 2004, p. 1, and David Held and Anthony McGrew, *Globalization/Anti-Globalization: Beyond the Great Divide*, Cambridge: Polity, 2007, p. 95.

nothing less than staggering."[10] Third, international immigration in this wave of globalization can be identified as the growing complexity of its origins, compositions, and destinations.[11] As two experts have pointed out, "Not only has immigration been rising; its composition is also changing. From North African venders in the streets of Florence to Mexican and Hmong meat packers in Iowa to Brazilian and Indonesian factory workers in Japan, immigrants are increasingly diverse in their origins, destinations, and characteristics."[12]

All of these developments are unprecedented; to this book, they have become realities only through the global triumph of capitalism.[13] International immigration, therefore, should be better understood in the context of the global expansion of capitalism; behind the dazzling and polychromatic developments, the force of the market at work is not

[10] Douglas S. Massey and J. Edward Taylor, "Introduction," in Douglas S. Massey and J. Edward Taylor eds., *International Migration: Prospects and Policies in a Global Market*, Oxford University Press, 2004, pp. 1–12 (p. 2).
[11] Held and McGrew, *Globalization/Anti-Globalization*, p. 95.
[12] Massey and Taylor, "Introduction," p. 1.
[13] Other economic systems often hinder movements of people in various ways. As a major rival of capitalism before its global triumph, the communist system in particular exercised strict state control and often prohibition over residents' geographic mobility. See such an example in China in Fei-Ling Wang, *Organizing Through Division and Exclusion: China's Hukou System*, Stanford University Press, 2005.

Table 4.2 *The Largest Suppliers of International Emigrants, 2005*

Country (in decreasing order)	GDP per capita (2005 US$)	Status of freedom / score of political rights (1 = best; 7 = worst)
Mexico	7,894	Free / 2
China	1,740	Not free / 7
Pakistan	714	Not free / 6
India	729	Free / 2
Iran	3,135	Not free / 6
Indonesia	1,264	Partly free / 3
Philippines	1,197	Free / 2
Ukraine	1,829	Partly free / 4
Kazakhstan	3,771	Not free / 6
Sudan	662	Not free / 7

Source: The author's composition based on the following information: for the list of the largest supplier countries of international emigrants, "UN Statistics Show Migration as a Dynamic and Diversifying Force in Global Development," press release, September 12, 2006, www.un.org/migratin/presskit/pressrelease12sept.pdf, accessed November 22, 2015; for GDP per capita, http://data.worldbank.org/indica tor/NY.GDP.PCAP.KD?page=2, accessed May 17, 2016; for status of freedom and score of political rights, The Freedom House, https://freedomhouse.org/report/free dom-world/freedom-world-2005, accessed May 8, 2016.

impalpable.[14] The global market explains the shape of international immigration in many ways, primarily the main direction of the flow of people around the globe that discloses how and why these people move. Although all nations at various levels of socioeconomic development see immigration flows, it is indisputable that the global mobility of people has largely been directed one way, from developing countries to industrialized nations.[15] Table 4.2 lists the ten largest suppliers of international emigrants in 2005, all being developing economies, most of which are economically poor.

On the other end of global immigration stand those destination countries belonging to the Global North. According to a 2006 United Nations report, 60 percent of the world's migrants live in developed countries, where almost 1 in 10 persons is an immigrant; while the ratio

[14] For labor relocation as a market function, see George J. Borjas, *Labor Economics*, New York: McGraw-Hill/Irwin, 2008, ch. 9.
[15] Segal, Elliott, and Mayadas, *Immigration Worldwide*, p. vii.

of migrants to native-born people worldwide is 1 in 35, in developing countries it is only 1 in 70.[16] Another source of information confirms this: "By 2005 approximately 60 percent of all recorded migrants were to be found in the world's more prosperous countries."[17] A slightly earlier survey showed a similar trend that "The major movement of immigrants is toward the developed world, where gradually the flow increased by 3 percent during the 1990s, with no increase in immigrants to the developing world."[18] North America, Oceania, and Europe are the major areas of net gain in migrant population; by contrast, the less developed areas of Latin America, Africa, and Asia show a net loss of population through migration.[19] That is why scholars conclude that "emigration states are post-colonial regions of the economically less developed and politically penetrated periphery, while the immigration states are thought to occupy the higher echelons in the political-economic hierarchy of the world economy."[20]

The United States, the largest industrial economy in the world and traditionally a country of immigrants, is doubtless a destination attracting most people in global mobility. It is reported that more than 20 percent of the entire world's migration population of 215 million immigrants, or 43 million people, have migrated to the United States.[21] Meanwhile, "what is surprising is that the foreign-born share now stands at record levels in countries that have little historical experience with immigration: 9 percent in Portugal, 10 percent in Norway and the United Kingdom, 13 percent in Germany, 14 percent in Spain and Sweden, and 16 percent in Austria. Much of the developed world is increasingly composed of 'nations of immigrants'."[22] However, experts, despite such a surprise, still find that "inward migration is somewhat

---

[16] United Nations, *International Migration 2006*, New York: Department of Economic and Social Affairs, Population Division, 2006.

[17] Report of the Global Commission on International Migration (New York, 2005), www.gcim.org/en/finalreport.html, p. 2.

[18] United Nations, *World Economic and Social Survey 2004: International Migration*, New York: Department of Economic and Social Affairs, 2004, p. vii.

[19] Elliott, Mayadas, and Segal, "Immigration Worldwide: Trends and Analysis," p. 19.

[20] Thomas Faist, *Volume and Dynamics of International Migration and Transnational Social Spaces*, Oxford University Press, 2000, p. 12.

[21] Borjas, *Immigration Economics*, p. 1.

[22] Borjas, *Immigration Economics*, p. 1; United Nations, *International Migration Report 2009: A Global Assessment*, New York: Department of Economic and Social Affairs, Population Division, 2009.

concentrated, in that 75 per cent of migrants were domiciled in just twenty-three countries in 1970 and some twenty-eight countries by 2000."[23] In fact, such developments simply signify how this intensive international immigration takes place from developing nations to the industrial world, as, first, "labour flows (especially unskilled) are geographically extensive and, in terms of direction, reflect an almost mirror image of capital flows in so far as they become primarily South to North";[24] second, due to such an intensity, now more countries in the North than before have become destinations for people flowing from the South. Together, these features have confirmed that South-North movements of people have become both intensive and extensive through the late twentieth to the early twenty-first century.

What accounts for the global movements of people from the South to the North? Demographic change in industrialized countries is often used to explain this trend in immigration to developed nations, "where because of the demographic consequences of declining fertility rates and longer life expectancy, populations are declining without immigration."[25] In 2005, migrants made up 3 percent of the global workforce but 9 percent of the workforce in the developed world.[26] However, such a perspective only explains why industrialized nations open their doors wider than before to welcome immigrants (i.e. because of those countries' demand for a labor force), not the motivations behind the immigrants leaving their home countries in the developing world.[27] The transportation and communication revolutions also help to explain global mobility of people, though it is this author's opinion that we should not mix the demonstration effect and the vehicle to immigrate with the inspiration behind immigration. It should not be difficult to understand the difference between the convenience of a

---

[23] Held and McGrew, *Globalization/Anti-Globalization*, p. 95.

[24] Ibid, pp. 94–5.

[25] Elliott, Mayadas, and Segal, "Immigration Worldwide: Trends and Analysis," p. 19.

[26] Held and McGrew, *Globalization/Anti-Globalization*, p. 95.

[27] Some experts have found that the causes of international immigration are not demographic, but political, social, and economic. See, for example, Hania Zlotnik, "Population Growth and International Migration," pp. 15–34; and Marek Okólski, "The Effects of Political and Economic Transition on International Migration in Central and Eastern Europe," pp. 35–58; both in Douglas S. Massey and J. Edward Taylor eds., *International Migration: Prospects and Policies in a Global Market*, Oxford University Press, 2004.

move provided by modern transportation and the significance of a decision to move that is inspired by one's life experience; it is very unlikely that there are many cases in which people are determined to migrant to a foreign country just because they happen to be able to obtain one-way air tickets to New York City from either Nairobi, Kenya, or Ningbo, China. In regards to the relevance of the information revolution to the increase of global migration, however, W. M. Spellman's interpretation sounds reasonable: "Thanks to the spread of electronic communications technologies (cinema, television and, most recently, the Internet), the material attractions of the developed world are now widely disseminated."[28]

Let's pay special attention to what Spellman refers to as "material attractions," and extend the argument to say that economic concerns and material inspirations are the most powerful and the most popular motivation behind the movements of people across national borders toward the North. For Spellman, there are two categories of transnational migrants, and "the overwhelming majority of these transnational migrants have relocated for simple economic reasons, for a better life. Such people normally respond to 'pull' factors, the potential opportunities for economic betterment in another country."[29] More specifically, for many who have come to make the once-in-a-lifetime decision for international immigration, it is the widening income gap between rich and poor countries that provides the most significant reason among various important considerations. For Spellman's second category of international migrants that "consists of those who are 'pushed' to depart their home country in the wake of natural disaster, civil conflict or out of fear of persecution due to their ethnic, political or religious identity,"[30] which is a much smaller group, economic concerns are also greatly involved in their dislocation. For example, though the request for asylum is political, "many applicants are in fact economic migrants seeking to expedite their relocation to the affluent countries of the northern hemisphere and Australasia."[31] Overall, it can be concluded that while the motivations of transnational migration vary, they are overwhelmingly due to immigrants' economic considerations for seeking the improvement of their material life.

---

[28] W. M. Spellman, *Uncertain Identity: International Migration since 1945*, London: Reaktion Books, 2008, p. 13.
[29] Ibid, p. 8.   [30] Ibid, p. 9.   [31] Ibid.

Such a materialist motivation of international mobility of people in the current wave of globalization is made even clearer when a historical perspective joins the analysis. The magnet of wealth in attracting international immigration is, in fact, not as natural as people today may have prevailingly supposed. "Speaking in very general terms," states a comparative study, "nineteenth-century migrants moved from densely settled and industrialized areas of Europe to sparsely settled and underdeveloped regions. Migrants after 1945 originated in densely populated and poor countries and sought material improvement in densely settled post-industrial states."[32] Therefore, that "the recent growth in immigration has mostly been to developed countries" is a relatively new phenomenon,[33] and we may argue that people's flow to the industrialized world does help to distinguish the latest wave of global immigration from earlier ones. This is not coincident with the rise of globalization, especially when one notices that recent flows are even more about the economic divergence between developing and industrial worlds. "Since the end of the Cold War, and especially with the collapse of the Soviet Union, points of departure have proliferated and the number of poor and unskilled migrants seeking to improve their standard of living has grown."[34] Considering the facts that now in the early twenty-first century rich countries have a per capita GDP 66 times greater than those of poor countries,[35] and that "outward flows of people are a phenomenon predominantly associated with developing countries,"[36] it is not difficult to follow Spellman to conclude that the contemporary phenomenon of international migration is "largely a function of a widening North-South divide."[37] The global triumph of capitalism, as will be investigated in Chapter 6, has accelerated and proliferated this widening divide, thus involving more nations and populations in the global flows of immigrants seeking a better life in developed countries.

---

[32] Douglas S. Massey, Joaquin Arango, Graeme Hugo, Ali Kouaouci, Adela Pellegrino, and J. Edward Taylor, *Worlds in Motion: Understanding International Migration at the End of the Millennium*, Oxford: Clarendon Press, 1998, p. 2.

[33] Massey and Taylor, "Introduction," p. 1.

[34] Spellman, *Uncertain Identity*, p. 13.

[35] GCIM, *Migration in an Interconnected World: New Directions for Action*, report of the Global Commission on International Migration, Switzerland, 2005.

[36] Held and McGrew, *Globalization/Anti-Globalization*, p. 95.

[37] Spellman, *Uncertain Identity*, p. 12.

International immigration is, of course, a heavy decision for those who are involved in the process, and it yields profound impacts on their lives, which often go beyond their initial imagination, and on the political economy of global capitalism, many of which will be discussed later. One prominent aftermath of international immigration, however, must be emphasized here, as it sets the fundamental ethos for understanding human mobility in the globalization age. This is the making of the "economic man," which this chapter attempts to define in a different sense from what is generally understood in economics as a person employing a rational calculation of his/her economic interest in decision-making and other behavior. Rather, following Herbert Marcuse's concept of the "one-dimensional man" in advanced industrial society,[38] this chapter highlights "economic man" as a human who is overwhelmingly concerned with his/her material, financial, and economic conditions of living as the single most important dimension of life against all other considerations. This "economic man" is not, of course, a new phenomenon in human history, but this chapter would argue that the global triumph of capitalism facilitates and enhances it by spreading the process of what may be called "one-dimensionalization" worldwide, well beyond advanced industrial societies.

Migration, prominently international immigration, is one of those major channels through which globalization "converts," so to speak, millions into the one-dimensional economic man; through this channel a person not only predominantly pursues material improvements of life, but must also be "squeezed" out of his/her rich, delicate, and complicated social, cultural, and other qualities as a well-rounded human being. This chapter has tried to show how global flows of people are by and large economically motivated; the discussion below will explore how the process and the impact are channeled and governed by the state-market nexus, more often than not out of economic considerations, and, moreover, how the life of the immigrant is deprived of many significant non-economic possessions in exchange for economic ones. Michael Samers, an expert on migration studies, is correct to assert that global capitalism is "a set of forces that has a

---

[38] Herbert Marcuse, *One-Dimensional Man: Studies in the Ideology of Advanced Industrial Society*, Boston: Beacon Press, 1964. For a contemporary discussion, see Harold Demsetz, *From Economic Man to Economic System: Essays on Human Behavior and the Institutions of Capitalism*, Cambridge University Press, 2008.

relatively fixed architecture" which "*does* impel people to migrate from poorer to richer countries."[39] This chapter would like to further point out the institutional nature of the "architecture" and its implications, which go beyond the geographic movement of people. Global capitalism, in this sense, is a set of institutions that induces and forces people, especially those people who are on the move via globalization, to become "economic men."

"Labor Flexibility" as a Response to the Oversupply Dilemma: Migrant Workers and Institutional Change of Capital-Labor Relations

In the reality of global capitalism, it is not necessary to be miserable from being squeezed into the mold of a "one-dimensional man" by the narrow door of international immigration. In many cases, immigrants who are able to catch the train (or, indeed, a ship or an airplane) to a developed country are simply lucky enough to have gained new hope in improving their material life through landing as residents in a much richer place. Many other people also hit the road, but in the move they often find themselves in a city within their native countries, or a foreign country in temporary status, or, more often than not, a coastal region where global capital finds advantages worthy of its investment in new operations. In any case, a huge number of people are involved in migration, not only in the channel of international immigration but in various categories all belonging to "migrant workers," which are, as an expert asserts, "an indispensable part of a global system."[40] This section will focus empirically on migrant workers in the broadest sense, either domestic, intraregional, or international in terms of their scale of mobility, either permanent, seasonal, or temporary in terms of their mode of residence and job tenure in their new destinations, and either legal or illegal in terms of the relationship of their mobility with relevant state authorities. The analytical concern of the investigation, however, will be on how institutions of capitalist employment have been reconfigured with a further weakening of positions of labor in dealing with capital.

---

[39] Michael Samers, *Migration*, London: Routledge, 2010, p. 34. Emphasis in original.

[40] David Bacon, *Illegal People: How Globalization Creates Migration and Criminalizes Immigrants*, Boston: Beacon Press, 2008, p. 70.

Max Weber once points out "the capitalistic principle of the 'cheaper hand'";[41] when capitalism goes global, this principle inevitably goes on to dominate the global labor market. The global triumph of capitalism, however, encounters a dilemma in expanding its global labor market: on one hand, it now enjoys an unprecedentedly huge supply of labor forces, as virtually every nation as well as, theoretically, every person in the world is involved in the global labor market; on the other hand, this gigantic supply, if it is mostly mobilized, can flood over the existing channels of market activities in particular, and the institutions of political economy of global capitalism in general, thus resulting in disastrous consequences by undermining and even destroying the status quo order of the world. In other words, this is a dilemma of the oversupply of labor. The increase of migrant workers, to this author, is a typical expression of the Weberian principle in global capitalism that encounters the labor oversupply dilemma, because it meets the economic demand of the global labor market, while the non-economic (legal, social, political, and more) restrictions and constraints over the labor supply are maintained. "Labor flexibility," a prevailing norm in globalization, thus arises in order for the state-market nexus to manage these labor issues.

According to Ronald Martin, an expert on the labor market, "there is no doubt that a key feature of emerging local labour market forms is the growing emphasis – by firms and governments – on *labour flexibility*."[42] This is a vague term, however, which may cover various aspects of the labor market ranging from flexible work hours for employees' convenience to an unfixed contract that can be discretionally terminated by the employer. What is analytically important in "labor flexibility" is the institutional change brought about by the increase of migrant workers to the labor-capital relationship in terms of it being institutionalized in the form of employment. Taking different types of service workers as an example, Martin points out that "flexibility" can have different meanings for professional and unskilled workers:

---

[41] Max Weber, "Capitalism and Rural Society in Germany," in H. H. Gerth and C. Wright Mills eds., *From Max Weber: Essays in Sociology*, Oxford University Press, 1958, pp. 363–385 (p. 384).

[42] Ronald L. Martin, "Local Labour Markets: Their Nature, Performance, and Regulation," in Gordon L. Clark, Maryann P. Feldman, and Meric S. Gertler eds., *The Oxford Handbook of Economic Geography*, Oxford University Press, 2000, pp. 455–476 (p. 458). Emphasis in original.

For service professionals, increased flexibility is likely to mean self-determined 'flexi-time,' split home-office working arrangements, high salaries, and generous social and non-wage benefits. For part-time cleaners, increased flexibility invariably means working unsocial shifts and hours, short-time contracts, loss of employment rights and entitlements, and depressed pay and conditions.[43]

In one sentence, "labor flexibility" favors those who already have better bargaining positions with employers, but it further disadvantages those workers who are in weaker positions – more often than not, those migrant workers.

One of the most significant institutional changes that has taken place in the name of "labor flexibility" is the growing trend of replacing permanent employment by various temporary contracts. Here the term "temporary workers" is used as a general category in contrast to relatively long-term or permanent workers. In relevant studies, it has been noticed that temporary workers have become an important phenomenon in globalization, but usually in a narrow sense of so-called dirty labor, and its institutional significance seems not yet to have gained full consideration. In fact, all migrant workers are temporary workers in one way or another. For a comprehensive study of globalization, this is stated in such a way:

Significantly, too, the huge expansion of temporary workers moving between world regions, facilitated by low cost transport infrastructures, is additional to these official figures and is of growing importance to certain sectors (for instance, construction and agriculture) within many developed economies (including the US/UK and even South Africa, which annually hosts 100,000 guest workers).[44]

The low income of migrant workers is a notorious issue, but this makes them "competitive" on the global labor market and, in a wider picture, facilitates capital to repress the price of other groups of employees. Let's take domestic migrant workers in China as an example, who suffer greatly from low incomes, often an absence of benefits, and unfavorable working conditions in this second largest economy in the world, which has experienced continuous prosperity for almost forty years. As international business has begun to warn of the "rising wages" of Chinese labor in recent years, it is worth emphasizing that

---

[43] Ibid, p. 467.   [44] Held and McGrew, *Globalization/Anti-Globalization*, p. 96.

these rising wages actually means, as of 2006, that on a per-capita basis, the average Chinese worker earned $230 a month, according to a report by *Forbes*.[45] If one traces back several years, to 2002, a quarter of a century after China started its long economic boom, the average Chinese worker earned as little as $136 a month.[46] The reliability of these numbers, however, is questionable, though not because they underestimate the reality. For the same year of 2006, for example, in Dongguan, Guangdong Province, one of the most prosperous regions in China, where workers earn high wages by Chinese standards, foreign businessmen complained that they now had to offer extremely high wages to attract labor, which were an average of $160 a month.[47] "The minimum wage," it is reported on a global scale, "is unstable in many countries, but particularly in the developing countries."[48]

There are groups of migrant workers that are even weaker than the generally weak, among which prominently stand female migrant workers, one of the cheapest labor groups, especially in developing areas. This helps to explain why females make up a huge percentage of migrant workers, nearly one-half of all migrants, in fact.[49] Many relevant studies have provided useful empirical examinations and often enlightening ideas in understanding the gender divide in migrant workers as the miserable circumstances of female migrant workers are highlighted in economically prosperous regions such as China's coastal areas.[50] In a similar vein, poverty has driven young women into plants

---

[45] Shu-Ching Jean Chen, "Chinese Wage Increases Outpacing Economic Growth," July 2007, *Forbes*, www.forbes.com/2007/07/02/china-wage-growth-markets-econ-cx_jc_0702markets1.html, accessed June 13, 2008.

[46] Ibid.

[47] Dexter Roberts, "How Rising Wages Are Changing the Game in China," *BusinessWeek*, 2006, http://businessweek.com/magazine/conten/06_13/b3977 049.htm, accessed June 13, 2008.

[48] Peter Brosnan, "The Minimum Wage in a Global Context," in Jonathan Michie ed., *The Handbook of Globalisation*, Chelteham: Edward Elgar, 2003 (pp. 179–190), p. 185.

[49] Population Division, Department of Economic and Social Affairs, United Nations, "World Population Prospect," http://esa.un.org/migrationP2K0data .asp; www.internal-displacement.org/8025708F004CE90B/(httpPages)22FB1 D4E2B196DAA802570BB005E7a&C?OpenDocument, accessed June 13, 2008.

[50] For example, in the case of China, see Ching Kwan Lee, *Gender and the South China Miracle: Two Worlds of Factory Women*, Berkeley: University of California Press, 1998; Anita Chan, *China's Workers under Assault: The Exploitation of Labor in a Globalizing Economy*, Armonk, NY: M. E. Sharpe,

and factories in many other places, such as Honduras and Mexico.[51] In fact, "migration tends to be an increasingly urban and gendered phenomenon," as a general study concludes.[52]

The low income of migrant workers in general, and the even lower income of female migrant workers in particular are among the most significant factors in the institutional change toward "temporization," or "labor flexibility," of the employment status of labor. As a relevant study reveals:

Today, women working on the line assembling printers for Hewlett-Packard mostly come from the Philippines, South and Southeast Asia, Mexico, and Latin America. But now they work for Manpower, a temporary-employment agency with an office in the plant. Sometimes they do the same job they did when they worked from HP directly, but now without healthcare or other benefits. They're paid a low wage, and they can be terminated at any time.[53]

This is, in fact, the tip of a huge iceberg, called by a variety of terms including "labor flexibility," "casualization," and "informalization," that has emerged in the global labor market; in essence, it is the process by which employment is pushed to be irregular, temporary, and nonpermanent and labor becomes casual, insecure, and unprotected. It is a

2001; Tamara Jacka, *On the Move: Women and Rural-to-Urban Migration in Contemporary China*, Cambridge University Press, 2004; Ngai Pun, *Made in China: Women Factory Workers in a Global Marketplace*, Durham, NC: Duke University Press, 2005; Tamara Jacka, *Rural Women in Urban China: Gender, Migration, and Social Change*, London: Routledge, 2006; Hairong Yan, *New Masters, New Servants: Migration, Development, and Women Workers in China*, Durham, NC: Duke University Press, 2008; Leslie T. Chang, *Factory Girls: From Village to City in a Changing China*, New York: Spiegel & Grau, 2008; Tiantian Zheng, *Red Lights: The Lives of Sex Workers in Postsocialist China*, Minneapolis: University of Minnesota Press, 2009; Arianne M. Gaetano, *Out to Work: Migration, Gender, and the Changing Lives of Rural Women in Contemporary China*, Honolulu: University of Hawaii Press, 2015. Also, Ann Brooks, *Gendered Work in Asian Cities: The New Economy and Changing Labour Markets*, Aldershot: Ashgate, 2006. For wider perspectives and theoretical debates around the gender divide and capitalism, see, for instance, Melissa W. Wright, *Disposable Women and Other Myths of Global Capitalism*, London: Routledge, 2006; Ann E. Cudd and Nancy Holmstrom, *Capitalism, For and Against: A Feminist Debate*, Cambridge University Press, 2011; Rania Antonopoulos ed., *Gender Perspectives and Gender Impacts of the Global Economic Crisis*, Abingdon: Routledge, 2014.
51 Bacon, *Illegal People*, p. 72.
52 Held and McGrew, *Globalization/Anti-Globalization*, pp. 95–6.
53 Bacon, *Illegal People*, p. 77.

trend on the rise, especially since the global triumph of capitalism, sweeping industrial, former communist, and developing economies across sectors.[54]

In addition to many factors that cause this world of job instability,[55] the pressure from migrant workers and the increasing supply of labor, this chapter would follow many to argue, has significantly contributed this general trend of "de-permanentization" or "temporization" of labor's employment. Migrant workers are, of course, struggling at the bottom of the socioeconomic pyramid of capitalism in terms of employment relationships with capital, but this phenomenon of de-permanentization is not limited to them. In the sense that the unavailability of a permanent or long-term job causes a laborer to remain mobile in order to look for the next employment opportunity, anybody who is involved in such a situation can be viewed as a "migrant worker," whether the laborer be a sweatshop worker, restaurant waitress, bank staffer, university teacher, or symphony musician.[56]

This is a truly global trend, having emerged in both developed and developing countries, as with it, "local labour markets in the advanced nations are now caught in a powerful predicament."[57] Even in a country like Japan, where employment stability for regular employees

[54] See some researches on the trend in, for example, Dave Broad, "The Periodic Casualization of Work: The Informal Economy, Causal Labor, and the *Longue Durée*," pp. 23–46; and Saskia Sassen, "The Demise of Pax Americana and the Emergence of Informalization as a Systematic Trend," pp. 91–115; both in Faruk Tabak and Michaeline A. Crichlow, eds., *Informalization: Process and Structure*, Baltimore: Johns Hopkins University Press, 2000. For a series of books by a single author on the topic, see Jan Breman, *Footloose Labour: Working in India's Informal Economy*, Cambridge University Press, 1996; Jan Breman, *Outcast Labour in Asia: Circulation and Informalization of the Workforce at the Bottom of the Economy*, Oxford University Press, 2010; and Jan Breman, *At Work in the Informal Economy of India: A Perspective from the Bottom Up*, Oxford University Press, 2013. For the trend in former communist countries, see, for instance, Sarosh Kuruvilla, Ching Kwan Lee, and Mary E. Gallagher, eds., *From Iron Rice Bowl to Informalization: Markets, Workers, and the State in a Changing China*, Ithaca: ILR Press, 2011; Mark Pittaway, *From the Vanguard to the Margins: Workers in Hungary, 1939 to the Present*, Adam Fabry ed., Leiden: Brill, 2014.

[55] For a comprehensive exploration of various factors in this regard, see Ulrich Beck, *The Brave New World of Work*, Cambridge: Polity, 2000.

[56] For example, see Robert J. Flanagan, "Symphony Musicians and Symphony Orchestras," in Clair Brown, Barry Eichengreen, and Michael Reich eds., *Labor in the Era of Globalization*, Cambridge University Press, 2010, pp. 264–294.

[57] Martin, "Local Labour Markets," p. 469.

has been well known, non-regular employees are now increasingly used across all industries: in 1982 they made up 17 percent of all employees but in 2002 had increased to 32 percent. From 1992 to 2002, non-regular employment was the only source of employment creation in Japan. In particular, non-regular employment involves more females than males. These trends have since continued in Japan, and these non-regular workers do not enjoy long-term careers or good fringe benefits.[58]

Accordingly, the consequence that the labor market has become increasingly characterized by risk or insecurity does not only apply to service sectors, as some have pointed out,[59] but has in fact expanded to all other "higher" professions, such as the innovative industries.[60] In general, company flexibility has been gained at the expense of employee job security;[61] many institutional arrangements in employment relationships that were developed during the past century, especially during the Cold-War capitalist era, have come to their end, leading to new gains for capital/employers but greater disadvantages for labor/employees. The labor market of global capitalism, therefore, becomes "a place of precarious employment" where at the extreme workers are "hired and fired at will by employers."[62]

[58] Yoshi-Fumi Nakata and Satoru Miyazaki, "Increasing Labor Flexibility during the Recession in Japan: The Role of Female Workers in Manufacturing," in Clair Brown, Barry Eichengreen, and Michael Reich eds., *Labor in the Era of Globalization*, Cambridge University Press, 2010, pp. 191–210. Also, Yoshi-Fumi Nakata and Satoru Miyazaki, "Has Lifetime Employment Become Extinct in Japanese Enterprise? An Empirical Analysis of Employment Adjustment Pracices in Japanese Companies," *Asian Business and Management* 6 (2007): 5–8. The similar trend is also observed in other East Asian nations such as South Korea. See, for example, Ki Seong Park and Donggyun Shin, "Income Polarization and Rising Social Unrest," pp. 83–109; Joonmo Cho, "Institutional Insecurity and Dissipation of Economic Efficiency from the Labor Market Flexibility in the Korean Labor Market," pp. 110–134; both in Joonmo Cho, Richard B. Freeman, Jae-Ho Keum and Sunwoong Kim eds., *The Korean Labor Market After the 1997 Economic Crisis*, London: Routledge, 2012.

[59] J. Allen and N. Henry, "Ulrich Beck's Risk Society at Work: Labour and Employment in the Contract Services Industries," *Transactions of the Institute of British Geographers*, 22, 2 (1997): 180–196; Suzanne Reimer, "Working in a Risk Society," *Transactions of the Institute of British Geographers*, 23, 1 (April 1998): 116–127.

[60] Gina Neff, *Venture Labor: Work and the Burden of Risk in Innovative Industries*, Cambridge, MA: MIT Press, 2012.

[61] Ibid.   [62] Martin, "Local Labour Markets," p. 468.

It is impossible for this chapter to present a comprehensive picture of migrant workers worldwide in terms of both intraregional and domestic fronts, but the brief discussion above helps to highlight how mobility of labor in its interaction with global capital's concentration is inclined to further disadvantage those weaker groups, in contrast to such groups' expectation of improving their life via mobility. In the Global South, the economic state is, as is often the case with ineffective democracies or without democratic participatory channels, even keener than its industrial democracy counterpart to promote economic performance and attract capital investment at the price of labor's pay, security, and rights. Sweatshops are such an example, which have proliferated in developing countries while also re-rising in the developed world with immigrants as workers.[63] All have pushed the entire labor market in the direction of more "flexible," or, in this chapter's interpretation, more unstable and less safe conditions for employees.

The advantage that capital has gained over labor through globalization, I would maintain, is institutionally rooted in the changing political economy of global capitalism, which can be analyzed in at least two aspects: first, the convenience of capital flow versus the inconvenience of labor mobility; second, the increasing involvement of labor in the global capitalist market. Global movements of capital are obviously

---

[63] There are already numerous empirical studies in this regard, thus, considering space limits, the current chapter chooses to not go into details. For the prevalence of sweatshops in the Global South, taking China as an example, see Michael A. Santoro, *Profits and Principles: Global Capitalism and Human Rights in China*, Ithaca: Cornell University Press, 2000; Chan, *China's Workers under Assault*; Pun, *Made in China*; Jaesok Kim, *Chinese Labor in a Korean Factory: Class, Ethnicity, and Productivity on the Shop Floor in Globalizing China*, Stanford University Press, 2013. For the resurgence of sweatshops in industrialized countries such as the United States, see, for example, Edna Bonacich and John Modell, *Behind the Label: Inequality in the Los Angeles Apparel Industry*, Berkeley: University of California Press, 2000; Daniel E. Bender and Richard A. Greenwald eds., *Sweatshop USA: The American Sweatshop in Historical and Global Perspective*, New York: Routledge, 2003; Robert J. S. Ross, *Slaves to Fashion: Poverty and Abuse in the New Sweatshops*, Ann Arbor: University of Michigan Press, 2004. Also, Ellen Rosen, *Making Sweatshops: The Globalization of the U.S. Apparel Industry*, Berkeley: University of California Press, 2002; Jennifer Gordon, *Suburban Sweatshops: The Fight for Immigrant Rights*, Cambridge, MA: Harvard University Press, 2009; Benjamin Powell, *Out of Poverty: Sweatshops in the Global Economy*, Cambridge University Press, 2014.

a major cause of this new arrangement of labor institutions. According to an expert:

> As global production lines are turned more and more closely to changes in the market, employers use the flexibility of the contract-labor system to adjust quickly. Capital has to be flexible, able to move where it can earn the greatest return, and permanent employment only gets in the way. When a garment goes out of fashion, or a piece of medical or electronic equipment becomes obsolete, the workers who produce it become expendable. Production of new product lines requires new workers, often in completely different locations.[64]

Yes, global competitive pressure explains why capital is inclined to move, leaving workers behind who lack the same convenience of moving without the jobs they previously had. Moreover, when the firms maximize profits and minimize costs in the move, the principal cost to minimize is labor; thus capital often finds cheaper labor in the new location where they have new employees. "Precisely because place matters, firms are able to 'cost hunt' by relocating and tapping into less costly and/or more pliant 'greenfield' local labour markets."[65] But that does not explain *how* capital can move so conveniently to meet the challenge of competitive pressure, especially in the age of globalization when labor mobility has also increased to respond to the pressure. The point this chapter would emphasize is that the contrast between different capabilities of movement of capital and labor should not be understood only in terms of the physical convenience that capital may possess over labor, but, more importantly, in terms of an institutional convenience facilitated by the state-market nexus for capital flow under neoliberalism. The impact of the state-market nexus on labor's mobility, however, is fundamentally different, and we will discuss this in a later section. Exactly because of the institutional convenience of movement, capital can successfully erode the strength of labor.

Only when such a possibility of relocation is not present, this chapter further argues, does the possibility of labor mobility emerge. In other words, when capital cannot move geographically to meet the challenges

---

[64] Bacon, *Illegal People*, p. 76.

[65] Trevor Barnes, Roger Hayter, and Eric Grass, "MacMillan Bloedel: Corporate Restructuring and Employment Change," in Marc de Smidt and Egbert Wever eds., *The Corporate Firms in a Changing World Economy: Case Studies in the Geography of Enterprise*, London: Routledge, 1990, pp. 145–165 (p. 147). Also, Doreen Massey, *Spatial Divisions of Labour: Social Relations and the Geography of Production*, London: Macmillan, 1995, 2nd ed.

and seize the opportunities of business operation, it has to turn to the promotion of labor mobility for its own benefits. The best demonstration of this point is that the rise of the service sector, which is usually labor intensive and location-bound, powerfully promotes labor mobility, but, on the other hand, limits migrant workers' choices on the job market. As an expert has observed, "migrants are now a vital part of the service industry workforce in most developed countries. As the most recent job seekers, they begin in the most marginal and contingent jobs."[66] Our earlier discussion of "labor flexibility" has also touched on this. The service economy, therefore, helps to explain the counterintuitive situation of labor mobility in which moving is often done for the sake of disadvantageous jobs.

The global triumph of capitalism means that many populaces in the world who previously lived outside of the capitalist system are now involved in the global labor market. Such a huge increase to the labor supply also helps to explain the institutional change in the employment relationship toward disfavoring labor. As mentioned earlier, no more than 3 percent of the world's population lives outside of their country of origin, a fact that often supports a cautious voice warning not to exaggerate the current global phenomenon of immigration.[67] In a similar vein, migrant workers, though a greater number than before, are still a small section of the entire labor population of the world. As emphasized at the beginning of this chapter, the global market cannot be fairly understood with attention given only to those in mobility; those who are in immobility are significant not only due to the logic that, as two experts point out, those who haven't migrated make up "a huge reservoir of potential emigrants,"[68] but, in my point of view, they constitute the largest, and often the cheapest, section of the global labor market. In other words, both those who are on the move and those who are not are simultaneously presented in the global labor market because of virtually every country's involvement in globalization; the global triumph of capitalism in this sense simply means the global inclusion of every laborer into its labor-market mechanisms. Therefore, as the same authors quoted above write, "newly emerging economies, in particular China, are beginning to enter the world labor market in a much bigger way than before."[69] This has unprecedentedly enlarged the supply of

---

[66] Bacon, *Illegal People*, p. 73.   [67] Samers, *Migration*, p. 299.
[68] Massey and Taylor, "Introduction," p. 2.   [69] Ibid.

labor to the global labor market, an advantage the employers shall definitely take.

Segmentation Enhanced in Transnational Integration: The Dialectic Dynamics of the Global Labor Market

The most populated supply of labor, this chapter would emphasize, lies with those who are not involved in geographic movement but are also covered by the global reach of capitalism in terms of production and consumption. In comparison with those people on the move examined above, who make up a small percentage of the world population, those who are not on move are the gigantic base of the iceberg beneath the surface of the water in the global labor market. This part of labor force, however, can easily be overlooked for their position and impact on the entire global labor market, especially when the increasing mobility of labor has, not unreasonably, attracted much attention in relevant studies.

Why and how do those who are not on move matter in understanding the global labor market? The answer can be explained primarily from a market angle: in the so-called price of labor on the market, this is the portion often with either the lowest price in the absolute sense, usually among those in the Global South who are not able to engage themselves in mobility to seek better opportunities on the global labor market, or, for many in the Global North, exactly due to their immobility, with lower competitiveness in the relative sense. As the global reach of capitalism in this context basically means the involvement of labor forces in the Global South in the global labor market, the discussion here will focus on those in the Global South, while the issues concerning Global North laborers will be analyzed in Chapter 6 mainly from a sociopolitical perspective. Although the discussions above have highlighted economic disadvantages that migrant workers in both international and non-international terms have to face in their relationships with capital, it must not be forgotten that the majority of the developing world who are not involved in international immigration or job-seeking migration may suffer more in the purely economic sense, as they can be stuck in what Carling calls an "involuntary immobility,"[70] namely, unable to pursue

---

[70] Jørgen Carling, "Migration in the Age of Involuntary Immobility: Theoretical Reflections and Cape Verdean Experiences," *Journal of Ethnic and Migration Studies*, 28, 1 (2002): 5–42.

and realize mobility even though many of them may desire it. Their income and material living conditions are often even lower and worse than those who are involved in migration.

It is easy to understand that those who haven't migrated form "a huge reservoir of potential emigrants"[71] and, thus, may actually provide a huge reservoir of potential competitors with those who are mobile within the global labor market, indirectly but negatively influencing the price of those who are in mobility. The underlying assumption for this chapter, therefore, is twofold: the increase of mobile labor has promoted the integration of the global labor market; it has also, in turn, helped to highlight the existence of the huge labor force on the global labor market in virtually immobility. In other words, the growing significance of the mobile elements of labor and the profound impacts of the immobile elements on the global labor market are complementary to each other. It is their linkage and interactions, therefore, rather than simply labor mobility, that must be the key for understanding the entire picture of the global labor market.

It is based on this assumption that this section would emphasize the segmentation of the global labor market brought about by the global triumph of capitalism. This is an updated and refreshed conceptualization of the traditional segmentation theory of the labor market, as this global segmentation theory emphasizes four new features of labor segmentation, which are: 1) the dynamic interactions between increasing transnational integration and deepening segmentation of the global labor market; 2) the linchpin position of labor mobility in creating new forms of segmentation of the global labor market; 3) the operating fluidity of such structural segmentation in accordance to the globalization of the capitalist economy; and 4) "comparative disadvantages" of different segments of labor in the face of capital on the global labor market. Below, each of them will be discussed.

Labor segmentation theory has existed for a long time in labor studies, with historical antecedents of the labor market segmentation thesis being traced back as early as to Alfred Marshall and even Adam Smith. It was systematically discussed first, however, by Clark Kerr in the 1950s, who employed the feudal metaphors of guild, manorial, and

---

[71]　Massey and Taylor, "Introduction," p. 2.

free agency to label each of the labor market segments.[72] His triple categories were developed into two different schemes in the early 1970s, with Gordon subsequently reducing the categories to two in his "dual labor market" theory,[73] while Doeringer and Piore at about the same time in effect re-labeled Kerr's original categories respectively as, primary independent, primary subordinate, and secondary.[74] Following a later line, Loveridge and Mok advocate the addition of a fourth labor market segment to the original trichotomous scheme of Doeringer and Piore by also subdividing the secondary segment into independent and subordinate components, making a quartet framework to explain segmentations of the labor market.[75] According to a summary in a literature review,

The argument for each one of these different typologies is in effect the same: the labor market is not perfectly competitive but is divided into non-competing segments. Each segment, however, provides a quite different set of employment relations. Crudely, the primary segment is characterized by "high wages, good working conditions, employment stability, chances of advancement, equity, and due process in the administration of work rules", while jobs in the secondary labour market tend to have "low wages and fringe benefits, poor working conditions, high labour turnover, little chance of advancement, and often arbitrary and capricious supervision."[76]

Different from the above emphasis on non-competing segments of the labor market, the current chapter suggests an understanding of the segmentation of the global labor market with dynamics primarily emerging between increasing transnational integration of the labor market via globalization, on one hand, and deepening segmentation

---

[72] Clark Kerr, "Labor Markets: Their Character and Consequences," *American Economic Review, Papers and Proceedings*, 40 (1950): 278–291; Clark Kerr, "The Balkanization of Labor Markets," in E. Wright Bakke ed., *Labor Mobility and Economic Opportunity*, Cambridge, MA: MIT Press, 1954, pp. 92–110.

[73] David M. Gordon, *Theories of Poverty and Underemployment*, Lexington: D. C. Heath, 1973.

[74] P. B. Doeringer and M. J. Piore, *International Labour Markets and Manpower Analysis*, Lexington: D. C. Heath, 1971.

[75] R. Loveridge and A. L. Mok, "Theoretical Approaches to Segmented Labour Markets," *International Journal of Social Economics* 7 (1979): 376–411; R. Loveridge and A. L. Mok, *Theories of Labour Market Segmentation: A Critique*, The Hague: Martinus Nijhoff Social Sciences Division, 1979. Also, Frank Wilkinson ed., *The Dynamics of Labor Market Segmentation*, New York: Academic Press, 1981.

[76] Barnes, Hayter, and Grass, "MacMillan Bloedel," p. 148.

of the same labor market on a global scale, on the other. Yes, global capitalism has made a trend of integration of the global labor market in the senses that all nations are connected to one another and that the global mobility of labor physically makes and reflects such connections. Various economic and social theories, accordingly, have emerged in belief that "the study of worker flows – across jobs, across cities, across industries, across occupations – is a core topic in labor economics."[77] They, of course, emphasize the integration and transnationalization of the global labor market:

These developments reflect tendencies towards the integration of distant labour markets. Such tendencies might be expected to produce some convergence in wage rates (both North and South), most especially for the skilled, but overall there is a growing divergence between rates for skilled and unskilled workers, given the preponderance of the latter among migrants and within the South ... Migration is of growing significance to the transnationalization of labour markets, and economic activity more generally.[78]

Some economic geographers, meanwhile, work on the concept of "local labor markets" that carries with it an assumption of the non-existence or at least insignificance of a general, global market of labor. Yet this point subscribes to the belief that

the labour market has an *intrinsically local level of operation and regulation*, that the creation and destruction of jobs, and the process of employment, unemployment, and wage setting, and the institutional and social regulation of these processes, to some extent at least, are locally constituted. It is within specific spatial settings and contexts – 'local labour markets' – that workers seek employment and employers hire and fire workers, that particular forms of employment structures evolve, that specific employment practices, work cultures, and labour relations become established, and particular institutionalized modes of labour regulation emerge or are imposed.[79]

This chapter, however, while neither denying the trend toward transnationalization and integration of the global labor market nor downgrading the importance of local labor markets, argues that, on one hand, the trend of transnationalization and global integration has been highly uneven and imbalanced, particularly alongside a central

[77] Borjas, *Immigration Economics*, p. 2.
[78] Held and McGrew, *Globalization/Anti-Globalization*, p. 96.
[79] Martin, "Local labour Markets," p. 456.

axis of mobility, where the so-called global hierarchy of mobility has emerged with the increase of labor's geographic movements;[80] on the other hand, local labor markets are now working under the general institutional framework of global capitalism rather than operating in separate worlds, thus the interconnections and interactions of local labor markets deserve emphatic attention. Global capitalism, therefore, dialectically links various local labor markets with each other and integrates them into the global labor market while creating greater tension than before and deepening cracks and gaps among local labor markets or within the global labor market, thereby shaping the division, segmentation, and fragmentation of the globally integrating labor market. In this sense, the insight of economist Dani Roderik on "social disintegration as the price of economic integration" in the globalization process can be extended to a point of view that integration and disintegration of the global market, economy, and society are simply two sides of the same token, mainly not for "economic" and "social" but for capital and labor.[81]

The second effort this chapter makes to reconceptualize labor segmentation theory lies in the highlighting of labor mobility as a central axis alongside which certain major demarcations of labor segments can be observed. As examined above, the rise of wide-scale yet still restricted human mobility in globalization connects together the various forms of labor markets in different parts of the world, integrates them in the sense that the laborers' fates are mutually influenced by each other and by their different bargaining positions with global capital, and, significantly, divides them in terms of their different degrees of freedom in choosing locations for maximizing their prices on the global labor market. Although this chapter is reluctant to suggest any fixed categorization of labor segments (the rationale will be elaborated upon later in this section), the different degrees of mobility actualized by laborers still stand out prominently, though roughly, as indicators for certain lines along which segmentation can be discussed. In fact, this chapter is basically structured in line with this consideration, starting its examination of labor in global capitalism with international immigrants, then other forms of migrant workers,

[80] Zygmunt Bauman, *Globalization: The Human Consequences*, New York: Columbia University Press, 1998.
[81] Dani Rodrik, *Has Globalization Gone Too Far?* Washington, DC: Institute for International Economics, 1997, p. 69.

and eventually taking into account labor in immobility as part of a wider picture by recognizing a fundamental divide among these non-movers into two groups, namely, those living in a place where many others come to join the local labor market, and those who are bound to the local labor market with a net outflow of labor.

The third feature of the global labor market, namely, the great diversity and the fluidity of labor segments, must be emphasized in conjunction with the above point on the significance of mobility in dominating the fundamental demarcation lines on the global labor market. Instead of suggesting a fixed scheme of labor segmentation as the intellectual tradition since Clark Kerr has done, I would argue that mainly due to both the rise of global capitalism and the existence of varieties of capitalism as well as extremely numerous and complicated non-economic factors, the global map of the labor market is teeming with tangled demarcations and countless segments, which it is impossible to exhaust. Only in a given empirical circumstance, or in the sense of something that may be termed micro-labor economics, is it viable and meaningful to present a context-specific categorization of labor segments. On the level that may belong to macro-labor economics, however, the thick lines of demarcation among segments can still be highlighted, which, this chapter maintains, appear along the axis of various forms of labor mobility wrought by globalization.

A number of examples can help to demonstrate the above principles of understanding labor market segmentation. One example appears between labor which has already established its status in industrial societies and all other forms of labor, including immigrants, having on one side of the demarcation the well-established work forces who have held citizenship for generations, in contrast to those new immigrants who, whether citizens or not, are unprivileged on the labor market. Numerous researchers have found, "whether manufacturing is exported to low-wage areas or migrants are imported to work in metropolitan service sectors, the distinctions between established workers, privileged foreigners and helot labourers have remained and may even have deepened."[82] Immigrant workers, therefore, in the case of the United States, gain access to US labor markets by either accepting low wages or taking jobs for which they are overqualified, despite

---

[82] Robin Cohen, *Migration and Its Enemies: Global Capital, Migrant Labour and the Nation-State*, Aldershot: Ashgate, 2006, p. 1.

society's mainstream cultural value of equity.[83] Furthermore, as the case of the United States also helps to show, "newly arrived immigrants and immigrants with some tenure in the United States are perhaps most likely to be in direct competition with one another in the U.S. labor market."[84] That is to say, individual qualifications such as education and skills can be overwhelmed by a social dividing based upon the duration for which the laborers have been in the local labor market; human capital alone does not account for the economic success of immigrants, but immigrants instead often encounter barriers based on group membership rather than on individual characteristics such as their skills. To this author, different lines of dividing present themselves in these cases, while the dominating significance of mobility in dividing labor is also palpable.

A similar example against migrant workers can be observed between native residents in less-industrialized nations and those who move into the local labor market via geographical mobility. For instance, Alicia Maguid contends that the Buenos Aires labor market has become segmented along immigration lines, as immigrants from neighboring countries are selectively inserted into manual jobs, particularly in construction and domestic service, the jobs rejected by the native population because of their low wages, instability, limited benefits, and hazardous working conditions.[85] According to editors of a leading volume on international migration in the global labor market, this is a general scenario across countries: "It seems that the space the labor market allows for immigrant workers narrows when the labour market contracts. In general, the concentration of immigrants is highest in

---

[83] Min Zhou, "Immigrants in the U.S. Economy," in Douglas S. Massey and J. Edward Taylor eds., *International Migration: Prospects and Policies in a Global Market*, Oxford University Press, 2004, pp. 131–153. Also, Michael J. Piore, *Birds of Passage: Migrant Labor in Industrial Societies*, Cambridge University Press, 1979; J. Edward Taylor, "Earnings and Mobility of Legal and Illegal Immigrant Workers in Agriculture," *American Journal of Agricultural Economics*, 74 (1992): 889–896.

[84] David Card and Steven Raphael, "Introduction," in David Card and Steven Raphael eds., *Immigration, Poverty, and Socioeconomic Inequality*, New York: Russell Sage Foundation, 2013, pp. 1–26 (p. 1).

[85] Alicia Maguid, "Immigration and the Labor Market in Metropolitan Buenos Aires," in Douglas S. Massey and J. Edward Taylor eds., *International Migration: Prospects and Policies in a Global Market*, Oxford University Press, 2004, pp. 104–119.

those sectors which have always been more flexible and unfavorable in terms of salary levels and working conditions."[86]

What deserves emphasis is that the above examples should not be regarded as fixed segment categories; this fluid approach is different from earlier attempts to identify and label a certain number of segments of the labor market. At the same time, these examples help to highlight how the increase of labor mobility has worked to affect local labor markets and, therefore, how it has worked as a major factor among various forces in reconfiguring the segmentation of the global labor market. Together, the approach employed here tries to avoid any attempt to grid those segments along fixed dimensions. Such a flexible approach helps to keep the segmentation theory more dynamic than otherwise, and that it leaves open the possibility for interpreting labor segmentations in different ways, such as, for example, the differentiation of skilled workers versus unskilled, professional versus blue-collar, and legal migrants versus illegal laborers. Due to global capitalism's great irregularities and internal gaps, there are too many segments on the global labor market to be neatly categorized in a general analysis; no fixed, single scheme can demarcate all existing labor segments.

Instead, context-specific investigations of segments should be adopted. For example, in addition to those differentiations alongside migrant workers mentioned earlier, regional differences within a nation and even a city also divide the labor market, as does the rise of the so-called new service economy. In the former regard, an expert summarizes in this way:

While some areas are attracting concentrations of highly skilled, highly paid employment, entrenched joblessness or inferior forms of low-skill, low-wage work have dominated others. Within most major cities, areas of mass unemployment, poverty, and social exclusion coexist with other areas of successful, high-income professional workers.[87]

In the latter, "the new 'service' economy is highly specialized and fragmented, and is characterized by strictly segmented labor markets, a growing differentiation in terms of labor conditions, salaries, security, or flexibility."[88]

---

[86] Massey and Taylor, "Introduction," p. 6.
[87] Martin, "Local Labour Markets," p. 457.
[88] Erik Swyngedouw, "Elite Power, Global Forces, and the Political Economy of 'Glocal' Development," in Gordon L. Clark, Maryann P. Feldman, and Meric S.

Even among those living in involuntary or natural immobility in the Global South, who, as this chapter constantly addresses, should not be left outside of an analysis of the global labor markets of capitalism, there is still substantial room for further segmentation in various manifestations, some of which are relevant to their different connections with those on the move. For these people, whom Paul Collier calls "the bottom billion," emigration, generally speaking, "helps those who leave, but it can have perverse effects on those left behind, especially if it selectively removes the educated."[89] Those among them, however, who have family connections with international immigrants to industrialized nations often receive remittance, and from this, accordingly, their economic status may benefit and their positions on the local labor markets could be somehow improved against those who have no such financial sources.[90]

Now let's turn to the fourth point of the refreshed labor segmentation theory, which suggests that such segmentations structurally and institutionally disfavor and disadvantage various and all groups of labor, especially in their competitive relationships that deal with capital and the state. Existing segmentation theories did pay special attention to the impact of labor market segmentation over labor-capital relations, but were often inclined to argue that different segments had discriminative relationships with capital. For example, in terms of "primary" and "secondary" labor markets, it is stated that

Because of the differences between the two labour markets, it is generally believed that lay-off decisions by firms discriminate between labour market segments. In particular, it is argued that because firms have made considerable "fixed" investment in terms of recruitment and firm-specific

Gertler eds., *The Oxford Handbook of Economic Geography*, Oxford University Press, 2000, pp. 541–558 (p. 545).

[89] Paul Collier, *The Bottom Billion: Why the Poorest Countries Are Failing and What Can Be Done About It*, Oxford University Press, 2007, pp. 93, 94.

[90] J. Edward Taylor, "Remittance, Savings, and Development in Migrant-Sending Areas," pp. 157–173; and Graeme Hugo and Charles Stahl, "Labor Export Strategies in Asia," pp. 174–200; both in Douglas S. Massey and J. Edward Taylor eds., *International Migration: Prospects and Policies in a Global Market*, Oxford University Press, 2004. Also, for the argument that remittances have large poverty-reducing effects, see, for instance, Pablo Acosta, Pablo Fajnzylber, and J. Humberto Lopez, "The Impact of Remittances on Poverty and Human Capital: Evidence from Latin American Household Surveys," in Çağlar Özden and Maurice Schiff eds., *International Migration, Economic Development, and Policy*, New York: Palgrave Macmillan and the World Bank, 2007, pp. 59–98.

training within the primary labour market (firms create an internal labour market), they are reluctant to shed this labour segment. In contrast, the secondary labour market consists of workers who either have general skills or very few skills, and are therefore extremely vulnerable to lay-offs (firms easily hire and fire because of an external labour market).[91]

Due to limited space, this is not a proper place to systematically analyze why such a differentiation of labor segments cannot benefit one segment at the cost of others. The discussion in the last section around "labor flexibility" leading to an overall trend of de-permanentization helps to demonstrate how the macro, structural feature works together with the micro, operational feature of the global labor market to cause a spiral effect that disfavors labor, in which certain segments of labor may temporarily gain better deals with capital than other segments; in the long run and in general, the internal competition within labor forces as such enhances capital's bargaining position against all laborers.

Some economists, however, believe that "The movement of workers from a low-paying to a high-paying sector creates competitive forces that tend to equalize wages in the two sectors."[92] According to a leading expert of labor economics,

A central lesson of economics is that the equalization of a worker's value of marginal product across markets yields an efficient allocation of workers to jobs, allocation that maximizes the total value of worker product in a competitive economy. From this perspective, migration is perhaps the key tool used by the labor market to iron out inefficiencies and to ensure that workers are allocated to those jobs where they are most productive.[93]

This might be true in a fully free, competitive market, but the labor market segmentation theory suggests that this market is far from free. The segmentation of the global labor market, therefore, helps to explain in a structural sense how mobility of labor cannot reach the goal of increasing economic equality. It must be pointed out that, in terms of consequences, labor segmentation greatly compromises the economic outcome of labor mobility in terms of equalization.

It has been clear that the global reach of capitalism can provide new momentum for the application, revitalization, and reconceptualization of labor segmentation theories, and, wrapping up our discussions on

[91] Barnes, Hayter, and Grass, "MacMillan Bloedel," pp. 148–149.
[92] Borjas, *Immigration Economics*, p. 2.   [93] Ibid.

labor-market segmentation, this section does not intend to contribute a new scheme of segment division with fixed boundaries among a certain number of segments, but simply attempts to highlight the following points: 1) The global labor markets are widely, deeply, and fundamentally segmented in many different ways; 2) it is the global reach of capitalism that intrinsically intensifies such balkanization, because it dialectically connects the significantly unbalanced world of labor; 3) segmentation as the internal dynamic of the global labor market has reduced the bargaining position of each and all groups of labor in dealing with capital.

The State in Enhancing Capital-Labor Power Imbalance: Triangular Interactions under Institutions of Global Capitalism

One of the most fundamental causes of the imbalance of labor segmentation and labor-capital relations, this chapter would further argue, lies in the institutional framework of global capitalism around the state-market nexus that has been discussed in Chapter 2. This section, therefore, extends the discussion of the global labor market to some general interactions among labor, capital, and the state, often around the niche of human mobility/immobility, especially in regards to how such interactions further disadvantage labor. It should be pointed out that I take the state as an analytical entity and wish to emphasize its conceptual relationships with capital, on one hand, and with labor, on the other hand. This is different from a perspective focusing on state-state relationships when considering the state in migration studies, with which the securitization of human mobility, especially of international immigration, has often become a major issue.[94] Instead, my approach is more similar to what the state-society perspective suggests,[95] as it likes

---

[94] See, for example, Aythan Kaya, *Islam, Migration and Integration: The Age of Securitization*, New York: Palgrave Macmillan, 2009; Rens van Munster, *Securitizing Immigration: The Politics of Risk in the EU*, New York: Palgrave Macmillan, 2009; Philippe Bourbeau, *The Securitization of Migration: A Study of Movement and Order*, London: Routledge, 2011; Ariane Chebel d'Appollonia, *Migrant Mobilization and Securitization in the US and Europe: How Does It Feel to Be a Threat?* New York: Palgrave Macmillan, 2015.

[95] Such as that is demonstrated in: Alfred Stepan, *The State and Society: Peru in Comparative Perspective*, Princeton University Press, 1978; Joel S. Migdal, Atul Kohli, and Vivienne Shue eds., *State Power and Social Forces: Domination and Transformation in the Third World*, Cambridge University Press, 1994.

to highlight how the state as one of the most significant institutional actors acts under globalization against labor's interests.

The state, first of all, hinders labor mobility with sovereign control of citizenship, which can be in sharp contrast with virtually all states' neoliberal policy of allowing the flow of capital with a much greater degree of freedom. Despite many disputes around globalization, experts have agreed on the point that labor mobility is much more inconvenient than capital. For example, Held and McGrew maintain that "by comparison with capital and goods, labour is relatively much more immobile."[96] What should be added, and indeed emphasized, is that such relative immobility of labor against capital is not only rooted in the physical and social inconveniences encountered by labor forces in geographic movements; institutional restrictions, mainly those imposed by the state, play a significant role in hindering labor's mobility across country borders and, in many cases, even within a nation. In fact, physical obstacles have obviously become much easier to overcome in the globalizing world with the conveniences provided by revolutions in transportation, communication, and relevant technologies; at least, they cannot be more effective in the twenty-first century than before in preventing people from moving around. State sovereignty and the state system in general, however, is able to mobilize coercive power for impeding human mobility across nations, especially human mobility in the sense of labor's movement (in contrast to travel etc.). While all states have more or less adopted neoliberal policies favoring and promoting capital flows, their policies toward labor mobility, by contrast, are much less liberal, and still fundamentally restrictive. As Massey and Taylor have observed, "There is a striking juxtaposition and, in some eyes, contradiction in the policies that increase the free movement of goods and capital across nations but leave migration – the movement of people – off the negotiating table."[97] In a similar vein, Elliott, Mayadas, and Segal make a contrast in which "goods and capital assets flow freely in the global market, while labor movement is severely restricted,"[98] and Spellman implicitly directs the reason of such to the state by saying, "at the very moment when ideas, money, business, manufacturing

---

[96] Held and McGrew, *Globalization/Anti-Globalization*, pp. 94–5.
[97] Massey and Taylor, "Introduction," p. 4.
[98] Elliott, Mayadas, and Segal, "Immigration Worldwide: Trends and Analysis," p. 18.

and products move ever more easily across international borders, restrictions on the movement of humans across those same borders have become more rigorous."[99]

Many states did relax their immigration policies in the globalization age, as best exemplified by Japan, a nation to which, traditionally, it has been extremely difficult for foreigners to migrate. This took place, however, predominantly because of the pressure of a fast aging population and, accordingly, for the purpose of revitalizing the economy with additional labor supplies.[100] This policy adjustment may also be regarded as a kind of "labor flexibility," what the state-market nexus promotes for the general benefit of capital in industrialized nations. Again, to quote Martin,

On the one side, advancing technologies and intensifying global competition are constantly restructuring regional and local economies, with destabilizing consequences for their workforces. On the other side, states are busy deregulating and reregulating local labour markets and decentralizing labour market policies so as to increase the flexibilities of regions and localities, whilst at the same time seeking ways of curbing expenditure on welfare and social security as part of their attempts to control public spending and reduce personal taxation. To the end, labour market policies have become more supply-side orientated and more targeted to the needs of labour market flexibility.[101]

In other words, it is a response made by the economic state to market demands, mainly in accordance with capital's needs.

A historical comparison may help to enforce the above argument. As a comprehensive system of sovereign power that has in the past century been dramatically expanding its coverage of more and more aspects of human life, the state regulates, constrains, and governs human mobility in general and migration in particular not only through its migration regime and relevant policies, but also through complicated, multifaceted arrangements. The state, as it is well known, has greatly expanded its role since the First World War. During the same historical period when

[99] Spellman, *Uncertain Identity*, p. 11.
[100] Reiji Yoshida, "Japan's Immigration Policy Rift Widens as Population Decline Forces Need for Foreign Workers," *The Japan Times*, November 25, 2015, www.japantimes.co.jp/news/2015/11/25/national/politics-diplomacy/japans-immigration-policy-rift-widens-population-decline-forces-need-for-foreign-workers/#.V09jPcvjQ_U, accessed March 4, 2016.
[101] Martin, "Local Labour Markets," p. 469.

the state has been expanding, human mobility has, in spite of its recent reemergence with globalization, actually been declining, if a comparison is drawn between the years prior to the First World Wars and those after. According to Raphael Kaplinsky, the rate of emigration was "startling" in many countries during the hundred years or so prior to the First World War, as

[A]pproximately 60 million Europeans emigrated to the USA between 1820 and 1914, and a similar number moved from China and India to surrounding countries ... [i]n the 1880s, more than 140 people in every thousand emigrated from Ireland, and almost 100 in every thousand from Norway. Between 1900 and 1910, more than 100 per thousand emigrated from Italy. At the same time, immigration rates into some countries were equally significant. In the first decade of the twentieth century, the rate of immigration was around 300 per thousand residents in Argentina, 160 per thousand in Canada, and more than 100 per thousand in the USA.[102]

But, "[T]here were no equivalent flows of people in the latter twentieth century. Whereas the proportion of global population living in countries in which they were not citizens was 10 per cent in 1900, in 2000 it was around 2 per cent."[103] Though there is no systematic research showing the direct causal line between the growth of state power and this historical reduction of international immigration, the parallel, obviously, is not coincidental.

The political and institutional dynamics of the segmentation of the global labor markets must also be considered against this background. This section argues that it is the measures taken by capital and the state that have created the segmentation of the global labor markets. Institutionally, the state sponsors a system in which a hierarchy of citizens and residents is developed to create a series of differentiations and discriminations, such as those among native citizens, aboriginal people, naturalized citizens, immigrants, visitors, and illegals. Politically, this helps to repress various fundamental rights of the non-citizens. From the point of view of market operations, together they repress the price of non-citizens on the labor market.

Capital plays a major role in this regard, of course; as discussed earlier, it does so often under the slogan of labor flexibility within the

---

[102] Raphael Kaplinsky, *Globalization, Poverty and Inequality: Between a Rock and a Hard Place*, Cambridge: Polity, 2005, p. 21.
[103] Ibid.

institutional framework of globalization. The so-called free global market described in Chapter 2 as that which is beyond possible popular influences rhetorically exercised by democratic participation provides a major facility in this regard. As an expert of the labor market has summarized,

One of the factors singled out by academics and governments alike as driving this new imperative of 'flexibility' is economic globalization. The growth of global markets, global companies, and global competition, so the argument goes, is 'delocalizing' local labour markets. The domestic prices of consumer goods, financial assets, and even labour are governed less and less by local and national conditions: they increasingly react to and reflect prices elsewhere in the global system.[104]

Nurtured by such macro-institutional conditions, big business can easily utilize and manipulate, as well as be adapted to, the combination of global integration and segmentation of the labor markets against labor. To continue a quotation from Martin:

Multinational companies break up the chains of production of their products or services and locate the links in different localities around the world, depending on what appears to be the most profitable at the time. Global capitalism is leading to the intensification of economic relations and the displacement of activities from their local connections and contexts into networks of relationships whose reach is distant or worldwide. Local labour thus becomes vulnerable to economic changes and developments happening in remote locations.[105]

On the side of labor, however, such global economic connections often stimulate and intensify internal conflicts among different groups, regions, and segments of workers. In addition to market competition that has been discussed in the last section, one such conflict is by nature social, which arises with increasing immigration to industrialized welfare societies, as new arrivals from foreign countries are often blamed as one of the major causes of the decline of citizens' social welfare. For example, in the United States, it is said that

Many of the newest immigrants have entered the country with low skills and low levels of education during an era when federal resources for fighting poverty are shrinking. In many areas of the country, the sheer volume of new immigrants has created enormous drains on educational

[104] Martin, "Local Labour Markets," p. 465.   [105] Ibid, pp. 465–6.

institutions, hospitals and clinics, jails and prisons, and the supply of low-income housing.[106]

The immigrants' benefits, in fact, are generally much worse than those of the citizens; the social conflict, however, is directed at these poor people for various political and cultural reasons.

In a similar vein, the participation of cheaper labor in developing countries in the global economy is frequently viewed by labor in industrialized nations as having robbed them of their employment opportunities, while capital's move into developing countries for the maximization of profits, justified by the promotion of competitiveness, can somehow be ignored for its responsibility in creating the problem. The state, especially with the rise of the economic state, which heavily depends on capital's profit-making for enhancing national competitiveness, often intentionally, in both the outflow and inflow of capital, promotes such a misperception, as pointed out by an expert in this way:

In the new battleground of global trade, local workers are forced into direct conflict with other, often geographically distant, local workers over jobs. Under the conditions, many argue, unless local labour is flexible – in terms of skills, working arrangements, employment conditions, and especially wages – local workers risk losing their jobs to other, more flexible, and cheaper workers elsewhere. Both the OECD and the European Commission subscribe to versions of this argument, and individual governments (as in the UK, for example) respond to public outcries stemming from the local closure of foreign plants by pleading that, while they sympathize, it is 'all part of the global economy,' and thus beyond their control.[107]

The absence of effective governance of the global economy is, ironically, cited as an excuse, as if the factories had been located nowhere before they were relocated for greater profits; the question of how outflow of capital easily takes place in its own interest at cost of labor's interest can simply be ignored by the state.

The decline of trade unions in the post–Cold War era has been widely observed across nations. For example, in Canada, a country traditionally having a high unionization rate, especially in comparison with the US,[108] the update statistics reveal an obvious declining curve of unionization rates from 1981 to 2014 (Figure 4.1), falling from 37.9 percent

---

[106] Swain, "Introduction," p. 3.　　[107] Martin, "Local Labour Markets," p. 466.
[108] Jason Clements, Niels Veldhuis, and Amela Karabegović, "Explaining Canada's High Unionization Rates," https://www.fraserinstitute.org/sites/

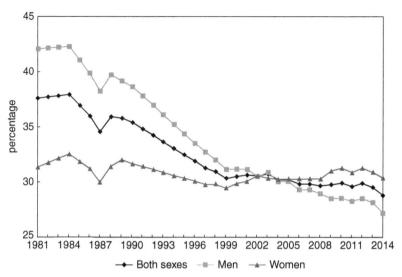

Figure 4.1 Declining Unionization Rate in Canada, 1981–2014
Source: www.statcan.gc.ca/pub/11-630-x/11-630-x2015005-eng.htm, accessed
March 4, 2016.

in 1984, the highest point in the period, to the lowest 28.8 in 2014.[109]
By contrast, the rate in the US in 2014 was 11.1 percent.[110] This trend
further demonstrates the weakening of labor in dealing with capital as
well as the state, since degree of unionization is a major indictor of
working-class strength and there is a positive correlation between
union strength and the development of welfare-state policies.[111]

Many factors explain such a decline, among which, this author
believes, the change of the labor market wrought by globalization
must not be underestimated. For example, this chapter has argued

        default/files/explaining-canadas-high-unionization-rates.pdf, The Fraser
        Institute, August 2005, accessed May 9, 2016.
[109]   Statistics of Canada, www.statcan.gc.ca/pub/11–630-x/11–630-x2015005-
        eng.htm, accessed May 9, 2016.
[110]   Bureau of Labor Statistics, United States Department of Labor, "Union
        Members Summary," www.bls.gov/news.release/union2.nr0.htm, accessed
        May 9, 2016.
[111]   Bo Rothstein, "Labor-Market Institutions and Working-Class Strength," in
        Sven Steinmo, Kathleen Thelen, and Frank Longstreth eds., *Structuring
        Politics: Historical Institutionalism in Comparative Analysis*, Cambridge
        University Press, 1992, pp. 33–56.

that globalization has fundamentally changed the supply of labor; labor fragmentation nevertheless increases the difficulties of collective action that labor may organize. "The main power resource unions possess is their control over the supply of labor power," according to a related study, and when unions are not able to control the supply of labor power, "capitalists are able to get labor power at a price below that which the unions have decided upon."[112] Immigration in particular helps to explain the weak momentum of unionization.[113]

The impact of the information revolution in this regard is also not evenly distributed to capital and labor. In contrast, it helps capital to be further globalized, more fluid, and more convenient in its coordination, while further balkanizing labor in a variety of ways. In fact, some experts have argued that the rise of post-Fordist capitalism with the information and communications technology revolution further disadvantages labor in general and trade unions in particular.

The power of trade unions to demarcate skill areas and negotiate employment levels was reduced, and the rewards given to the high-skilled computer whizz-kids substantially exceeded those given to the hamburger flippers. Income inequality increased as firms faced niche markets replacing mass markets. This emphasis on the technological basis of capitalist production finds further expression today in analyses of, for example, capitalism in the 'information age' in which the technological requirements of ICT are shown to have altered the way work takes place and the forms that it takes.[114]

Though space is limited here for further discussion in this regard, it should not be difficult to understand how various changes of the global market in particular, and globalization and its institutions in general weaken workers' unionization, strength of trade unions, and collective power of labor in dealing with capital.[115]

The triangular interactions of labor vis-à-vis capital and the state are far more complicated than what this section has been able to cover.

---

[112] Ibid, p. 37.

[113] Immanuel Ness, *Immigrant, Unions, and the U.S. Labor Market*, Philadelphia: Temple University Press, 2005.

[114] Paul Bowles, *Capitalism*, Harlow: Pearson Longman, 2007, p. 18.

[115] There are efforts to battle against this trend, of course. For example, see, Jeffrey Harrod and Robert O'Brien eds., *Global Unions? Theory and Strategies of Organized Labour in the Global Political Economy*, London: Routledge, 2002; Lowell Turner and Daniel B. Cornfield eds., *Labor in the New Urban Battleground: Local Solidarity in a Global Economy*, Ithaca: ILR Press, 2007.

However, it can be generally argued that the global labor market is, on a grand scale, shaped or reshaped powerfully by the institutions of global capitalism. The state-market nexus and the economic state, on one hand, facilitate capital's global movement in the latter's interest, but simultaneously create obstacles against labor's corresponding movement to counterbalance capital's predominant power in the bargaining game between capital and labor. As movements of capital are promoted by the state, have generally increased the concentration and density of money in economic and non-economic decision-making and have strategically strengthened the power of investment and production, various human movements, including international immigration, regional and domestic migration of workers, and other forms of the dislocation of peoples, result in the creation of new tensions and fragmentations not only within labor forces but also in labor's relationships with the state, thus putting labor in both its mobile and immobile forms at an economic, social, and political disadvantage versus capital. Moreover, institutions of global capitalism empower capital to negotiate new norms to rule the global labor market, leading to new uncertainties over labor's fate, even in purely economic realms. Overall, fundamental institutions of globalization greatly contribute to the segmentation of the global labor market while integrating the capital market, thus further reducing labor's bargaining power in general and each labor group's bargaining power in particular in dealing with well-coordinated global capital. The double splits of global capitalism, namely, the disjuncture between global capitalism and nation-state democracy, and the split between mixed national economies and the global free economy, have trapped labor in an institutional circumstance of being powerless to mobilize its collective strength.

From Social Poverty to Political Inability: Human Capital of Capitalism Against Social Capital of Democracy

Labor is not only labor; laborers are human beings, members of social groups, and citizens to public affairs. The "economic man" is still a human in all psychological, spiritual, cultural, social, and political aspects, rather than a robot that capital prefers to run without non-mechanical complicities. To understand the labor of global capitalism, therefore, the discussion must be extended to non-economic spheres, especially cultural, social, and political realms where the consequences of our one-dimensional "economic man" can be more fully spelled out under the lens of the institutional political-economy perspective. Systematic discussions of how globalization reshapes social stratification and undermines citizen power in public affairs will be presented in Chapter 6; below the analysis shall return to the current chapter's early focus on the small part of global labor that is in high mobility, namely, international immigrants and migrant workers, because they are the groups enjoying and often actualizing the greatest freedom of mobility among labor, having supposedly achieved their sought-after better life. Are they really successful in the economic sense? What do they pay in non-economic realms for the freedom of mobility as laborers? As both laborers and humans, how do their movements in globalization affect the fate of their own life and society?

Methodologically, this approach contradicts economic approaches that think the questions concerning immigration can all be "addressed through economic analysis."[116] Whereas economist Borjas views "immigration as a human capital investment; a person migrates whenever the gains from migration (such as the expected wage gain) exceed the costs" with "the income-maximization hypothesis,"[117] this chapter's analysis emphasizes a migrant person as an rounded human-being who lives not only with an income but an identity, social ties, and a role in public life. Non-economic consequences must be included in the analysis, especially cultural, social, and political consequences.

Such an analysis, in our inter-institutional approach, can begin with an irony, this being the fact that the economic man cannot always make his economic dream into reality via global, interregional, or domestic mobility. As a scholar has observed, "many migrant workers are still locked into forms of labour exploitation that marked the birth of global capitalism"; thus, "employer demand for cheap, often illegal, labour has not abated despite the spread of an evangelical form of neo-liberal capitalism proclaiming that opportunity and fairness are available to all."[118] In industrialized countries, therefore, the increase of immigrants becomes a major cause of inequality, as new immigrants are often at the bottom of the income hierarchy. In the United States, for example, it is reported that

---

[116] Borjas, *Immigration Economics*, pp. 1–2.   [117] Ibid, p. 5.
[118] Cohen, *Migration and Its Enemies*, p. 1.

In the early 1970s, noncitizens were quite a small share of the population of the United States, and their income profiles were close to those of citizens. Increasingly, however, noncitizens became a larger, poorer share of the population. From 1990 on, this change placed a number of ineligibles at the bottom of the income distribution, sufficient to make a substantial impact on the redistributive preferences of the median income voters.[119]

In general, immigration prompts inequality. As the above cited authors point out, "economists have recognized that immigration, through low wage competition, has had an effect on inequality," and, for some, immigration explains as much as 25–70 percent of the growth in the Gini coefficients.[120] "The immigration series, like the income series, largely parallels our polarization measures."[121] Chapter 6 will emphatically explore the issue of inequality; here the point is: as laborers seek job opportunities with better pay and pursue possible improvement of material life, though mobility may help them upgrade their status to some extent on the global labor market, leading to a higher income than if they were to not move, their desirable economic goal by principle is not likely to be realized in the new place. In fact, "international labour migration at the turn of the twenty-first century has created a large underclass with limited opportunities for upward mobility and access to universal human rights," a phenomenon historically different from what history saw in migration in the nineteenth century.[122]

More importantly, the cost for them is extremely high if cultural, social, and political factors are taken into account, as the mobility of laborers makes these people culturally lost, socially uprooted, and

---

[119] Nolan McCarty, Keith T. Poole, and Howard Rosenthal, *Polarized America: The Dance of Ideology and Unequal Riches*, Cambridge, MA: MIT Press, 2008, p. 138.

[120] McCarty, Poole, and Rosenthal, *Polarized America*, p. 116. There are numerous data indicating the same trend in other regions of the Global North. For a side note, in British Columbia, Canada where this author lives and where a huge number of immigrants are regularly received, local media report that immigration, "which has increased significantly in the last thirty years," is "part of reason" causing the general decline of work income. Tara Carman, "Men's work income falling," *Times Colonist*, October 10, 2014, p. B1.

[121] McCarty, Poole, and Rosenthal, *Polarized America*, p. 9.

[122] Amarjit Kaur and Dirk Hoerder, "Understanding International Migration: Comparative and Transcultural Perspectives," in Dirk Hoerder and Amarjit Kaur, eds., *Proletarian and Gendered Mass Migrations: A Global Perspective on Continuities and Discontinuities from the 19th to the 21st Centuries*, Leiden: Brill, 2013, pp. 3–18; (p. 8).

politically impotent in the public life of their destination societies. Identity is among those issues attracting much attention in cultural studies in general, and migration scholarship in particular: "When group membership comes into question, then doubts arise also about identity."[123] While the problem of identity arises everywhere with globalization, international immigrants are doubtless among those who meet the most serious challenges in this regard, as they have to "abandon their own language, culture and religion" in settling into new destinations.[124] As two leading scholars of globalization point out, the globalists are "at their most vulnerable when considering the movements of people, their allegiances and their cultural and moral identities"; one of reasons is that "the role of national (and local) cultures remains central to public life in nearly all political communities."[125] Other scholars also argue that "while religious ethicists have long-standing frameworks for dealing with such complex issues as war and peace and beginning and end of life issues, we have found no such ethical frameworks constructed on the topic of migration. Yet the perils of migration, arguably, impact the lives of more people today than most other ethical issues."[126] In fact, global human mobility, especially its impact on those who have moved to industrialized countries in the physical sense but have felt disappointed about their identification within the host societies, becomes one of the most severe sources of global intensification of religious and ethical conflicts, even leading to the rise of terrorism not only in global peripheries but also in the Global North.[127]

Circumstances in which immigrants have "remained psychologically unsettled"[128] can be, perhaps, termed the "immigrant mentality," with which they constantly feel themselves to be aliens in host societies. To this chapter, this is not simply a psychological problem; it is more

---

123 Wolfgang Schluchter, "Foreword," to Reinhard Bendix, *Force, Fate, and Freedom: On Historical Sociology*, Berkeley: University of California Press, 1984, pp. vii–xv (p. xiv).
124 Cohen, *Migration and Its Enemies*, p. 8.
125 Held and McGrew, *Globalization/Anti-Globalization*, p. 208.
126 Elizabeth W. Collier and Charles R. Strain, "Introduction," in Elizabeth W. Collier and Charles R. Strain eds., *Religious and Ethical Perspectives on Global Migration*, Lanham: Lexington Books, 2014, pp. 1–10 (p. 3).
127 Samuel P. Huntington, *Who Are We? The Challenges to America's National Identity*, New York: Simon & Schuster, 2004.
128 Cohen, *Migration and Its Enemies*, p. 8.

social, and even institutional. The central issue here is that the immigrants are uprooted from their social fabrics. Immigration transforms those who make the exodus to settle (or unsettle) down in a new land in terms of their reconfigured position in the distributions of income and benefit, voice and power, education and life chances; it actually redefines the meaning and goals of their life, or, more often than not, creates crises in the meaning and purposes of their life. Solid things become precarious; hopes can be turned to disillusions. Such a feeling of ontological loss in life has profound institutional implications for these people's social and political life, which will be analyzed later.

Their adaptation to new social-cultural surroundings in a host country, however, can be tricky in terms of its trade-off effect with their maintenance of close connections with the nations from which they originate, often for economic considerations as well as for non-economic ones. Alejandro Portes and his collaborators have connected network analyses with the economic success of self-employed immigrants in the United States; their argument goes that the higher the stock of social capital in the form of reciprocity and solidarity, the more successful these immigrants are in inserting themselves into the American economy.[129] However, as Thomas Faist emphasizes, "resources inherent in ties between people – within networks, groups, and communities – are often locally specific," and "these ties and corresponding resources are not easily transferred from one place to another, especially across borders of nation-states."[130] In other words,

Social capital is location-specific. Local assets include economic resources, such as money or physical capital, human capital, such as educational credentials, vocational training and professional skills, and social capital, i.e. the content of ties and the resources inherent in social transactions ... Social capital denotes the transactions between individuals and groups that facilitate social action, and the benefits derived from these mechanisms. It is primarily a local asset and can be transferred cross-nationally only under specific conditions.[131]

It is, therefore, also a trade-off between the utilization of an economic advantage in the home country and the losing of social opportunity and

---

[129] Alejandro Portes ed., *The Economic Sociology of Immigration: Essays on Networks, Ethnicity, and Entrepreneurship*, New York: Russell Sage Foundation, 1995.

[130] Faist, *Volume and Dynamics of International Migration and Transnational Social Spaces*, p. 1.

[131] Ibid, p. 15.

political involvement in the new home. In analyzing the tendency of immigrant communities to geographically cluster in enclaves, David Card and Steven Raphael are fully aware of this difficult situation among immigrants:

To the extent that such geographic clustering provides ready social networks rich with information on negotiating U.S. institutions and finding work, the existence of enclaves may increase employment and reduce poverty among newer immigrants. On the other hand, such geographic clusters may inhibit English-language acquisition and perhaps make immigrants less willing to migrate internally for jobs in cities and states with smaller co-national populations.[132]

So, what Cohen calls the "propensity to link 'home' and 'away'"[133] is actually an effort by immigrants to maintain their social networks, not only for economic resources but, more importantly to my analysis, for social belonging and the meaning of life. The irony is double: Immigrants come to foreign countries seeking, for the most part, an improvement of their economic conditions, but soon after they come to the new place they find that they have to utilize their ties with the emigration country to build up their possible competitiveness against native residents in the host economy; furthermore, as they seek and possibly gain a better economic life, their integration into the social life of the host country is compromised or even sacrificed, which, in turn, puts the immigrants into lasting social poverty.

The logic for immigrants, therefore, does not always move in a linear fashion from becoming wealthy to gaining social capital in the host country; rather, standing in either good or bad economic statuses, immigrants can be in social poverty, as social poverty can be defined in terms of the loss of social capital. There have been many studies in this regard, leading to the conclusion that immigrants are seriously challenged in maintaining or promoting their social capital. For example, Faist regards social capital as the content of network ties, in which "certain positions within a web of ties," "symbolic ties, embodied in shared or common meanings, memories, future expectations, and symbols" are all significant. As the content of social and symbolic ties, "obligations, reciprocity, and solidarity are dimensions of social capital; resources of others, information, and control are benefits derived

---

[132] Card and Raphael, "Introduction," pp. 1–2.
[133] Cohen, *Migration and Its Enemies*, p. 8.

from social capital."[134] He particularly emphasizes those significant functions of social capital in international migration, such as the selection function, the diffusion function, the bridging function, and the adaptation function,[135] indicating that the understanding of social capital in international migration should go beyond the discussion of the concept in a normal social context that lacks fundamental change in terms of mobility.

The social irony immigrants face clearly indicates that many of those things that are seemingly natural to native citizens can become huge difficulties in the daily, cultural, and social lives of newcomers, some of which are often insurmountable. In the political realm this is particularly so, because politics means public life and public involvement, which is beyond imagination for someone whose involvement in social life is already thin and weak. Generally speaking, "political engagement of migrants abroad needs a basis in ties and social capital."[136] In particular, I would like to make several points to further the analysis concerning the political inability of immigrants to participate in the host country's politics. First, the making of "economic man" makes an immigrant's life inevitably centered on private issues such as struggles for improving incomes and the unity of the family.[137] The high priority of such issues and the concern and energy required for dealing with them, I would argue, further "privatize" immigrants' lives and reduce the possibility and capability of them to be concerned with public affairs.[138] Though the image of "economic man" is argued in this chapter to fit virtually everybody in general, mobility, primarily including international immigration, is also particularly pointed out to be a narrow door for "economization" of men and women who are involved in the move. Through such a squeezing process, they are

---

[134] Faist, *Volume and Dynamics of International Migration and Transnational Social Spaces*, p. 15. For a definition of social capital and a discussion of it in social theory, see James S. Coleman, *Foundations of Social Theory*, Cambridge, MA: Belknap Press of Harvard University Press, 1990, ch. 12; for the significance of social capital for political democracy, see Robert D. Putnam, *Making Democracy Work: Civic Traditions in Modern Italy*, Princeton University Press, 1993.

[135] Faist, *Volume and Dynamics of International Migration and Transnational Social Spaces*, p. 121.

[136] Ibid, p. 16.   [137] Spellman, *Uncertain Identity*, pp. 8–9.

[138] As pointed out earlier, here I also follow E. E. Shattsneider's concept of "privatization," which is in a contrast with "socialization." See ft. 25, ch. 2.

often greatly deprived of their concerns over and ability in the participation in public affairs.

Second, some institutional constraints in the destination countries work specifically against immigrants' participation in public life. Take the United States as an example: In such an advanced, often exemplary democratic polity, rights and benefits that are conferred to immigrants are not guaranteed; they are under debate.[139] While some experts point out "a democratic deficit around immigration policymaking in the United States,"[140] I would add that a general democratic deficit exists for immigrants in their participation in a host democracy. And, thirdly, in adapting to their new social and political circumstances in the destination countries, immigrants have a weakness in translating their newly obtained legal rights, assuming such rights are often more sufficient than in their native countries, into capability and action for participating in public life. Relevant publications indicate that these often economically poor people are not able to utilize democracy to protect and promote their interests. For example, in studying immigrants and economic inequality in the United States, a group of scholars has asked: "Why has the increased importance of income not translated into policies that would curtail the sharp growth in inequality?" Their research found an intimate connection between democratic participation and economic income in a back-and-forth way: "At least in part, noncitizens who are ineligible to vote are concentrated at the bottom of the income distribution, so politicians feel little pressure to respond to their interests."[141]

In addition, international immigrants coming to the Global North are often from places where they have had little to no opportunity to practice democracy in their native countries, and where individualism is usually weak; as such, a non-democratic political culture can be reinforced in immigration due to what Emma Lazaru termed the "huddled masses,"[142] referring to their propensity to compose an enclave. In a more general sense, that immigrants have been increasing in the Global North actually makes even a mature democracy more dysfunctional.

All of these non-economic qualities are essential to human beings. Many of them, as Robert Putnam puts it, provide social capital for

[139] Swain, "Introduction," p. 1.   [140] Ibid, p. 4.
[141] McCarty, Poole, and Rosenthal, *Polarized America*, p. 115.
[142] As quoted in Faist, *The Volume and Dynamics of International Migration and Transnational Social Spaces*, p. 3.

making democracy work;[143] moreover, their incapacity in those regards can lead to the immigrants, an already privileged section of the hierarchy of labor in terms of mobility, being trapped in an unpleasant circumstance of making a livelihood but losing the meaning of life. Immigration is, of course, a life-changing move rather than simply an economic action, even though it can be, in reality and in the theory of global capitalism, a cost-benefit decision primarily driven by economic motivations. The life implications of immigration and mobility are all-embracing beyond what their motivations might have anticipated; when immigrants are squeezed in the process of immigration into "economic men," as human beings they still require non-economic life, but they are incapable of actualizing such life. Those non-economic dimensions of life, after all, also influence their economic benefits; trade-offs often emerge to trap them into dilemmas of gaining uncertain economic benefits while suffering definite sociopolitical losses.

"The effects of migration," as some experts have pointed out, "are becoming increasingly multifaceted, both at places of migrant origins and migrant destinations."[144] One such effect, parallel to the deprivation or significant weakening of immigrants' cultural, social, and political abilities in the host countries, is that the existing status of citizens in these host countries, often developed democracies, in terms of security and welfare has come under increasing pressure because "the 'Third World' comes to the North through migration and leads to conflicts when migrants primarily act as and are seen by the natives not only as economic but also political and cultural agents."[145] The securitization of international immigration, in addition, cannot help newcomers feel at home in the host countries, but further makes them alienated from host social and political circumstances. In another line of reasoning, migration studies emphasize human mobility's challenges to the state, especially the fiscal impact of immigration and the interaction between immigration and the modern welfare state.[146] Of these, the fiscal challenges the developed nations encounter in providing social welfare to new immigrants have been further stressed.

---

[143] Putnam, *Making Democracy Work*.
[144] Massey and Taylor, "Introduction," p. 3.
[145] Faist, *Volume and Dynamics of International Migration and Transnational Social Spaces*, pp. 12–13.
[146] Borjas, *Immigration Economics*, p. 3.

In this distressing endeavor to overcome the fate that is termed to be "born poor," poverty cannot be easily tackled; alternatively, they have to pay the cost of social and political poverty to improve their material and financial situations, and they are institutionally, that is, by the rule of the game, turned into "human capital," a conception that Collier regards as "one of the ugliest phrases in economics,"[147] with little social capital as democratic citizens. When such qualities are weakened and deprived, the human capital of global capitalism is turned against the social capital of democracy.

Concluding Remarks

Many have argued that this wave of globalization has powerfully propelled various movements of human capital around the world. It is around this mobility, its effect in reconfiguring the global labor market, and its economic, social, and political consequences that the above chapter has been organized to analyze how labor as one of the fundamental elements of capitalism has been reshaped in globalization. Based on existing studies of the labor market in general and migration in particular but following this book's inter-institutionalist methodology, the chapter has positioned labor's mobility and immobility, laborers' economic pursuits and their sociopolitical losses, and labor and capital as well as the state into the perspective of mutual contextualization, thus trying to draw a big picture of the political economy of labor under global capitalism.

The chapter has accordingly made three arguments regarding, respectively, economic, institutional, and sociopolitical reconfigurations of the global labor market. Laborers are humans, rather than purely economic animals, but global capitalism squeezes primarily those who are on the move in regards to the global labor market into one-dimensional "economic men" – international immigrants and various migrant workers are either motivated by economic and materialist incentives or are pushed to become more greatly concerned with economic and materialist benefits than they otherwise would be. Together with the rise of the economic state, this is a fundamental reconfiguration of not only the global system of human mobility but, perhaps, also the fundamental organization of human societies. Such "economic

---

[147] Collier, *The Bottom Billion*, p. 93.

men" actually provide a mass foundation to global capitalism, a point we will come back to in the next chapter when discussing how consumption also works to a similar effect in making the version of "economic man 2.0."

The institutional change of the global labor market brought about by the increasing mobility of various types of migrant workers can be analyzed upon three layers, as the above chapter has attempted to do. On the operational layer, the changing labor-capital relationship has been increasingly crystalized in the displacement of permanent employment by a variety of temporary contracts, the latter being termed in labor studies, and promoted by both capital and governments, as "informal" work, or, in a more general sense, "labor flexibility," but in reality meaning job insecurity, decreased pay, deteriorating welfare, and many other disadvantages for workers. This change has fundamentally undermined labor in its relationships vis-à-vis capital and the state.

At the structural level, the global labor market is further balkanized due to the dialectic dynamism of increasing global connections among different parts of labor and, accordingly, a deepening segmentation and an intensifying internal competition among those parts. The segmentation theory is not new to labor-market studies, and in fact has been there long before this wave of globalization, but now what we see is labor segmentation on a global scale. Being aware of the many different possibilities in mapping such multidimensional segmentations, this chapter has emphasized an interpretation that runs along degrees of freedom and scales of mobility and in which a labor hierarchy has been configured, which helps to better reflect the impacts of globalization and to highlight the contrast between labor and capital in terms of freedoms they have gained or not gained against the institutional framework of global capitalism.

The third level concerns the external linkages between labor, on one hand, and capital and the state on the other. Although it is impossible in a short section to comprehensively outline the complicated triangular interactions among them, the chapter has made an effort to discuss some points in this regard, in order to offer a glimpse into the institutional connections between the balkanized labor market and the general, fundamental institutions of global capitalism with the state-market nexus as its backbone.

All of the above-discussed processes, structures, and institutions, this chapter has maintained, lead to the traps into which labor has fallen, as exemplified in the fate of international immigrants, the group arguably with a freedom of movement beyond state borders and therefore somehow occupying a privileged position within the hierarchy of the segmented global labor market. The chapter has discussed how such mobility traps labor in a cycle of social poverty due to constant striving for better material wellbeing, thus depriving the laborers of social and political capabilities. It has also argued that geographical movements of these people still cannot substantially improve and overcome their economic poverty, or, when such improvements are more or less achieved, they pay extremely high costs that go beyond economic realms, in particular costs of cultural alienation, social poverty, and political inability. The ramifications for democracy and democratization are obviously profound, and will be analyzed in Chapter 6, where they will be discussed in the context of interactions among capital, labor, and consumption.

5 | The Shaping of the Caged Anarchy

Standardized Consumption, Atomized Consumers

Consumption is a miracle of capitalism; it is also a myth to institutional studies of political economy. As a miracle it is via the seemingly cosmopolitan activity of consumption that capitalism, especially in its global triumph, involves virtually everybody on this globe in the market mechanism with, more often than not, a level of participation that is not only willing but often passionately so; it is also advocated by economists and politicians as the ultimate engine of the capitalist economy, "the sole end and object of all economic activity," and the democratic soul of market operations.[1] In both the socioeconomic and political-institutional sense, therefore, consumption lies at the core of capitalism, around which market activities unfold to actualize the values of both capital's investment and labor's engagement in production, services, and sales. In the epistemological sense, however, it is a myth, as general studies of the political economy of capitalism and/or globalization have not so frequently as one might expect paid sufficient attention to consumption and its role in the bigger picture of global capitalism,[2] in spite of the recent appearance of a separate and flourishing field of consumption studies, whose particular focus concerns

---

[1] The quotation is from John Maynard Keynes, *A Tract on Monetary Reform*, London: Macmillan, 1923, p. 95. For the democratic meanings of consumption, see, for example, Peter N. Stearns, *Consumerism in World History*, London: Routledge, 2006, 2nd ed., p. 25.

[2] For example, those comprehensive books on globalization usually contain no chapter or section on consumption, as in David Held, Anthony McGrew, David Goldblatt, and Jonathan Perraton, *Global Transformations: Politics, Economics and Culture*, Stanford University Press, 1999; Frank J. Lechner and John Boli eds., *The Globalization Reader*, Malden, MA: Blackwell, 2004, 2nd ed.; Jonathan Michie ed., *The Handbook of Globalisation*, Cheltenham: Edward Elgar, 2003; Gordon L. Clark, Maryann P. Feldman, and Meric S. Gertler, eds., *The Oxford Handbook of Economic Geography*, Oxford University Press 2000.

cultural consumptions and consumption as culture.[3] Does consumption have anything to do with the political economy of globalization? Is it primarily a cultural and, in its widest sense, a behavioral phenomenon with little institutional meaning? How has the global triumph of capitalism restructured consumption, and what implications does such restructuring have for a general, macro-level understanding of global capitalism?

Through the lens of both inter-institutionalism and political economy, this chapter is designed to explore the above questions with emphases on two angles in analyzing consumption: First, it will highlight the interconnections and interactions of consumption with other fundamental political-economic elements of global capitalism, namely, capital, labor, and the state; second, it focuses on the role, functions, and contributions of consumption in and to the institutional reconfiguration of capitalism in its global triumph. In the first line of reasoning, regarding the relationships among three fundamental elements of capitalism, this book argues that there is a diminishing curve stretching from capital's concentration and coordination to labor's segmentation and consumer's atomization. To sketch out the third section of this curve, that is, how consumption is atomized, will therefore be a central task of this chapter subsequent to the proceeding chapters that have investigated capital and labor. The global coverage of the capitalist consumer markets, to this chapter, is a fundamental change that globalization has brought to human societies, even more fundamental

---

[3] As in the tradition of the Frankfurt school of social critiques and the publications contributed by the Birmingham school of cultural studies. See some introduction and summary in, for example, Graeme Turner, *British Cultural Studies: An Introduction*, New York: Unwin Hyman, 1990; Ben Agger, *Cultural Studies as Critical Theory*, London: Routledge, 1992; Rolf Wiggershaus, *The Frankfurt School*, Cambridge: Polity, 1994; Ioan Davies, *Cultural Studies and After*, London: Routledge, 1995; Ann Cvetkovich and Douglas Kellner, *Articulating the Global and the Local: Globalization and Cultural Studies*, Boulder: Westview Press, 1997; Simon During, *Cultural Studies: A Critical Introduction*, London: Routledge, 2005; Simon During ed., *The Cultural Studies Reader*, London: Routledge, 2007, 3rd ed.; Emma A. Jane and Chris Barker, *Cultural Studies: Theory and Practice*, Thousand Oaks, CA: Sage, 5th re. ed., 2016. In utilizing existing studies to inform our discussion, this chapter attempts to overcome an ideological gap between two parallel but generally non-interactive research traditions, namely, that between the ignorance regarding consumption in political economic studies of globalization and the richness of findings and understandings of consumption contributed by consumption studies, particularly by cultural studies of consumption.

than capital's movement, a phenomenon that is not, in fact, totally new, and more so than labor's mobility, which, as investigated in the last chapter, is greatly counterbalanced by the larger existence of immobility. The expansion of the global consumption system, by contrast, has reached virtually every remote corner of the world and every person in human society, which, as a new phenomenon that has emerged in the post–Cold War era, can be regarded as one of the most powerful and effective parameters of the global triumph of capitalism. How this consumption system works; how it interacts with other capitalist political-economy elements, especially with capital and, under the state-market nexus, with the state; and what the implications of such workings and interactions are for globalizing societies, are all significant questions for understanding the political economy of global capitalism.

The second line of analysis will focus on institutional implications of consumption to global capitalism. The globe as *agora*, in fact, highlights both the involvement of essentially every person worldwide in globalized consumption and the limitations now encountered by the global market in exhausting its last frontiers. The latter stimulates capital to strengthen its occupation of the consumer markets and, more importantly to squeeze consumers more powerfully than it would otherwise for its interest return, while the former "institutionalizes" the globe in terms of marketing, consumption, and, via both, human life. Consumption has been increasingly standardized in tandem with large corporations taking greater and greater shares of the global market; consumers are, accordingly, becoming increasingly similar to each other while simultaneously losing their organic connections with one another: this is the process of consumers' atomization. Thus emerges the anarchy of capitalist consumption.

This happens in the name of market freedom and a consumer's autonomous decision-making power. In this context, a resident-as-consumer in the global village lives in circumstances that are in a sharp contrast with the surroundings he/she faces as a laborer, in which he/she is, at best, an employer in a capitalist firm where authority, discipline, and organization dominate. The two organizational and political bodies of global capitalism are thus further epitomized in the human being as a Janus-faced "economic man": as a laborer, he/she works within a firm (if this person is lucky enough to get a job), where the principle of state capitalism now prevails, thereby successfully promulgating authority; as a consumer, he/she lives within the confines of the market, where neoliberalism governs for the purpose of promoting capital's ill-regulated dominance of consumption. Putting these two aspects together, it is clear that the consumer is "liberated" to pursue material desires but suppressed from being a citizen, and the anarchy of consumption is, ironically, organized and governed by the state-capital synthesis.

In the pages below, this chapter will first investigate how the rise of the global consumption market promotes through its geographic expansion an encompassing of consumerism to commercialize everything, often beyond people's immediate needs. It will subsequently move to emphasize, however, the imbalance of power between consumers and capital in disfavoring the former, particularly how such an imbalance is embedded in the political economic institutions of global capitalism despite the appearance of consumers being fetishized. Consumerism, the chapter shall continue to argue, constrains an individual consumer by turning this prototypical human being into an "economic man" in the sense of being overwhelmingly concerned with the acquisition of commodities; this personality is termed "economic man 2.0" in comparison with the earlier version of "economic man" discussed in Chapter 4 concerning labor in global capitalism. The chapter will emphatically analyze how globalization helps to standardize first the consumer markets, then the methods of consumption, and, inevitably, all consumers, thus concluding that such consumerist standardization leads to the atomization of consumers. As the chapter will argue, standardization of consumption and atomization of consumers together lay down the micro foundation of the anarchy of global capitalism in the consumption realm, and such consumption complements the entire picture of the political economy of global capitalism in its organization, operation, and institutionalization.

Commercializing Everything: The Expansion of the Global Consumption System and the Global Rise of Consumerism

The global expansion of consumption is, perhaps, the most visible and the most significant indicator of the global triumph of capitalism: It is more visible than capital's global movement, and, at least in terms of quantity, much more significant than labor's global mobility. Analytically, it can be inspected in two dimensions. First, it is the geographic expansion of the global consumption system, meaning the global involvement of virtually everyone on Earth in this system; it also implies the exhaustion of the external limit of the global consumer markets. Second, it is the cultural expansion over the globe of capitalist consumption, culture being used here in its broadest sense to refer to a way of life, a philosophy of living, and a series of habits and styles of human actions in daily activities. The rise of consumerism on the global scale, to this author, is the most obvious and dominating parameter of such a cultural expansion of the global consumption system. Though consumption is perhaps necessary for all societies and cultures to some extent, not all societies and cultures have been inclined to promote consumption to the degree that human beings are mentally encouraged and institutionally pushed into passionate engagement or even limitless indulgence in consumption.[4] Such engagement or indulgence is the trademark of consumerism, originating from industrial capitalist societies but now spread across the world. These two dimensions are, of course, often overlapping and entangled with one another, but both the conceptual and practical distinctions between them remain discernable. If we regard the geographic expansion of the global consumer market as the physical growth of a body, the consumerism that arises worldwide can be viewed as the soul of such physical development. Together they have made a contemporary giant of the global consumption system.

Interactions between these two dimensions have provided a dynamic that drives the overall expansion of capitalist consumption to its eventual global coverage. As an historian of consumerism points out,

Western consumerism had itself depended heavily on global context. It had been stimulated in part by access to new goods from other parts of the world: sugar, Indian silk, cotton. It depended also on the profits from world trade . . . But the full world history of modern consumerism also involves the spread of consumer styles and interests from the West to other places.[5]

---

[4] For the historical development of consumerism, see, for instance, Gary Cross, *Time and Money: The Making of Consumer Society*, London: Routledge, 1993; David Horowitz, *The Morality of Spending: Attitudes Toward the Consumer Society in America*, Chicago: I. R. Dee, 1993; John Benson, *The Rise of Consumer Society in Britain, 1880–1980*, New York: Longman, 1994; Victoria de Grazia with Ellen Furlough, *The Sex of Things: Gender and Consumption in Historical Perspective*, Berkeley: University of California Press, 1996; Martin Daunton and Matthew Hilton, *The Politics of Consumption: Material Culture and Citizenship in Europe and America*, New York: Berg Press, 2001; Matthew Hilton, *Consumerism in Twentieth-Century Britain*, Cambridge University Press, 2003.

[5] Stearns, *Consumerism in World History*, p. 79.

From this short quotation we glean the significance of three factors for promoting consumerism: new goods, tremendous profits, and the cross-nation spread of consumer styles and interests originating from the West. Today it is easy to see the presentation of all three factors in global capitalism, though often in renewed and upgraded forms. New goods nowadays are often artificial goods invented by the information revolution and by the new, continuous industrial revolution; these goods can be physical in form, as they have been traditionally, but many of the new goods appear more and more in the form of various novelties of visual, virtual, and fictitious economies, or at least come with increasing elements in this regard.[6] As the global division of labor has been developed worldwide through movements of capital on a global scale in the hunt for cheaper costs, primarily cheaper labor, this combined with other factors such as the gigantic pool of consumers of a given product, profits have in general become tremendous. The spread of consumerism, therefore, is easily conquering every corner of the world.

In order to better catch the essence of the global expansion of the consumption market, here I propose three indicative scenarios alongside which our discussion can be unfolded. These scenarios are: 1) consumption as a norm of the commercialization of every need in life, to the extreme that consumer acquisitions go well beyond immediate necessity; 2) cultural consumption as a rising domain of expenditure, through which those traditionally non-material dimensions of life are quickly materialized in the sense that they are turned into goods and commodities, often as artificially invented items designed for a level of consumption that involves various activities of human minds, brains, feelings, spirits, relationships, communications, time-filling, etc., rather than purely for human beings' physical needs; 3) accordingly, consumption as a culture or a life style that greatly contributes to the defining or redefining of personal identities in the global age. Intimately connected to one another, these scenarios can be viewed as an expanding loop that continues to enlarge the scope and scale of capitalist consumption in terms of both the rise of the global consumption markets and the global spread of consumerism.

[6] Cross, *Time and Money*; Jonathan Beller, *The Cinematic Mode of Production: Attention Economy and the Society of the Spectacle*, Hanover, NH: Dartmouth College Press, 2006; Vili Lehdonvirta and Edward Castronova, *Virtual Economies: Design and Analysis*, Cambridge, MA: MIT Press, 2014.

Consumption is, of course, necessary for daily life, but, with the global expansion of the capitalist consumption system, it now often stretches in two overlapping and interacting directions: first, in the direction of commercializing basic needs in various renewed, global ways rather than maintaining a form of consumption based on traditional, local ways; second, in the direction of going far beyond the acquisition of living necessities alone. Following the first direction, one can easily find an example in the expansion of American fast food into developing countries, including many nations traditionally proud of their own food and culinary culture as being distinguished from America. Chapter 3 already touched on this when discussing chain stores, and later I will revisit it for further analysis. Such a phenomenon not only occurs through geographic expansion, but also through market expansion in the sense of involving an increasing number of basic needs in refreshed methods of consumption. Take bottled water as an example in this regard, which is, according to a pundit,

now the fastest growing market in the global beverage industry with consumption highest in countries that have access to safe drinking water. It is the second largest beverage sold in the US with per capita consumption doubling between 1993–2003. In Canada bottled water outstrips coffee, tea, apple juice and milk. Markets are also growing in countries that are rapidly modernizing, and where water infrastructure is unsafe and/or underdeveloped.[7]

Such examples, to our discussion, mean both the further commercialization of basic human needs and the increasing standardization of consumption worldwide.

In the second direction, consumption is well developed to stretch beyond the normal subsistence levels of life, often creating new needs for consumers. If the last point is about the new way of commercializing traditional, basic needs, here we are talking about something essentially "useless" for human beings' physical existence; the invention of novel demands unneeded and unimaginable to ancestor generations; goods to meet the needs of human beings' mind, spirit, and other, so to

---

[7] Gay Hawkins, "More-than-Human Politics: The Case of Plastic Bags," *Australian Humanities Review*, 46 (May 2009), www.australianhumanitiesre view.org/archive/Issue-May-2009/hawkins.htm, accessed September 22, 2015.

speak, "soft" aspects.[8] Although here cultural consumption immediately becomes topical, it will be left for a later, systematic discussion, as it deserves special attention. Here a seemingly insubstantial realm of consumption will serve as an example of such novel demands: that of luxury, or the goods that people "clearly do not need for subsistence or for traditional display."[9] In fact, the growth of luxury consumption, according to two experts of Carlson School of Management, University of Minnesota, is "one of the biggest trends in consumer behavior over the last two decades,"[10] during which time sales of luxury goods have skyrocketed from 80 billion US$ to over 500 billion per year and the number of luxury consumers has more than tripled from 90 million to 330 million worldwide.[11] A market statistics agent, Statista, reports the increase of the value of the personal luxury goods market worldwide from 77 billion euros in 1995 to 253 billion of 2015.[12] Accordingly, it has also become a flourishing field of business and academic research,[13] with many findings and insights that endorse this chapter's arguments in later discussions.

[8] Even intimacy is commodified. See Lauren Berlant, *The Female Complaint: The Unfinished Business of Sentimentality in American Culture*, Durham: Duke University Press, 2008.
[9] Stearns, *Consumerism in World History*, p. vii. For a comprehensive investigation of luxury, see Christopher J. Berry, *The Idea of Luxury: A Conceptual and Historical Investigation*, Cambridge University Press, 1994. "Luxury consumption" can be a biological term, which is defined as "the absorption of nitrogen or potash from the soil by a crop in excess of crop needs." See www.merriam-webster.com/dictionary/luxury%20consumption, accessed May 10, 2016. To this author, this biological definition is also helpful for understanding the social phenomenon of "luxury consumption."
[10] Yajin Wang and Deborah Roedder John, "Louis Vuitton and Conservatism: How Luxury Consumption Influences Political Attitudes," http://bbr2015.brandrelationships.org/wp-content/uploads/sites/3/2015/05/Luxury-Consumption-and-Political-Attitudes_BBR_Yajin-Wang.pdf, accessed May 10, 2016.
[11] Claudia D'Arpizio, "Luxury Goods Worldwide Market Study," Bain & Company, www.bain.com/about/press/press-releases/worldwide-luxury-goods-continues-double-digit-annual-growth.aspx; Statista, "Value of the Personal Luxury Goods Market Worldwide From 1995 to 2013," The Statistics Portal, www.statista.com/statistics/266503/value-of-the-personal-luxury-goods-market-worldwide/; both accessed November 11, 2015.
[12] Statista, "Value of the Personal Luxury Goods Market".
[13] See, for example, Berry, *The Idea of Luxury*; Patrizia Calefato, *Luxury: Fashion, Lifestyle and Excess*, New York: Bloomsbury Academic, 2014; David Cloutier, *The Vice of Luxury: Economic Excess in a Consumer Age*, Washington, DC: Georgetown University Press, 2015.

The "embrace of faddism,"[14] or the extreme interest in fashions, also helps to demonstrate such fatal attractiveness of luxuries; moreover, it empowers those fashion-related brands to expand at a speed and size beyond ordinary imagination. Let's take Hello Kitty as an example, whose "power," a researcher comes to realize, is concealed in "her very innocuousness"; in fact, behind this power lies Sanrio, a Japanese corporation of which Hello Kitty is the best known product, whose profits in 1998 totaled 120 million yen, equaling approximately 1 billion US dollars.[15] Another example comes from Adidas, which, in 2008 when Beijing sponsored the Olympic Games, took the opportunity to open a new store in Sanlitun – several miles away from the Bird's Nest Stadium – the largest Adidas store in the world, with 3,170 square meters of retail space over four floors. By the end of the year, Adidas owned 5,000 stores in China.[16]

The rise of cultural consumption also belongs to this general trend of consumption beyond immediate material utility, but I list it as a distinctive expansion of consumption because of its extreme weight in both commercial power and conceptual significance. There can be two categories of this phenomenon, depending on whether the concept of "culture" is defined narrowly or broadly. Following the first line, "culture" is often understood not in the wider anthropological sense of the term but in the narrower sense of, to quote a formulation by Gans, "the practices, goods and ideas classified broadly under the arts (including literature, music, architecture and design etc., and the products of all other print media, electronic media, etc.) whether used for education and aesthetic and spiritual enlightenment or for entertainment and diversion."[17] How society consumes history, from computer games to daytime television, from blockbuster fictional narratives such as *The Da Vinci Code* to DNA genealogical tools, is a good example in this regard.[18] "Culture" in

---

[14] Stearns, *Consumerism in World History*, p. 54.
[15] Brian J. Mcveigh, "How Hello Kitty Commodifies the Cute, Cool and Camp: 'Consumutopia' versus 'Control' in Japan," *Journal of Material Culture*, 5, 2 (July 2000): 225–245.
[16] Tania Branigan, "The Real Olympics Competition: Nike and Adidas Claim China's Heroes," *The Guardian*, https://www.theguardian.com/sport/2008/aug/18/olympics2008.retail, posted August 18, 2008, accessed November 12, 2015.
[17] Herbert J. Gans, *Popular Culture and High Culture: An Analysis and Evaluation of Taste*, New York: Basic Books, 1999, rev. ed., p. 5.
[18] Jerome de Groot, *Consuming History: Historians and Heritage in Contemporary Popular Culture*, London: Routledge, 2009.

"cultural consumption" and especially "consumer culture," however, is often given a wider definition to emphasize what Celia Lury sees in "the tendency for more and more aspects of human life to be made available through the market." For her, "one instance of this is the marketization of what were previously state or publicly provided services in the UK. Examples include health, housing and education – such that it is said that Britain is now a home-owning nation and that students are consumers of education."[19] This is echoed by two other experts: "Education and health provisions have become yet more commodified, with students and patients viewing themselves as consumers."[20] In any case, the current chapter's point here is to highlight the increasing commoditization of human activities, not only beyond physical and immediate needs, but also stretching into those traditionally non-commercial domains, which can be put into the conceptual basket of "cultural consumption."

Yes, with the rise of cultural consumption, everything is commercialized and supposedly consumed. In 2006, two experts of consumption studies claimed that "the last 10 years have seen a substantial expansion of consumerism into new areas, countries and homes ... "[21] Although this sounds as though it has more to do with spatial expansion, what must be stressed here is the expansion of consumerism beyond the geographic into new aspects, domains, and dimensions of life. Leisure, for example, has fully entered the consumer orbit with the rise of terms such as "commercial leisure" and "consumerist leisure," including sports;[22] and people have seen the emergence of "forms of retail therapy such as spas, health treatments and shopping itself,"[23] meaning simply that every hour of human life has become commercialized. Indeed, as an historian of consumerism points out, "the triumph of consumerist leisure simultaneously transformed recreation and greatly extended the reach of consumerism overall"; "leisure, once associated with traditional continuity as the basis for community life, now reversed direction."[24] Moreover, "consumerism even began to affect emotional life directly," for example, grief.[25]

---

[19] Celia Lury, *Consumer Culture*, New Brunswick, NJ: Rutgers University Press, 2011, 2nd ed., p. 2.
[20] Yiannis Gabriel and Tim Lang, *The Unmanageable Consumer*, London: Sage Publications, 2006, 2nd ed., p. vi.
[21] Ibid.   [22] Stearns, *Consumerism in World History*, pp. 53–4.
[23] Lury, *Consumer Culture*, p. 4.
[24] Stearns, *Consumerism in World History*, p. 54.
[25] Ibid, p. 59. Also, Berlant, *The Female Complaint*.

Shopping in itself, in this line of reasoning, has become a culture of consumption. In fact, it is a major activity of life in many places in the world, especially in industrialized countries and in urban areas of developing nations. It is reported that

The expansion of shopping as a leisure pursuit – in the United States, shopping is the second most popular leisure pursuit – six hours per person a week – after watching television, while already in 1987 the country had more shopping malls than high schools. More recently, annual retail sales add up to more than $3 trillion a year, while consumer spending is thought to account for two thirds of US national economic growth.[26]

Accordingly, space is further commercialized, as the above trend calls for a constant increase in sites for purchase and consumption, including but not limited to the spread of shopping malls. According to a relevant study,

between 1986 and 1990 almost 30 million square feet of shopping centre space was opened in the UK while the amount of retail space per person in the USA has quadrupled over the last thirty years – and the emergence of so-called 'third spaces', in between home and work such as the Starbucks chain of coffee shops, but also gyms and clubs . . . The growth in size of retail chain stores, with stores in chains such as Walmart, Target, Home Depot and The Gap occupying up to 200,000 and even 300,000 square feet; the growth in number of retail parks, leisure complexes, and consumption environments, from the increase in "themed" pubs and restaurants to the setting up of Niketowns and Disneyworlds.[27]

The developing world has not been far behind in this regard, where, as Adidas in China has helped to indicate, such an expansion can occur at a greater rate.

As both time and space are further commercialized, the life of every-body is occupied almost entirely by consumption, and, accordingly, everybody is now primarily identified by the capitalist system as a consumer rather than anything else. To quote two experts,

By the beginning of the 21st-century, we had learnt to talk and think of each other and of ourselves less as workers, citizens, parents or teachers, and more as consumers. Our rights and our powers derive from our standing as consumers; our political choices are votes for those promising us the best deal as consumers; our enjoyment of life is almost synonymous with the

---

[26] Lury, *Consumer Culture*, p. 2.   [27] Ibid, pp. 2–3.

quantities (and to a lesser extent qualities) of what we consume. Our success is measured in terms of how well we are doing as consumers. Consumption is not just a means of fulfilling needs but permeates our social relations, identities, perceptions and images.[28]

This directly leads to the third dimension important to my discussion of the global expansion of consumerism, which is that consumption now greatly defines personal identity in everyday life. Or, more exactly, consumption arises to redefine personal identities in shaping, actualizing, and displaying a life style that a specific person adopts, with which this person clarifies his/her own social status, cultural tastes, financial plans, and many other aspects of his/her way of life. It is in this sense that the concept of "consumer culture" should be considered in this last line of reasoning. According to a relevant study, "consumer culture is central to identity," and "consumer culture has contributed to the emergence and growth of object worlds that encourage forms of reflexivity in individual and collective identity."[29] When consumerism went global, in fact, "consumerism meant more than acquisition, it meant association with a larger set of images."[30] Stearns maintains that the "first causes of consumerism" included people's reevaluation of "what the goals in life should be, and what brought happiness."[31] Other experts emphasize that "identity construction has come to be viewed increasingly through the prism of lifestyles."[32] And, moreover, lifestyle has been largely shaped by consumption, as evidenced in the fact that in the contemporary world it is extremely difficult to avoid "making choices in relation to goods and services, and the associated celebration of self-fashioning or self-transformation and the promotion of lifestyle as a way of life."[33] Therefore,

Consumerism describes a society in which many people formulate their goals in life partly through acquiring goods that they clearly do not need for subsistence or for traditional display. They become enmeshed in the process of acquisition – shopping – and take some of their identity from a procession of new items that they buy and exhibit. In this society, a host of institutions both encourage and serve consumerism, from eager shopkeepers trying to lure customers into buying more than they need, to product

[28] Gabriel and Lang, *The Unmanageable Consumer*, p. 1.
[29] Lury, *Consumer Culture*, p. 7.
[30] Stearns, *Consumerism in World History*, p. 81.   [31] Ibid, p. 27.
[32] Gabriel and Lang, *The Unmanageable Consumer*, p. vi.
[33] Lury, *Consumer Culture*, p. 4.

designers employed to put new twists on established models, to advertisers seeking to create new needs.[34]

Such power of consumption in shaping identity can even overwhelm the search for national identities that arises in tandem with the process of globalization as a balance against global "flattening." For example, "without question, a consumer revolution was occurring in China by the late twentieth century, in a surprisingly short span of time."[35] Significantly, this took place in great part by adding the consumption of Western-style goods and lifestyles to individual identities in daily life, simultaneously set against a background in which nationalism has reportedly become very strong in the country since the 1990s, often in a mood that is hostile to the United States and Japan, China's leading trade partners.[36] A scholar vividly describes a social scene like this:

American fast-food outlets were a new rage, with a few Chinese wannabes, such as Red Sorghum, lagging a bit behind. Interestingly, the patrons did not particularly like the food involved. One loyal patron noted, "The Big Mac doesn't taste great; but the experience of eating in this place makes me feel good. Sometimes I even imagine that I am sitting in a restaurant in New York or Paris." Here was a key way for successful young professionals to *define* themselves, creating a display and a fantasy at the same time. The fast-food outlets suggested modernity and quality as well as unusually friendly service and hygiene. Many people, belying the fast food part, sat in the restaurants for hours, soaking up the atmosphere, seeing and being seen.[37]

[34] Stearns, *Consumerism in World History*, p. vii.
[35] Ibid, p. 100. Also, Debora S. Davis ed., *The Consumer Revolution in Urban China*, Berkeley: University of California Press, 2000; Karl Gerth, *As China Goes, So Goes the World: How Chinese Consumers Are Transforming Everything*, New York: Hill & Wang, 2010; Shuguang Wang, *China's New Retail Economy: A Geographic Perspective*, London: Routledge, 2014; LiAnne Yu, *Consumption in China: How China's New Consumer Ideology is Shaping the Nation*, Cambridge: Polity, 2014.
[36] Yongnian Zheng, *Discovering Chinese Nationalism in China: Modernization, Identity, and International Relations*, Cambridge University Press, 1999; Peter Hays Gries, *China's New Nationalism: Pride, Politics, and Diplomacy*, Berkeley: University of California Press, 2004; Susan Shirk, *China: Fragile Superpower*, Oxford University Press, 2007; Guoguang Wu, "From Post-Imperial to Late Communist Nationalism: Historical Change in Chinese Nationalism from May Fourth to the 1990s," *Third World Quarterly*, 29, 3 (March 2008): 467–482; Zheng Wang, *Never Forget National Humiliation: Historical Memory in Chinese Politics and Foreign Relations*, New York: Columbia University Press, 2012.
[37] Stearns, *Consumerism in World History*, p. 100. Emphasis added.

Yes, consumption, or more exactly, what one buys and how one consumes on the markets, now defines an individual in this globalizing world in substantial ways. A person is often categorized according to his/her consumption, or one's "secret" to life can easily be disclosed by the processes and consequences of this person's recent history of consumption as reflected in the encompassing ethos in which this person lives. You buy therefore you are – this is a world in which what you consume makes you. Thus, to a consumer living in the age of the global triumph of capitalism, no matter where you live, consumption embodies the existence of life, and defines its meaning.

Unbalanced Power: The Institutional Asymmetry between Capital and Consumers

Do the expansion of the global consumption markets and the rise of consumerism mean the increasing power of consumers? For many, consumers are said to be like kings and emperors to the markets; some relevant studies, in fact, talk about the "fetishization of the consumer."[38] Two leading experts started their introduction with the declaration that "the consumer is a god-like figure, before whom markets and politicians alike bow." They continue:

Everywhere it seems, the consumer is triumphant. Consumers are said to dictate production; to fuel innovation; to be creating new service sectors in advanced economies; to be driving modern politics; to have it in their power to save the environment and protect the future of the planet. Consumers embody a simple modern logic – the right to choose. Choice, the consumer's friend, the inefficient producer's foe, can be applied to things as diverse as soap-powder, holidays, healthcare or politicians.[39]

It sounds as though the triumph of capitalism is the triumph of consumers.

Certainly this is just one side of the story. The same authors have also noticed that "the consumer is also seen as a weak and malleable creature, easily manipulated, dependent, passive and foolish. Immersed in illusions, addicted to joyless pursuits of ever-increasing living standards, the consumer, far from being a god, is a pawn, in games played in invisible boardrooms."[40] It appears to be a well-balanced analysis of the

---

[38] Gabriel and Lang, *The Unmanageable Consumer*, p. vi.   [39] Ibid, p. 1.
[40] Ibid.

consumer, as they put the two sides together by arguing that "the notion of the consumer was an intellectually unstable entity, which summed up a central dilemma for late 20th-century capitalism – whether to treat people as controllable or free," and emphasizing that "in spite of the best attempts to seduce them, coax them or chide them, consumers consistently proved themselves unpredictable, contradictory and unmanageable – that they displayed many different faces and images."[41]

This section, however, places doubt in this seemingly perfect balance and combination of the different faces of the consumer. Instead, it argues that the global triumph of capitalism does not mean the triumph of consumers, and maintains that a variety of imbalances between consumers and capital has been created, reinforced, and institutionalized through globalization to the degree that the powerful appearance of the consumer can be an illusion. It further highlights the institutional reasons for why the consumer is not empowered by the global expansion of the capitalist consumption system and the global rise of consumerism, and how the various imbalances are embedded in the *institutions* of global capitalism that favor capital over consumers.

Consumer, consumption, and consumerism have been intensively studied, but often through the so-called cultural approach and social approach that emphasize the cultural and social aspects of consumption.[42] This chapter, however, has taken an institutional approach to explore the question of how consumption has been transformed by the global triumph of capitalism; it is also a political-economy perspective, which focuses on how the political economic institutions are shaping and, in turn, are shaped by the geographic and mechanic expansion of the global capitalist consumption system. In other words, consumption here is analyzed as a political economic phenomenon occurring within and being constrained by the given institutions of global capitalism. Behavioral readings, it argues, could vary in measuring the power of consumers, as the millions of consumers in various consumption circumstances could provide different empirical bases for every possible interpretation in this regard.

---

[41] Ibid, p. vii.
[42] Stearns, *Consumerism in World History*, pp. 31–6. For the cultural approach, see, for example, Colin Campbell, *The Romantic Ethic and the Spirit of Modern Consumerism*, Oxford: Basil Blackwell, 1987; for the social approach, see, for instance, Tak Wing Chan ed., *Social Status and Cultural Consumption*, Cambridge University Press, 2010.

Placing emphasis on the institutional facets of consumption helps to make for a less confusing read of the complicated kaleidoscope of consumption.

This section, therefore, will draw readers' attention to fundamental institutional arrangements in the global consumption system that lend support to its observation on unbalanced power between consumers and capital, the latter being predominant in shaping the former's choices. The global reach of multinational corporations, the rise of international retailing chain stores, and various forms of "colonization" of the markets in developing countries by existing commercial empires through methods such as franchising – some of them discussed in Chapter 3 – can all be regarded as belonging to institutional channels that are actualizing the geographic expansion of the global consumption markets. The section below, however, will analyze the power imbalance in three particular aspects: first, the asymmetry in the possession and availability of information for consumers and capital; second, organization or coordination of interests and behavior, and accordingly, the capacity for collective action by consumers and capital; and third, consumers' and capital's different connections with and influences over the state.

The Information Asymmetry between Capital and Consumers

The fundamental institutional imbalance between consumers and capital lies in the extremely unequal availability of information for the two sides and the capability of information processing at a similar level of inequality between them. A fundamental assumption of "free market" is, to quote an expert, that "the producers and consumers behave competitively when they are price takers; they are perfectly informed when they possess all information relevant to their transactions," but, as the quoted scholar emphasizes, these conditions do not exist in reality.[43] And while both producers/sellers and consumers are not "perfectly" informed, moreover, consumers in general are much worse informed than producers/sellers, and an individual consumer is extremely less informed than an individual producer/seller. The reasons are various, primarily including the mechanism of pricing, degrees of

---

[43] Julian Reiss, *Philosophy of Economics: A Contemporary Introduction*, London: Routledge, 2013, p. 230.

organization, and the weight of relevant action in decision-making. Immediately below I will discuss the price mechanism, leaving the other two factors to later analyses.

Economist Friedrich Hayek, a well-known defender of the market mechanism, emphasizes that the price mechanism communicates massive amounts of information that is dispersed among many actors, and that changes in prices coordinate the production and consumption decisions of economic agents without their knowledge.[44] This can be termed the "price-centered" approach to the market information mechanism. With such an approach, according to another defender of the ideal market,

The big company, with its resources, can afford the planning and the technology which enable it to increase the number of units produced per manhour and machine and so decrease unit costs. Thus the big company can afford to lower prices where a small producer cannot. Low prices increase consumption, and the increased consumption in turn leads to more production on a gamble that the market is virtually insatiable – which sometimes happens to be the case. The dynamic increase in earnings out of penny savings at volume sales justifies more investment in plant, still more production at higher wages, and still lower prices. Meanwhile, society becomes more and more consumer-oriented. With such a dynamic process at work, it would be sheer idiocy for an "oligopolist," or even a monopolist, to stick to the price policies of small-scale industry; sheer insanity to "charge all the traffic will bear" for the first items off the production line.[45]

It sounds perfect; but it is merely utopia, mainly because the price-centered mechanism is obviously far from being sufficient in interpreting all information communication of the market. Market information, first of all, is much richer than what the price of a good carries, even without consideration of the frequent possibility that the price does not correctly reflect the value of the good. Mechanically, furthermore, it is the side of capital, including the producer and the seller, that determines the price of a given good; a consumer's intervention, if there is an intervention, is simply in the form of feedback in response to the already-decided-upon price, and such feedback will have to wait to be taken into account by the producer and the seller, if they do, for

[44] F. A. Hayek, "The Use of Knowledge in Society," *American Economic Review* 35, 4 (1945): 519–530.
[45] John Chamberlin, *The Roots of Capitalism*, Princeton, NJ: D. Van Nostrand, 1965, rev. ed., p. 173.

future price adjustment. This is an obvious imbalance between the producer and the consumer in terms of power to determine the price, a fundamental guiding factor for those market fundamentalists. Moreover, the purpose of both the producer and the seller in pricing, no one would deny, is profit-making, which can also be realized via, simplistically speaking, setting a higher price and selling more goods – not necessarily solely through, as the quotation above suggests, lowering the price. Whether a price is low or not low in comparison to its cost, after all, is a truth that only the producer and the seller know, not the consumer.

In addition to the pricing mechanism, several other significant institutional arrangements of the market also put the consumer at a disadvantageous position in comparison with the producer, the seller, and the service-provider in terms of the availability of information. Advertisement and branding can be examples for this discussion. In regards to the former, obviously there is now a "pervasiveness of advertising in everyday life" and, accordingly, a "growing importance of packaging and promotion in the manufacture, display and purchase of consumer goods."[46] It is said that a child today sees over 20,000 commercials annually.[47] This necessity of advertising helps to demonstrate the insufficiency of price for providing market information; however, the increase of advertisements does not necessarily mean a sufficiency of information for a consumer to make his/her decision on the acquisition of a good. Mechanically, like pricing, it is also the producer and the seller who decide upon all matters regarding advertisement, including what information is carried to the consumer; this means that advertisement works to promote the market target of the producers, sellers, and service-providers, while consumers' inputs, if there are some at all, only emerge at a later stage and work marginally to have an effect over advertising. In market practice, the consumer can easily get lost in the ocean of advertisements; ironically, his/her capacity for information processing can be further reduced with the increase of advertisements.[48]

---

[46] Lury, *Consumer Culture*, pp. 3, 4.
[47] Jack Yan, "The Brand Manifesto: Why Brands Must Act Now or Alienate the Future's Primary Consumer Group," in Nicholas Ind ed., *Beyond Branding: How the New Values of Transparency and Integrity are Changing the World of Brands*, London: Kogan Page, 2003, pp. 199–221 (p. 200).
[48] Sut Jhally, *The Codes of Advertising: Fetishism and the Political Economy of Meaning in the Consumer Society*, New York: Routledge, 1990.

216 The Shaping of the Caged Anarchy

The domination of capital in market communication, therefore, is not remedied with advertisement, but only reinforced.

In regards to branding, nowadays one can easily see the "rise of brands, their increasing visibility inside and outside the economy."[49] In fact, branding is simply a significant strategy of advertising which itself promotes brand loyalty, often an important factor of marketing for monopoly. Listen to Warren Buffet, one of the richest capitalists in America who supposedly said "I'll tell you why I like the cigarette business. It costs a penny to make. Sell it for a dollar. It's addictive. And there's fantastic brand loyalty."[50] With such successful brand loyalty, the influence of price in a consumer's consideration of consumption can be reduced further to the degree that the consumer develops blind trust in making his/her decision.[51] Moreover, branding can effectively stimulate the monopoly or oligopoly of those leading brands on the market, a point to which we will return below.

The global expansion of the consumption markets simply strengthens these institutional arrangements that cause such inequality of information between producers/sellers and consumers in favor of the former. It contributes two additional factors in particular that can work powerfully to promote this information inequality, which are: the constant appearance of new products, often at a fast pace, and the sudden involvement of numerous new consumers. In regards to goods, the rise of consumerism has often "resulted from a number of factors operating concurrently, from new products and new earnings to new needs, framed by changing culture including growing urban influence."[52] Fashion is a good example in this regard, although nowadays it is easily overshadowed by those cutting-edge products brought about by the information revolution, which joins in perpetuating trends such as consumption beyond immediate need and the rise of cultural consumption, thereby providing powerful momentum and infinite possibilities for new, renewed, and novel

---

[49] Lury, *Consumer Culture*, p. 3.
[50] Quoted in Michael Albert, "The Parecon Proposal," in Jeff Shantz and Jose Brendan Macdonald eds., *Beyond Capitalism: Building Democratic Alternatives for Today and the Future*, New York: Bloomsbury, 2013, pp. 25–44 (p. 27).
[51] Martin Lindstrom, *Brand Sense: Sensory Secrets Behind the Stuff We Buy*, New York: Free Press, 2010.
[52] Stearns, *Consumerism in World History*, p. 36.

products.[53] Think about the constant issuing and reissuing of a new generation of the same product (do you use an iPhone?); one can vividly sense such a progression of a good. These products are inevitably new commodities for consumers, which implies that the consumer's knowledge of them is even weaker than in usual circumstances. On the other hand, the producers are well equipped with the necessary information concerning these products. This contrast thus pushes the information inequality between consumers and producers to a further degree at which the latter can easily dominate and manipulate the former.

Globalization has involved millions of new consumers almost overnight in the global consumption system, and these new consumers are especially ill informed (and poorly experienced, as experience provides information) when suddenly faced with the abundance of commodities available on global consumption markets. Scholars point out that the spread of global consumer culture is conditioned by the transnational flow of cultural resources,[54] which involves branded goods and the associated symbolic and cultural meanings that consumers internalize.[55] Branding is an especially effective strategy to convince these inexperienced consumers, as evidenced in the near-worship of big brands among customers in developing countries.[56] The relative incapability of information processing concerning numerous versions of the same product can be a reason for them to take this approach: when they don't really know how to choose, it is assumed to be a safer choice to choose those big-brand products.

---

[53] Teri Agins, *The End of Fashion: The Mass Marketing of the Clothing Business*, New York: William Morrow, 1999; Elizabeth L. Cline, *Overdressed: The Shockingly High Cost of Cheap Fashion*, New York: Portfolio, 2012; Tansy E. Hoskins, *Stitched Up: The Anti-Capitalist Book of Fashion*, London: Pluto Press, 2014.

[54] Eric Arnould, "Global Consumer Culture," in Jagdish N. Sheth and Naresh Malhotra eds., *Wiley International Encyclopedia of Marketing*, New York: Wiley, 2011, as posted on http://www.uwyo.edu/sustainable/recent-research/docs/global%20consumer%20culture%20arnould.pdf.

[55] Wanhsiu Sunny Tsai, Qinghua Yang, and Yu Liu, "Young Chinese Consumers' Snob and Bandwagon Luxury Consumption Preferences," *Journal of International Consumer Marketing* 25, 5 (2013): 290–304.

[56] See, for example, Paurav Shukla, "A Closer Look at Luxury Consumption in Asia," http://luxurysociety.com/articles/2015/07/a-closer-look-at-luxury-consumption-in-asia, posted 16 July 2015, accessed May 10, 2016; Tsai, Yang, and Liu, "Young Chinese Consumers' Snob and Bandwagon Luxury Consumption Preferences."

It helps explain the nearly ludicrous infatuation with luxuries in many developing countries.[57] To highlight such an effect, experts refer to the phenomenon with terms such as "bandwagon," "snob," and "signaling,"[58] particularly in luxury consumption but, this author believes, suitable to discussions of general consumption.

The Inequality in Organizational Capacities between Capital and Consumers

A consumer is by nature an individual in his/her consumption, but he/she usually comes to encounter an organization or more possibly a set of organizations that provide the commodity. In the contemporary world, it is rare that a production or sale or service provision is a business of literally an individual person, while, at the same time, it is equally rare to see an act of daily consumption being performed as a collective decision beyond a core family size. Furthermore, such a decision regarding daily consumption is usually pretty casual, especially in comparison to the decision of a producer or a seller to invest in producing or selling a product; the latter often makes a careful decision with a volume of information involved in the decision-making process that is far greater than the consumer's in his/her effort to search for relevant information – this has more to do with information processing, but what has been analyzed here discloses the greatly different degrees of organization between consumption and capital. I would argue that such inequalities between capital and consumers in terms of organizational capacity further extend themselves onto a wider scale, where, as examined in Chapter 3, capital has been increasingly developing its various methods of coordination of interests and

---

[57] There are, of course, many other reasons to explain this big-brand-worship and luxury-worship phenomenon, among which the emergence of the superrich due to huge inequality in developing economies is one that will be touched upon later.

[58] See, for example, Minas Kastanakis and George Balabanis, "Bandwagon, Snob and Veblen Effects in Luxury Consumption," *Advances in Consumer Research* 38 (2011): 609–611; Minas N. Kastanakis and George Balabanis, "Between the Mass and the Class: Antecedents of the "Bandwagon" Luxury Consumption Behavior," *Journal of Business Research*, 65, 10 (2012): 1399–1407; Minas Kastanakis and George Balabanis, "Signalling Effects in Luxury Consumption," Association for Consumer Research, http://acrwebsite.org/volumes/1007091/eacr/vol9/E-09, accessed May 10, 2016; Tsai, Yang, and Liu, "Young Chinese Consumers' Snob and Bandwagon Luxury Consumption Preferences."

behavior through national and international connections and global networks; by contrast, consumers are psychologically and institutionally individual-oriented in consumption with a trend of being suppressed into atomization.

Yes, there are movements in the consumption world that are rising against the institutional imbalance between capital and consumers for the purpose of enhancing consumers' power and impact in both the market sense and the political sense. Experts, therefore, began to talk about the "new orthodoxy" of the "active consumer" or "citizen consumer," defining such a consumer as "a creative, confident and rational being articulating personal identity and serving the public interest."[59] Political consumerism has been suggested; organizations such as the Consumers' Council are set up; movements like "Fair Trade" are advocated; and various proposals are made, as exemplified by the so-called "Parecon proposal".[60] Resistance, as an expert points out, can arise among "many ordinary individuals [who] worried about their own engagement in consumerism, seeking to find some outlet for real guilt about indulgence even *as they continue to indulge.*"[61]

To this author, the rise of various social movements among consumers is definitely a desirable development in global capitalism in the normative sense,[62] but, in the epistemological sense of understanding the reality of global capitalism, such a rise is, regretfully, not powerful

[59] Frank Trentmann, "Knowing Consumers – Histories, Identities, Practices: An Introduction," in Frank Trentmann ed., *The Making of the Consumer: Knowledge, Power and Identity in the Modern World*, Oxford: Berg, 2006, pp. 1–27 (pp. 2–3).

[60] For political consumerism, see, for example, Michele Micheletti, *Political Virtue and Shopping: Individuals, Consumerism, and Collective Action*, New York: Palgrave Macmillan, 2010, rev. ed.; Dietlind Stolle and Michele Micheletti, *Political Consumerism: Global Responsibility in Action*, Cambridge University Press, 2013. For Fair Trade, see, for instance, Daniel Jaffee, *Brewing Justice: Fair Trade Coffee, Sustainability, and Survival*, Berkeley: University of California Press, 2007; Sarah Lyon and Mark Moberg eds., *Fair Trade and Social Justice: Global Ethnographies*, New York University Press, 2010; Keith R. Brown, *Buying Into Fair Trade: Culture, Morality, and Consumption*, New York University Press, 2013. For other proposals and efforts in the regard, see, for example, Jeff Shantz and Jose Brendan Macdonald eds., *Beyond Capitalism: Building Democratic Alternatives for Today and the Future*, New York: Bloomsbury, 2013.

[61] Stearns, *Consumerism in World History*, p. 67. Emphasis added.

[62] In the final chapter, this book will follow this line of reasoning that emphasizes the significance of change in the sphere of consumption and consumers' action to discuss the future of global capitalism.

enough to alter the fundamental institutions of the global political economy. For example, by 2008, total Fair Trade purchases in the developed world reached nearly $3 billion, a fivefold increase in four years. Consumers pay a "fair price" for Fair Trade items, which is meant to generate greater earnings for family farmers, cover the costs of production, and support socially just and environmentally sound practices. Yet it is, according to a group of experts, still constrained by existing markets and the entities that dominate them, which often cause the Fair Trade movement to deliver material improvements to producers that are much more modest than the profound social transformations the movement claims to support.[63] In fact, the overwhelming power of the giant corporations in international trade seeks to improve their image by co-optation and dilution of the standards when faced by the challenge of Fair Trade.[64]

Moreover, the assumption that underlines the effectiveness of such consumer resistance is somehow unrealistic, as stated in the so-called Parecon proposal for building a democratic alternative beyond capitalism:

> Another defining feature of capitalism is that the amount of any particular good or service produced and the relative valuations of different products are largely determined by competitive markets. Buyers and sellers each aggrandize themselves essentially oblivious to the impact of their choices on others. I sell at the highest price I can impose the least costly items I can provide. You buy at the lowest price you can impose the most valuable items you can find. We fleece each other.[65]

This is, to our discussion, not a realistic assumption, because it is practically impossible for a buyer to "impose" something over the seller, as a buyer is an individual who in every single transaction faces the organizational power of production, sale, and service-provision. Perfect market competition is never fully in practice, as it is assumed; a consumer, as emphasized earlier, has much less information about everything concerning the transaction than the seller has. Therefore, in addition to the information asymmetry, the buyer and the seller also possess asymmetric bargaining power that is rooted in their asymmetric organizational strength.

---

[63] Lyon and Moberg, *Fair Trade and Social Justice.*   [64] Jaffee, *Brewing Justice.*
[65] Albert, "The Parecon Proposal," p. 26.

These efforts, therefore, indicate a counteraction against the institutions of global capitalism much more than a fundamentally new configuration of the institutions themselves; as social initiatives, they are attempting to remedy the negative social impacts of capitalist consumption, but, at least so far, they are far from being globally effective enough to overcome the impacts, let alone alter the institutional path leading to these impacts. In fact, anti-consumerism is not a totally new effort, as it has existed and developed for centuries;[66] capitalism, however, has still been able to gain its global triumph, including its triumph in attaining the global expansion of the capitalist consumption system and the global rise of consumerism. It seems that, to use a metaphor, the existence of counter-currents is not able to divert the path of the riverbed. For this author, therefore, the rise of various consumer movements does not invalidate the argument regarding the general inequality between capital and consumers in terms of organizational capacities, and the particular difficulties for consumers in comparison with capital to take collective action in the institutional circumstances set up by global capitalism.

The Power Imbalance between Capital and Consumers in Relations with the State

The state is definitely a decisive intervening factor for balancing, rebalancing, or unbalancing in the relationship between consumers and capital. With the state-market nexus, the state in general joins capital, rather than consumers, in this power imbalance, further giving greater favor to capital against consumers. This argument can be discussed from two angles: historical and institutional.

From the historical perspective, the state's resistance to the market mechanism is often associated with this state's hostility to consumerism, as recorded and exemplified in Nazi and fascist resistance to consumerism during the Second World War and, similarly, communist resistance to consumerism during the Cold War.[67] With post–Cold

---

[66] See some records and analyses in Cross, *Time and Money*; Horowitz, *The Morality of Spending*; de Grazia with Furlough, *The Sex of Things*; Daunton and Hilton, *The Politics of Consumption*; Hilton, *Consumerism in Twentieth-Century Britain*.

[67] For Nazi Germany's anti-consumerism, see, for example, Stearns, *Consumerism in World History*, pp. 72–73; Victoria de Grazia, *Culture of Consent: Mass*

War globalization, which is defined in this book as all states having embraced the market mechanism, no state any longer takes the stance of opposing consumerism. Instead, the state in the developing world today may resist Western values but will still welcome foreign (Western) goods. Here is an interesting comparison: According to the historian Stearns, "King Frederick the Great of Prussia condemned popular coffee drinking, arguing that beer should be good enough for his subjects; here, simple traditionalism plus a reaction against foreign products motivated concern."[68] In the twenty-first century, "coffee in China" can serve as an example, as well as Coca-Cola, beer, wine, bottled water, etc., of the controversy of Western beverages coming into China to conquer the land of tea, Chinese alcohol, and boiled water.[69] This demise of the anti-consumerist state, however, does not necessarily mean the state's endorsement of consumers' interests and power. Quite the opposite, it supports the expansion of markets, primarily the interest of producers and sellers; namely, of capital.

Organization of Leisure in Fascist Italy, Cambridge University Press, 1981. For communist anti-consumerism, see, for instance, Alec Nove, *An Economic History of the U.S.S.R.*, London: Penguin Books, 1982, pp. 358–359; Janos Kornai, *The Socialist System: The Political Economy of Communism*, Princeton University Press, 1992; Richard Curt Kraus, *The Cultural Revolution: A Very Short Introduction*, Oxford University Press, 2012; Paulina Bren and Mary Neuburger eds., *Communism Unwrapped: Consumption in Cold War Eastern Europe*, Oxford University Press, 2012.

[68] Stearns, *Consumerism in World History*, p. 26.

[69] See some reports in: Jennifer Duggan, "Spilling the Beans on China's Booming Coffee Culture," *The Guardians*, May 18, 2015, www.theguardian.com/sustain able-business/2015/may/18/spilling-the-beans-chinas-growing-coffee-culture, accessed May 12, 2016; The Coca Cola Company, "Celebrating 35 years of Coca-Cola in China," www.coca-colacompany.com/stories/celebrating-35-years -of-coca-cola-in-china, posted November 24, 2014, accessed May 12, 2016 (it reported that China as "one of the world's fastest-growing markets today is the third-largest market in the Coca-Cola system"); Katharine Song, "The China Beer Market: A New Era," Rabobank Food & Agribusiness Research and Advisory (Utrecht, the Netherlands), https://far.rabobank.com/en/sectors/beverages/the-china-beer-market.html, posted May 2015, accessed June 3, 2016 (in reporting "the continuous growth of imported beer," the survey says "Chinese consumers see imported premium beers as part of a modern lifestyle"); Kim Willsher, "China Becomes Biggest Market for Red Wine, with 1.86bn Bottles Sold in 2013," *The Guardians*, January 29, 2014, www.theguardian.com/world/2014/jan/29/ china-appetite-red-wine-market-boom, accessed October 2, 2015; Kenneth Rapoza, "Bottled Water Market Quickly Turning Chinese," *Forbes*, www.forbes.com/sites/kenrapoza/2013/08/13/bottled-water-market-quickly-turning-chinese/#3807e7d050d9, posted August 13, 2013, accessed June 3, 2016.

Why is it so? We need to return to our earlier discussion of the economic state to find an institutional explanation about the inclination of the state when it embraces consumerism toward supporting capital rather than consumers. With the rise of the economic state in globalization, the state now plays more roles in the economy than before; it has an increasing concern over economic activities as a response to increasing materialist concerns of the populace everywhere in the post–Cold War era. This is to say, prevailing commodity fetishism both entices and enforces the state to actively make corresponding responses in delivering economic goods to citizens. That is why, after September 2001, American government leaders "hastened to urge people to keep their consumer activities going rather than asking citizens to sacrifice."[70] This, perhaps, can serve as an example of "the active role of the state in organizing collective and individual forms of consumption."[71]

Such a role, however, is not necessarily consistent with consumers' preferences and interests. Everybody knows that capital regularly invests huge money in advertising for the purpose of promoting consumption; it is, therefore, not difficult to conclude that the state's promotion of consumption is much in accordance to capital's interests. Here the difference is only this: a producer and a seller promote consumption of a specific commodity, usually by boasting the attractiveness of its product, but, with coercive power as its nature, the state promotes consumption in general. In this sense, therefore, the state in this context acts as the general agent of capital's collective interests.

Standardization of Consumption, Atomization of Consumer: The Mass Foundation of Global Capitalism

The above three developments, namely, the involvement of the entire global populace into the capitalist consumption system, the global rise of consumerism, and the power imbalance between consumers and capital, this chapter would argue, have provided the mass foundation for global capitalism. Despite varied resistance, consumers in general "continue to indulge" in consumerism, as an early quotation indicates. Or, in other authors' sentences, there is an increasing visibility of so-called "consumer

[70] Stearns, *Consumerism in World History*, p. vii.
[71] Lury, *Consumer Culture*, p. 6.

illness" linked to what have been called "maladies of agency"[72] and pathologies or "maladies of the will," such as addiction,[73] "whether it be addiction to alcohol, sex, food, shopping, kleptomania, 'binge shopping' or compulsive buying."[74] "Economic man" again emerges in this context of consumption, in addition to his earlier setting around labor, as the consumer is increasingly standardized and atomized. Before turning to elaborate upon the conceptualization of the consumer as "economic man," in this section we should first analyze how the consumer is standardized and atomized.

Cultural consumption deserves special discussion in this context, as it commercializes the cultural, spiritual, and even moral lives of consumers, the last territories of human life invaded and conquered by the power of money, materialism, and the market; these are also supposedly the domains in which diversity and individuality are by nature more rigorous than in the domains of humans' material life. In this regard, sociological debates on cultural consumption can be relevant to our understanding, as they, according to a fine review of relevant literature provided by Chan and Goldthorpe, "have engaged in research to increase the body of empirical evidence on the nature and extent of differences in cultural tastes and consumption across social strata; and they have tried to provide some theoretical explanation and understanding of the interrelations that can thus be shown to exist between cultural and social hierarchies."[75] A central theme of the debate is about whether there is a corresponding connection between cultural consumption and social stratification, for which the so-called homology argument and its rivals have provided contending perspectives. For our consideration, however, as will be discussed immediately below, these different arguments have all provided support in differing ways to the assertion that the commercialization of cultural life has yielded a significant social consequence; that is, the standardization of consumption.

---

[72] Mark Seltzer, "Series Killers (1)," *Differences: A Journal of Feminist Cultural Studies* 5, 1 (1993): 92–128.

[73] Eve Kosofsky Sedgwick, *Tendencies*, London: Routledge, 1994; quoted in Lury, *Consumer Culture*, p. 5.

[74] Lury, *Consumer Culture*, pp. 4–5.

[75] Tak Wing Chan and John H. Goldthorpe, "Social Status and Cultural Consumption," in Tak Wing Chan ed., *Social Status and Cultural Consumption*, Cambridge University Press, 2010, pp. 1–27 (p. 2).

In the "homology" argument, "a close correspondence exists between social and cultural stratification."[76] In this line of reasoning, Herbert Gans presents a range of research findings in support of the view that "highbrow," "lowbrow," as well as versions of "middlebrow" cultural tastes and consumption do systematically map the socioeconomic stratification of American society.[77] Similarly, Pierre Bourdieu maintains that social classes display different patterns of cultural taste and consumption along with closely related patterns of material consumption, and emphasizes that

[T]he cultural field, no less than the economic field, is one in which class competition and conflict are always present. The "dominant classes" of modern societies use their superior "cultural capital," no less than their superior economic capital, in order to maintain their position of dominance. Differentiation inevitably serves as a means of underwriting hierarchy. More specifically, members of dominant classes seek to demonstrate and confirm the superiority of their own lifestyle over those of other classes by arrogating to it cultural forms that they can represent as "canonical," "legitimate" or otherwise "distinguished" – while maintaining "aesthetic distance" from other forms deemed to be inferior.[78]

Bourdieu coins the term "symbolic violence," through which "cultural capital can in fact be converted into economic capital, and cultural reproduction thus serves as a crucial component in social reproduction more generally."[79]

These imply, for our discussion, that "economic capital" has been extending to cultural domains, thus turning cultures into extended forms of economy and further squeezing a consumer of cultures into an "economic man." As Chan and Goldthorpe have synthesized, income and education are "important stratifying forces in regard to cultural consumption," as "income may be taken as a good indicator of more immediately available economic resources, and education of

---

[76] Ibid, p. 3.

[77] Gans, *Popular Culture and High Culture*. Also, Lawrence Levine, *Highbrow/ Lowbrow: The Emergence of Cultural Hierarchy in America*, Cambridge, MA: Harvard University Press, 1988.

[78] Pierre Bourdieu, *Distinction: A Social Critique of the Judgment of Taste*, London: Routledge & Kegan Paul, 1984; quoted in Chan and Goldthorpe, "Social Status and Cultural Consumption," p. 4.

[79] Quoted in Chan and Goldthorpe, "Social Status and Cultural Consumption," p. 4.

cultural resources."[80] They also acknowledge the importance of "information processing capacity that can independently exert an influence on cultural consumption," though only regarding it as something belonging to "individual psychological attributes,"[81] with which this chapter does not agree, as we have already pointed out the institutional essence of information processing under global capitalism. Moreover, Chan and Goldthorpe highlight the "individual motivations *that are grounded in specifically status concerns* – whether these are directed towards status enhancement or exclusion or simply towards confirmation of membership in social networks or circles that are seen as expressing a valued lifestyle."[82]

This argument can be developed further into two more points that reinforce the materialistic concern of a consumer. First, such "status concerns" are inevitably, though not purely, income-based, which join other factors to further motivate the shaping of the "economic man." Secondly, and more importantly, although these motivations are "individual," they must ironically lead to the decline of individuality as long as such "status concerns" prevail, let alone in the event that such concerns are actualized through consumption, because such concerns imply a consumer's desire to become similar to members of a certain social network or circle through either cultural or material consumption. As every consumer is by principle motivated to do so, the logical conclusion is their inclination toward further resembling one another in the continuous process of daily consumption – this signifies a social trend toward the standardization of consumers in both the material and cultural domains.

The arguments in cultural consumption studies challenging the homology perspective can also be understood as complimentary rather than rival to the above points concerning standardization of consumption, especially in the diachronic sense of observing the historical development of cultural consumption. One such argument, in an attempt to challenge the idea of a simple matching of social and cultural hierarchies, highlights "massification" of cultural consumption, for which H. L. Wilensky produced evidence decades ago to show that participation in cultural consumption – via TV, newspapers, magazines etc. – was extensive across all strata of American

---

[80] Ibid, p. 15   [81] Ibid.   [82] Ibid. Emphasis in original.

society.[83] This argument and its accompanying example directly support our standardization thesis.

In the process of post–Cold War globalization, this trend of consumer standardization in cultural consumption has been confirmed by various observations. Different from the historical development by the 1980s in which the earlier cultural eclecticism and openness had become increasingly rare but cultural space was more sharply defined and less flexible than it had been,[84] the old cultural distinctions among highbrow, middlebrow, and lowbrow now cease to exist, which leads scholars to suggest "nobrow" for describing this flattening, great category of all standardized consumers of theater, cinema, music, fiction, and more.[85] It is, especially, the power of market that drives this onrushing cultural phenomenon, as it is argued to be the melding of culture along with "the marketing of culture and the culture of marketing."[86]

Social stratification, however, does not disappear in this trend toward "nobrow," as financial constraints at the very least cannot easily be escaped for many in their consumption. Such constraints, I would further argue, often create a spiral effect enforcing the standardization of consumption. Let's analyze this effect by discussing the so-called omnivore-univore argument that arose in the 1990s which maintained that members of higher social strata do not shun popular or lowbrow culture; rather, they participate in it regularly and even more actively than members of lower strata.[87] The cultural consumption of individuals in more advantaged social positions, according to this

---

[83] H. L. Wilensky, "Mass Society and Mass Culture: Interdependence or Independence?" *American Sociological Review*, 29, 2 (1964): 173–197.
[84] For this historical development in the United States, see Levine, *Highbrow/Lowbrow*.
[85] John Seabrook, *Nobrow: The Culture of Marketing, the Marketing of Culture*, New York: Knopf, 2000; Peter Swirski, *From Lowbrow to Nobrow*, Montreal and Kingston: McGill-Queen's University Press, 2005.
[86] Seabrook, *Nobrow*.
[87] See especially Richard A. Peterson, "Understanding Audience Segmentation: From Elite and Mass to Omnivore and Univore," *Poetics*, 21, 4 (1992): 243–258; Richard A. Peterson and Albert Simkus, "How Musical Tastes Mark Occupational Status Groups," in Michèle Lamont and Marcel Fournier eds., *Cultivating Differences: Symbolic Boundaries and the Making of Inequality*, University of Chicago Press, 1992, pp. 152–186; Richard A. Peterson and Roger M. Kern, "Changing Highbrow Taste: From Snob to Omnivore," *American Sociological Review*, 61, 5 (1996): 900–907.

perspective, is "both greater and wider in its range" than that of individuals in less advantaged positions, creating a "crucial contrast" of cultural omnivore versus cultural univore that is dissimilar to the traditional concept of "snob versus slob."[88] To our discussion, this argument helps to add some sophistication to the conclusion on the inherent dynamics of "massifization" or standardization. Yet, a subtle indictor of status hierarchies emerges in which a member of the so-called plutocrats is not as easily recognizable; while he or she will frequent universally popular places such as McDonald's, a non-plutocrat will be refused the opportunity to so much as glance at, let alone frequent, a fine restaurant in which the plutocrat will dine when he or she no longer wants to eat at McDonald's. Moreover, the average person would also do these things when able to do so; it may not necessarily involve the same restaurants, but it would follow the same pattern of eating out that involves occasionally having meals at fine restaurants and at other times buying a Big Mac.

Here, three points can be drawn to enrich our discussion of the standardization of consumption: First, consumers at lower statuses must reduce the scope of their consumptive choices, and a uniformity of lifestyles thus emerges and prevails for this overwhelming majority of global consumers. Such uniformity is, of course, the primary meaning of standardization. Second, assuming there is a constant progression of an increasing number of people joining the "upper" echelons of consumption, the result is that the mode of omnivore consumption prevails over univore and, I would argue, that social diversity is definitively reduced, although the diversity of an individual's choices may increase. More exactly, the diversity within an individual's lifestyle may increase slightly, but the diversity of lifestyles as a whole in a society will be narrowed down. Considering the increasing inequality promoted by globalization, such a progression is suspicious, at least in the current world. We have already acknowledged that there is a strong "status concern" among consumers in the capitalist consumption system; the lower echelons' imitation of the "upper" echelons in consumption patterns, therefore, is always powerfully motivated. Thus, we arrive at our third point: does imitation in any form promote diversity, or does it instead lead to standardization? The answer is obviously the

[88] Peterson, "Understanding Audience Segmentation," p. 252. See a discussion in Chan and Goldthorpe, "Social Status and Cultural Consumption," p. 8.

latter. According to Chan and Goldthorpe's summary of those perspectives against the homology argument, "no expectation can be maintained that different patterns of cultural consumption will stand in some systematic relationships to structures of social inequality";[89] therefore the standardization of consumption reaches a new level in which it occurs not only in material consumption but in cultural consumption as well.

A two-way effect, therefore, emerges in reinforcing standardization: on one hand, the higher strata always extend their consumption downward, making them "standardized" in consumption in line with other social groups; on the other hand, the lower strata intend to imitate the higher strata's consumption whenever they can do so, thus jumping on the bandwagon for the purpose of following the standard of higher consumption. To our discussion, the snob effect and the bandwagon effect in, for example, luxury consumption, are thus dialectically propping up each other, both strengthening the momentum of standardization of consumption against the social background of increasing inequalities.

The information revolution also contributes greatly to the standardization of consumption. Experts have already taken full note of the impacts of the information revolution on the promotion of consumerism: "A proliferation of spaces, platforms and modes of consuming, including, for example, an increase in the range of different forums of shopping, from Internet shopping (including eBay and Amazon), retail tourism, mail-order, shopping malls, rummage sales, car-boot fairs, farmers' markets, vintage, pop-up and second-hand shops."[90] Moreover, information technologies have changed the concrete nature of commercial deals, and this has often resulted in a standardization of the commercial method. For example, the rise of the use of the barcode to monitor and manage the sales of products now prevails; in 2005, it was already estimated that five billion barcodes were scanned every day across the world.[91] This helps to standardize the format of all transaction deals worldwide across nations, cultures, and different types of commodities. In terms of the contents of consumption, the standardization impact of the

---

[89] Chan and Goldthorpe, "Social Status and Cultural Consumption," p. 6.
[90] Lury, *Consumer Culture*, p. 2.
[91] Bruce Sterling, *Shaping Things*, Cambridge, MA: MIT Press, 2005.

information revolution is perhaps not quite as straightforward, but it is more easily observable: just think about how TV has attracted immigrants through the sought-after lifestyle and level of consumption experienced in industrialized nations.[92] Such desirability does make these people's consumption increasingly similar to that which they are seeking. In fact, the latest studies of the music industry reveal that the information and communication technology revolution has the powerful effect of making the production, marketing, and consumption of cultural products, such as music products, simply like junk food.[93]

"Individualization" forms the core of another line of argument against the homology perspective; the authors carrying this line believe that social stratification has a declining influence on the formation of lifestyles and of patterns of consumption, material and cultural.[94] In these respects, class no longer provides an adequate "context of orientation" and status-based social milieus lose their luster.[95] This also works in consent with the standardization argument, at least in the sense that a consumption action can take place in ignorance of the consumer's social status, if not his/her financial status. Anthony Giddens, however, carries this line of reasoning further to conclude that rising standards of living, greater geographical and social mobility and exogamy, as well as a growing awareness of alternative social bases of identity – for example, gender, ethnicity or sexuality – all help to free individuals from class constraints and status preoccupations and allow them to develop their own lifestyles as a matter of personal choice and so as to give expression "to particular narrative of self-identity."[96] With a similar line of reasoning, it is said by another heavy-weight contemporary thinker of sociology that consumption forms new "patterns of success," opening up the possibility for achievement of symbolic distinction through consumer rivalry and "taste contests" that

---

[92] Spellman, *Uncertain Identity*.

[93] John Seabrook, *The Song Machine: Inside the Hit Factory*, New York: W. W. Norton, 2015. Also, Stephen Witt, *How Music Got Free: The End of an Industry, the Turn of the Century, and the Patient Zero of Piracy*, New York: Viking, 2015.

[94] Chan and Goldthorpe, "Social Status and Cultural Consumption," p. 5.

[95] Ulrich Beck, *Risk Society: Toward a New Modernity*, London: Sage, 1992, pp. 88–89.

[96] Anthony Giddens, *Modernity and Self-Identity: Self and Society in the Late Modern Age*, Cambridge: Polity, 1991, pp. 80–81.

can be pursued "not just in ideologically induced fantasies but in practical life, by the *majority* in capitalist societies."[97]

Here the crucial problem is the possible conceptual confusion between "individualization" and "atomization"[98] – whereas Giddens and Bauman argue for the former, this chapter sees the latter. The distinction between the two phenomena, in fact, can be found alongside at least two dividing lines. First, in terms of the individual motivation for being engaged in consumption, Giddens admits that nowadays individuals are increasingly *forced* to choose their lifestyles.[99] In my point of view, "being forced" may imply that consumers are forced to consume under the guise of the "choice" of selecting commodities that exist on global markets. In the sense that no one can escape from making such choices, all consumers are institutionally standardized in their behaviors. Second, what can a consumer choose on the consumption market? Can the weight of the consumer's individual autonomy in this regard overwhelm the options provided by the markets or vice versa? In the global markets that have been shaped by the institutions and movements analyzed by this book, it is quite obvious that an individual consumer's "choice" in consumption is more fundamentally constrained by institutional and macropolitical economic factors rather than being based on his/her own autonomous willingness. Yes, at a given moment you may decide if you would like to have a cup of coffee or not, which could be celebrated as a consumer's power of choice; you can even decide upon which type of coffee you would like. In many, actually more and more, places in the present world, however, you have no choice except to go to Starbucks for the purpose of actualizing your "autonomous" decision. In the end, as more and more consumers actualize their choices in the same way, it seems more proper to conceptualize the trend as "standardization" rather than "individualization."

[97] Zygmunt Bauman, *Freedom*, Milton Keynes: Open University Press, 1988, pp. 58–61. Also, Zygmunt Bauman, *The Individualized Society*, Cambridge: Polity, 2001.

[98] Chan and Goldthorpe also criticize that "individualisation arguments cannot themselves claim any strong research basis"; that their leading proponents are "social theorists," writing in "a largely data-free mode" without "empirical compelling." Chan and Goldthorpe, "Social Status and Cultural Consumption," p. 7. But, due to space limitations, here it is impossible to follow that line of argument.

[99] Giddens, *Modernity and Self-Identity*, p. 81.

In the sense of highlighting the fact that the same decision by these consumers is made and actualized individually without any purpose of collective action, the trend can be further argued as "atomization." In fact, cultural consumption is now seen as essentially reflecting more than the highly personalized choices and self-identity projects that individuals pursue in a way that is definitely not free of constraints "imposed by, and of motivations grounded in, the positions that they hold within structures of social inequality."[100] In other words, putting the two sides together, a consumer is flanked by, or even squeezed between, making personal choices within the constraints that must be confronted by his/her own status of finance, education, etc. and follow-ing mass, market, and commercial trends that are standardized often across social strata. Yes, a consumer is an individual in making choices of consumption, but not in the sense of individualism; rather, it is in the sense of being an atomized person imitating all others while lacking an organic connection to those others.

The atomization of consumers, to sum up, means that virtually all consumers are similar to each other but without inherent coordination, nor does their similar behavior form any collective action; rather, they are similar to each other as are atoms, or, to borrow a classic metaphor, as are potatoes within a sack: among them they appear to have virtually no differences, yet they are not connected or organized coherently. Atomization, to repeat, is not individualization, though they can be easily confused. Whereas the individualization argument sees consump-tion at large becoming celebrated as "the focus and playground for individual freedom" and even "self-assertion" without facing "the dan-ger of imminent and conclusive defeat,"[101] atomization implies a vulnerability of consumers in the face of the global market, or more exactly, the producers, sellers, or service-providers, the human agents of capital on the global market, especially in terms of following the hints, guides, symbols, or any other kinds of information provided by the latter in the consumer pursuing his/her seemingly "individualized" behavior of consumption. A typical consumer in global capitalism, therefore, is a person who acts alone in mass consumption, often struggling to simultaneously create his/her own style/identity/individuality while,

---

[100] Chan and Goldthorpe, "Social Status and Cultural Consumption," p. 10.
[101] Bauman, *Freedom*; Zygmunt Bauman, *Society under Siege*, Cambridge: Polity, 2002.

ironically, following a relevant global fashion/trend/standard. It is such consumers, numbering in the millions, as will be further maintained, who compose the mass foundation of global capitalism.

"Economic Man 2.0" in the Caged Anarchy: The Two Organizational Bodies of Capitalism Revisited

At the core of both consumption's standardization and consumer's atomization stands the "economic man" who is now in the incarnation of a consumer. This is the persona we have encountered in the last chapter when discussing labor's predicament. Now, however, in circumstances shaped by the global expansion of the capitalist consumption system, the "economic man" possesses quite a different personality. Let's term it "economic man 2.0" and refer it as a general identity and a personified expression of the consumer in global capitalism.

"Economic man 2.0" distinguishes himself from the "economic man" of a laborer in many ways. As "economic man," a laborer always struggles to find a job and gain a better income, thus his/her mental state is predominated by concerns over the often scant opportunity of selling his/her own labor on the global labor market with a relatively good price and by the pursuit of the actualization of his/her price as "human capital" through various means, most prominently upward mobility. As this person is lucky enough to sell his/her labor, he/she will often find him/herself in a capitalist firm intensively competing with other firms and extensively imposing discipline, authority, hierarchy, and even repression over its employees. This is an "economic man" who has been turned, in the historical process of centuries eventually advanced by the global triumph of capitalism, into something resembling a moneymaking machine.

"Economic man 2.0" as a consumer, however, appears to be much more autonomous, individualistic, and focused on enjoyment, as he/she now has valuable opportunities to appreciate material affluence and take pleasure in life. Here the subtlety lies mainly in two elements that shape consumption: consumption as an enjoyment, unlike tedious, onerous, and often insufferable labor; and consumption as a seemingly individual, autonomous decision-making process and, accordingly, an expression of individuality that carries social independence, in contrast to labor often being reluctant, disciplined, and supervised. The subtlety of "economic man 2.0," therefore, is much better developed, as the "economic man" in the last chapter who fiercely struggles to make a living now comes to enjoy the achievements of the struggle, as well as the process and even freedom of living per se.

The consumer as "economic man 2.0," however, is not a chronological and technical upgrade of the "economic man" as laborer; rather, it indicates both the upgrading of materialization and commercialization, on one hand, and the refinement and sophistication of one-dimensionalization of human beings, on the other. "Economic man 2.0" structurally and synchronously takes the effects of "economic man" in the capitalist production system further to the degree that the expansion of global capitalism covers everything, not only geographically but socially. Capitalism by nature aims to create such an economic man, but it is its global triumph that has made capitalism a powerful enough machine to make "economic man 2.0" a "global citizen."

Clearly, there is a parallel and complementariness between the "economic man" in the global production system and the "economic man" in the global consumption process; they are two manifestations of the same essence of global capitalism. Emerging against the same background of globalization, they are psychologically, socially, and institutionally similar in the way that they are directed to single-mindedly pursue and enjoy material life, and they reinforce each other in these many aspects. Moreover, despite the apparent advantages, individual consumers are equally weak in their status as laborers. As the laborer, he/she is a "cog" in the machine; as the consumer, he/she is standardized, isolated, and atomized. The former is forced to be in a highly organized system, and the latter often appears to be part of an autonomous decision-making process but without any actual powerful organizational support. It is nonetheless in these two elements, namely, consumption as an enjoyment and consumption as a seemingly autonomous activity, this chapter argues, that the expansion of the global consumer markets has brought the rise of global consumerism and the fall of individual consumers, and that, as our common universal identity in daily life, "economic man 2.0" possesses a great significance for understanding the mass foundation of global capitalism.

The standardization of consumption and the atomization of consumers, this chapter would further argue, are expressions of the process in which the caged anarchy of capitalist consumption is being shaped. Caged anarchy would appear to be a self-contradictory term; therefore, let me explain. First, "anarchy" is used here in the sense that there is no central authority coordinating a trillion people's consumption on the global market.[102] This is an argument that stands distinct from an earlier criticism contributed by Karl Marx of capitalism as the anarchy of production. According to James Fulcher's summary,

Marx argued that capitalism was prone to crises because production was separated from consumption. In pre-capitalist societies they were closely related, since most production was for more or less immediate consumption. Under capitalism, goods were increasingly produced for sale in markets and this relationship became more distant. Goods were produced in the expectation that they could be sold, but the market might be unable to absorb them. Marx described capitalism as anarchic because production was no longer directly regulated by the needs of those consuming its products.[103]

When global capitalism develops, as this book has maintained, due to many factors including monopoly and networking, capitalist production has immensely increased its concentrative movements on the global scale, and has considerably enhanced its institutional coordination across firms, sectors, nations, and the mechanical boundaries between the state and the market. In one sentence, capitalist production today is becoming well organized. Instead, it is in the realm of consumption that anarchy now arises with the global expansion of capitalism.

Second, this is an anarchy contained within the institutional boundaries of global capitalism, within which the state-market nexus in general and capital in particular rule over everything, including consumption; thus, it is a caged anarchy, as the boundaries form this institutional cage. When an inter-institutional perspective is applied to highlight interconnections and interactions between consumer and capital for understanding consumption, the awkwardness of the term "caged anarchy," I would claim, actually helps to accurately portray the awkwardness of global capitalism that combines two sides of capitalist consumption, namely, the side of well-organized capital dominating consumption in general and, ironically, the other side composed of consumers who consume anarchically.

---

[102] In studies of international relations, such "anarchy" is assumed to be a fundamental situation in which states interact with each other without a central authority. See ft. 81, ch. 2.

[103] James Fulcher, *Capitalism: A Very Short Introduction*, Oxford University Press, 2004, pp. 106–107.

Emphasizing both sides of consumption anarchy and capital coordination, the argument of the new anarchy presented here is fundamentally different from a thesis of the "end of organized capitalism." Years ago, Scott Lash and John Urry declared such an end, defining what was described by Marx and Engels in *Manifesto of the Communist Party* as "organized capitalism," and suggesting that "this era" of "organized capitalism" is coming to an end. They argued that "there is a set of tremendously significant transformations which have recently been literally 'disorganizing' contemporary capitalist societies – transformations of time and space, of economy and culture – which disrupt and dislocate the patterns that Marx and Engels so brilliantly foresaw."[104] They announced, therefore, that "we are moving into an era of *'disorganized* capitalism'."[105] Theoretically, they claim to oppose both Marxist and Weberian traditions, which "generally contend that we are living in increasingly *organized* societies," as Marxists speak of a "monopoly capitalism" that is characterized by the increasing concentration of constant and variable capital complemented by the unidirectional tendency toward centralization of money capital. Marxists also speak of 'state-monopoly capitalism' or 'late capitalism', in which "a low-growth and low-profitability phase of capitalist development is counteracted through a combination of state economic subsidies and growth in size of the public sector." "Weberians," these two authors assume, "will similarly claim that contemporary society is imbued with increased levels of organization. They will point to the seemingly teleological growth of state bureaucracy in both capitalist and state socialist countries."[106]

The current book agrees with *both* Marxist and Weberian perspectives of capitalism, though it finds some criticisms with each; the state-market nexus, in fact, well demonstrates that only the combination of *both* perspectives beyond the traditional ideological dichotomy, rather than the reliance upon one or the other or neither, can concisely interpret the essence of global capitalism.[107] Lash and Urry, however,

---

[104] Scott Lash and John Urry, *The End of Organized Capitalism*, Cambridge: Polity, 1987, p. 2.

[105] Ibid. Emphasis in original.   [106] Ibid.

[107] They set out what is meant by "disorganized capitalism" with fourteen points, including primarily: "1. The growth of a world market combined with the increasing scale of industrial, banking and commercial enterprises means that

did mistakenly assert that there is an "increasing contradiction between the state and capital."[108] The state-market nexus acts as the backbone to bolster the organizational side; the observation of the new anarchy of consumption has to be understood in this institutional context. The anarchy, therefore, does not imply a disorganization of capitalism as a system; rather, it highlights how such organization is well developed to the degree that it levies a cost to average consumers' interest, namely, the cost of ordinary people's benefits.

As both sides of the anarchy have been analyzed above, namely, the intrinsic anarchy of consumption in terms of consumers' behavior and the high degree of organization and coordination of capital, what deserves repeated emphasis is the overwhelming influence of capital in framing global consumption, especially through market manipulation. The market is supposed to run as an "invisible hand" out of the management or control of any specific person or organization, in a way that is almost similar to a natural phenomenon. When a specific person or organization is able to alter such an idealized mechanism through the showing of a specific "hand" that can disturb and distort the so-called "invisible hand," this, I would argue, can be defined as market manipulation.[109] In the reality of global capitalism, the market is obviously not "natural," nor neutral enough to be "fair" to all who participate in its exchange activities. Instead, the market is manipulated

national markets have become less regulated by nationally based corporations. From the point of view of national markets there has been an effective *de*-concentration of capital. This tendency has been complemented by the nearly universal decline of cartels. Such deconcentration has been aided by the general decline of tariffs and the encouragement by states, particularly the USA., to increase the scale of external activity of large corporations. In many countries there is a growing separation of banks from industry." Lash and Urry, *The End of Organized Capitalism*, p. 5.

[108] Lash and Urry, *The End of Organized Capitalism*, p. 5: "Decline in the importance and effectiveness of national-level collective bargaining procedures in industrial relations and the growth of company and plant-level bargaining. This accompanies an important shift from Taylorist to 'flexible' forms of work organization."

[109] For the "invisible hand," see Adam Smith (1776), *An Inquiry into the Nature and Causes of the Wealth of Nations*, New York: Modern Library, 1937. For some discussions of it in general and of it as "natural," see John Eatwell, Murray Milgate, and Peter Newman eds., *The Invisible Hand*, London: Macmillan, 1989; E. K. Hunt and Mark Lautzenheiser, *History of Economic Thought: A Critical Perspective*, New York: Routledge, 2011, 3rd ed., p. 44.

by specific persons and organizations to gain the advantage, at least in the following ways:

First, markets are not only expanded; markets are often created. Globalization has virtually exhausted the geographical expansion of markets; but the populace's demands are limitless in the social-psychological sense, because there is a subtle lying in the unclear demarcation between natural and artificial demands. As this chapter earlier discussed, one of the major expressions of the global triumph of capitalism is embedded in the successful pushing of the market beyond consumers' immediate, physical, and natural demands. In this process, a consumer's autonomous articulation of his/her demand is increasingly replaced by a collective mentality that has been constantly configured by the capitalist consumption system. In other words, many seemingly basic, natural consumer demands for commodities are simply invented, created, and perpetuated by producers, sellers, and service-providers for their market profits. I would, therefore, term this as the "inventive mobilization of consumption."

Second, global capitalism also enhances "extensive mobilization of consumption," which means that demands can also be promoted in the quantitative sense to a degree that goes far beyond the necessity of consumption for living. This is usually referred to as overconsumption; global capitalism, as analyzed earlier, stimulates overconsumption. Traditionally, Marxian political economy criticizes capitalism for a tendency in which monopoly causes over-accumulation and under-consumption.[110] Yes, "a tendency to overproduce was in fact built into capitalist production. Competition between producers generated a pressure to expand production, since higher volume reduced costs, cheapened prices, and enlarged market share."[111] For the interest of capital, however, overproduction is mechanically remedied by overconsumption. In other words, capital manipulates the market for the purpose of promoting purchases of its products beyond consumers' needs.

Moreover, the financial system as it operates nowadays provides the facility to actualize such a promotion of overconsumption. For example, in terms of personal consumption, "the lifting in restrictions on

---

[110]   Foster, *The Theory of Monopoly Capitalism*, esp. "Introduction to the New ·
        Edition."
[111]   Fulcher, *Capitalism*, p. 107.

borrowing money and the associated change in meaning of being in debt" helps to simulate "a shift from the dubious respectability of the 'never-never,' through the anxieties of hire purchase to the competitive display of credit cards – to a situation in which an Access card could be your 'flexible friend' and a Platinum American Express card is a symbol of elite exclusivity."[112] This can be the third point concerning market manipulation for promoting consumption, namely, capital's providing of facilities and conveniences to entice and smooth consumers' spending and overspending.

Thus, market demands can be discovered, amplified, and encouraged; consumption is accordingly channeled, modeled, and manipulated; consumers are nevertheless subtly educated, configured, and controlled. Yes, various forms of resistance have emerged from consumers protesting against this caged anarchy, as exemplified in the rise of political consumerism and many other consumer-oriented social movements, all indicating "the growth of a range of different forms of consumer politics, which seek to mobilize consumers to influence the state, producers and other consumers."[113] The capitalist consumption system, however, is not running in adherence to their norms and rules; it is, in the institutional sense, in other words, according to the rules of the game, organized and dominated by capital and its various agents. As an historian observes,

Consumerism has always been hard to protest against ... Collective action against consumerism has proved even more difficult, at least in the Western world ... Consumer boycotts have historically been hard to pull off, because they depend on an elusive loyalty; many people break the boycott precisely because they yearn to buy.[114]

Even in individual forms, there are huge difficulties in waging action against such an addiction to or obsession of consumerism.[115] Therefore,

Whether personal or political, attacks on consumerism rarely slowed the advance of consumer behavior in Western Europe or the United States ... Simply put, in most situations, from the eighteenth century onward, the

---

[112] Lury, *Consumer Culture*, p. 3.   [113] Ibid, p. 6.
[114] Stearns, *Consumerism in World History*, p. 66.
[115] See a personal story of such an individual effort in Avis Cardella, *Spent: Memoirs of a Shopping Addict*, New York: Little Brown, 2010; for a discussion of American obsession with shopping, see Arthur Asa Berger, *Shop 'til You Drop: Consumer Behavior and American Culture*, Lanham: Rowman & Littlefield, 2004.

forces propelling consumerism were stronger than those opposing it in the Western world. Criticisms of other people's consumer behavior, relatively, proved easier than criticisms of one's own.[116]

For the age of global capitalism, the same historian even asks, "[H]ad the anxieties about consumerism disappeared in the Western world by the advent of the twenty-first century?"[117] The rise of those social movements orchestrated by consumers may provide an answer of "no" to this pessimistic question, but there are also arguments and rich evidence that highlight the increasing difficulties in protesting against consumerism. Even the information revolution is argued to be a powerful factor in people "bowling alone," meaning that it makes society further fragmented rather than more social, collective, and cooperative, thus making it more difficult to incite collective action.[118] The multiplicity of consumers, after all, creates huge negotiating costs. In other words, in addition to factors such as "institutional oligopolies" that are discussed in Chapter 3, the atomization of consumers also empowers market manipulation by capital.

The issue of two organizational bodies of capitalism must be revisited in this context, as the caged anarchy of consumption adds one more powerful element that is embedded in capitalism to favor authoritarianism rather than democracy. Earlier, this book has maintained that between the two major institutional elements of capitalism, namely the firm and the market, the latter resonates with democracy but the former resembles authoritarianism. Now it can be extended to make two significant points for understanding the general consequences of the developments around the consumption system over the institutions of global capitalism. The first point refers to the contrast emerging between two versions of "economic man": while a laborer seeks employment in a firm, and accordingly to be organized into this authoritarian system, a consumer on the market lives under an anarchy that is disguised as a system of actualizing freedom, a freedom of one-dimensional devotion to material and commercial activities with little public concern, and a freedom to seek standardization through atomized consumption. If the "economic man" of a laborer is usually aware of his/her disadvantageous and often depressing position in the

---

[116] Stearns, *Consumerism in World History*, p. 77.   [117] Ibid.
[118] Robert D. Putnam, *Bowling Alone: The Collapse and Revival of American Community*, New York: Simon & Schuster, 2000.

capitalist system, "economic man 2.0," however, habitually lives in the illusion of enjoyment that is consumption. Where laborers may contend with each other under the fragmented labor market but may also be connected to each other by the production process, consumers, though a new trend is emerging to resist such materialization and privatization of consumption, are virtually atomized.

Secondly, it can be further argued that due to the emergence of the caged anarchy of consumption, the market as an institution is now also altered to favor authoritarianism more than democracy. Anarchy never means freedom; manipulation implies that the seemingly individual autonomy embedded in consumption is actually harnessed by capital, primarily for fulfilling its interests. It is in this political economic context that the so-called "consumers' plebiscite" simply cannot stand. It is said that, under the capitalist system, "every day," "a consumer's plebiscite is held, the vote being counted in whatever money unit is the handiest. With his votes the consumer directs production, forcing or luring energy, brains, and capital to obey his will."[119] The caged anarchy argument contradicts this illusion. Consumption is turned to be a hidden war against everybody by capital; global capitalism enforces capital in this regard through its institutions, cultures, and operations. The "consumerist orgy,"[120] therefore, is much more the feast of capital than a carouse of consumers.

Concluding Remarks

The global triumph of capitalism can be said to be primarily a triumph of capitalist consumerism against any other possibly contending ideologies or lifestyles. Keynes propounds that consumption is the motor of the economy;[121] in a similar logic, we may say that consumption is also the motor of the capitalist economy in conquering the globe. The assertion that "Western influence in the world at large rested on consumer standards more than anything else, outlasting military and colonial predominance"[122] remains accurate in the current age. This triumph, in return, has reconfigured capitalism by

[119] Chamberlin, *The Roots of Capitalism*, p. 165.
[120] Gabriel and Lang, *The Unmanageable Consumer*, p. vi.
[121] Quoted in Richard A. Posner, *The Crisis of Capitalist Democracy*, Cambridge, MA: Harvard University Press, 2010, p. 154.
[122] Stearns, *Consumerism in World History*, p. ix.

rousing worldwide popular consumption that has reached a level often going well beyond immediate, in other words, hard living, though poverty and even famine are still, shamefully, a pressing problem for many parts of the world. This nature of consumption beyond immediate need creates markets by manufacturing human beings' new and novel needs, involving consumers numbering in billions into a huge race of consumerism.

Yes, many basic features of capitalist consumption have maintained their historical roots and developmental trends for a long time; but, this chapter above has tried to highlight how the global expansion of the capitalist consumption system, that is, the global limit reached by capitalist markets, has institutionally and inevitably intensified all of the lasting trends and intrinsic features. It has been found that, with globalization, the consumption markets meet their eventual limits. Their intramural, deepening expansions, which can be defined as intensive developments of the consumption potential of existing consumers, thus accompany the external, outwardly spreading expansions of consumption that target the involvement of more and more consumers in the consumption system. The "propensity to consume"[123] in a natural sense for supporting human lives, therefore, is transformed into the rise of consumerism worldwide. In the age of global capitalism, "I spend therefore I am."

Consumption, therefore, must not be overlooked in a comprehensive analysis of global capitalism; it is a complicated, multifaceted phenomenon that is far more encompassing than simply the extension of its geographic, commercial coverage. In appearance, consumption teems with contradictions. In the neoliberal climate of the past several decades, the consumer has been constructed "as an engine of wealth and representative of the public interest," said to be "close to becoming a quasi-natural being" "in contemporary politics and discourse."[124] As market spending is said to be the actualization of individual choice, and "the political identification of freedom" is intimately associated with individual choice,[125] being a consumer can mean being a free citizen: in the age of global capitalism, it would seem that "I spend therefore I enjoy freedom." The above chapter, however, has looked at

---

[123] Posner, *The Crisis of Capitalist Democracy*, p. 154.
[124] Trentmann, "Knowing Consumers," pp. 1, 2.
[125] Lury, *Consumer Culture*, p. 6.

consumers and consumption from an institutional perspective, with a particular emphasis on "inter-institutionalism" for paying special attention to interactions of different sets of institutions, suggesting that, beneath her/his appearance, the consumer is fundamentally constrained by the political economic institutions of global capitalism. A contemporary consumer, through the lens provided by the analyses above, is not only stretched but split in two contradictory directions: commercially, a consumer is encouraged, indulged, and even fetishized simply for capital's, as well the state's, promotion of consumption, which often results in overconsumption or consumerism; institutionally, by contrast, the consumer is overwhelmed by the asymmetry of available information, the disorganization and the difficulties of collective action, and an inability to influence the state. As a result, the consumer is engaged in a manner that is socially, behaviorally, and institutionally compressed to become, by principle, one-dimensionally inclined toward being commodity-fetishist and materialistic.

Sitting at the center of this picture is the consumer as "economic man 2.0," the personification of the political economy of global capitalist consumption. One who lives in the age of global capitalism, under this conceptual lens, is primarily an economic person with two interconnecting fundamental engagements, namely, engagements simultaneously in work and consumption. As a laborer, one is tightly attached to an organization of production, selling, or service-providing that is often dominated by authoritarian, hierarchical principles; as a consumer, he/she feels released from such disciplines, stresses, and repressions, having seemingly gained freedom through individual choice. The institutional imbalances of power between a consumer and capital, however, have already constructed a cage in which a consumer, docile or rebellious in personal mentality, is structurally tamed, behaviorally standardized, and socially atomized.

For the purpose of highlighting the institutional expression in consumption of such a connection and contrast between the influence of well-coordinated capital and the well-tamed and atomized consumers, the above chapter has suggested "caged anarchy" to term the structural configuration of consumption in global capitalism. The term means that on one hand, consumers live in an anarchy in which they have an illusion of autonomous decision-making power in their consumptive behavior; on the other hand, producers, sellers, and service providers, or, together as capital, are well networked and coordinated in organizing production and service, and, accordingly, in dominating consumption. Global capitalism, therefore, has a face like that of Janus: one side is anarchic, that of consumers, while the other side is organized, that of capital.

Freedom of a consumer, therefore, is an illusion of the institutional anarchy rooted in capitalist consumption, while the anarchy is created and, ironically, governed by capital, the state-market nexus, and the economic state. This new anarchy of capitalist consumption has been arising at the cost of social, political, and ecological integrity of human societies, under which "economic man" resonates to the rise of the economic state in a spiral effect to, first of all, define a fundamental ethos of global capitalism and, accordingly, to carry out the commercialization of life often beyond economic domains and into social, cultural, and political life. The marketization of everything simply implies the poverty of public goods.

In all, the chapter has completed the final section of the diminishing curve concerning the unbalanced power among the three fundamental elements of capitalism, namely, capital, which is well coordinated toward oligopoly; labor, which falls into further fragmentation with global integration; and consumption, which is creating standardization among consumers in terms of social behavior and atomization in the political economic sense. Now we will turn to the next chapter in an attempt to draw the three elements together with the institutional features of global capitalism for the purpose of systematically spelling out how they jointly undermine democracy.

6 | Global Inequalities Challenge Democracy

Sociopolitical Impacts of Transnational Stratification

As globalization has reconfigured capitalism in both its "internal" operation and "external" connections, all new institutional and operational features of global capitalism point to disadvantaging democracy in profound ways. In the preceding chapters, this argument has been discussed at two levels: Chapter 2 presents an institutionalist framework which generally outlines the logical path leading to the rise of globalization at the great expense of democracy; subsequent chapters then explore the movements of each particular but fundamental element of global capitalism, namely, capital, labor, and consumption, and demonstrate how their dynamics result in the sabotage of the socioeconomic factors that favor and support democracy. Following these lines of reasoning but focusing on a single fundamental socioeconomic aftermath, the current chapter is designed to analyze how this aftermath, namely, increasing inequalities, undermines democracy and impairs the momentum of democratization.

The coming crisis of democracy has been a repeated warning at least since the last quarter of the twentieth century;[1] this book would argue that the crisis has now arrived in the most fundamental sense with its

---

[1] See an early publication of such in Michel Crozier, Samuel P. Huntington, and Joji Watanuki, *The Crisis of Democracy: Report on the Governability of Democracies to the Trilateral Commission*, New York University Press, 1975. Very recently there have been a bunch of books claiming the crisis of democracy, though they define "crisis" differently, as exemplified in Richard A. Posner, *The Crisis of Capitalist Democracy*, Cambridge, MA: Harvard University Press, 2010; Yannis Papadopoulos, *Democracy in Crisis? Politics, Governance and Policy*, New York: Palgrave Macmillan, 2013; Nolan McCarty, Keith T. Poole, and Howard Rosenthal, *Political Bubbles: Financial Crises and the Failure of American Democracy*, Princeton University Press, 2013; Todd Huizinga, *The New Totalitarian Temptation: Global Governance and the Crisis of Democracy in Europe*, New York: Encounter Books, 2016. For a historical investigation into how modern democracy is living with crises, see David Runciman, *The*

final victory having been declared, a crisis embedded in the global triumph of capitalism. As our initial theoretical assumption has highlighted, democracy and capitalism are historically coupled together rather than intrinsically and institutionally inseparable from one another; the global triumph of capitalism, however, has uncoupled them in a direction that disfavors democracy in profound ways. It should be pointed out that, although agreeing with many authors who have suggested the revitalization of democracy to be the remedy of globalization's problems,[2] this chapter, and indeed this book in general, takes an approach emphasizing an opposing logic that the stalling of democracy is fundamentally and specifically rooted in the political-economic institutions and dynamics of global capitalism. In fact, both capitalism and democracy are jeopardized in their institutional separation from one another. Democracy is impaired due to its inherent restriction within the scope of the state, the erosion of its social bases, and its disadvantage in competition with any form of authoritarianism; capitalism, at the same time, becomes vulnerable without a "political shell" and can easily be hijacked by political authoritarianism. Diagnoses on either political democracy or global capitalism, therefore, are not sufficient; instead, an inter-institutional approach of political economy is needed for focusing on the juncture between capitalism and democracy.

The issue of increasing socioeconomic inequalities alongside globalization, this chapter believes, is one of the most significant junctures as such. The sections below, therefore, will further discuss the thesis of globalization-versus-democracy around this issue in the following structure: First, we will briefly investigate the increasing of economic inequalities during the globalization age, and try to highlight its feature as a tandem between the inequality growing within every society across groups and, simultaneously, that which prevails globally across nations. Then we will proceed to outline a personified transnational picture of such inequalities by suggesting a notional scheme of "three

Confidence Trap: A History of Democracy in Crisis from World War I to the Present, Princeton University Press, 2013.
[2] For such a line of reasoning, see, for example, Ellen Meiksins Wood, *Democracy Against Capitalism: Reinventing Historical Materialism*, Cambridge University Press, 1995; Richard Wolff, *Democracy at Work: A Cure for Capitalism*, Chicago: Heymarket Books, 2012; Colin Crouch, *Making Capitalism Fit for Society*, Cambridge: Polity, 2013.

worlds" of global social stratification, in which a great divergence of wealth, power, and life qualities rises among global elites as the first world, citizens of industrial nations as the second, and populaces of the Global South as the third.

Struggling in what can be termed the "jungle political economy" of global capitalism, these different "worlds" of people, the chapter will argue, whether gainers or losers in globalization, all now turn to disfavor democracy, thus causing the global landslide erosion of social foundations for democracy and democratization. Within a democracy, these deepening social cleavages substantially impair the functioning of democracy as a governance system. The attractiveness of democracy is accordingly reduced for those non-democratic nations, and the potential momentum of a democratic transition from political authoritarianism inevitably declines. Taken together, how global inequalities challenge democracy and democratization will be contemplated from three angles: from the bottom up, namely, concerning social bases; internally, regarding the capacity of democracy per se as a political system in such an unequal society; and externally, that is, vis-à-vis democracy's competition with authoritarianism in dealing with socioeconomic inequalities and their impacts.

The Great Transnational Divergence among "Three Worlds": Mapping Global Social Stratification with Growing Inequality

Rapidly increasing economic inequality has been one of the most striking phenomena since the world entered the globalization age. Many relevant studies have already demonstrated and analyzed this phenomenon;[3] what this chapter aims to add is twofold: First, in an attempt to go

---

[3] This is a huge body of literature, with some leading and latest examples found in: Joseph E. Stiglitz, *The Price of Inequality: How Today's Divided Society Endangers Our Future*, New York: W. W. Norton, 2013; Joseph E. Stiglitz, *The Great Divide: Unequal Societies and What We Can Do About Them*, New York: W. W. Norton, 2015; Anthony B. Atkinson, *Inequality: What Can Be Done?* Cambridge, MA: Harvard University Press, 2015; François Bourguignon, *The Globalization of Inequality*, Princeton University Press, 2015; Thomas Piketty, *The Economics of Inequality*, translated by Arthur Goldhammer, Cambridge, MA: Belknap Press of Harvard University Press, 2015; Branko Milanovic, *Global Inequality: A New Approach for the Age of Globalization*, Cambridge, MA: Belknap Press of Harvard University Press, 2016.

beyond the one-dimensional perspective in either addressing inequality between different nations or highlighting class divisions within a nation, this chapter will emphasize both, namely, the increasing inequalities now existing *both* between societies and within a society. Second, the chapter will propose a scheme of three worlds as a macro-picture of global social stratification in order to highlight both types of inequality, and, taking account of the factors in political-economic interactions rather than employing a purely sociological or economic classification, emphasizes the institutional positions of different groups in the world dominated by the state-market nexus. Limited in space, the presentation of empirical data below will be restricted to sketching only a basic picture of inequality in general and providing direct evidence in support of the particular arguments.

According to *The Economist*'s 2012 special issue on inequality, the world witnessed "a dramatic concentration of incomes over the past 30 years, on a scale that matches, or even exceeds, the first Gilded Age." For example, in the United States, the largest economy in the world,

Including capital gains, the share of national income going to the richest 1% of Americans has doubled since 1980, from 10% to 20%, roughly where it was a century ago. Even more striking, the share going to the top 0.01% – some 16,000 families with an average income of $24 m – has quadrupled, from just over 1% to almost 5%. That is a bigger slice of the national pie than the top 0.01% received 100 years ago.[4]

A similar situation occurs worldwide in most countries, as *The Economist* continues:

This is an extraordinary development, and it is not confined to America. Many countries, including Britain, Canada, China, India and even egalitarian Sweden, have seen a rise in the share of national income taken by the top 1%. The numbers of the ultra-wealthy have soared around the globe. According to *Forbes* magazine's rich list, America has some 421 billionaires, Russia 96, China 95 and India 48. The world's richest man is a Mexican (Carlos Slim, worth some $69 billion). The world's largest new house belongs to an Indian. Mukesh Ambani's 27-storey skyscraper in Mumbai occupies 400,000 square feet, making it 1,300 times bigger than the average shack in the slums that surround it.[5]

---

[4] *The Economist*, "Special Report: For Richer, for Poorer," http://www.economist .com/node/21564414, posted October 13, 2012, accessed September 7, 2015.
[5] Ibid.

Table 6.1 *Growing Inequality Worldwide, 1965–2007*

	Percentage of Total World Income over Years					
Population	1965	1970	1980	1990	2000	2007
Poorest 20%	2.3	2.2	1.7	1.4	0.8	1
Second poorest 20%	2.8	2.7	2.2	1.8	1.6	2.1
Third richest 20%	4.2	3.9	3.5	2.1	3.2	4.2
Second richest 20%	21.2	21.2	18.2	11.3	7.6	9.9
Richest 20%	69.5	70.0	74.4	83.4	86.8	82.8

Note: Special thanks go to Jack John Hoskins for his research assistance in composing the columns of "2000" and "2007."
Sources: The author's composition based on the information available in Robert P. Korzeniewicz and Timothy P. Moran, "World Economic Trends in the Distribution of Income, 1965–1992," *American Journal of Sociology* 102, 4 (1997): 1000–1039; Isabel Oritz and Matthew Cummins, "Global Inequality: Beyond the Bottom Billion," Working Paper 1105, Unicef, Division of Policy and Strategy (2011): 1–65.

Some long-term, general statistics presented in Table 6.1 can sketch a global picture of this growing inequality. In 2010, three billion individuals, more than two-thirds of the world's adult population, had net assets worth under $10,000, while twenty-four million millionaires accounted for less than 1 percent of the global adult population but owned more than a third of the world's household wealth.[6]

Yes, "the concentration of wealth at the very top is part of a much broader rise in disparities all along the income distribution."[7] Taking the Gini index as the indicator, *The Economist* states, "America's Gini for disposable income is up by almost 30% since 1980, to 0.39. Sweden's is up by a quarter, to 0.24. China's has risen by around 50% to 0.42 (and by some measures to 0.48)."[8] Table 6.2 lists such changes in the G20 economies, which collectively account for around 85 percent of the gross world product (GWP) and two-thirds of the world population.[9] Though a variety of trajectories exist across

---

[6] Credit Suisse, *Global Wealth Report 2010*, prepared by James Davies and Andrew Shorrocks, quoted in Richard Pomfret, *The Age of Equality: The Twentieth Century in Economic Perspective*, Cambridge, MA: Belknap Press of Harvard University Press, 2011.
[7] *The Economist*, "Special Report: For Richer, for Poorer."   [8] Ibid.
[9] Wikipedia, "G20," https://en.wikipedia.org/wiki/G-20_major_economies, accessed May 14, 2016.

Table 6.2 *Increasing GINI Index of G20 Economies, the Mid-1970s to the Early 2010s*

Economy	GINI Index (World Bank estimate)				
	Mid-1970s	1981	1991	2001	2011
Argentina	–	42.8 (1986)	46.8	53.3	43.6
Australia	–	31.3	33.2 (1989)	34.1	34.9 (2010)
Brazil	–	57.9	60.5 (1990)	59.3	53.1
Canada	30.4	32.6	31.2	33.7 (2000)	33.7 (2010)
China	–	29.1	32.4 (1990)	42.6 (2002)	46.9 (2014)*
France	–	30.0 (mid-80s)	–	30.8 (2004)	33.4
Germany	–	25.1 (mid-80s)	–	–	30.1
India	–	31.1 (1983)	31.9 (1987)	33.4 (2004)	33.9 (2009)
Indonesia	–	30.5 (1984)	29.2 (1990)	29.7 (2002)	36.8 (2009)*
Italy	–	30.9 (mid-80s)	–	34.5 (2004)	34.5
Japan	–	30.4 (mid-80s)	–	–	37.9 (2011)*
Korea, South	–	–	–	–	30.2 (2014)*
Mexico	–	49.0 (1984)	54.3 (1990)	51.7 (2000)	48.1 (2012)
Russia	–	23.8 (1988)	48.4 (1993)	39.6	41.0
Saudi Arabia	–	–	–	–	45.9 (2013)*
South Africa	–	–	59.3 (1993)	57.8	63.0 (2008)

Turkey	–	43.5 (1987)	41.3 (1994)	41.4 (2002)	40.0
United Kingdom	26.8	–	–	36.2 (2004)	33.7
United States	31.6	37.7 (1986)	38.4	40.5 (2000)	45.0 (2007)*
European Union	–	–	–	–	30.9 (2014)*

Notes: 1) "–" indicates unavailability of information; 2) in the brackets is the year the closest to the selected year of the column but the information is available; 3) the entries with "*" are from the CIA source of information.

Sources: The author's composition based on the information available in, mostly, The World Bank, http://data.worldbank.org/indicator/SI.POV.GINI; for those for the mid-1970s and the mid-1980s, https://en.wikipedia.org/wiki/List/of/countries/by/income/equality; for those with *, from the Central Intelligence Agency (CIA) of the United States, https://www.cia.gov/library/publications/the-world-factbook/rankorder/2172rank.html; all accessed May 14, 2016.

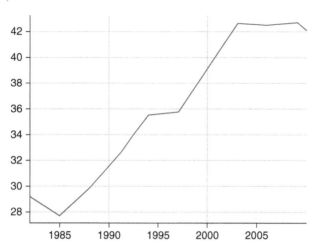

Figure 6.1 The Great Surge of Income Inequality in China since the 1980s (measured with GINI index)
Source: Quandl, https://www.quandl.com/collections/demography/gini-index-by-country, accessed May 14, 2016.

countries and over time, the general trend of increasing inequality has been clear since the mid-1970s, even for those nations enjoying the greatest equality of income, such as Australia, Canada, Japan, and some European countries. Newly emerging market economies during the globalization era, as exemplified by Brazil, China, and South Africa, particularly suffer from this high level of inequality, either as a chronic problem or as a great surge that has been experienced in more recent decades (see Figure 6.1 for China as a case in point).

That the "majority of the people on the planet live in countries where income disparities are bigger than they were a generation ago"[10] is an indisputable conclusion, though interpretations of its implication vary. For example, two French economists, as *The Economist* has cited, think that the development "does not mean the world as a whole has become more unequal," but that "global inequality – the income gaps between all people on the planet – has begun to fall as poorer countries catch up with richer ones." For them, "in a world of nation-states it is inequality within countries that has political salience."[11]

Interstate inequality, however, has persisted in many measures. For example, of those millionaires mentioned above, 41 percent lived in the

---

[10] *The Economist*, "Special Report: For Richer, for Poorer."   [11] Ibid.

United States, 32 percent in Europe, 10 percent in Japan, 4 percent in Canada, 3 percent in China, 3 percent in Australia, and 7 percent in the rest of the world.[12] Today the ratio between the richest country and the poorest country is 50:1.[13] IPE studies, accordingly, often emphasize interstate inequality worldwide. In fact, as we have seen in Chapter 4, such international inequality of income does propel major global movements of labor, namely, international immigration from low-income to high-income countries.

For this chapter, both types of inequality, namely, interstate inequality in the world and inter-group inequality within a nation, are eye-catching phenomena; there is no zero-sum game between the two types of inequality. Instead, they can both increase simultaneously, as we are witnessing in the current era. A combination of statist and class perspectives, therefore, is necessary for highlighting a transnational pattern of social stratification in the globalization age. Roughly speaking, this pattern can be outlined as the divisions among three worlds, as elaborated below.

"Three Worlds" of Transnational Social Stratification: A Political Economic Scheme

It is not difficult in this globalizing world to recognize a group of people who live in extraordinary wealth, a relatively small group that often makes dazzling appearances in public and causes tantalizing feelings of envy in many others. Existing studies have already observed the rise of such a group, labeling it with a variety of terms such as the "superrich," "plutocrats," or the "upper crust."[14] The social boundary of the group,

---

[12] Pomfret, *The Age of Equality*, p. vii.

[13] *The Economist*, "Special Report: For Richer, for Poorer."

[14] See, for example, Stephen Haseler, *The Super-Rich: The Unjust New World of Global Capitalism*, New York: Palgrave Macmillan, 2000; Chrystia Freeland, *Plutocrats: The Rise of the New Global Super-Rich and the Fall of Everyone Else*, New York: Penguin Books, 2013; Iain Hay ed., *Geographies of the Super-Rich*, Cheltenham: Edward Elgar, 2013; Darrell M. West, *Billionaires: Reflections on the Upper Crust*, Washington, DC: Brookings Institution Press, 2014; Ronald P. Formisano, *Plutocracy in America: How Increasing Inequality Destroys the Middle Class and Exploits the Poor*, Baltimore: Johns Hopkins University Press, 2015. In addition, there are many popular readings, as exemplified by Sam Wilkin, *Wealth Secrets of the One Percent: A Modern Manual to Getting Marvelously, Obscenely Rich*, Boston: Little, Brown, 2015. My analyses below are often based on the observations and investigations contributed by the above titles.

however, may not be so clear cut; to define it, relevant studies employ different indicators, referring, for example, to the top one percent of wealthiest people, or instead to some social and/or occupational backgrounds such as those of business tycoons.[15] This chapter chooses to categorize the group as the "first world" of global social stratification, and essentially agrees with the demarcation of this group from other people using the indicator of extraordinary wealth and its expression in a lifestyle of material, cultural, and social luxury. In a strict analysis, however, this chapter is not completely satisfied with such a definition, due to the reasons discussed immediately below.

This "first world," in addition to its possession of huge wealth, does have a series of distinct features in terms of political economy and political sociology. First of all, this is a truly global group in multiple senses. These senses may include its intimate connection with globalization in fortune-making, and the life radii of these people in various aspects that are not confined within a nation but instead exist on a global level – in fact, their national citizenries are often not as important to them as they would be to the majority of people in terms of locating their properties, defining their interpersonal networks, exercising their power and influence, and living their daily life. Globalization does increase the scope and scale of most people's lives in terms of wider global involvement, but this distinctive group's globalization of life is extraordinary to a degree that goes far beyond ordinary people's imaginations. This is, however, still an expression of deeper causes, often institutional; behind their true globalization of life lies not only the possession of wealth but also the capability and privilege to transcend various borders that could be linguistic, cultural, financial, and sovereign. It is in the sense of easily crossing state borders that this group is by nature global, which can lie in a sharp contrast with the tremendous difficulties labor encounters in its geographic mobility.

The second, and much more important, character of this group is its intimate and simultaneously diverse connections to political power, especially state power but also including many other forms of organizational power and public authority. These connections can be manifested in the holding of a public office, a tight affiliation to government or other public organizations and their administrators, a weight of

---

[15] Danny Dorling, *Inequality and the 1%*, New York: Verso, 2014; West, *Billionaires*; Wilkin, *Wealth Secrets of the One Percent*.

influence in public decision-making processes beyond the capacity possessed by an average citizen through normal participation, intimate networking with public officials, or various collaborations with political powers in doing one's own business, be it the business of fortune-making or fame. These connections can be either legal or illegal, or, as is often the case, both, as primarily reflected in the prevalence of various two-way patron-client relationships in government-business relations, and in the rise of crony capitalism worldwide from the US and the UK to Latin America, and from Russia and India to East Asia.[16]

This is a group, therefore, that must not be defined simply in terms of income and wealth, but also in consideration of those factors concerning its connections to public power and its involvement in the exercise of public power.[17] From an institutional perspective, the privileges and advantages of this group, furthermore, should not be viewed only in terms of outcomes of the game of the political economy of global capitalism, but must be analyzed with emphasis given to the process of the game, namely, the group's power in making rules for the political economy of global capitalism. An individual member of the group may lose a play to another member of the group, but the group as a whole will never lose to other groups under the established rules of the political economy of global capitalism; likewise, the group may be

---

[16] For the US, see Luigi Zingales, *A Capitalism for the People: Recapturing the Lost Genius of American Prosperity*, New York: Basic Books, 2012, ch. 3; Hunter Lewis, *Crony Capitalism in America: 2008–2012*, AC2 Books, 2013; David A. Stockman, *The Great Deformation: The Corruption of Capitalism in America*, New York: Public Affairs, 2013; James T. Bennett, *Corporate Welfare: Crony Capitalism that Enriches the Rich*, Piscataway, NJ: Transaction, 2015. For the UK, Tamasin Cave and Christopher Rowell, *A Quiet Word: Lobbying, Crony Capitalism and Broken Politics in Britain*, London: Random House, 2015. For Latin America, Stephen Haber ed., *Crony Capitalism and Economic Growth in Latin America: Theory and Evidence*, Stanford: Hoover Institution Press, 2002. For Russia, Gulnaz Sharafutdinova, *Political Consequences of Crony Capitalism Inside Russia*, University of Notre Dame Press, 2011; David E. Hoffman, *The Oligarchs: Wealth and Power in the New Russia*, New York: Public Affairs, 2011. For India, Naresh Khatri and Abhoy K. Ojha eds., *Crony Capitalism in India: Establishing Robust Counteractive Institutional Frameworks*, New York: Palgrave Macmillan, 2016. For East Asia, David C. Kang, *Crony Capitalism: Corruption and Development in South Korea and the Philippines*, Cambridge University Press, 2002; Minxin Pei, *China's Crony Capitalism: Dynamics of Regime Decay*, Cambridge, MA: Harvard University Press, 2016.

[17] David Rothkopf, *Superclass: The Global Power Elite and the World They Are Making*, New York: Farrar Straus and Giroux, 2008.

not able to win every move in global capitalism, but they have the power to make rules for the game that in general favor their overall gains. In this line of reasoning, a proper defining phrase for this "first world," in order to reflect state-capital collaboration under the state-market nexus as the institutional backbone of global capitalism, should be the "state-capital establishment."

Due to the characters above, the composition of the "state-capital establishment" stretches across nations. In other words, the borderlines dividing the members do not cause their mutual differences to be more distinctive than the divisions between this world and the other two worlds that we will discuss. While many members of this "first world" may herald from more economically advanced countries, it is equally true that many others herald from the poorest countries on the globe, where they stand as ruling elites, and are, by global standards, among some of the richest even in their own class, let alone in comparison with people in the other two worlds.

An extreme example is the Kim family of the North Korean dictator, whose members fit into this "first world" despite their political, ideological, and even military confrontations with the majority of the same group. There are similar examples easily found in African and Arabian nations, where a dictator can be deeply, indeed, much more deeply than North Korea's Kim family, involved in operations of global capitalism to make his fortune and his possession of wealth may reach a level parallel to that of the richest banker in Wall Street.[18] Contending ideologies, nationalisms in conflict, or state-centered competition may cause various confrontations and clashes among members of this "first world," but they never prevent the emerging of this "state-capital establishment" that rules the globe through the triumph of global capitalism. The North Korean dictator Kim's enjoyment of Western luxuries is no different from that of capitalists in New York City;[19] "Armani communist," a term coined by a BBC blogger describing a 14-year-old Chinese boy who

---

[18]   For example, see Craig Unger, *House of Bush, House of Saud: The Secret Relationship Between the World's Two Most Powerful Dynasties*, New York: Scribner, 2004.

[19]   North Korea's controversial supreme leader Kim Jong-un has an estimated US $5 billion at his disposal, according to the *Huffington Post*. As the UN says, this money should be spent on raising standards in the impoverished country and on its people, but much of it, as much as US $600 million a year, is expended for providing Kim a life of luxury. He reportedly spends an average of $30 million each year on importing liquors into the country for his elite circles. His favorites

tied a red scarf, a political symbol of being a young communist, over his Armani suit, is not really a "wardrobe malfunction as a clash of ideologies in a single outfit," but rather a daily-life symbol of the well-functioning combination of money and power that exists beyond ideological clashes within the "first world."[20]

The rest, in a comparison to the "first world," should be divided into two categories, especially from a political-economic perspective rather than a purely economic one. Roughly speaking, they live in the "second world" and the "third world," respectively, alongside the economic demarcation between developed and developing nations and, simultaneously, the political boundary between mature democracies on one hand and non-democracies, instable democracies, and various hybrid regimes on the other. In the "second world" of global social stratification, therefore, live ordinary people of the Global North, whose relative economic statuses have been in decline during these decades of globalization, but, in general, are still much better than residents of the Global South. People of this world also benefit from globalization, but they pay dearly for it in visible ways, such as declining incomes, increasing taxes, deterioration of the quality of daily life, and in deeper but often impalpable ways, such as environmental degradation, prevalence of commodity fetishism, and, due to the rise of global terrorism, evaporation of peace of mind and life, especially when travelling abroad. Yes, people in the Global North usually live with beneficial political and social arrangements, primarily democracy and social welfare, but it is these ordinary people in the "second world" who

are whisky and cognac; he prefers the more expensive kinds such as Hennessy, which can cost up to US $2,145 for the best bottle. See "Kim Jong-un's Unbelievable Life of Luxury," MSN News, http://www.msn.com/en-ca/news/photos/kim-jong-uns-unbelievable-life-of-luxury/ss-BBp8fdA, posted and accessed June 21, 2016. Also, see Ryan Lipman, "Pianos, Cars and a 1,000 Person Private Theatre: How North Korean Tyrant Kim Jong-un Blew £386MILLION in Just a Year While His People Starved," *Daily Mail*, http://www.dailymail.co.uk/news/article-2563421/UN-records-Kim-Jong-uns-control-645-spending-spree-luxurious-items-including-dozens-pianos-1-000-person-private-theatre-North-Koreans-suffer-appalling-conditions-control.html, posted February 20, 2014, accessed June 21, 2016; Soo Kim, "Inside the Luxury World of Kim Jong-un," *The Telegraph*, http://www.telegraph.co.uk/travel/destinations/asia/north-korea/articles/Inside-the-luxury-world-of-Kim-Jong-un/, posted August 27, 2015, accessed June 21, 2016.

20 Anisa Subedar, "'Armani Communist' Divides China," http://www.bbc.com/news/blogs-trending-35496562, posted and accessed February 6, 2016.

pay the high cost for supporting such institutions. Everywhere in the industrial world, including the United States, the most powerful nation in the world, Europe, where social democracy has prevailed, and East Asia, where capitalist economies have often been known for their relative economic equality, the gap between the rich and the poor has been fast and enormously widening in recent decades, and the middle class has been squeezed in terms of both its size and income, thus resulting in a small minority rising into the "first world" of the rich while the greater majority falls to a lower status against the general increase of national and global wealth.[21] As indicated by the shift of their daily consumption from goods of relatively high quality to something from Wal-Mart, what the classic Marxist economists referred to as the "lumpenproletariat"[22] is now seemingly being replaced by the trend of the "lumpen-middle-class."

The ruled, the ordinary, and the disadvantaged in the Global South compose the "third world" of our scheme of global social stratification. The physical presence of this vast group is so obvious and discriminable that perhaps it is not necessary to demonstrate its empirical existence; rather, the question here is conceptual. As the "state-capital establishment" or the superrich is definitively distant from "everyone else,"[23] why are the rest not categorized together as a single entity, rather than highlighting the distinction between the "second" and the "third world"? My answer can be elaborated upon from a number of perspectives. First, from the economic perspective, levels of income and quality of life in general for ordinary citizens in the Global North, on one hand, and the Global South, on the other, are obviously and substantially different, as a simple fact reveals that "the gap in incomes between countries is of the order of 50:1."[24] As earlier discussed, interstate inequality is still prominent in the global picture of wealth distribution; more importantly, rather than being demonstrated through abstract statistics, such cross-nation inequality must be personified as being embedded in ordinary people's lives. Because of the

[21] See, for example, Sawako Shirahase, *Social Inequality in Japan*, London: Routledge, 2015; Leo F. Goodstadt, *Poverty in the Midst of Affluence: How Hong Kong Mismanaged Its Prosperity*, Hong Kong University Press, 2013.
[22] Anthony Brewer, *Marxist Theories of Imperialism: A Critical Survey*, London: Routledge, 1990, 2nd ed., p. 10.
[23] Freeland, *Plutocrats*.
[24] Gregory Clark, *A Farewell to Alms: A Brief Economic History of the World*, Princeton University Press, 2007, p. 3.

"democratisation of living standards" within the industrial world, in countries like the United States "even poor people have televisions, air conditioners and cars,"[25] which can be unimaginable for many in the Global South. Thus, the economic divide should be highlighted between residents in the Global North and the Global South.

Second, from the sociological perspective, the differences in the lives of ordinary people in the Global North and their counterparts in the Global South are also obvious and fundamental in many aspects, ranging from the benefits of social welfare to the convenience of geographical mobility across the north and the south. Take mobility as an example: The superrich everywhere, including those who are affiliated in various ways with developing countries, may easily ignore and overstep state borders when they deem it necessary to do so (think about Kim Jong-un, the current North Korean leader, who studied and lived in Switzerland for years when he was a teenager as a son of his preceding North Korean leader, let alone stories of secret bank accounts in Western countries of similar non-Western elites[26]). Ordinary citizens of industrial nations may also overcome the hindrance of state borders with ease, coming to developing nations for visits, work, or even to take up residence if they like, in sharp comparison to the difficulties and, for the majority, the impossibilities of ordinary citizens in developing countries of enjoying such mobility. As discussed in Chapter 4, global mobility of people to seek better economic and other opportunities is not evenly distributed to everyone, and its availability or lack thereof is a fundamental issue in the political economy of global capitalism that puts those who are not able to move at their own will at a great disadvantage on the global labor market. Here the argument must be extended to mobility in the sphere of daily life, in which such disadvantages are also prominent.

The third is from the political perspective: the civic and political rights that citizens enjoy in the "second world," despite how superficial they might be, are far from being matched by what the populace in our

---

[25] *The Economist*, "Special Report: For Richer, for Poorer."

[26] As revealed by the Panama Papers, which disclosed 11.5 million documents that illustrate how wealthy individuals worldwide, including public officials, utilize the financial mechanism of global capitalism to keep their wealth, often in illegal ways such as fraud, kleptocracy, tax evasion, and evading international sanctions. See International Consortium of Investigative Journalists (ICIJ), https://panamapapers.icij.org, accessed April 8, 2016.

"third world" possess in this regard. This difference matters greatly in this book's inter-institutional analysis, as political rights interact with economic statuses. Wealth distribution, after all, is never a purely economic issue; it is a political-economic game.

This scheme of three worlds, however, leaves leeway through which to recognize the huge diversity within each of the worlds; it is for this reason that the term "world" is adopted rather than other possible choices such as "class." For example, in the "first world," the smallest in terms of its size, there live capitalist bankers of Wall Street, business tycoons in Hong Kong and Dubai, coal mine owners in Shanxi, China, democratically elected leaders in the Philippines and Portugal, monarchs in the United Kingdom and Saudi Arabia, tribe patriarchs in western Africa, and communist party secretaries in Vietnam and North Korea. They can be enemies to each other for various reasons, but that does not exclude or weaken their social distance from and, at least, socioeconomic confrontation with people of the other two worlds. In a similar vein, the categorization of an individual into a particular world is not entirely determined by the individual's economic income, although income is a significant factor. Being logically consistent with the emphasis being placed on those grand institutional elements of global capitalism, this term "world" is an attempt to express how those institutions such as the state-market nexus are significant in shaping transnational social stratification.

The Rise of Another Great Divergence: How Is the Globalizing World Deeply, Widely, and Lastingly Divided?

The category of three worlds aims to suggest a truly transnational scheme, which echoes various existing theories on transnational class. Some prominent scholars have already produced thoughtful works in this regard, as exemplified in Robinson's emphasis of the rise of a transnational capital class and Sassen's portrait of emergent, different global classes that include "transnational elites," "transnational networks of government officials," and "the new global class of the disadvantaged."[27] Although they correctly seize upon the feature of the

---

[27] William I. Robinson, *A Theory of Global Capitalism: Production, Class, and State in a Transnational World*, Baltimore: Johns Hopkins University Press, 2004, esp. ch. 2; Saskia Sassen, *A Sociology of Globalization*, New York: W. W. Norton, 2007, ch. 6.

declining importance of state borders in class formations in global capitalism and accordingly highlight what can be called "transnational-ness," they may underestimate the impacts of the state system and state power over dynamics, processes, and the shape of global capitalism, especially in regards to the differentiated relationships of separate groups of people with both the state system and the state-market nexus. State sovereignty may have declined greatly as a hindrance to capital and to those who are closely attached to it, but it still powerfully controls and disadvantages the others. The "three worlds" version of global social stratification proposed above is hoped to be of help in remedying this shortcoming while equally emphasizing transnationalness.

To an extent this scheme of "three worlds" can be compared with the historian Arnold Toynbee's "schism in the body social," with which he suggests there are "dominant minorities," "internal proletariats," and "external proletariats."[28] There are many things that our scheme does not share with Toynbee, however, including his Eurocentric approach, his universal application of the trifold schism to individual human societies over different historical eras, and his proposition of analyzing the schism against the background of "the disintegrations of civiliza-tions." Our "first world," despite these disagreements, is similar to Toynbee's "dominant minorities" in the sense that it rules the world, also often in both predatory and creative ways. "Internal" and "exter-nal proletariats" can parallel our "second" and "third world" if one follows Toynbee to view the world from today's Global North, as our "second world" does refer to the ruled in the "internal" domains of the Global North, while the "third world," namely, the ruled in the Global South, is "external." This comparison, therefore, can help to empha-size what Toynbee stresses as "schism in the body social," but in our picture the body social is global, or more exactly, the transnational human society as a whole under global capitalism.

From a historical perspective, this scheme of understanding transna-tional inequalities can be viewed as another Great Divergence, which may be compared to the Great Divergence that emerged with the Industrial Revolution dividing the West from the rest in achieving progress through modernization.[29] Economic historians and international-studies scholars

[28] Arnold J. Toynbee, *A Study of History*, abridged by D. C. Somervell, Oxford University Press, 1946, ch. xviii.

[29] For the Great Divergence of the Industrial Revolution, see, for instance, Kenneth Pomeranz, *The Great Divergence: China, Europe, and the Making of the*

alike emphasize that the Industrial Revolution and developments since then have increased income inequalities between societies, while reducing them within a society.[30] As this inequality between industrial societies and the others is labeled the Great Divergence, the different historical paths of economic development by Western nations and non-Western nations and their different outcomes across states are highlighted. In other words, this is a nation-state-centered divergence, or, at most, a civilization-centered divergence. In recent years, Paul Krugman and others also refer to the rising economic inequality in the United States as "the great divergence."[31] Their scale of discussion, however, is still national, being strictly within the United States. To this book, the global triumph of capitalism that has now conquered all states, all nations, or, to a lesser degree, all civilizations, has stimulated the emergence of the ultimate answer to the Great Divergence of the Industrial Revolution, which is, by essence, non-Western nations' adoption of the industrialization program that originated from the West in order to catch up, though the concrete methods of implementation of the program may differ, the actual accomplishments in doing so can vary, and the non-economic responses from the late-comer nations and civilizations can be diverse and negative. Though following Krugman, this chapter further argues that it is in this circumstance that virtually all nations are involved in globalization but transnational inequalities prevail, thus emerges the second, new Great Divergence occurring on a global scale.

This is the Great Divergence of the Globalizing Revolution, which features the rise of the state-capital establishment along with globalization in confrontation with the rest of the world populace, who are disadvantaged in various ways by the same globalization. This new Great Divergence has to a significant extent transformed the pre-globalization

Modern World Economy, Princeton University Press, 2000. Also, Jared Diamond, *Guns, Germs, and Steel: The Fate of Human Societies*, New York: W. W. Norton, 1999; David S. Landes, *The Wealth and Poverty of Nations: Why Some Are So Rich and Some So Poor*, New York: W. W. Norton, 1999; Robert C. Allen, *Global Economic History: A Very Short Introduction*, Oxford University Press, 2011.

[30] See, for example, Clark, *A Farewell to Alms*, p. 3.

[31] Paul Krugman, *The Conscience of a Liberal*, New York: W. W. Norton, 2007, p. 5; Timothy Noah, "The United States of Inequality," http://www.slate.com/articles/news/and/politics/the/great/divergence/features/2010/the/united/states/of/inequality.html, posted Sep 16, 2010; accessed May 14, 2016. Joseph Stiglitz also constantly emphasizes this is the great divide in our time, as in *The Price of Inequality* and *The Great Divide*.

cross-nation divergence into the global transnational divergence of the richest versus the rest, while the legacies of the last Great Divergence remain powerful in effectively dividing the rest into our "second" and "third" worlds. In one sentence, it is a divergence that emerges not only within but across societies, along with which a small portion of human societies has become the richest ever to have occurred in human history, and the gap of wealth between this section and the overwhelming majority of people has widened to the largest ever seen.[32]

The "Jungle Political Economy" of Global Competitiveness: Institutional Roots of Transnational Inequality

The total wealth of the world has dramatically multiplied with the latest wave of globalization, let alone since the Industrial Revolution centuries ago. It is in this reality that the huge gaps of wealth in terms of distribution across states, regions, groups, and families become epistemically surprising and ethically shameful. Why have poverty and inequality dramatically risen alongside rapidly growing wealth? Why is it that the material abundance of human societies in general cannot be shared and enjoyed by all members of human societies? The answer lies in the institutional and operational dimensions of global capitalism that have been analyzed in the preceding chapters. Institutions of capitalist globalization, to repeat, feature the state-market nexus, in which all states cooperate with the market mechanism, an arrangement powerful in promoting both the growth of wealth and inequalities of distribution; the economic state, which indicates a shift of legitimacy of the state from other possible sources to its materialist performance; the uncoupling between nation-state democracy and global capitalism, which makes citizens' influence over capital via democratic institutions impotent and restricted; and a disconnection between mixed domestic economies and the under-regulated global economy, which further re-contours state interventions from functioning to balance the market and correct its failures to strengthening state-capital collaborations for the purpose of global competitiveness. With overlapping and complicated interactions, these major institutional features of global capitalism have omnipresent impacts and implications, one of which is their

---

[32] In an economic historian's words, "There walk the earth now both the richest people who ever lived and the poorest." Clark, *A Farewell to Alms*, p. 3.

significant contributions to the shaping of the greatly unequal global social stratification. Furthermore, movements of and interactions among each of the three fundamental elements of capitalism, namely, capital, labor, and consumption, operate and actualize those impacts, thus carrying out the dynamics with which the three worlds of the transnational divergence have been created.

Let's start the analysis with the consequence of capital concentration for socioeconomic distribution with a reference to its different influences over the three worlds proposed above. Apparently it is easy to become rich through monopoly, the most extreme form of capital concentration. The story of Thales of Miletus in ancient Greece, with whom Western philosophy is often said have begun, well illustrates this point:

> According to one anecdote, Thales became tired of people poking fun at him for his poverty, which was supposedly due to the practical uselessness of philosophy. To demonstrate that philosophy wasn't necessarily an unprofitable enterprise, one winter he bought, at small value, all the olive presses in Miletus after predicting a particular good harvest on the basis of his knowledge of astronomy. When harvest came presses were in enormous demand, and Thales could charge any price he wanted.[33]

Aristotle cited this story for a discussion of monopoly; he also pointed out that states can secure a monopoly for their interests.[34] Early critical thinkers of capitalism, such as Hobson, further identify monopoly as one cause of inequality, because monopoly not only increases the share of profit, but also concentrates it into fewer hands.[35] At the other end of this logic are those people who are concurrently both laborers and consumers, who are inevitably preyed upon in the process of capital concentration. As Kalecki's analysis of the degree of monopoly suggests, the overall chain of interactions is ultimately "passed on to consumers who would predominantly be wage-earners, with the profit margins on intermediate products being passed on from one capitalist to another until the products made their way to the market as consumption goods." This suggests a theory of the distribution of income,

---

[33] Julian Reiss, *Philosophy of Economics: A Contemporary Introduction*, London: Routledge, 2013, p. 231.
[34] Aristotle, *The Politics*, translated by T. A. Sinclair and revised by Trevor J. Saunders, London: Penguin Books, 1981, p. 90.
[35] Brewer, *Marxist Theories of Imperialism*, pp. 77, 73.

in which "profits [are] gained and wages lost with an increasing degree of monopoly."[36]

The global triumph of capitalism does not change this principle, but has significantly promoted the phenomenon due, as Chapter 3 has demonstrated, to capital's increasing concentration, coordination, oligopoly, and monopoly on an unprecedented gigantic, global level. In his "self-help" manual for making oneself a billionaire, Sam Wilkin lists "establish a monopoly" as the number-one "secret" of becoming wealthy. In fact, his other advice and examples, such as "expand as quickly as possible as Amazon did and learning from Bill Gates's Microsoft which at one point had a 95 per cent share of the operating systems market," also imply this or that kind of, or this or that way to, monopoly.[37] In other words, monopoly most easily creates the super-rich that constitute the "first world" of transnational social stratification of the globalization age.

How can monopoly be achieved? Wilkin does not mention anything about this real "secret" behind the secret, but one can find many clues in our Chapter 3 analysis. Collaboration with the state, for example, is definitely an effective way to do so; technological innovations also help. With regard to collaboration with the state, the state-market nexus and the rise of the economic state have opened the door much wider for such collaboration than in the pre-global age of capitalism. This is especially the case when there is involvement in global competition, either by state supports or by admission to a foreign nation's market by that nation's government, particularly when such a government is actively authoritarian and interventionist; this involvement can be more crucial than other factors in achieving monopoly.

Concentration of capital means the diminishment of small business, which is intimately connected with the existence, development, and prosperity of the middle class, a social base of democracy.[38] With emphasis placed on global competitiveness, as Chapter 3 has demonstrated, gigantism in businesses prevails. The structural change of the size of business firms, namely, the concentration of capital into the

---

[36] Ben Fine and Andy Murfin, *Macroeconomics and Monopoly Capitalism*, Brighton: Wheatsheaf Books, 1984, p. 80.

[37] Wilkin, *Wealth Secrets of the One Percent*, p. 3.

[38] This is a well-established argument since the publication of Moore, *Social Origins of Dictatorship and Democracy* in 1966, though counterarguments have emerged in recent decades – a point which will be discussed later.

hands of big businesses while small factories, shops, and stores are either swallowed or excluded, means a large-scale shrinking and weakening of small-business owners, the major section of middle class composition. Look at the retail sector, for instance, which had traditionally been composed of countless small businesses.[39] In global capitalism, as showed in Chapter 3, retail is no longer a small-shop business. An additional factor is the difficulty for small business to gain financing due to the institutional arrangements of the global financial system. Even in the wave of reflection upon the shortcomings of global capitalism that followed the 2008 world financial meltdown, this discrimination against small businesses has not been remedied, but simply deepened. As of spring 2009, "credit card delinquency among small business [was] more than 12 percent" greater than that before the financial crisis.[40] Furthermore, "unlike big businesses, small businesses and consumers cannot borrow at affordable rates outside the banking system; they cannot issue bonds or commercial paper."[41] Economist Hetzel thus asks: "Did banks limit credit to small businesses because they had become riskier *given* the recession or did banks limit credit to small business and thereby *exacerbate* the recession?"[42] This, however, is often regarded as a policy or management problem, while the fundamental structural flaw embedded in the rise of global capitalism is easily ignored.

Big businesses do not only prey on small businesses in market competition, but, in terms of capital-labor relations, also impair and impoverish labor more than small businesses might be able to do so. When the concentration of capital arises on one hand but there is a structural fragmentation of the labor markets on the other, labor's position is inevitably weakened in bargaining with capital in general and with big businesses in particular. It is found that firms have pulled back significantly in their provision of occupational defined benefit pensions everywhere in the world; in explaining how and why, Adam Dixon concludes that "the decline of corporate-sponsored occupational

---

[39] Britain was once said to be "a nation of small shoppers," for example. See the discussion of chain stores in Chapter 3.

[40] *New York Times*, "Small businesses suffer in crackdown of credit," June 19, 2009, p. B1.

[41] Posner, *The Crisis of Capitalist Democracy*, p. 84.

[42] Robert L. Hetzel, *The Great Recession: Market Failure or Policy Failure?* Cambridge University Press, 2012, p. 252. Emphasis in original.

defined benefit pensions is, in part, an outcome of the globalization of financial markets and the globalization of supply chains. Large firms in particular are hardly constrained by their history and geography."[43] A theory of Social Structure of Accumulation Theory (SSA) echoes in a wider perspective:

The new SSA was characterized by a weakening of labor relative to capital, with a corresponding gap between productivity and wages; by a qualitatively different globalization of competition, setting the terms of a transnational economy of complex commodity chains and diversification of manufacturing venues rather than the previous international economy characterized by differential manufacturing in the core and commodity production in the periphery; the upsetting of the previously settled position and prospects of oligopolies and national champions formerly protected within nation-states; and by movements of loan and investment capital.[44]

Therefore, as a group of scholars who study inequality in the United States has observed, "for each story about successful people like Bill Gates and Sam Walton, there are contrasting stories about low-wage, no-benefit workers."[45] According to them, in 1967 a household in the 95th percentile of the income distribution had six times the income of someone in the 25th percentile, but, by 2003 the disparity had increased to 8.6 times.[46] This means that the middle class has encountered huge challenges to maintaining their income and quality of life.[47] Robert Reich, who once serves as labor secretary in the Clinton

[43] Adam D. Dixon, *The New Geography of Capitalism: Firms, Finance, and Society*, Oxford University Press, 2014, p. xiii.

[44] William K. Tabb, "Financialization in the Contemporary Social Structure of Accumulation," in Terrence McDonough, Michael Reich, and David M. Kotz eds., *Contemporary Capitalism and Its Crises: Social Structure of Accumulation Theory for the 21st Century*, Cambridge University Press, 2010, pp. 145–167 (pp. 145–146).

[45] Nolan McCarty, Keith T. Poole, and Howard Rosenthal, *Polarized America: The Dance of Ideology and Unequal Riches*, Cambridge, MA: MIT Press, 2008, p. 1.

[46] Ibid, p. 2.

[47] Randall Collins, "The End of Middle-Class Work: No More Escapes," in Immanuel Wallerstein, Randall Collins, Michael Mann, Georgi Derluguian, and Craig Calhoun, *Does Capitalism Have a Future?* Oxford University Press, 2013, pp. 37–69. Also, David Held and Ayse Kaya eds., *Global Inequality: Patterns and Explanations*, Cambridge: Polity, 2007; Ian Goldin and Kenneth Reinert, *Globalization for Development: Meeting New Challenges*, Oxford University Press, 2012.

administration, in 1991 insightfully observed that the USA had a large and growing "underclass" against an "overclass" on top, with those in between becoming the new "anxious class."[48] An expert on poverty concludes that "to a significant extent this growing anxiety and unease is a direct consequence of the imperative for continual 'reinvention' forced by global competition."[49] According to him, for those middle class members, "it is a world of insecurity, fear and anxiety, and one which threatens to engender opposition to globalization, the more so as the professional classes in the high-income economies are now being threatened by the offshoring of their own jobs to India and other lower-wage economies."[50]

Domestic inequality, ironically enough, is often larger in lower-income economies than in industrial nations, as Table 6.3 helps to tell. Among thirty economies that suffer the most serious inequality in the world, more than twenty-five are low-income countries with the exception only of Hong Kong and two or three Latin American nations; some are indeed the poorest countries in the world. The superrich of these economies, who belong to the first world of our transnational social stratification, can be equally rich to, if not richer than, their counterparts based in industrial societies, while ordinary residents in these economies can only dream of matching the quality of life of an average citizen in an industrial country. An expert on international immigration has criticized that most relevant studies lay their focus on the professional elite in NICs who have bene-fitted from the emergence of the global economy, while less attention is paid to the laboring poor.[51] In fact, even such professionals in developing nations often have the intention of migrating to the Global North to seek a better life. Furthermore, such global movements of labor do not work much to reduce inequality, as, according to a study of economic polariza-tion in the United States, the "massive wave of immigration" is one of the factors contributing to the increase of inequality.[52] The expansion of the

---

[48] Robert B. Reich, *The Work of Nations: Preparing Ourselves for 21st-Century Capitalism*, New York: Simon & Schuster, 1991.

[49] Raphael Kaplinsky, *Globalization, Poverty and Inequality: Between a Rock and a Hard Place*, Cambridge: Polity, 2005, p. 255.

[50] Ibid.

[51] W. M. Spellman, *Uncertain Identity: International Migration since 1945*, London: Reaktion Books, 2008, p. 17.

[52] McCarty, Poole, and Rosenthal, *Polarized America*, p. 2. Also, Rafada Dancygier, *Immigration and Conflict in Europe*, Cambridge University Press, 2010.

Table 6.3 *The Economies with the Most Unequal Income in the World,*
2014–2015

Rank	Country	GINI Index For Family Income	GDP Per Capita (US$)	Rank by GDP Per Capita
1	Lesotho	63.2	3,000	190
2	Botswana	63.0	17,700	96
3	Serra Leone	62.9	1,600	215
4	South Africa	62.5	13,400	116
5	Central Africa	61.3	600	228
6	Micronesia	61.1	3,000	191
7	Haiti	60.8	1,800	211
8	Namibia	59.7	11,300	133
9	Honduras	57.7	5,000	169
10	Zambia	57.5	4,200	177
11	Hong Kong	53.7	57,000	17
12	Colombia	53.5	14,000	113
13	Paraguay	53.2	8,800	140
14	Guatemala	53.0	7,900	150
15	Chile	52.1	23,800	77
16	Panama	51.9	20,900	86
17	Brazil	51.9	15,800	101
18	Papua New Guinea	50.9	2,800	193
19	Swaziland	50.4	9,800	138
20	Costa Rica	50.3	15,500	105
21	Gambia	50.2	1,700	212
22	Zimbabwe	50.1	2,100	201
23	Sri Lanka	49.0	11,200	134
24	Ecuador	48.5	11,300	131
25	Thailand	48.4	16,100	100
26	Mexico	48.3	18,500	92
27	Madagascar	47.5	1,500	218
28	Dominican Republic	47.1	14,900	108
29	China	46.9	14,300	112
30	El Salvador	46.9	8,300	146

Note: The base year for Gini index information is 2014, and for the GDP per capita is
2015, or any possible previous year when the relevant information is available.
Source: The author's composition based on the information available in CIA the World
Factbook; for Gini index, https://www.cia.gov/library/publications/the-world-fact
book/rankorder/2172rank.html, accessed May 14, 2016; for GDP per capita, https://
www.cia.gov/library/publications/the-world-factbook/rankorder/2004rank.html,
accessed May 15, 206.

poor alongside globalization, therefore, cannot be substantially remedied by globalization itself. Rather, these global movements simply highlight the cross-fertilization between global inequality and domestic inequality, and clearly outline the demarcation between ordinary residents in the Global North and the Global South, namely, the second and third world in our lexicon, in terms of socioeconomic inequality.

It is impossible for such a short section to exhaust the numerous impacts of capitalist globalization on the promotion of inequality, but the point is clear: The global triumph of capitalism has empowered the market mechanism in promoting the growth of wealth but unbalancing the distribution of wealth; now this is being reinforced by the state, which would otherwise maintain a check over such consequences. This is going on particularly under the slogan of enhancing global competitiveness. On the micro level that concerns business firms,

Competition is dictated by an impersonal market which demands there be a constant alert for every businessperson to take measures which aim at minimizing costs and maximizing profits. It can demand the dismissal of laborers, the intensification of work even when that harms the laborer's health, deceitful advertising, the increase of red tape methods, and so on.[53]

At the macro level of the political-economic-social system, as two leading observers of capitalism have once emphasized, "international competition among national social systems of production may cut deeply into a country's social and political fabric," thus,

As the social sciences increasingly recognize that noneconomic domestic institutions are important determinants of success in world markets, economic competition is increasingly becoming competition over different forms of social systems of production, and competitive pressures for better economic performance are more and more often translated into pressures for broad social change.[54]

---

[53]   Jose Brendan Macdonald, "The Challenge of a Democratic Economy," in Jeff Shantz and Jose Brendan Macdonald eds., *Beyond Capitalism: Building Democratic Alternatives for Today and the Future*, New York: Bloomsbury, 2013, pp. 1–23 (p. 7).

[54]   J. Rogers Hollingsworth and Robert Boyer, "Coordination of Economic Actors and Social Systems of Production," in J. Rogers Hollingsworth and Robert Boyer eds., *Contemporary Capitalism: The Embeddedness of Institutions*, Cambridge University Press, 1997, pp. 1–47 (p. 38).

In general, therefore, what might be termed the "jungle political economy" has come to dominate global capitalism, a political economy that focuses on economic gain with as little consideration as possible of the social, political, environmental or any other costs of such gain. This has, to a great extent, sent capitalist civilization back to the jungles, in which the strong are free to prey on the weak.

From Social-Capital Erosion to Institutional Decay: Why Is Democracy Increasingly Dysfunctional?

Mainly because of its aftermath of increasing inequalities, globalization greatly erodes the social bases of democracy. "How does a 'democratic' system work amid inequality of resources?"[55] Robert Dahl, a leading expert on democracy, asked decades ago. In his formalized and updated research, Carles Boix employs systematic data to support the conclusions that "increasing levels of economic equality bolster the chances of democracy" and, furthermore, that "democratization, and, particularly, democratic consolidation have been systematically bolstered by high levels of income equality and a fair distribution of property in the countryside across the world in the last two centuries."[56] Following this line of argument in the context of globalization fostering inequality, this section chooses to first highlight how each of the three worlds of global social stratification portrayed earlier has become less pro-democracy than before for different reasons, then discuss the institutional implications of this multilayer sociopolitical change for democracy as a governance mechanism.

Apparently the winner of globalization, the "first world," greatly benefiting from the uncoupling between nation-state democracy and global capitalism, is growingly anti-democratic in both its value orientation and practical propensity. In theory, democracy means an institutional arrangement that involves the poorer and the powerless in the public decision-making process, allowing these people as the majority of a society to influence public affairs and government policy with their weight in numbers. Naturally, this is a constraint over the rich, the powerful, or the state-capital establishment. This is why Plato sees the

---

[55] Robert A. Dahl, *Who Governs? Democracy and Power in an American City*, New Haven: Yale University Press, 1961, p. 3.

[56] Carles Boix, *Democracy and Distribution*, Cambridge University Press, 2003, pp. 10, 11–12.

conflict between oligarch and democrat as the conflict between rich and poor, though in terms of value he prefers the rich and, therefore, oligarchy.[57]

In the globalization age, moreover, those belonging to the first world now enjoy authoritarianism in at least two senses: in the statist sense, those effective authoritarian governments can promote their profit-making better than democracy; in the institutional sense, they like to impose their power and management on their own firms in the author-itarian spirit. In practice, globalization empowers these people, in the case that in the legal sense they are citizens of a democracy, to, first of all, care less than otherwise about the domestic popular preferences in their home democracy, and, furthermore, as they deem necessary to do so, utilize their fortune, power, and autonomy gained in the global sphere against those domestic popular preferences. In the worst case, they are able to hijack a democracy with their financial power for their own interest.[58] In a leading scholar's conclusion, "the power of big money, especially superrich TNCs, is subverting and obstructing the consolidation of democracy everywhere. In many cases, the most powerful government in the world, namely, the G7 (G8 if we add Russia) governments seem to be acting as agents of these superrich corporations."[59]

Those who are the haves in the developing world, furthermore, are of course authoritarian elites; economically they support world capitalism but politically and ideologically they oppose the leading countries of capitalism which are democratic. In the latter sense, they share their subjects' nationalism, as two examples can help to disclose: Bin Laden and his terrorist organization, and the Chinese Communist Party ruling elite.[60] Therefore, as winners of globalization, they are simply more empowered than they were before as an enemy of democracy.

---

[57] Plato, *The Republic*, ed. by G. R. F. Ferrari, translated by Tom Griffith, Cambridge University Press, 2000, pp. 266–280.

[58] For how capital in general and big businesses in particular impair US democracy, see, for example, Peter Dale Scott, *The American Deep State: Wall Street, Big Oil, and the Attack on U.S. Democracy*, Lanham: Rowman & Littlefield, 2014; for a general analysis, see Noreena Hertz, *The Silent Takeover: Global Capitalism and the Death of Democracy*, New York: Free Press, 2002.

[59] Amiya Kumar Bagchi, *Perilous Passage: Mankind and the Global Ascendancy of Capitalism*, Lanham: Rowman & Littlefield, 2005, p. xxi.

[60] For a brief discussion of Bin Laden's opposition to democracy, see Del Dickson, *The People's Government: An Introduction to Democracy*, Cambridge

The ordinary citizens in the Global North, namely, those of our "second world," are in the most direct sense the loser in the political game described above, as they have accordingly lost their bargaining power in the face of the state-capital establishment, and as average voters their influence in such a democracy has substantially declined. The vast population of the ruled in the Global South, which is our "third world," is a victim to the double repressions of local political-business elites and global capital, its "comparative advantage" of lower wages over second world peers being the only hope of improving livelihoods. In addition, these "third-world" peoples' struggle to defend their cultural identities against globalization can be mixed with anti-Western and anti-democratic traits. In order to analyze specifically the growing anti-democratic mentality of the second and the third world wherein runs a democracy, at least in the formal sense, three overlapping issues must be emphatically discussed.

The first issue here is increasing poverty in mature democracies against those impoverished groups' substantial participation in the democratic process. While the entire world has become much richer with globalization than before, a most ironic aftermath is the increasing poverty in the Global North, the region where industrialization first took place centuries ago leading to a well-established "modernized" society, and the region in which, moreover, mature democracies have been running for many years. Earlier sections have shown how severe the relevant issues are and why such impoverishment occurs against the general background of increased world wealth; here the point is taken further with the argument that such impoverishment simply means the de facto deprivation of these impoverished people from their de jure democratic rights.

This connection between socioeconomic poverty and democratic underrepresentation, or, more precisely, the disconnection between

University Press, 2014, p. 118. The Chinese Communist Party (CCP)'s stance on democracy is quite complicated and even confusing, often due to the split between rhetoric and practice, the gap between formal institutions and real politics, and changes over history. Its opposition to competitive, participatory democracy (could there be a democracy without competition and participation?), however, is clear and strong. For the "institutional inconsistency" in CCP politics against democracy, see Guoguang Wu, *China's Party Congress: Power, Legitimacy, and Institutional Manipulation*, Cambridge University Press, 2015; for China's current resistance to democratization, see Minxin Pei, *China's Trapped Transition: The Limits of Developmental Autocracy*, Cambridge, MA: Harvard University Press, 2006.

the poor and democratic participation, is often highlighted from a normative perspective to call for the strengthening of impoverished people's participation in public affairs. As an expert on African American people has pointed out, "when one considers the socioeconomic situation of black communities, with their high rates of poverty, crime, unemployment, and disease, their need for effective political representation takes on an added sense of urgency."[61] The logic, however, can also be true when it is reversed to emphasize that the poverty of African Americans in the economic sense greatly undermines their capacity in democratic participation, Congressional representation, and political influence. This book, therefore, turns to emphasizing that the problems of democracy are, generally speaking, often fundamentally rooted in the rise of global capitalism and the socioeconomic phenomena brought about by globalization. This is so not only in the sense of restricting impoverished people's ability and will for participation, but also in a more fundamental sense regarding their alienation from the idea and system of democracy. It can be concluded, therefore, that the more citizens in a democracy are troubled by poverty, the more the democracy is troubled as a political system.

Secondly, the shrinking or downgrading of the middle class yields tremendously negative consequences for democracy, especially in the eroding of "social capital" of democracy. Democracy, as commonly acknowledged, is bolstered by the middle class; moreover, mature democratic societies are without exception societies comprised of an overwhelming proportion of the middle class in terms of socioeconomic compositions.[62] As socioeconomic disparity becomes a major problem for a democracy simultaneous to an accelerating

---

[61] Carol M. Swain, "The Congressional Black Caucus and the Impact of Immigration on African American Unemployment," in Carol M. Swain ed., *Debating Immigration*, Cambridge University Press, 2007, pp. 175–188 (p. 176).

[62] Seymour Martin Lipset, "Some Social Requisites of Democracy: Economic Development and Political Legitimacy," *American Political Science Review* 53, 1 (March 1959): 69–105; Barrington Moore, Jr., *Social Origins of Dictatorship and Democracy: Lord and Peasant in the Making of the Modern World*, Boston: Beacon Press, 1966; Robert A. Dahl, *Polyarchy: Participation and Opposition*, New Haven: Yale University Press, 1971; Samuel P. Huntington, *The Third Wave: Democratization in the Late Twentieth Century*, Norman: University of Oklahoma Press, 1991; Daron Acemoglu and James A. Robinson, *Economic Origins of Dictatorship and Democracy*, Cambridge University Press, 2006.

globalization,[63] the expansion of the poor, as discussed earlier, primarily means that previously middle class families are now squeezed by both the state and oligopolistic capital into the process of moving downward in their socioeconomic statuses. On the other hand, although the economic state in a mature democracy is often obliged to provide some social welfare to the impoverished, the superrich move beyond state sovereignty into a global sphere where they are relied upon by the economic state to promote a nation's competitiveness while also avoiding fiscal responsibility to the welfare system, resulting in the economic state choosing to rely upon the squeezing of the middle class for the fiscal resources of governance.

Social coherence that supports a mature democracy, therefore, has been dissolved in a variety of ways: this is the third point that deserves special attention. "Globalization has fueled a rapid process of social polarization worldwide,"[64] and within democratic societies, the shrinking of the middle class obviously implies that the social spectrum moves to the two extremes while those in the middle have become fewer in number and weaker in influence.[65] Moreover, globalization brings many other factors to established democracies, such as global immigration, which have contributed intensely to deepening social, ethnic, cultural, and religious cleavages to the degree that identities are confused and distorted.[66] We may say, to a certain extent, if following Samuel Huntington's seminal assertions about the clash of civilizations and about "who are we" in US politics,[67] that this global clash of civilizations is inevitably internalized through global migration and other globalizing factors into domestic cleavages within a mature democratic society, such as in the United States. The social coherence of democratic societies, therefore, has been substantially reduced; instead arises a variety of social polarizations not only in the shape of growing economic inequality but also in intensified social, ethnic, cultural, religious, and political cleavages that enkindle social polarization.

---

[63] Larry M. Bartels, *Unequal Democracy: The Political Economy of the New Gilded Age*, Princeton University Press, 2008.

[64] Robinson, *A Theory of Global Capitalism*, p. 152.

[65] McCarty, Poole, and Rosenthal, *Polarized America*.

[66] Samuel P. Huntington, *Who Are We? The Challenges to America's National Identity*, New York: Simon & Schuster, 2004.

[67] Samuel P. Huntington, *The Clash of Civilizations and the Remaking of World Order*, New York: Simon & Schuster, 1997; Huntington, *Who Are We?*

A similar situation also emerges in those new democratic NICs. For example, in South Korea, according to experts, the recent trend of neoliberal globalization has significantly encroached on "liberal democracy" by weakening labor forces and restricting civil rights. It has widely expanded the political economic power of big businesses such as *chaebol* across various fields in the country; the weakening of progressive social forces and the strengthening of capital has been promoted by various neoliberal reforms in South Korea. Two local scholars, therefore, conclude that "South Korea's experience shows the complicated possibilities and difficulties of democratic progress in the process of globalization."[68]

In the boldest sense, it can be argued that globalization has created three enemies to democracy and democratization, including all losers and winners in the grand game of global capitalism. This sociopolitical challenge to democracy, furthermore, has institutional ramifications, which can be analyzed on two tiers: the impotency of democracy as part of the grand institutional arrangements around the state-capitalism-democracy system, and, accordingly, the incapability of democratic institutions in governance. Chapter 2 has already outlined the first tier, where it is emphasized that the grand institutional structure shared by capitalism, democracy, and the nation-state has been reconfigured with the advent of the global triumph of capitalism, and that the previous historical institutional match between capitalism and democracy has been dismantled, mainly because the rise of globalization advances market victory further while simultaneously restricting democracy even more substantially than before.

Global capitalism now lives with two political bodies, namely, democracy and authoritarianism, but its relationships with them are imbalanced. On one hand, national democracies are not only weak in their ability to govern global capitalism with their "local" democratic procedures and "local" citizens' preferences, but are in return undermined by a variety of local impacts from global capitalism; effective authoritarianism, on the other hand, has gained leverage vis-à-vis both democracy and global capitalism, locking them in a two-link chain, together termed "dependency reversed." In the first link global capital is dependent on

[68] Hyun-Chin Lim and Jin-Ho Jang, "Whither Democracy? South Korea under Globalization Revisited," in Jan Nederveen Pieterse and Jongtae Kim eds., *Globalization and Development in East Asia*, New York: Routledge, 2012, pp. 166–181 (p. 178).

the effective authoritarian state, which, through political repression, provides favorable circumstances for global capital to gain financial success and, joined by other factors like the global limit of capitalist expansion, strengthens its bargaining position in dealing with global capital. In the second link, however, the democratic but now economic state depends on capital for enhancing its materialistic legitimacy. This makes possible the new political economy of development in the globalization age: economic prosperity is often achieved with a strong state working together institutionally with the world market and, in consequence, growing economic inequality, social injustice, and a tremendous ecological cost. It also casts a political shadow on civil rights and political freedoms at home and abroad. Authoritarian advantages work as a fundamental feature of capitalism in pursuing efficiency via well-managed corporations, but they sacrifice ordinary populations' rights and interests in particular and human public goods in general.

The relationship between capitalism and democracy, therefore, has been fundamentally reconfigured to one in which the latter is not able to contain the former, but has been undermined by various social, economic, political, and even cultural and ideational impacts of globalization to the degree that it has become increasingly dysfunctional. First of all, international capital gains more leverage than before due to its "freedom" in stretching globally to undemocratic territories, and, in return, becomes more dominating in its home political bases of democracy for the purpose of reducing democracy's accountability to ordinary citizens. Democracy, therefore, increasingly falls prey to capital, thus creating a power play in which money penetrates, influences, and even controls public authorities. Second, as economic and social life is globalizing and, especially, running "free" based on the neoliberal global market, it often becomes a distant territory beyond the reach of effective governance by a nation-state democracy. Thirdly, the rise of the economic state means the shift of state legitimacy toward its material performance and, accordingly, the weakening of procedural legitimacy provided by democracy; democratic accountability becomes an accountability to banknotes rather than ballots. Due to all of these reasons, the capability of democratic governance has inevitably been declining. In general, democracy as a value, as an institution with popular accountability, and as an effective form of governance is seriously and even fundamentally challenged by both globalization as a set of institutions and its political-economic aftermaths.

Paradise Lost, Momentum in Decline: "Repressive Capitalism" at Work, Democratization Hindered

The increasing dysfunction of the democratic system cannot mean anything positive for democratization. Contrary to the prevailing celebration of the "end of history" through the ultimate victory of the market and democracy in the late-twentieth century, this book argues that the victory of the global market instead hinders the further spread of democracy over the world, and in particular impedes democratic transitions from existing authoritarian regimes. The theoretical framework presented by this book in Chapter 2 already explicitly argues that capitalist expansion depends both on the smooth functioning of the repressive state in global peripheries and on the authoritarian organizational principle in the capitalist firm; the relationship between market globalization and state democracy, on the other hand, is fractured, as democracy is confined within its shape of stateness. This is a fundamental dilemma of market globalization with a series of implications that have transformed the political economy of development and, in a broader sense, the triangular relationship among capitalism, authoritarianism, and democracy as three sets of institutions.

Following the above line of reasoning, a further discussion will be supplied here in order to enrich the understanding of why and how capitalist globalization and its major aftermath of inequalities run against possible democratization of existing authoritarian states. Due to space limits, the discussion will simply be a sketch; for organizational convenience, it will be unfolded along three overlapping aspects: 1) the declining attractiveness of democracy in authoritarian politics in terms of the "demonstration effect" and, by the same token, the weakening momentum of democracy in "exporting" its political model to non-democracies; 2) the comparative advantages of political authoritarianism over democracy created by global capitalism in performing the role of the economic state; and 3) the negative impacts of globalization within authoritarian nations, leading to increasing local resistance to democracy, and the broader internal dynamics in political authoritarianism disfavoring democratic transition. These points, especially the last one, are also a continuation of the analysis on the anti-democracy impact of transitional social stratification of global capitalism regarding how the "third world" of those ruled in the Global South now turns in opposition to the values and institutions of democracy.

Less Attractiveness, Less "Export": The Decline of Democracy Both as a Model and as a Mission

Increasing dysfunction of democracy inevitably means the decline and even the demise of the attractiveness of democracy to those peoples living under non-democratic polities. As some experts on democratization have pointed out, the demonstration effect of democracy often plays a significant role in promoting a democratic transition from authoritarianism.[69] When established democracies are undermined and impaired, the appeal of democracy as an idea and a model can be seriously questioned and challenged, especially to currently existing non-democratic nations where the authoritarian regimes have survived the so-called third wave of democratization with their extraordinary reason, resources, determinants, and political skills. More specifically, this "declining attractiveness" thesis can be understood from roughly two angles against the political economic background of globalization, that is, regarding a political regime's economic performance, and regarding state capacity of democracy and its perception in authoritarian nations.

From the angle of less desirable socioeconomic performance of democracy, the declining attractiveness of democracy should be considered in the institutional context of globalization, especially with the rise of the economic state, and in the value orientation of authoritarian nations. As a democracy is not able to help greatly in overcoming increasing economic inequalities, though it still has to more than its authoritarian counterpart consider the balance between economic efficiency and social distributions, its performance in both economic development and social equity cannot claim a model desirable for residents in non-democratic developing countries who are simultaneously concerned with, in terms of life goals, becoming rich quickly and, in terms of reality, suffering from perilous inequalities. Regarding the possibility of a democratic transition, the question for them can be simple: how does a democracy do better in these regards than what we have now?

The debate around so-called "Asian values" is relevant here, as it confronts democracy and authoritarianism with each other in their

---

[69] Laurence Whitehead ed., *The International Dimensions of Democratization*, Oxford University Press, 2001, expanded ed.; Laurence Whitehead, *Democratization: Theory and Experience*, Oxford University Press, 2002.

economic performance. For those advocates of "Asian values," an overwhelming of, so to speak, rights for rice or freedom to food is reasonable, as in these cultures rice or food is often taken as the basic symbol of material abundance, for which other values must be compromised, abased, or even abandoned.[70] When those non-democratic developing nations are economically backward in a comparison with industrial democracies, this mentality is often cited to support the priority of economic development over democracy on national agendas; when the economic prosperity has been achieved without democracy, however, the mentality finds an even stronger ground to endorse the argument that democracy is useless but economic development must be favored over any other possible pursuits. The economic state, with the prevalence of which political authoritarianism can compete advantageously against democracy, thus lends economic-performance-based legitimacy to political repression; democracy, by the same token, is devalued and even regarded as a negative arrangement that disfavors economic development.

The second angle is that of less reliable capacity of democracy in governance. This is a real scenario that democracies have increasingly experienced in various fields of public affairs, including, to name a few, the quality of public management, the economic, financial, and unemployment crises, the governmental responses to social and natural disasters, the challenges concerning human security issues, dilemmas between civic freedoms and national-security considerations in the age of anti-terrorism and cyber warfare, all suffering from the deterioration of democratic governance.[71] Such problems of democratic governance

---

[70] For "Asian values" and relevant debates, see, for instance, United Nations University, *"Asian Values" and Democracy in Asia*, proceedings of a conference held on March 28, 1997 at Hamamatsu, Japan, http://archive.unu.edu/unu press/asian-values.html, accessed November 20, 2015; Josiane Cauquelin, Paul Lim, and Birgit Mayer-Köenig eds., *Asian Values: Encounter with Diversity*, London: Routledge, 1998; Leena Avonius and Damien Kingsbury eds., *Human Rights in Asia: A Reassessment of the Asian Values Debate*, New York: Palgrave Macmillan, 2008.

[71] For example, see Robert C. Paehlke, *Democracy's Dilemma: Environment, Social Policy, and the Global Economy*, Cambridge, MA: MIT Press, 2003; Douglas Kellner, *Media Spectacle and the Crisis of Democracy: Terrorism, War, and Election Battles*, New York: Routledge, 2005; Papadopoulos, *Democracy in Crisis?*; Eran Vigoda-Gadot and Shlomo Mizrahi, *Managing Democracies in Turbulent Times: Trust, Performance, and Governance in Modern States*, Berlin: Springer, 2014.

are loomed out especially to those residents of non-democratic countries, as they live in a tricky situation in terms of information acquisition: the global information revolution, on one hand, helps them to get
more outside information than otherwise, but both institutionally and
technically they are still under control and surveillance in information
acquisition, exercised by their authoritarian governments.[72] Because of
information censorship, they are much more handicapped than citizens
in a democracy to gain necessary information, let alone sufficient
information, to roundly comprehend the reality of foreign democratic
governance; because of the involvement in the global information
revolution, however, with the fresh feeling of being partially released
from the previous state of non-freedom of information, they intend to
believe that they now know the world well, thus they don't know that
they don't know the truth, in a contrast with the typical situation in this
regard under pre-globalization authoritarianism when they knew that
they didn't know.[73] Moreover, the democratic press is often devoted to
what might be called "negative reporting;" according to the saying,
"no news is good news" is the underlying rationale of journalism. For
those receivers living under authoritarian politics, however, this can be
misleading as they are usually inured to the "positive report" – when
the bad news is published, they tend to believe that the real situation is
much worse than they read. Weak state capacity of a democracy,

---

[72] Not all authoritarian regimes are able to control mass media as effectively as
they would prefer, but it is safe to conclude that in general, authoritarian politics
exercise information censorship much more than a democracy might. For
alternative resources of information as a fundamental feature of democracy, see
Robert A. Dahl, *Democracy and Its Critics*, New Haven: Yale University Press,
1989, p. 222; for authoritarian control of information flow in the current age,
see, for example, Chin-Chuan Lee ed., *Power, Money, and Media:
Communication Patterns and Bureaucratic Control in Cultural China*,
Evanston, IL: Northwestern University Press, 2000; Anna Arutunyan, *The
Media in Russia*, Maidenhead: Open University Press, 2009; Daniela
Stockmann, *Media Commercialization and Authoritarian Rule in China*,
Cambridge University Press, 2012; Edward Webb, *Media in Egypt and Tunisia:
From Control to Transition?* New York: Palgrave Pivot, 2014; David Satter,
*The Less You Know, The Better You Sleep: Russia's Road to Terror and
Dictatorship under Yeltsin and Putin*, New Haven: Yale University Press, 2016.

[73] In fact, citizens under a democracy also have problems in gaining sufficient
information for making decisions on public issues. For this information limit
and its implication for democratic politics, see Arthur Lupia and Mathew D.
McCubbins, *The Democratic Dilemma: Can Citizens Learn What They Need to
Know?* Cambridge University Press, 1998.

therefore, is even much weaker in perception of the authoritarian audiences than in the democratic reality; this issue thus has a doubled effect of reducing the desirability of these audiences for democracy.

Foreign influence in terms of democratization cannot take place without agents or, so to speak, missionaries and their democracy-promoting activities. It is such activities stretching from democracy to non-democracy, especially those performed by democratic states, that take a major role in spreading to non-democracies those ideas, norms, and other elements favoring democratic transition.[74] The global expansion of capitalist activities to non-democracies was once regarded as one of the most significant channels through which such expansion could become a reality. This turns out to be an illusion, however, as the modernization logic of economic development inevitably leading to political democratization does not apply to the world of global capitalism – a point we will discuss later. Instead, this channel is flooded over any possible uttered concerns about democratization by a complicated interdependence in economic, investment, trade, financial, technological, cultural, material, institutional, diplomatic, global-governance, and many other aspects between capitalist democracies and market authoritarianism, thus causing the diminution of international pressures over existing authoritarian regimes to push and urge them to improve human rights, enlarge civic freedoms, and undergo democratization.[75] With such deep institutional constraints embedded in capitalist globalization, the political mission of global democratization that the democratic states might have is apparently less committed and much weaker to the degree that any possible effort of democracy to "export" its political values, norms, and institutions to authoritarianism is quickly declining in both willingness and effectiveness.

The Emergence of "Repressive Capitalism": How "Social Contract of Materialism" Empowers Authoritarianism

The other side of the same story is the growing magnetism of political authoritarianism due to its institutional advantages in global capitalism;

---

[74] Whitehead, *The International Dimensions of Democratization*; Tony Smith, *America's Mission: The United States and the Worldwide Struggle for Democracy in the Twentieth Century*, Princeton University Press, 1994.

[75] Michael Mandelbaum, *Mission Failure: America and the World in the Post-Cold War Era*, Oxford University Press, 2016.

in fact, the decline of democratic attractiveness is simply a reflection of such profound advantages of political authoritarianism created by global capitalism against democracy. This theme has been repeatedly discussed in previous chapters; here it can be analyzed around a concept of "social contract of materialism" for further exploration.

In economic terms, contemporary authoritarian regimes live unexceptionally in developing nations, where residents often seek progress in economic development more enthusiastically than both in other circumstances and other values. Such seeking has become especially overwhelming and impatient due to these nations' involvement in globalization, through which, as mentioned earlier, residents are exposed to greater knowledge about the quality of life in advanced economies and, accordingly, demand such quality. As long as the authoritarian regime claims to make every effort for improving the quality of life of its people, especially when the regime is able to deliver such a promise despite any costs, a "social contract of materialism," as some scholars have observed, can be reached between the regime and its subjects. According to Xiaonong Cheng, an expert on China's capitalist transition, China has experienced a huge change in terms of social contract from Mao's "command and obedience" to Deng's "feeding and compliance,"[76] thus ideological control has been replaced by a developmental mechanism that functions to, ironically, control material deliveries. In Eastern European countries, Przeworski has noted "an implicit social pact in which elites offered the prospect of material welfare in exchange for silence."[77] Ludlam's study of reformed communist regimes has also highlighted a social contract that was established as an exchange relationship in which the regime provides material benefits and security, and subjects agree to acknowledge the legitimacy of the government, and to support, at least passively, the established authoritarian political order.[78] Generally speaking, the prevalence of state-led development in the Global South can be understood in these terms, where the bases of political

[76] Xiaonong Cheng, "Back from Honeymoon to Political Tension: Reform Politics from Zhao Ziyang to Hu Jintao," in Guoguang Wu and Helen Lansdowne eds., *Zhao Ziyang and China's Political Future*, London: Routledge, 2008, pp. 135–150.

[77] Adam Przeworski, *Democracy and the Market: Political and Economic Reforms in Eastern Europe and Latin America*, Cambridge University Press, 1991, p. 2.

[78] Janine Ludlam, "Reform and the Redefinition of the Social Contract under Gorbachev," *World Politics* 43 (January 1991): 284–312.

legitimacy are shifted in varying degrees from other possible sources to the regime's delivery of material progress to its society.

This social contract of materialism, I would further argue, has become possible because of two fundamental conditions, which seem contradictory in the traditional ideological spectrum but are, in fact, complementary for our analysis. The first condition is involvement in globalization with the capable employment of the market mechanism by the state; otherwise the state is not able to deliver economic progress. Such an inability was already witnessed previously under those communist regimes that acted against the market and in many developing countries with access only to a primitive version of market.[79] In other words, it is the state-market nexus that provides the institutional tool for these authoritarian regimes to utilize global capitalism in seeking or making economic prosperity.

The second condition is political repression, or, in perhaps a morally neutral language, state capacity in maintaining the existing political order, namely, the authoritarian political order, by silencing and scrubbing away any possible demands for regime change. It is easy to imagine that, if there was no such repression at work, the residents' knowledge of the outside world of non-authoritarianism, albeit how limited it might be, would stimulate both material and political requests upon their rulers to improve the quality of life and provide increasing rights; it is only with effective political repression that all requests from the populace are engineered to be materialistic to such a degree that it overwhelms their efforts towards improvement of other things, things that may include civic freedoms and basic human rights.[80] These two conditions actually mean the ironic coalition between state sovereignty and economic liberalization, which, though seemingly contradictory, operates to fend off the potential of any political globalization. This institutional feature also helps to differentiate political authoritarianism in the globalization age from earlier authoritarian regimes, as authoritarianism now generally abandons its anti-consumerist stance, instead aiming to fan the fires of the populace's inclination toward avarice and unscrupulousness.

---

[79] For a case in the latter category, see, for instance, Jean Ensminger, *Making a Market: The Institutional Transformation of an African Society*, Cambridge University Press, 1992.

[80] As exemplified by post–Tiananmen China, see Cheng, "Back from Honeymoon to Political Tension."

In the globalization age, moreover, such an authoritarian-materialist social contract is not limited to governing authoritarian developing nations, but has now increasingly become relevant and even prevalent in global political economy. Globalization implies growing connections between democratic and authoritarian states through the global market mechanism; global capital, as investigated earlier, increasingly depends on effective authoritarianism for financial success. The chains of "dependency reversed," suggested in Chapter 2, can be viewed as a global form of the social contract that is highlighted above, via which not only does political authoritarianism become the political and institutional sponsor of capitalist expansion to those parts of the globe where political authoritarianism rules, but also capitalist vitality in fostering material prosperity turns out to be a powerful endorsement behind political authoritarianism.

In addition, as the victory of the market stemming from democracy is misinterpreted as the victory of democracy, those rising markets in which there is no accompaniment of democracy are greatly released from international pressure for democratization. As in the case of China, the largest non-democratic nation in the world, openness to the world economy has helped to effectively delay democratization of the nation.[81] The end of the Cold War released people from, or, at least relaxed, the vigilance against political repression, illustrated by the fact that an emphasis on the existence of an enemy to democracy can be scorned as the so-called Cold War mentality. Material benefits now occupy a central concern of citizens everywhere; the means to achieve these benefits are often not seriously questioned or pondered. In democracies, therefore, popular resistance to political authoritarianism is modified, partly because contemporary authoritarianism is no longer able to threaten democracy as Nazi Germany or the Soviet Union once did. State-market collaboration, furthermore, paints those authoritarian states in liberal colors as they embrace market globalization, which helps to create a relaxation of distrust between democracy and authoritarianism. Deeper changes, too, take place on the side of political authoritarianism, including such a state's learning from, and adjustment and adaptation to, the new international environment of globalization and domestic economic liberalization. The interdependence

---

[81] Mary Gallagher, "Reform and Openness: Why Chinese Economic Reforms Have Delayed Democracy," *World Politics* 54, 3 (April 2002): 338–372.

discussed above, of course, also greatly helps to create a post–Cold War mentality that pays less attention to political repression in dictatorship countries than to the international economic cooperation they offer to the leading industrialized nations. The negative side of political authoritarianism is put aside together with any ideological scruples in the heady experience of market success. The Chamberlain foreign policy of appeasement toward market-authoritarian regimes has prevailed, by citing the outdated logic of modernization theory that the extension of the market into authoritarian states can be expected to drive authoritarian states onto a trajectory toward democracy, as if the question of democratization is only about time and speed.

This capitalist collaboration of leading industrial democracies with market authoritarianism is a phenomenon so new to the contemporary world, and so strange and ironic to existing ideologies, Rightist and Leftists included, that rarely does consideration of it occur in the plural, diverse, and robust new developments of social sciences in the post–Cold War era. In terms of the political economy of democratization, they still believe in the basic logic that is rooted in the assumption of democracy's coupling with capitalism, thus seeing a linear inevitability from economic liberalization through political liberalization to political democratization.[82] With the global triumph of capitalism, however, the somehow positive connection between marketization and democratization in terms of challenging authoritarianism has been greatly reduced, and even institutionally annihilated. Instead, the market-oriented transition in many countries is not leading to a democratic transition of the polity, but to a variety of hybrid regimes in developing nations or "market Leninism," "communist capitalism," or "repressive capitalism" in former or sustaining communist regimes.[83]

[82] See a criticism of the linear assumption concerning the transition from communism in Guoguang Wu, "'Repressive Capitalism' as the Institutional Crystallization of China's Transition," in Guoguang Wu and Helen Lansdowne eds., *China's Transition from Communism – New Perspectives*, London: Routledge, 2016, pp. 190–210.
[83] Xiaonong Cheng, "Capitalism Making and Its Political Consequences in Transition: A Political Economy Analysis of China's Communist Capitalism," in Guoguang Wu and Helen Lansdowne eds., *China's Transition from Communism – New Perspectives*, London: Routledge, 2016, pp. 10–34; Wu, "'Repressive Capitalism' as the Institutional Crystallization of China's Transition."

The Rise of Local Resistance to Democracy: How Globalization Enhances the Authoritarian Political Dynamics Against Democratization

The third major aspect of globalization impairing democratization lies in the impacts that globalization has brought to the internal dynamics of authoritarian politics in increasing local resistance to democracy not only from the authoritarian state but also from ordinary residents, or the "third world" in our scheme of transnational social stratification. This is touched on earlier in this way or that, but here it will be analyzed with two linkages created or enhanced by globalization.

The first linkage can be termed "cultural resistance" to global capitalism, in which the penetration of globalization into local life against existing local cultures, social fabrics, etc., tensions between universal capitalist norms and local diversities, and impersonal market rules and social heritages, rouse local resistance. As globalization often implies a profound "Westernization" of local cultures, it is easy to observe the rise of nationalism in the Global South among the populace for defending their cultural traditions and national identities.[84] The authoritarian regimes which embrace economic globalization often find good reason, or at least a plausible excuse, to mobilize such nationalism against the spread of "Western" values, especially "Western" political values, primarily democracy. As the illusion of the "end-of-history" softens and even omits the antagonism of democracy against authoritarianism, it helps to alarm existing authoritarian states that the threat to their survival is pending and pressing, thus, ironically enough, often making authoritarian regimes highly vigilant and deeply confrontational towards democracy. When the have-nots in the developing nations are exploited economically and deprived politically by the alliance between global capital and local political authoritarianism, such

---

[84] Peter L. Berger and Samuel P. Huntington eds., *Many Globalizations: Cultural Diversity in the Contemporary World*, Oxford University Press, 2002; Harald Barrios, Martin Beck, Andreas Boeckh, and Klaus Segbers, *Resistance to Globalization: Political Struggle and Cultural Resilience in the Middle East, Russia, and Latin America*, Hamburg: LIT Verlag, 2003; Thomas D. Hall and James V. Fenelon, *Indigenous Peoples and Globalization: Resistance and Revitalization*, New York: Routledge, 2009; James Petras and Henry Veltmeyer, *Social Movements in Latin America: Neoliberalism and Popular Resistance*, New York: Palgrave Macmillan, 2011; Valentine M. Moghad, *Globalization and Social Movements: Islamism, Feminism, and the Global Justice Movement*, Lanham: Rowman & Littlefield, 2012, 2nd ed.

mobilization reinforces their turn to nationalism; together popular and official nationalisms can join each other in resisting Western democracy. National authoritarianism and its vigilance against democracy, therefore, can be reinforced by popular support in a developing nation in order to oppose the cultural effect of globalization in particular and the western imperialist penetration in general.

In this regard, the discussion of retail franchising in Chapter 3 can be extended here to cultural domains as an example of how global capitalism arouses local resistance. In emerging markets, it is clear that "retail franchising can sometimes supplant traditional and local cultural elements, which over time can lead to homogenization and westernization of preferences, especially among the youth population."[85] The older generation and the political establishments, therefore, often resist such "cultural shifts."[86] Although nationalism arises in a political authoritarian polity along with globalization, it is political authoritarianism whose will wins against either the penetration of global cultures or local protests, or both. At the very least, nationalism can help to sway local residents in terms of appreciating the value of the authoritarian regime by which their civic rights are often deprived, simply due to the authoritarian regime's resistance to Western values in politics and cultures.[87]

The second linkage concerns global human mobility and its negative impacts on democratization of authoritarian polities.[88] In Table 4.2, five countries of the ten largest suppliers of international emigrants are non-democracies, and two are only "partially free" according to the Freedom House's assessment. How does such emigration affect the political development of these non-democratic source countries? Here we must briefly consider two points, one empirical and another conceptual. In the empirical sense, relevant studies have found that more educated people than undereducated have emigrated from the Global South to developed countries. According to an economist,

---

[85] Illan Alon, Dianne H. B. Welsh, and Cecilia M. Falbe, "Franchising in Emerging Markets," in Illan Alon ed., *Franchising Globally: Innovation, Learning and Imitation*, New York: Palgrave Macmillan, 2010, pp. 11–35 (p. 20).

[86] Ibid.

[87] Berch Berberoglu, *Nationalism and Ethnic Conflict: Class, State, and Nation in the Age of Globalization*, Lanham: Rowman & Littlefield, 2004.

[88] For example, Jonathon W. Moses, *Emigration and Political Development*, Cambridge University Press, 2011.

It suggests that these countries will hemorrhage their educated people to a far greater extent than their uneducated people ... Our analysis predicts that the exodus of capital from the bottom billion was only phase one of the global integration of the bottom billion. Phase two will be an exodus of educated people ... Emigration will be selective: the brightest and the best will have most to gain from moving. They are also the ones most likely to be welcomed in host countries.[89]

This is often analyzed as the issue of "brain drain" in globalization that disfavors the developing countries' economic development in general and global competitiveness in particular,[90] but its political implications to democracy and democratization are also obvious: with such human movement from south to north, the quality of democracy in the north declines because of various reasons including identity problems, ethnic tensions, increasing economic inequalities, and low participation in politics from new immigrants.[91] In the Global South, possible social bases for supporting democratization are undermined, if we believe that educated people often have higher personal autonomy, more cosmopolitan value inclinations, and greater demands for freedoms, rights, and participation in public life than their undereducated counterparts.[92] In the conceptual sense, one can be reminded of a classic statement that "exit" reduces the domestic momentum of voice for change.[93] Taking

---

[89] Collier, *The Bottom Billion*, p. 94.

[90] Collier, *The Bottom Billion*. He certainly notices the aftermaths of such emigration in governance of a developing country: "Where as migration has generally been helpful as part of the development process, I am skeptical of it as a force for transforming the bottom billion. I think that by draining these countries of their talent, migration is more like to make it harder for these nations to decisively escape the trap of bad policy and governance." (pp. 94–95).

[91] Huntington, *Who Are We?* Also, Natan Sharansky, *Defending Identity: Its Indispensable Role in Protecting Democracy*, New York: Public Affairs, 2008; Douglas S. Massey and Magaly Sánchez R., *Brokered Boundaries: Immigrant Identity in Anti-Immigrant Times*, New York: Russell Sage Foundation, 2010; Rafada Dancygier, *Immigration and Conflict in Europe*, Cambridge University Press, 2010.

[92] This is, of course, a classic idea from John Dewey. See John Dewey, *Democracy and Education*, New York: Free Press, 1916/1997. Also, Lipset, "Some Social Requisites of Democracy"; Eamonn Callan, *Creating Citizens: Political Education and Liberal Democracy*, Oxford: Clarendon Press, 1997; Jim Garrison, Stefan Neubert, and Kersten Reich, *Democracy and Education Reconsidered: Dewey After One Hundred Years*, New York: Routledge, 2016.

[93] Albert O. Hirschman, *Exit, Voice, and Loyalty: Responses to Decline in Firms, Organizations, and States*, Cambridge, MA: Harvard University Press, 1970. Also, Moses, *Emigration and Political Development*, pp. 10–12.

together both the empirical and conceptual points, it can be argued that human mobility as a global linkage has negative impacts on the potential of democratization of existing authoritarian politics.

Both linkages have helped to demonstrate that the domestic dynamics of authoritarian nations have gained from their involvement in globalization some positive changes that favor the sustaining of authoritarian rule. In a broader picture, it must be emphasized that such changes tilt to favor the state in state-society relations. This picture is, of course, not one-dimensional in which the state predominates while societal factors are silenced and even eliminated. Instead, the political dynamic of an authoritarian nation involved in globalization nowadays is always much more complicated; it is, perhaps, better to describe such a dynamic in which both social activism and state repression grow simultaneously. Moreover, both social movements and state control are benefitted from their nation's growing integration with global capitalism.[94] In most cases, however, and in principle of analysis, globalization empowers those effective authoritarian regimes more than their domestic social protesters, especially concerning the dynamic toward possible democratic transition.

As space is limited, here let's just mention two factors of such an imbalance in the dynamics. The first is structural, with which stands the middle class's dependence on the authoritarian state. Such dependence has been widely observed in nations where the authoritarian leadership has played a significant role in stimulating economic prosperity, as in Latin America of the 1970s, East Asia of the 1980s, and China in the early twenty-first century.[95] The second is strategic, concerning the

[94] John A. Guidry, Michael D. Kennedy, and Mayer N. Zald eds., *Globalizations and Social Movements: Culture, Power, and the Transnational Public Sphere*, Ann Arbor: University of Michigan Press, 2000; Hank Johnston and Paul Almeida eds., *Latin American Social Movements: Globalization, Democratization, and Transnational Networks*, Lanham: Rowman & Littlefield, 2006.

[95] For Latin America, see David Collier ed., *The New Authoritarianism in Latin America*, Princeton University Press, 1979; for East Asia, David Martin Jones, "Democratization, Civil Society, and Illiberal Middle Class Culture in Pacific Asia," *Comparative Politics* 30, 2 (January 1998): 147–169; for China, Bruce J. Dickson, *Red Capitalists in China: The Party, Private Entrepreneurs, and Prospects for Political Change*, Cambridge University Press, 2003; Jie Chen and Bruce J. Dickson, *Allies of the State: Democratic Support and Regime Support among China's Capitalists*, Cambridge, MA: Harvard University Press, 2010. Also, Victoria E. Bonnell and Thomas B. Gold eds., *New Entrepreneurs of*

ability of the state in exercising political oppression, which has generally grown in tandem with the authoritarian state effectively embracing and managing its involvement in globalization. For example, with economic prosperity and rapidly growing fiscal revenues, the Chinese state has been able to maintain a huge budget for what is called "stability maintenance" (*weiwen*). This term is notoriously known as suppression over any expression of citizen's discontent, ranging from a mass protest against environmental pollution to a publication of a piece critical of the government, and the amount of this budget scandalously surpasses the country's national defense budget, despite the fact that the latter has also been growing fast, often with an annual increase of two digits.[96]

The new political economy of development with globalization, therefore, curtails democratization by both reducing the possible internal momentum of democratic transition, as exemplified in the middle class's authoritarian attachment to the state, and by strengthening the authoritarian state, which, with its highly concentrated political and economic power, is able to hijack economic prosperity that is propelled by market globalization for the purpose of maintaining and exercising political repression. Overall, democracy as an attractive alternative of political authoritarianism is questioned, and democratization is successfully contained and delayed through "repressive capitalism," which works well in both promoting economic development and maintaining the existing political order.

Concluding Remarks

Nobel laureate economist Joseph Stiglitz asserts that "inequality is behind a lot of what you see as a dysfunctional behavior and extremism in the United States."[97] The above chapter, agreeing with his point of view, pushes the argument further in both geographic coverage and institutional logic. In the first sense, the judgment not only applies to the United States, but also fits virtually every nation in the world and

Europe and Asia: Russia, Eastern Europe and China, Armonk, NY: M. E. Sharpe, 2002.

[96] Yue Xie, "Rising Central Spending on Public Security and the Dilemma Facing Grassroots Officials in China," *Journal of Current Chinese Affairs* 42, 2 (2013): 79–110.

[97] "The Interview," *MacLean's* magazine, September 14, 2015, pp. 14–15.

the entire globe in the current age of globalization; secondly, inequality is particularly behind the dysfunction of democracy, a fundamental and often preferred political institution that is supposed to work with capitalism to govern human life after the so-called "end of history." This chapter has been, accordingly, structured with two parts: it first summarizes how globalization has caused the constant and increasing intensification of inequality in various, comprehensive ways; it then moves to a synthesis of how and why growing inequality joins other globalization effects to impair democracy and to impede democratization.

It is impractical to sketch an exhaustive list of the social consequences of globalization for a chapter, but it is absolutely necessary to provide a macro picture of how globalization increases socioeconomic inequality. The above chapter's contribution in this regard has, perhaps, been threefold: First, rather than highlighting a single aspect of inequality, it has clarified the multifaceted manifestation of inequality in the globalization age, which primarily includes both the growing interstate gap of wealth and increasing intra-society class divides in virtually every nation, be it democratic or authoritarian, developing or industrial. Second, recognizing the overlapping and interconnections between these two dimensions of inequality, the above chapter has attributed the dilemma of increasing inequality with growing wealth to the global triumph of capitalism, especially to the new institutional framework of global capitalism that has been outlined in Chapter 2 and the new operational trends of global capitalism in capital, labor, and consumption under this institutional framework. Thirdly, the chapter suggests a transnational scheme of "three worlds" in its globalization module for mapping global social stratification around multiple inequalities across and within societies, and further argues that this is a great divergence of wealth distribution paralleling the early Great Divergence that emerged when the industrialized West had left other continents and countries far behind. The first half of the chapter, putting the above contributions together, attempts to reach beyond the confrontation between the state-centered approach and class analysis in studies of inequality, and highlights instead a turning point of human societies in pursuing growth, development, and wealth since the late eighteenth and early nineteenth centuries.

The latter half of the chapter turns to the effects of globalization, especially the increase of inequality, on democracy and democratization, and argues that all consequences of global capitalism, such as those discussed in the proceeding sections and chapters, make democracy handicapped and dysfunctional, and democratization hindered and victimized. For democracy, inequality and other consequences of globalization primarily undermine its social bases in both substantial and structural senses. Generally speaking, the substantial sense means that every major social strata's enthusiasm toward democracy is reduced by the rise of globalization, which this chapter has elaborated upon as a disappointing picture of one winner and two losers in the grand global social stratification which have all become decreasingly supportive to democracy; the structural sense implies that those structural changes, such as the decline of the middle classes and the polarization of social stratification, point further to a drain of social capital that is argued to be critical for democracy at work. Furthermore, also as exemplified by the issue of transnational and national inequalities, globalization challenges the ability and quality of democratic governance in various ways, as global governance appears on the agenda but national democracies are impotent to respond and manage.

The deterioration of democracy cannot mean anything positive for a democratic transition of non-democratic polities. Contrary to popular belief that the extension of market liberalization to authoritarian nations definitively promotes democratization in those nations, the above chapter has analyzed why and how global capitalism has altered this positive linkage that had existed in the pre-global capitalist age, as well as trying to spell out the sociopolitical implications of those institutional and operational features of global capitalism for democratization, such as global mobility of labor, and has argued that the political economy of globalization has decreased motivation but increased obstacles toward democratic transition.

The global triumph of capitalism, therefore, is not a global victory of democracy; by contrast, the rise of global capitalism and its various impacts fundamentally undermine democracy and hinder democratization, and have essentially finished the age of democracy by opening the age of globalization. Meanwhile, globalization enforces authoritarianism. The general argument of this book on "dependency reversed" has been further reinforced in this chapter by highlighting global capitalism's sociopolitical consequences: in the social realm, transnational inequality in particular forms a major source of various problems that are now confronting the fate of human societies; in the political domain, the decline and dysfunction of democracy is maintained to be the institutional root of various crises of our age. In summary, the gulf between political democracy and global capitalism brought about by globalization signals a fundamental transformation of human institutions, and the impact of this transformation is so profound that our understanding of it is far from sufficient. The next chapter, therefore, will continue to explore many aspects of the impact, especially those going beyond social realms into the wider domains, such as ideological, human-nature interactive (or ecological), and other general consequences of global capitalism.

7 | Conclusion

Drawing conclusions from preceding investigations and arguments, with a particular focus on extending the penultimate chapter's discussion on democracy, this chapter emphasizes that the future of capitalism depends on the power of ideas and a public engagement in discussions to stimulate institutional innovations in human societies that allow global capitalism as a system of creation of material wealth to play to its strengths, while curbing its negative penetration into noneconomic realms and, furthermore, harnessing this system with various sociopolitical arrangements that enhance public interests. The chapter will first summarize the book's major arguments and, in light of these arguments, will attempt to redefine our time with a special emphasis on theorizing and problematizing global capitalism as a system running without a political shell. Then, in the hope of spelling out some fundamental implications of the book and possibly shedding some light on theoretical debates and practical remedies around globalization, the chapter will briefly discuss five themes that are deemed to be extremely significant, namely, economic development and growth, global governance, the authoritarian option, ideational reorientation, and the future of capitalism.

The chapter will question the "development" paradigm that values the state-market nexus for the purpose of increasing material wealth but underestimates the various costs of such development, especially in its ignorance of the incapability of the state-market nexus in providing public goods on both national and global scales. Accordingly, it will boldly suggest the legitimization of stationary economic growth as a desirable goal for industrial economies, and, for developing economies, the replacement of growth- and-wealth-centered governmentality with equality- and-ecology-centered development.

The absence of a "political shell" for global capitalism has obviously left a huge vacuum of public affairs; challenges loom large, especially in the sphere where global governance is expected to work. Various political impulses have indeed emerged to respond to the challenges, including attempts at new imperialism. Often emphasizing the role of power, these impulses, however, have provoked varied resistance from global peripheries rather than providing global governance. These instances of resistance primarily take the form of nationalism, religious fundamentalism, and/or terrorism, which in turn fuel the reactive momentum in the Global North of returning to the exclusive state system for the purpose of reducing the globalization impact. This is a great dilemma; thinking beyond power may help to overcome it.

Also in emergence is a tendency towards effective market authoritarianism to cope with global challenges. China is often considered exemplary in this regard, whose state capacity in promoting economic prosperity and dealing with external pressures is appreciated as a viable exit from the globalization paradox. This chapter, indeed this book by and large, argues against such an authoritarian option as a match for globalization; in doing so, it will trace the relevant debate back to the beginning of human political thinking over the perplexing question of alternatives between prosperity and repression, on one hand, and liberty and dignity on the other.

So, does global capitalism have a future? The answer depends on the human capacity of thinking beyond the existing ideational framework centered on the dichotomy of the state/Left versus the market/Right. The chapter argues that the framework is obsolescent in understanding global capitalism. The state-market nexus as the institutional core of global capitalism poisons the virtues of both the state and the market while magnifying their vices; the search for possible remedies must aim for the strengthening of political and public mechanisms in order to promote "public spirits" to match, balance, and harness "private pursuits." With this as a tenet, the chapter shall propose to accentuate the inherent democratic elements within the organizational bodies of capitalism for the purpose of overcoming globalization's subversive impact on democracy while promoting its enhancing function for democracy.

Global Capitalism without a Political Shell: Theorizing and Problematizing the Now

The end of the Cold War has, of course, changed international political economy tremendously, but it seems that human thinking on how this change can be defined is unclear, notwithstanding that more than a quarter of a century has passed since the change began. This book has attempted to outline a series of findings and arguments for identifying, locating, and comprehending this era that has been the now. These findings and arguments can be summarized as below:

1) We are living in the age of global capitalism. This age has been created through post–Cold War globalization; this latest incarnation of globalization distinguishes itself from earlier waves of globalization in human history by its institutional essence that is the global triumph of capitalism, signaled in the acceptance of the market institutions by virtually all states. The historical stage of "world resistance" to capitalism, specifically dating from the World Wars to the Cold War through the twentieth century, has become a thing of the past, the collapse of practical communism in the late 1980s and early 1990s having eliminated the type of state that worshiped an ideology of confrontation with the market, and, accordingly, the state-planned economy that communism had practiced as a system to organize human economic life has been placed into the museum of humanity. Capitalism, therefore, has become the only ideology, institution, and practice in organizing human economic activities; capitalism has conquered the entire globe in its institutional triumph, thus being reborn as global capitalism.

2) Its global triumph has reconfigured the institutional connections of capitalism with other human organizations, especially the state. The conquering of all states by the market does not dissolve the state as a fundamental institution of monopolizing coercive power;[1] instead, the state system and the market system have now been intimately twisted, mutually penetrated, and powerfully influenced by one another through what this book has termed "the state-market nexus," which replaces the ideological confrontation, institutional separation, and operational counterbalance between the state and the market. Now the institutional inter-transplantation between the state and the market is increasingly crystallizing into the state-sponsored or the state-promoted market on one hand, and, on the other hand, the "economic state." Combining two of the most powerful human institutions, this

---

[1] See ft. 4, ch. 2.

state-market coupling is able to forcefully promote global competitiveness and economic growth.

3) Global capitalism is politically "nude," as it suffers from the absence of a coherent, integrating, effective political body. A fundamental uncoupling emerges with globalization, as capitalism becomes global but its previous "political shell," democracy, is still confined within "stateness." In other words, the rise of global capitalism has broken the historically established institutional linkage between capitalism and democracy, making global capitalism grow without a political match and nation-state democracy become dwarfed before global market forces.

4) Another disconnection also arises to frame the institutions of global capitalism, that between the global market that is ineffectively regulated and the national economies, all of which have mixed state governance and market apparatuses. This gap structurally parallels the two organizational bodies of capitalism, namely, the market and the firm; it reinforces both the corporatizing trend of the economic state and neoliberal deregulations of the global economy. Neoliberalism and state capitalism simultaneously prevail worldwide as dominating ideologies to resonate this global split, in the seemingly self-contradictory way of modeling the national economy increasingly after the firm while fostering a level of "jungle" competitiveness among firms and states on the global market.

5) Capitalist coverage of the globe inevitably means the geographic exhaustion of the global expansion of capitalism and, therefore, the global limitedness capitalism has now encountered. As the market reaches its final boundaries, the introversive mobilization of institutional resources for global competition becomes more intensive than before. It also stimulates the rise of both neoliberalism and state capitalism, as the former allows capital to be further empowered through tremendous freedom in its global movements, while the latter supports various organizational forms of resource concentration and authoritarian management, especially the firm in its global form, namely, multinational corporations, to maintain and strengthen competiveness on a global scale.

6) All major elements of capitalism, that is, capital, labor, and consumption, now operate under the above institutions of globalization,

but with different momentums of power and divergent paths of movement, thus resulting in a curve of decline from capital's increasing concentration and coordination, through labor's fragmentation and segmentation, to consumer's standardization and atomization. Alongside the curve emerges the two extremes corresponding to those institutional differentiations that feature global capitalism: on one extreme there are global oligopolies of capital with facilities and conveniences endorsed by the state for the purpose of a growing gigantism; on the other, an ordinary resident as "economic man" struggles between being economic prey within the suppressive firm system and a gleeful materialist wonderer navigating the global consumption market.

7) Economic inequality and social polarization, therefore, prevail in globalization to the degree at which on one end of the spectrum stands the state-market establishment that includes those people who have a share in the monopoly of capital power or state power, and on the other end the poverty grows quickly in an increasingly wealthy world, and between the two sides the middle classes are squeezed, undermined, and shrinking. The state system in terms of the difference between an industrial democracy and others stands to further divide those who do not belong to the state-capital establishment. Transitional social stratification, therefore, can be mapped into "three worlds," as the divide between ordinary peoples in the Global North and the Global South is drawn against the global ruling class of the state-market establishment. None of these "three worlds," as either a winner or loser of globalization, lends its political support to democracy, thus making democracy everywhere hollowed out and democratization hindered from making progress.

8) Political authoritarianism thus regains vigor in the form of both a political regime of the state and its institutional elements of organization and management. Mirroring the capitalist firm, effective political authoritarianism now often operates within the institutional form of state capitalism, which combines those trends of the state-market nexus and the economic state while punctuating the concentration of resource and power, corporatization of human organizations of all types, and competition of government-backed firms on the global markets. Moreover, authoritarianism tends to prevail in other organizations, including within a democratic

system; it does so in multiple senses that may include the concentration of resources and decision-making power with less diffusion and diversification, the tightening of control over members while neglecting their autonomy, freedoms, and rights, and the exclusion of ordinary members with pull and push from effectively influencing public affairs.

9) Emerging with the decline of democracy and the rise of authoritarianism is the chain of "dependency reversed," in which democracy of the economic state depends on capital but global capital depends on effective authoritarianism. In the global political economy, this chain has reshaped domestic and international relations of power, with which the fundamental political ethos of the age of global capitalism can be encapsulated into AA versus DD, that is, authoritarian advantage versus democracy's dysfunction. It makes global capitalism vulnerable to all harm it may encounter, including from political authoritarianism and from all domains concerning the exercise of public power.

10) The rise of globalization, overall, brings democracy into a fundamental crisis. This is a landmark turn in the linear path of and often-positive connections between capitalism and democracy that had unfolded in human history since the Industrial Revolution and the European and American democratic revolutions, the revolutions together having created the fundamental institutional framework of global political economy featuring the combination of a capitalist market and political democracy within sovereign states. The effects and consequences of the rise of global capitalism are obviously fundamental, profound, and encompassing; it is this absence of a coherent, effective, and appropriate political framework for global capitalism that has laid itself deep as the institutional root of tremendous problems, troubles, and challenges now facing human societies.

Rethinking the Paradigm of Development: Would the "Stationary Economy" Be Recommendable?

All above findings and arguments, though they sound negative, do not imply a moral blame or a practical denouncement of globalization and capitalism. With the fundamental methodology of inter-institutionalism, this book fully recognizes the capacity and credits of global capitalism in creating material, economic, and technological benefits. Meanwhile, the book's emphasis is on the other side of this capacity and creation, which is argued to be going rampant without effective checks from the state and other human institutions, thus causing huge problems such as increasing inequality and deepening ecological crises. This is why the time of our material prosperity is marching hand in hand with increasing public perils; it is global capitalism that makes both.

Obviously this is not a linear approach that sees positive and reciprocal connections between material and technological progress and successful economic development, on one hand, and social wellbeing, cultural dignity, public virtues, political rights, and human-nature harmony on the other. Quite the opposite, the institutional features and operational mechanisms of global capitalism by essence cost the latter to the benefit of the former. Democracy, as a realistically preferable political institution governing public life, is undermined and handicapped, which, in return, furthers the crises caused by globalization but tremendously reduces human capabilities to deal with these crises. The unbearable costs of unprecedented development, therefore, suggest a necessity of rethinking the paradigm of development.

"Development" has been a central theme since the end of the Second World War through the Cold War era, around which distinguished schools of thought have risen to shape the academic disciplines of political economy and comparative politics as well as public policies and popular mentality. These schools, including modernization theory, the dependency school, world-system theory, and state-centered approaches,[2] have contributed enormously to human understandings

---

[2] For some representative works of modernization theory, see Seymour Martin Lipset, "Some Social Requisites of Democracy: Economic Development and Political Legitimacy," *American Political Science Review* 53, 1 (March 1959): 69–105; Gabriel A. Almond and James S. Coleman eds., *The Politics of the Developing Areas*, Princeton University Press, 1960; David E. Apter, *The Politics of Modernization*, University of Chicago Press, 1965; also, Samuel P. Huntington, *Political Order in Changing Societies*, New Haven: Yale University Press, 1968; Robert A. Dahl, *Polyarchy: Participation and Opposition*, New Haven: Yale University Press, 1971; Myron Weiner and Samuel P. Huntington eds., *Understanding Political Development*, Boston: Little Brown, 1987. For dependency theory, see, for example, Fernando Henrique Cardoso and Enzo Faletto, *Dependence and Development in Latin America*, Berkeley: University of California Press, 1979; Peter Evans, *Dependent Development: The Alliance of Multinational, State, and Local Capital in Brazil*, Princeton University Press, 1979; also, David G. Becker, *The New Bourgeoisie and the Limits of*

of political economy of economic progress and social/cultural change in the form of "development."[3] Globalization has changed a series of relationships with which they are concerned, however, primarily including the relationship between the market and the state by turning them from institutional rivals to political allies; that between global capital and developing states, which have reversed their dependency connections; that between liberal democracy and market authoritarianism, which now compete and cooperate around a new axis instead of their previous ideological and political confrontations; and that between economic development and human welfare/human security, which are not necessarily reciprocal in a positive way. Therefore, it is time to refresh and reorient our conception of "development."

There have been skeptical perspectives on development, which emphasize various limits to growth, especially those restrictions in natural resources and social domains that the pursuit for unlimited growth inevitably encounters.[4] Their warnings are turning out to be truer and

Dependence: Mining, Class, and Power in "Revolutionary" Peru, Princeton University Press, 1983; Thomas J. Biersteker, *Multinationals, the State, and Control of the Nigerian Economy*, Princeton University Press, 1987. For the world system theory, see works by Immanuel Wallerstein, such as: *The Modern World-System*, Vol. I: *Capitalist Agriculture and the Origins of the European World-Economy in the Sixteenth Century*, New York: Academic Press, 1974; *The Capitalist World-Economy*, Cambridge University Press, 1979; *The Modern World-System*, Vol. II: *Mercantilism and the Consolidation of the European World-Economy, 1600–1750*, New York: Academic Press, 1980; *The Modern World-System*, Vol. III: *The Second Great Expansion of the Capitalist World-Economy, 1730-1840s*, New York: Academic Press, 1989; *World-Systems Analysis: An Introduction*, Durham, NC: Duke University Press, 2004. For state-centered approach, see, for instance, Peter Evans, Dietrich Rueschemeyer, and Theda Skocpol eds., *Bringing the State Back In*, Cambridge University Press, 1985; Migdal, *Strong Societies and Weak States*; Peter Evans, *Embedded Autonomy: States and Industrial Transformation*, Princeton University Press, 1995; Atul Kohli, *State-Directed Development: Political Power and Industrialization in the Global Periphery*, Cambridge University Press, 2004.

[3] For some general reviews of studies of development, see Deepak Lal, *The Poverty of 'Development Economics'*, Cambridge, MA: Harvard University Press, 1983; H. W. Arndt, *Economic Development: The History of an Idea*, University of Chicago Press, 1987; Michael P. Todaro, *Economic Development in the Third World*, New York: Longman, 1989, 4th ed.; Gerald M. Meier and Joseph E. Stiglitz eds., *Frontiers of Development Economics: The Future in Perspective*, Oxford University Press, 2001.

[4] A well-known example is Donella H. Meadows, Dennis L. Meadows, Jørgen Randers, and William W. Behrens III, *The Limits to Growth: A Report for the Club of Rome's Project on the Predicament of Mankind*, New York: New

more urgent in the age of global capitalism than before, as reality is even worse than what the warnings once predicted, especially due to two prominent phenomena wrought with the global triumph of capitalism: First, virtually all nations are now involved in the global pursuit for economic growth through the state-market synergy. Under the pressure of global competition, they, especially those late-comers, intend to mobilize every possible resource to accomplish this pursuit with little concern for its ecological, social, and political costs, and such costs increasingly become the great burden of the globe. Second, the institutions of globalization, as analyzed in this book, especially those exemplified in the economic state and the concentration of capital, intend to exhaust every possible energy, be it material and non-material, for actualizing the pursuit. Together, these phenomena turn economic development into the "red shoe" human societies wear for a perpetual dance: at the micro level individuals dream of becoming richer and richer, and firms seek unlimited economic expansion; at the macro level, nations strive for a stronger and stronger global competitiveness, and governments value and prioritize the highest possible annual economic growth rate they can achieve. The constant pursuit of growth becomes politically and even naturally correct for state policies and global governance without being effectively questioned.[5]

As an effort to correct such a reality and mentality, this book would extend its investigation to the making of a proposition that concerns the value of growth, or more exactly, the devaluation of growth. For the Global North, where by principle an average resident already leads a

American Library, 1972. Also, Dennis Meadows, Jorgen Randers, Donella Meadows, *Limits to Growth: The 30-Year Global Update*, White River Junction, VT: Chelsea Green, 2004; Dennis Pirages and Ken Cousins eds., *From Resource Scarcity to Ecological Security: Exploring New Limits to Growth*, Cambridge, MA: MIT Press, 2005. For a classic scholarly work in this regard, see Fred Hirsch, *Social Limits to Growth*, Cambridge, MA: Harvard University Press, 1999 [1976]. For a concise, general review of the predicament of growth and progress, see Ronald Wright, *A Short History of Progress*, Toronto: Anansi, 2004.

5   A latest example can be found in the G20 leaders' joint declaration of the 2015 Antalya summit, which in its first short paragraph highlights growth three times with words such as "strong" and "robust" and with the leaders' "determination" and "resolve." See http://www.consilium.europa.eu/en/press/press-releases/2015/11/16-g20-summit-antalya-communique/, accessed December 7, 2015. In intellectual reflections of the issue on growth, some began to recognize the so-called age of stagnation, but normatively think it is not preferable. See Satyajit Das, *The Age of Stagnation: Why Perpetual Growth is Unattainable and the Global Economy is in Peril*, Amherst, NY: Prometheus Books, 2016.

considerably comfortable life while demographic growth has already slowed down to, in some cases, a negative birth rate, this book would suggest placing value in a stationary economy virtually without substantial growth. Social consensus must be explicitly, widely, and firmly established among individuals, groups, governments, and society as a whole on the discontinuation of seeking further economic growth. Instead, distribution reform for the improvement of socioeconomic equality and institutionalized efforts for ecological preservation must be the priority of governance, including economic governance. For the Global South, a similar rationale is also recommended: though the pursuit of moderate economic growth can be legitimate for these peoples in order to lift the material level of their life to that which is similar to what industrial societies currently enjoy, economic growth should not be the exclusive goal of development and governance; instead, the preferred annual growth rate must be moderate, well-balanced, and sustainable, as it must be conditioned simultaneously with socioeconomic equality and ecological protection.

As the idea of pursuing a stationary economy might be viewed as radical or unrealistic, it deserves some discussion and, perhaps, justification. In fact, it is not as novel as it looks; rather, it is a classical idea in the history of economic thought, foreseen more than a century ago by John Stuart Mill. To quote him,

> We have still to consider the economical condition of mankind as liable to change and indeed ... as at all times undergoing progressive changes. We have to consider what these changes are, what are their laws, and what their ultimate tendencies; thereby adding a theory of motion to our theory of equilibrium – the Dynamics of political economy to the Statics.[6]

From an economist perspective that considers the declining return of capital, Mill believed that the growth of material welfare cannot go on indefinitely.[7] More importantly, he regarded such a stationary status of the economy as a positive factor, for it may imply that humans, liberated from the idea of incessant material progress, may find peace of mind for loftier purposes.[8]

---

[6] John Stuart Mill, *Principles of Political Economy, Collected Works of John Stuart Mill*, Vols. 2–3, University of Toronto Press, 1965 [1848], p. 705.

[7] Agnar Sandmo, *Economics Evolving: A History of Economic Thought*, Princeton University Press, 2011, pp. 103–105.

[8] Bo Sandelin, Hans-Michael Trautwein, and Richard Wundrak, *A Short History of Economic Thought*, London: Routledge, 2014, p. 33.

Almost 170 years have passed since Mill raised the issue; during this long historical span the most spectacular progress human societies have made, indeed since the Industrial Revolution, is material affluence in the general sense for human beings as an entity.[9] It is, this book would propose, the time for human societies to shift our focus on "the struggle for riches" to other "better things," to use Mill's phrases.[10] In this sense, here this book suggests a theory not about "development"; more exactly, it advocates a fundamental shift in the realm of development or wealth and production from a growth-centered approach to an equality-centered approach. The human mentality must be altered from unconditionally valuing economic growth to setting up a red line for questioning, criticizing, and even, if possible in practice, prohibiting further growth beyond this line.[11]

The pages here are not an appropriate place to discuss the technical details of such a line or standard, nor to explore how this idea can be implemented in the global political economy, but the logic is clear: growth must not be a legitimate goal for which all nations strive in constant pursuit, nor the sources with which governments self-legitimize. In one

---

[9] Gregory Clark, *A Farewell to Alms: A Brief Economic History of the World*, Princeton University Press, 2007; Robert J. Gordon, *The Rise and Fall of American Growth: The U.S. Standard of Living since the Civil War*, Princeton University Press, 2016.

[10] These quoted phrases are from Mill, *Principles of Political Economy*, as recited in E. K. Hunt and Mark Lautzenheiser, *History of Economic Thought: A Critical Perspective*, London: Routledge, 2015, p. 195.

[11] This author clearly knows that there has been for a long time a strong upholding of the prioritization of economic growth over public goods, including environmental protections, with the argument that it is impossible to effectively preserve natural environments without the growth of wealth. At this stage of human history, however, although natural disasters still threaten human beings in various ways, the speeding up of economic development per se has often become a major source of human security crises. Furthermore, in the globalization age, challenges to human security issues, most prominently in regards to climate change and wider environmental degradation, are concerned more than ever with the nature of human security equating to global public goods, in contrast to national economic growth that is equated to "private goods" for a given economy. As those institutional elements that provide advantages in promoting development are simultaneously and increasingly the causes of human insecurity crises, the worship of development must be reexamined from its institutional roots and its philosophical foundations. For a discussion, see Guoguang Wu, "Human Security Challenges with China: Why and How the Rise of China Makes the World Vulnerable," in Guoguang Wu ed., *China's Challenges to Human Security: Foreign Relations and Global Implications*, London: Routledge, 2013, pp. 1–27.

sentence, the paradigm of development must be reconsidered in the direction of departing from its concern over the increasing production of wealth toward a better utilization and distribution of wealth, thereby allowing for the possibility that "development" be transformed from being a system of constant resource-drawing for human consumption to being ecology-oriented for the purpose of making the globe a better place for humanity in a comprehensive way.

Dilemmas of Global Governance: Power Politics, New Imperialism, and Double Resistance

The absence of a coherent political match to global capitalism, this book would maintain, is a central problem from which various troubles emerge in the contemporary world. Though this absence may not have been conceptually acknowledged until the current book's attempt to do so, the various challenges rooted in it have perplexed human societies for decades and, accordingly, have nourished many human efforts to address the problem.

Global governance is a natural and prominent response to the absence of a political match to global capitalism. Being a legitimate impulse in this regard, it is often demanded and promoted with the rise of international regimes through their increasing functioning in global affairs.[12] Multilateralism becomes more acceptable than before;[13] intergovernmental organizations (IGOs) and nongovernmental organizations (NGOs) are playing increasingly significant roles in international affairs.[14] Their limits, however, are obvious and fundamental,

---

[12] Stephen D. Krasner ed., *International Regimes*, Ithaca: Cornell University Press, 1983. Also, Volker Rittberger with Peter Mayer eds., *Regime Theory and International Relations*, Oxford: Clarendon, 1993; Andreas Hasenclever, Peter Mayer, and Volker Rittberger, *Theories of International Regimes*, Cambridge University Press, 1997; Oran R. Young, *Governance in World Affairs*, Ithaca: Cornell University Press, 1999.

[13] John Gerard Ruggie ed., *Multilateralism Matters: The Theory and Praxis of an Institutional Form*, New York: Columbia University Press, 1993; Guoguang Wu and Helen Lansdowne eds., *China Turns to Multilateralism: Foreign Policy and Regional Security*, London: Routledge, 2008.

[14] Michael Barnett and Martha Finnemore, *Rules for the World: International Organizations in Global Politics*, Ithaca: Cornell University Press, 2004; Thomas G. Weiss and Rorden Wilkinson eds., *International Organization and Global Governance*, London: Routledge, 2013; Brian Frederking and Paul F. Diehl eds., *The Politics of Global Governance: International Organizations in*

while they also create further problems in themselves through power abuse and corruption. As Robert Gilpin, a leading expert of global political economy, has realized, "while an international regime could prove beneficial, there is no ready and permanent solution to the problems generated by concentrations of wealth and power in economic, social, and political affairs, so constant vigilance is required to prevent abuses."[15] This is certainly a weak statement, because it is apparent that "constant vigilance" does not work effectively to prevent those problems. In general, international regimes in either their current state or a more desirable updated version cannot match global capitalism in the domains of politics and governance.

More often than not, a power-centered approach in international politics in general and global governance in particular stands behind the effective functioning of international regimes, thus requiring the cooperation of world powers to do so. This trend is clearly exemplified in the rise of state groups such as "G8" and "G20" states, let alone those more traditional IOs such as the United Nations and its Security Council.[16] Ironically enough, it often lends further attention to state security and state-centered global competitiveness while causing continued impotence in providing human security; the ignorance of political differences in terms of regime type also has the effect of downplaying the significance of citizens' rights in any possible mechanisms of global governance. Furthermore, it obviously neglects the role of less powerful nations in global governance.[17] This power-centered approach reminds us of the reasons why Immanuel Kant takes a pessimistic view of global governance: the diversity of nations is greatly

an Interdependent World, Boulder, CO: Lynne Rienner, 2015, 5th ed.; Margaret P. Karns, Karen A. Mingst, and Kendall W. Stiles, *International Organizations: The Politics and Processes of Global Governance*, Boulder, CO: Lynne Rienner, 2015, 3rd ed.; Stephen Macekura, *Of Limits and Growth: The Rise of Global Sustainable Development in the Twentieth Century*, Cambridge University Press, 2015.

[15] Robert Gilpin, *The Challenge of Global Capitalism: The World Economy in the 21st Century*, Princeton University Press, 2000, p. 192.

[16] For example, see David L. Bosco, *Five to Rule Them All: The UN Security Council and the Making of the Modern World*, Oxford University Press, 2009.

[17] For instance, Stephen Buzdugan and Anthony Payne, *The Long Battle for Global Governance*, London: Routledge, 2016, highlights how the Global South is often excluded from participation in global governance, but they still pay major attention to the role of the "Southern" powers in this regard such as China, India, and Brazil.

reduced; the whole world is becoming a "closed society" within which "further strife" prevails.[18]

A related, and even more power-centered, political impulse responding to the absence of a political match to global capitalism is the new, or renewed, trend of imperialism, especially what may be termed "democratic imperialism."[19] In terms of the relationship between the West and the rest, globalization can be viewed as a new wave of colonization, though in practice it remains at best a partial program, as it takes place in economic, social, cultural, and international-relations domains, rather than the domestic domains of rights, politics, and governance in the "rest." Problems in global governance, therefore, are expectedly dealt with effectively as the power of industrial democratic states is extended onto the global stage. With the dominance of state sovereignty in many domains in today's world, democratic imperialism seems a realistic option for improving global governance, but the conceptual questions it raises and the practical resistance it rouses are huge, often creating more conflicts than providing solutions.

In concept, can democracy as people's self-governance and imperialism as power from external, coercive sources be compatible with each other? In ancient Greece, when democracy prevailed for the first time in human history (though on a highly limited scale in terms of global geography), democracy was associated with empire or imperialism.[20] This historical practice failed, however, as democratic Greek city-states were eventually defeated and destroyed by non-democratic empires. Moreover, this connection was fundamentally changed in the centuries that followed; globalization, especially, has created a new circumstance in which tensions between democracy and imperialism reach a new height. That the weaker is the prey of the stronger is "the philosophy of

---

[18] For a brief discussion of Kant's opposition to world government, see Hans Reiss, "Postscript," in Immanuel Kant, *Kant: Political Writings*, ed. by Hans Reiss, Cambridge University Press, 1991, 2nd ed. (pp. 250–272), pp. 270–271. For an optimistic view in terms of increasing diversity in the world that prevents powers' dominance, see Charles A. Kupchan, *No One's World: The West, the Rising Rest, and the Coming Global Turn*, Oxford University Press, 2012.

[19] G. John Ikenberry, *Liberal Leviathan: The Origins, Crisis, and Transformation of the American World Order*, Princeton University Press, 2011; Leo Panitch and Sam Gindin, *The Making of Global Capitalism: The Political Economy of American Empire*, London: Verso, 2012.

[20] Francis MacDonald Cornford, "Introduction," in *The Republic of Plato*, Oxford University Press, 1978 [1941], pp. v–xxix.

imperialism";[21] by contrast, democracy is built upon an opposite principle that argues for the collective power of the weak being institutionalized against, or at least acting as a check and balance to, the power of the strong. This implies, at least conceptually, that when democracy functions well, imperialism will be contained. And, vice versa, when imperialism gains, democracy pays – it is exactly this relationship that this book has observed in the predominance of globalization.

The practical obstacles that "democratic imperialism" has encountered in its attempts to improve global governance are also huge and even more disastrous than its inherent logical inconsistency. In fact, as the market or capitalism has successfully conquered all the states on the globe, forms of resistance increasingly come from non-economic realms and from non-state factors such as ethnic or religious groups. Any attempt at democratic imperialism simply intensifies further confrontations, resistance, and conflicts, rather than effectively remedying them, thus deepening the crises of democracy and global governance. Some disastrous challenges in global politics under the ethos of the so-called "clash of civilizations,"[22] specifically, religious fundamentalism, cultural, economic, and political nationalisms, and extremism and terrorism have arisen in the traditional global peripheries to empower such forms of resistance to a degree that now highlights the inability of the democratic state in the global age to defend even the basic security that it otherwise promises to its citizens.

In reaction to both the rise of nationalism and fundamentalism in global peripheries, on one hand, and, on the other, the mounting problems and challenges to industrial democracies wrought through globalization, such as international immigration, industrial hollowing, and socioeconomic inequality, a trend often calling for the strengthening of state exclusion has gathered momentum in industrial democracies, highlighted by this book at its very beginning, namely, the rise of ultra-rightist political forces in Europe and the United States. Different from but also parallel to the rise of nationalism in the Global South, this

---

[21] Social Darwinism? In fact, centuries ago Thucydides had the idea already, as expressed in the famous "Melian dialogue" in Thucydides, *History of the Peloponnesian War*, New York: Penguin Books, 1972, pp. 400–408, and Plato also focused on the idea in Part I of *The Republic* (Plato, *The Republic of Plato*, Oxford University Press, 1978).

[22] Samuel P. Huntington, *The Clash of Civilizations and the Remaking of World Order*, New York: Simon & Schuster, 1997.

nationalistic and isolationist voice in the Global North can be also viewed as a political impulse to remedy the problems of global capitalism by shrinking back to the pre-global scheme of state sovereignty, localizing global governance, and, in essence, reducing and even eliminating the momentum of globalization.

In appearance, the political developments in leading countries of the Global North such as the UK, the US, and France seem to be a victory of democracy, as a considerable portion of voters successfully expressed their discontent with globalization through their democratic rights. A severe dilemma exists, however, in at least two senses: first, voters in each case are deeply divided, and such social cleavages, especially in the rise to cause political polarization, wouldn't benefit the quality of a democracy;[23] second, the cost of the backlash of globalization can be high, thus harming the socioeconomic bases of the democratic state. In any case, the collectively imagined global governance is twisted to a breaking point within this political-economic and global-local (domestic) spiral; democracy is crushed at the center of the spiral from both global challenges and domestic polarization (a polarization that is now

---

[23] The interrelationship between democracy and social division is complicated and subtle, as a democracy, on one hand, works as a political mechanism for competition among diverse groups and often stands on political divisions – this may be called the "divided we stand" thesis, as a famous slogan indicates, and there are many publications so entitled, as exemplified by a textbook, James A. Percoco, *Divided We Stand: Teaching About Conflict in U.S. History*, Portsmouth, NH: Heinemann, 2001; a classic study of American democracy, David R. Mayhew, *Divided We Govern: Party Control, Lawmaking, and Investigations, 1946–1990*, New Haven: Yale University Press, 1991; and a recent publication directly relevant to what we have discussed in this book, Organization for Economic Cooperation and Development, *Divided We Stand: Why Inequality Keeps Rising*, Paris: OECD, 2012. The opposite argument, on the other hand, is equally well researched and elaborated upon for supporting the point emphasized here, as seen in, for instance, a classic book, Robert A. Dahl, *Democracy and Its Critics*, New Haven: Yale University Press, 1989, and some updated publications, Angel E. Alvarez, "Social Cleavages, Political Polarization and Democratic Breakdown in Venezuela," *Stockholm Review of Latin American Studies* 1 (November 2006): 18–28; Pippa Norris, "The 'New Cleavage' Thesis and the Social Basis of Radical Right Support," a paper presented at the American Political Science Association Annual Meeting, Washington DC, September 2, 2005, http://www.cses.org/plancom/module3/2005plenary/Norris2005.pdf, accessed July 14, 2016. In short, this author believes that "one cleavage of overwhelming salience," as highlighted by Nicholas R. Miller in his "Pluralism and Social Choice" (*American Political Science Review* 77: 734–747; quotation is from p. 740) while being seen in the recent cases we have listed here, reduces the leverage of democracy.

becoming political rather than only socioeconomic); democratization is easily caricatured, politically, as a Western imperialist plot and, principally, as a naïve joke without a realistic touch of cultural and national characteristics of existing authoritarian polities. Even as the democratic mechanism that has been undermined by globalization is mobilized in turn against globalization, both democracy and globalization are hurt without a winner. The exit, therefore, must be sought in a direction that looks beyond the institutional deadlock of global capitalism versus nation-state democracy.

Fatal Attractiveness: The Gravity of Repressive Capitalism and Its Philosophical Implications

It is understandable in such a background to see the emerging inclination of favoring political authoritarianism as a match to global capitalism, though this book disputes this response in both a normative and positive sense. Merging with the chain of "dependency reversed" in transnational political economy, the spiral effect described above strengthens the authoritarian advantage in global governance against democracy, because the centralization of power is often sought for exercising global governance and political authoritarianism is frequently claimed to be more efficient in taking action than its democratic counterpart in this regard. Such a recommendation may appear without explicitly mentioning authoritarianism; rather, it chooses to pay no heed to the regime difference between democracy and authoritarianism, thus valuing effective authoritarianism for its economic accomplishment and state capacity. China is, of course, a most notable and exemplary case in this regard. In a collaborative book by a number of leading contemporary social scientists, for example, Craig Calhoun thinks that, for the future of capitalism, "a centralized socialist economy is one possibility, but Chinese-style state capitalism may be even more likely."[24] Though a thorough treatment of this theme needs at

---

[24] Craig Calhoun, "What Threatens Capitalism Now?" in Immanuel Wallerstein, Randall Collins, Michael Mann, Georgi Derluguian, and Craig Calhoun eds., *Does Capitalism Have a Future?* Oxford University Press, 2013, pp. 131–161; the quotation is from p. 3, as that is summarized in Immanuel Wallerstein, Randall Collins, Michael Mann, Georgi Derluguian, and Craig Calhoun, "The Next Big Turn: Collective Introduction." In fact, some other authors of the collection such as Michael Mann and Georgi Derluguian have expressed a similar point of view.

least a book, the current discussion would be greatly incomplete without some brief analysis on the relevant points.

The most obvious question concerning the China recommendation is about its empirical validation, or more exactly, its ignorance or underestimation of the social, ecological, political, and many other costs that the economic prosperity of the China style brings to human beings. How economic development in China has been achieved with increasing social injustice; what price China and the world must pay for China's material progress in regards to environmental degradation, including the pollution of water, air, and other critical elements for human survival; and how political repression is required and enforced by China's economic prosperity, are all well researched and demonstrated in relevant studies.[25] In the institutional sense, how the expanding size of big corporations, which is a great asset for Chinese economic competitiveness and is institutionally nursed by the Chinese state, promotes social injustice in income distribution and social welfare;

---

[25] There are many publications in these regards. See some examples for social injustice in: Michael A. Stantoro, *Profits and Principles: Global Capitalism and Human Rights in China*, Ithaca: Cornell University Press, 2000; Mary Elizabeth Gallagher, *Contagious Capitalism: Globalization and the Politics of Labor in China*, Princeton University Press, 2005; William Hurst, *The Chinese Worker after Socialism*, Cambridge University Press, 2009; Dorothy J. Solinger, *State's Gains, Labor's Losses: China, France, and Mexico Choose Global Liaisons, 1980–2000*, Ithaca: Cornell University Press, 2009; Martin King Whyte, *Myth of the Social Volcano: Perceptions of Inequality and Distributive Injustice in Contemporary China*, Stanford University Press, 2010; for the production cost and environmental challenges, Elizabeth C. Economy, *The River Runs Black: The Environmental Challenge to China's Future*, Ithaca: Cornel University Press, 2004; Alexandra Harney, *The China Price: The True Cost of Chinese Competitive Advantage*, New York: Penguin Books, 2008; Paul Milder, *Poorly Made in China: An Insider's Account of the Tactics Behind China's Production Game*, New York: Wiley, 2009; Judith Shapiro, *China's Environmental Challenges*, Cambridge: Polity, 2012; Bryan Tilt, *Dams and Development in China: The Moral Economy of Water and Power*, New York: Columbia University Press, 2014; for political corruption and repression, Melanie Manion, *Corruption by Design: Building Clean Government in Mainland China and Hong Kong*, Cambridge, MA: Harvard University Press, 2004; Minxin Pei, *China's Trapped Transition: The Limits of Developmental Autocracy*, Cambridge, MA: Harvard University Press, 2006; James Mann, *The China Fantasy: How Our Leaders Explain Away Chinese Repression*, New York: Viking, 2007; Andrew Wedeman, *Double Paradox: Rapid Growth and Rising Corruption in China*, Ithaca: Cornell University Press, 2012; Zhaohui Hong, *The Price of China's Economic Development: Power, Capital, and the Poverty of Rights*, Lexington: University Press of Kentucky, 2015.

how China's competitiveness in the global market has demanded the victimization of labor's rights and local/global ecological environments, how the political-economic alliance of power and money makes such victimization feasible and inevitable; how the high speed of economic growth requires the virtual absence of political and civic freedoms; and how such a model makes governmental corruption rampant, are all too familiar stories for an informed global citizen. In addition, developmentalism as governmentality and statecraft in China powerfully helps to curb public expression and popular participation, which remarkably reduces the human capacity to deal with the above problems.[26] China's success, therefore, has been built up upon the institutional weaknesses of global capitalism; it simply benefits from the pitfalls of globalization. In other words, what China has achieved in recent decades accurately represents what the global triumph of capitalism can accomplish, while the huge negative consequences of China's development epitomize the typical problems, challenges, and disasters that the global triumph of capitalism has brought to human life. Chinese-style capitalism, therefore, is a fruit of, rather than a cure for, the crisis of global capitalism; its political function is to enhance the vice of global capitalism against public interests, which, in this book's analysis, is the exact root of those problems demanding remedies – how can it be an alternative to global capitalism?

The greatest relevance of the issue, however, is theoretical and even philosophical, concerning the basic values of human life. Prominent economist Amartya Sen criticizes so-called Asian values in this way:

There have been strong claims in East Asia about the contribution of the respect for "order," "discipline," and "loyalty" (allegedly embodied in 'Asian values') in promoting capitalist success ... Some among the new theorists also see the need for order as requiring authoritarian governments (and perhaps the suspension of human rights) ... its subject matter is at this very moment altogether topical in that part of the world which is trying to establish its claim to be the center of new capitalism.[27]

Sen is correct to denounce such "Asian values" in finding them "often based on badly researched generalizations and frequently uttered by

---

[26] Wu, "Human Security Challenges with China."
[27] Amartya Sen, "Foreword," to Albert O. Hirschman, *The Passions and the Interests: Political Arguments for Capitalism before Its Triumph*, Princeton University Press, 1997, 20th anniversary ed., pp. ix–xix (p. xv).

governmental spokesmen countering accusations of authoritarianism and violations of human rights."[28]

For this book's analysis, the relationship between capitalism and authoritarianism is rather complicated and they are often institutionally entangled with each other. From an institutional and historic perspective, capitalism does have a propensity toward authoritarianism in general, and global capitalism is dependent on effective authoritarianism in particular. This may contradict conventional perception, but our earlier discussion of the English countryside of the sixteenth century has helped to demonstrate it. In addition, Max Weber observed that, when capitalism began to emerge on the European continent, European capitalism had a "peculiar authoritarian stamp," which contrasted with citizens' equality of rights. For Weber, old traditions and socioeconomic elements like the density of population can explain such an authoritarian stamp.[29] This book has further identified the Janus feature of capitalism as institutions, in which the intrinsic requirement for effective management of firms lies in an institutional resonance with political authoritarianism. In consequence, this propensity in general, and the "reversed dependence" in particular may help capitalism to spread and even prosper, but they also powerfully promote the vices of capitalism while oppressing the virtues of it in non-economic spheres. In other words, effective political repression benefits capitalism in achieving material accomplishments but deprives it from contributing to public welfare.

This dilemma, furthermore, can be traced back as far as the starting point of political philosophy, at which, according to Alan Ryan at the very beginning of his massive history of political thought, stands the ancient contrast between effective, prosperous, powerful, despotic Persia, and democratic Athens where citizens enjoyed rights and freedoms.[30] Leading thinkers of the time are rarely enthusiasts of democracy, but the democratic principle lives through history and eventually prevails in very late practice to the degree that at the end of the twentieth century it could be plausible to claim its final victory as the "end of history." The counterargument, however, revives itself after this claim, as global capitalism helps to make not only effective

---

[28] Sen, "Foreword," p. xvi.
[29] Max Weber, "Capitalism and Rural Society in Germany," in H. H. Gerth and C. Wright Mills eds., *From Max Weber: Essays in Sociology*, Oxford University Press, 1958, pp. 363–385 p. 372.
[30] Alan Ryan, *On Politics: A History of Political Thought, Book I: Herodotus to Machiavelli*, New York: Liveright, 2012, "Introduction" and ch. 1.

authoritarian states like China prosperous and powerful while simultaneously making even mature democracies deeply troubled, but also, in a more fundamental sense concerning institutions as rules of the game, authoritarian elements prevail or become desirable alongside capitalism in nearly all human organizations, activities, strategies, and values. The question now challenging human societies is, therefore, ancient as well as contemporary, lasting while newly refreshed, and fundamental but also urgent: do people prefer the combination of material prosperity and political repression to dignity, freedom, and justice?

Keynes once noted that it was "better that a man should tyrannize over his bank balance than over his fellow citizens," expressing a hope that the former might serve as "an alternative to the latter."[31] However, if a man or regime tyrannizes over both? This is not unimaginable, as Sen already mentioned: "given appropriate circumstances, a Mafia can forcefully combine moneymaking with violence and brutality."[32] Globalization, unfortunately, provides such "appropriate circumstances" to those who possess effective authoritarian measures in the form of the state, the firm, or other possible entities, because, generally speaking, when economics becomes politics, political repression, in turn, may become an advantage in economic competition due to its enhancement of discipline, efficiency, and resource concentration. Must human societies fall into a paradox of making choices for their future between either material prosperity with deprivation of rights or the degradation of governance with preservation of rights; or between the predatory state with the ability to prosper or the democratic state with disorder?

Reorienting Our Ideational Compass: Beyond the Ideological Scheme of the State versus the Market

In order to find an exit from the dilemma, this book would emphasize the power of ideas, specifically the human ability in thinking beyond the existing but obsolete framework of ideology centered on the assumption of the state versus the market. This book's institutional analysis has argued that the state-market nexus and other institutional arrangements of global capitalism have fundamentally reconfigured the

---

[31] Quoted in Sen, "Foreword," p. xii.   [32] Sen, "Foreword," p. xiii.

state-market relationship in the globalization age, thus challenging the state-market confrontation assumption in concept. A question is, therefore, how could our thinking be reoriented now that this long-time, basic axis of the state confronting the market has disappeared?

The state and the market are two extremes on opposing sides of the existing ideological map. As people are aware that "in a free market public goods are undersupplied,"[33] and that "to allow the market mechanism to be the sole director of the fate of human beings and their natural environment ... would result in the destruction of society,"[34] they often turn to the state for a remedy. This line of reasoning was especially reinforced by the human experience during the Cold War, where market-oriented ideas on one end of the spectrum were confronted with ideas calling for the state's increasing role in regulating, remedying, remodeling, and/or even replacing the market. The global triumph of capitalism, however, means ideological conciliation and practical convergence between the state and the market, thus the shaping of the state-market nexus that has emerged to frame the unfolding of globalization. The highly concentrated state power that enables effective control of many economic and noneconomic elements becomes a major institutional advantage in global capitalism, obviously over both the previous statist-without-market mechanism and those market-oriented economies with a less powerful state. It is in the intellectual tradition that still sees the state and the market as conceptually and institutionally confrontational that such recommendations for remedying the pitfalls of globalization prevail to value state interventions to correct market failures, to the degree that they greatly appreciate the high concentration of state capacity at the level of what effective authoritarianism like that of China now possesses.

Such a line of reasoning, this book would point out, is anachronistic; it has essentially ignored the state-market syncretism of global capitalism, its harmful consequences in practice, and its transformative implications to social epistemology. As market globalization has crystallized the mutual acceptance between the state and the market into a set of new institutions, many observers, with the outdated ideational map as their reference, are puzzled and confounded by the parallel yet

[33] Reiss, *Philosophy of Economics*, p. 242.
[34] Karl Polanyi, *The Great Transformation: The Political and Economic Origins of Our Time*, Boston: Beacon Press, 1957 [1944], p. 73. Also, Gareth Dale, *Karl Polanyi: The Limits of the Market*, Cambridge: Polity, 2010.

conflicting trends of the prevailing market and increasing state economic functions. With this binary of the state versus market framework of political economy, moreover, even the various efforts in studies of political economy that emphasize the compatibility of the state and the market often fall into a conceptual trap which regards the state and the market as complementary mechanisms for checking one another, thus their institutional collaboration is seen to be not only desirable but even ideal for the mechanism of governing human societies, especially in promoting economic development. That is also why it is extremely difficult for many to understand the rise of neoliberalism and statist capitalism in tandem and, more importantly and ironically, their working together, albeit often awkwardly, to take the lead of global capitalism.

Analytically, that is why, with new changes in the globalization age, the traditional ideological demarcation between the Left and Right is often confused. Such changes can take place in a decisive role like that played by the French Socialists under Francois Mitterrand, rather than Wall Street and the US Treasury, as an expert has discovered, in making the global turn toward financial liberalization.[35] Confusions are especially embedded in the recommendation of the state to remedy a significant market failure, specifically, monopoly, without an awareness of another trap in which monopoly is easily reinforced, if not expanded, by the state-market nexus. Many responses to the 2008 global financial crisis, therefore, simply went in the direction of increasing state intervention against neoliberalism while reinforcing capital concentration.[36] People have been habituated to turn to the state in an attempt to find rescue, or at least a remedy for market problems, being unaware of the fundamental change that the state is now in collusion with the market. With the state sponsoring the market and the market dominating the state, the two most powerful human institutions are able to collaborate in promoting capitalist development, often

---

[35] Rawi Abdelal, *Capital Rules: The Construction of Global Finance*, Cambridge, MA: Harvard University Press, 2007.

[36] "The financial crisis has also led several European governments to rethink their industrial policies. For example, in the UK, Peter Mandelson's active industrialism is being interpreted as implying more clusters." Gilles Duranton, Philippe Martin, Thierry Mayer, and Florian Mayneris, *The Economics of Clusters: Lessons from the French Experience*, Oxford University Press, 2010, p. 13. Peter Mandelson was Secretary of State for Trade and Industry in Tony Blair's Labor Party government.

successfully. To repeat, as the function of the market in maximizing private wealth has been galvanized, the responsibility of the state, now in collaboration with the market, in protecting public interests is greatly undermined and compromised. As these ideologies are confined within the state-market dichotomy, many seek a strengthening of the state to remedy the shortage of public goods; as the democratic state is actually undermined and becoming dysfunctional, they move further towards placing their demands on the authoritarian state.

The implications of the state-market nexus are profound and fundamental, as primarily reflected in the alternations of two basic relationships, namely, the relationship between material accomplishment and human progress, and that between industrialization and democracy. In the first relationship, the state-market nexus is the institutional secret of economic success, but it is also what makes development unsustainable due to its inevitable consequences of social inequality, ecological degradation, and political repression. The expansion of economic freedom in globalization is turned against the interests of the majority of citizens; the privileged minority's economic freedom lays heavy costs on the social development of the majority and the ecological sustainability of the globe. This is the challenge to human capabilities in managing the wealth that human societies have created and in accommodating this wealth within the natural ecological systems from which they draw it and in which they live. This challenge identifies two key words of the time: distribution and sustainability – not growth and wealth.

The mutual acceptance between the state and the market has been crystallized into institutions that differ from the fundamental institutional framework that once brought about the rise of industrialization and it has, therefore, shaped the new politics of development in the age of global capitalism. Yes, rural England, a preferred location of industries in the sixteenth century, later became a territory of democracy, born along with national democracy. Today's situation, however, has a fundamental difference from such a development mainly because nowadays' "global rural" is protected by state sovereignty to resist the spread of rule of law and democracy. In return, as capital comes to this "world countryside," it further empowers the state to undertake such resistance in the political domain, though it may reduce economic barriers. The modern political economic order, in which the sovereign state system constitutionally guarantees property and civic rights, and elected representative assemblies and governments are accountable to the voters, thus becomes fractured in post–Cold War globalization.[37]

The state-market nexus, in this book's analysis, poisons the virtues of both the state and the market but magnifies their vices. This state-market synergy is not only the institutional secret of the global triumph of capitalism, but has also transformed the institutional and conceptual landscapes on which the expectation of the state's increasing participation in market operation to correct market failures is now wrongly grounded. It calls for an ideational transformation concerning state-market relations. Decades ago, Hannah Arendt expressed the insight that "capitalism and communism are systems that are both based on expropriation, and neither is the remedy for the other."[38] In a wider yet changed circumstance of global capitalism, we may further maintain that neither neoliberalism nor state capitalism is the remedy for the other, nor is the oscillation between market functions and state actions the way to escape from the dilemma. The answer to market failure, this book dares to assert, does not lie in the state; furthermore, the answer to the incapability of the state cannot be found in the repressive, predatory, authoritarian state if the goal of state capacity is the promotion of benefits for every member of society.

Making Democracy a Built-In Mechanism for Capitalism: The Consumer Stock Market and Searches for Reformist Institutional Innovations

What will be, if not the state for the market, the direction of remedying the pitfalls of global capitalism while promoting its possible merits? There have been many ideational and practical contributions to answering the question, especially following the 2008 crisis that prompted various diagnoses of the crisis in particular and global capitalism in general, but it is impossible to have an exhaustive discussion of the diagnoses with limited space here. In fact, this author does not believe there is a one-shot scheme for working out the future of global capitalism; instead, numerous and diverse institutional innovations are needed for making improvements. This book, in principle, would

---

[37] See ft. 19, ch. 1.
[38] Hannah Arendt, *Crises of the Republic*, San Diego: Harcourt Brace Jovanovich, 1972, pp. 211–215; the quotation is from the back cover.

emphasize that the central challenge is how to support the market's merits while restricting its pitfalls, having recognized, going beyond the Cold War ideological spectrum, the merits of the market in material production and economic life while denying any possible form of market fundamentalism. Specifically, it suggests a way of thinking in democratizing capitalism from within and from below, especially with the mobilization of public power of consumers.

Here it is capitalism per se that is the recipient of democratization, meaning the building up of democratic mechanisms as inherent parts of capitalist operation. The expectation would be to update and internalize the external linkage between pre-global capitalism and political democracy as two different sets of institutions by integrating and institutionalizing bottom-up participation of citizens into the decision-making mechanisms of not only the state but also the market. In other words, it suggests a reconfiguration of the market mechanisms in order to enhance the power of non-capital elements, especially consumers. One possible practice in this regard, this chapter would propose, is to set up what may be termed the "consumer stock market," in which as a consumer buys a consumer good, the consumer, without additional pay, is also buying stock of the final producer company. It is expected to balance the financial power of global capitalism but increase consumers' weight, first, by reducing the pure speculation that is the spirit of current institutions of capitalist finance in dominating the economic life of global capitalism; second, by adding weight to every daily-life decision of consumers' consumption, making it like a vote to elect firms, with a level of frequency and an unavoidability that voting in a political democracy usually lacks.

This is, of course, still an infant idea; its viability and practicability need further studies and, especially, empirical tests and experiments. The idea is not as novel or ridiculous as it might appear to be, as Joseph Schumpeter has pointed out the similarity of the market choices among firms to the democratic voting mechanism used to choose political parties.[39] In focusing attention on the institutional essence and weaknesses of global capitalism that are elaborated upon in proceeding chapters, and with the aim of actualizing this book's fundamental ethos into practical explorations, however, this "neo-Schumpeterian" design, so to speak, emphasizes the following two practical and theoretical factors that have been updated in global capitalism.

[39] See ft. 18, ch. 1.

First, following this book's discussion of two organizational bodies of capitalism and aiming at the institutional mobilization of consumers' power to check capital's power from within the capitalism system, the idea distinguishes itself from two significant attempts to restructure capitalism that emphasize the role of labor within the domain of the firm. As everybody knows, the Marxist tradition calls for the proletarian revolution of capitalism; in our point of view, it is a theoretical devotion to labor's power demanding radical change of capitalism. The institutional measures of doing so and its practical effects in both utilitarian effectiveness and moral justice are highly controversial and historically failed, as already showed in the history of the Cold War. The theory of "economic democracy" and practices of "workplace democracy" open another line of thinking which aims to increase laborers' democratic participation within the firm.[40] It seems to me that this idea contradicts the nature of the capitalist firm, thus, if the firm is successfully reformed in that direction, capitalism would not function well. By contrast, my proposal recognizes the tension between the two organizational bodies of capitalism, but attempts to enhance the market's inherent resonance with democracy in order to rein in, rather than terminate, the firm's inclination to authoritarianism, thus, in a more general sense, further institutionalizing the democratic elements embedded in market operation for checking over the inherent authoritarian elements of capitalism.

Second, it takes the global rise of consumerism as an underlying development of doing so. The recent rise of "political consumerism" has provided a creative way in which citizens, consumers, and political activists use the market as their arena for politics in order to meet the challenges wrought by globalization.[41] Moreover, various grassroots movements of consumers and laborers have tried some practical designs as "democratic alternatives" to capitalism, as exemplified in the so-called Parecon Proposal which advocates "workers and consumers councils" that may provide an institutional platform for workers

---

[40] Robert A. Dahl, *A Preface to Economic Democracy*, Berkeley: University of California Press, 1985; Edward S. Greenberg, *Workplace Democracy: The Political Effects of Participation*, Ithaca: Cornell University Press, 1986; Joyce Rothschild and J. Allen Whitt, *The Cooperative Workplace: Potentials and Dilemmas of Organisational Democracy and Participation*, Cambridge University Press, 1989; Seymour Melman, *After Capitalism: From Managerialism to Workplace Democracy*, New York: Knopf, 2001.

[41] See ft. 60, ch. 5.

and consumers "to express and pursue their preferences."[42] All of these efforts have followed the principle of increasing consumers' public concerns and everyday power. Possible advantages of the idea of the "consumer stock market," however, are rooted in its easier viability, as it does not need to particularly "enlighten" consumers in order to do so; its wider universality beyond specific consumer groups; and its "institutionality" as a built-in mechanism for capitalism that is consumption being democratized.

Such a simple idea is, of course, alone insufficient for curing the fundamental problems caused by global capitalism and its lack of a political framework. The suggestion of it does not imply opposition to other possible, different lines of effort to reform capitalism. It must be emphasized that political democracy, even though it is undermined and weakened by the alliance of global capitalism and revived authoritarianism, and is becoming increasingly dysfunctional in dealing with various challenges to human public life, still provides the most vital and fundamental political condition for human progress; this condition offers the spirit and institutions that allow public debates over the most sensitive political issues and stimulate competition, criticism, and compatibility of different, even conflicting, ideas and experiments.[43] By contrast, authoritarianism does not allow these; thus, for this very reason, it cannot offer any possible option for human societies to improve our future. As new challenges emerge and increase to a critical degree at which the fate of human beings is seriously tested, we desperately need new ideas, new perspectives, and new initiatives, which democracy allows and promotes.[44] The global triumph of capitalism, after all, is just the beginning of a new history of human societies; the

[42] Michael Albert, "The Parecon Proposal," in Jeff Shantz and Jose Brendan Macdonald eds., *Beyond Capitalism: Building Democratic Alternatives for Today and the Future*, New York: Bloomsbury, 2013, pp. 25–44 (p. 35). The whole collection (Shantz and Macdonald, *Beyond Capitalism*) is about various cooperatives as capitalism's "democratic alternatives."

[43] Kant thinks only this condition gives the possibility of reform and progress. For a discussion of Kant's ideas in this regard, see Hans Reiss, "Introduction," in Hans Reiss ed., *Kant: Political Writings*, translated by H. B. Nisbet, Cambridge University Press, 1991, 2nd ed., pp. 1–40, esp. pp. 21–26, 32–33.

[44] For how ideas change history in the economic realm, see Mark Blyth, *Great Transformations: Economic Ideas and Institutional Change in the Twentieth Century*, Cambridge University Press, 2002; for the significance of critique in refreshing human life, Luc Boltanski and Eve Chiapello, *The New Spirit of Capitalism*, translated by Gregory Elliott, London: Verso, 2005.

ideational cage that has attached, restricted, and imprisoned our thinking within the existing but obsolete ideological framework established
along with the origin, struggle, and development of pre-global capitalism must be unlocked and opened. As many have already contributed
various diagnoses of capitalism in debating how to deal with the issues
of inequality, ecological challenges, and the declining quality of democracy, this book is simply another attempt at doing so by arguing that
the future of capitalism, and, by and large, the future of human societies, does not depend on any form of monopoly, commodity fetishism,
and political repression under any possible beautiful name including
concentration of power and resources for promoting development,
but on the power of creativity and diversity, of ideas and idealism,
and of freedoms and participations that generate ideas, creativity, and
diversity.

Index

accountability, and authoritarian
  advantage, 72–74
Adidas, 206
advanced industrial economies, 35–36
advertising, 215–216
Africa, 151, 153
African Americans, 274
Agricultural Bank of China, 93–94
Algeria, 93–94
Alibaba, 99
Amazon.com, 98–99, 135–136
Ambani, Mukesh, 248
American Revolution, 10, 300
anarchy of consumption, 200–201,
  234–241, 243–244
anti-consumerism, 219–221,
  239–240
anti-democratic mentality, 271–276
AOL, 89
Apple, 115, 136, 138
Arendt, Hannah, 319
Argentina, 181
Aristotle, 264
Armani communist, 256–257
Asia, 153. *See also specific countries*
"Asian tigers", 35
Asian values, 279–280, 313–314
atomization of consumers, 19,
  200–201, 232–233, 239–240
Auchan, 100
Australia, 249–252
  Australian capitalism, 140
Austria, 93–94
authoritarianism
  advantages in globalization, 32–33,
  68–78, 282–286, 299–300
  capacity of democracy in governance,
  280–282
  democratization, obstacles to,
  278–291

demonstration effect of democracy,
  279–282
dependency reversed, 76–78,
  276–277, 300
in developing countries, 52
effective, 70–76, 276–277, 299–300
in first world of social stratification,
  272
gap between global capitalism and
  nation-state democracy, 55–56,
  60–61
global limit thesis, 9
local resistance to democracy,
  287–291
relationship with global capitalism,
  14–16, 296, 311–315
and social contract of materialism,
  282–286
split between national mixed
  economies and global market,
  66–68
autonomy, individual, 56

Baidu, 99
Bangladesh, 93–94
Bank for International Settlements
  (BIS), 112
Bates, Robert, 70–71
Bauman, Zygmunt, 231
Belgium, 88, 93–94
Bell, Daniel, 8–9
Bendix, Reinhard, 18–19, 121, 149
Berlin, Isaiah, 39
big brands, and monopolization, 142
big business, capital concentration
  caused by, 265–267. *See also*
  multinational corporations
Bin Laden, Osama, 272
Biovalley (Strasbourg, Basle, and
  Freiburg), 105–106